British Political Culture and the Idea of 'Public Opinion', 1867–1914

Newspapers, periodicals, pamphlets and books all reflect the ubiquity of 'public opinion' in political discourse in late nineteenth- and early twentieth-century Britain. Through close attention to debates across the political spectrum, James Thompson charts the ways in which Britons sought to locate 'public opinion' in an era prior to polling. He shows that 'public opinion' was the principal term through which the link between the social and the political was interrogated, charted and contested, and reveals how the widespread conviction that the public was growing in power raised significant issues about the kind of polity emerging in Britain. He also examines how the early Labour party negotiated the language of 'public opinion' and sought to articulate Labour interests in relation to those of the public. In so doing he sheds important new light on the character of Britain's liberal political culture and on Labour's place in and relationship to that culture.

JAMES THOMPSON is a senior lecturer in modern British history at the University of Bristol. His research focuses primarily upon the political and intellectual culture of nineteenth- and twentieth-century Britain. He has published articles on a wide variety of aspects of modern British history, including trade union law, class and political language, and political posters.

British Political Culture and the Idea of 'Public Opinion', 1867–1914

JAMES THOMPSON

CAMBRIDGE
UNIVERSITY PRESS

CAMBRIDGE
UNIVERSITY PRESS

University Printing House, Cambridge CB2 8BS, United Kingdom

Published in the United States of America by Cambridge University Press, New York

Cambridge University Press is part of the University of Cambridge.

It furthers the University's mission by disseminating knowledge in the pursuit of education, learning and research at the highest international levels of excellence.

www.cambridge.org
Information on this title: www.cambridge.org/9781107026797

First published 2013

Printed and bound in the United Kingdom by Clays, St Ives plc

A catalogue record for this publication is available from the British Library

Library of Congress Cataloguing in Publication data
Thompson, James, 1973–
British political culture and the idea of 'public opinion', 1867–1914 / James Thompson.
  pages cm
Includes bibliographical references and index.
ISBN 978-1-107-02679-7
1. Political culture – Great Britain – History.   2. Public opinion – Great
Britain – History.   3. Great Britain – Politics and government.   4. Press – Great
Britain – History.   I. Title.
JN216.T46   2013
306.20941'09034 – dc23   2012042952

ISBN 978-1-107-02679-7 Hardback

To my mother and father

Contents

Acknowledgements

The origins of this book lie, longer ago than I care to remember, in New York City. David Cannadine provided sage advice then, and has been unfailingly generous ever since. The project took shape in Cambridge under the wise supervision of Peter Clarke. Its completion was aided by the responses of the readers for Cambridge University Press and the editorial work of Michael Watson.

The research and writing were supported by the British Academy, the Institute of Historical Research, King's College and Jesus College, Cambridge and the University of Bristol. I am grateful to archivists and librarians at the British Library, Cambridge University Library, the London School of Economics, the Bodleian Library and Houghton Library at Harvard University.

My research has benefited from the comments of colleagues at seminars and conferences at the University of Cambridge, the University of Oxford, the Institute of Historical Research, the University of Bristol and the Ecole Normale Supérieure. I owe a particular debt to the insights of Jon Lawrence, Jon Parry, Gareth Stedman Jones and Miles Taylor. The intellectual comradeship of Max Jones, Adam Tooze, Lawrence Black, Josie McLellan, Kirsty Reid and Richard Sheldon helped revive spirits and clarify ideas. David Craig has been a stalwart friend and a source of excellent advice – more of which I should have followed – over many years. Ann Fielding provided love and patience in the face of considerable provocation.

Introduction

Rethinking public opinion in late nineteenth-century Britain

'There is no word that has played so important and conspicuous a role in the politics of recent times, as Public Opinion. None more often occurs, and there is none on which cases of difficulty more often turn, than this. The word, if not the thing it expresses, is new; and the thing, if not new, is new in the importance it plays.'[1]

'Such a disquisition, if it is to accomplish anything, must be prefaced by some analysis of public opinion itself. A multitude of persons, who employ the phrase continuously and often rightly, would nevertheless be puzzled to define it.'[2]

Writing at the middle and end of the nineteenth century respectively, Joseph Moseley and Frank Taylor noted the pervasiveness of the language of 'public opinion' in the political discourse of their times. They were right to do so. Few terms occupied such a central and enduring place in the political life of late nineteenth-century Britain. Dispute over the boundaries of the public recurred throughout a period which witnessed significant growth in the electorate. Debate over the character and quality of 'public opinion', about its reasonableness and vigilance, was equally persistent. In an era prior to opinion polling, the location of 'public opinion' gave rise to considerable discussion. This book recovers and reconstructs these debates.

The language of 'public opinion' in the second half of the nineteenth century has received less attention from historians than might be expected, and less than has been devoted to the debates of the late eighteenth and early nineteenth centuries. This is surprising for two main reasons: the importance of the idea of 'public opinion' in

---

[1] J. Moseley, *Political Elements, or The Progress of Modern Legislation* (London, 1852), p. 119.
[2] F. Taylor, *The Newspaper Press as a Power Both in the Expression and Formation of Public Opinion* (London, 1898), p. 4.

contemporary political argument and the relevance of its history to both established and recent historiographical concerns.

Newspapers, periodicals, pamphlets and books all reflect the ubiquity of 'public opinion' in the political discourse of late nineteenth-century Britons.[3] Historians of the late eighteenth century have highlighted the rise of 'society' as a category of thought, and the rapid growth of interest in the relationship between social change and political arrangements. In the second half of the nineteenth century, these debates gained urgency from the conjuncture of sustained economic growth, urbanisation and technological change, particularly in communications, with the growing accessibility of and participation in the political system. 'Public opinion' was the principal term through which the link between the social and the political was interrogated, charted and contested. The widespread conviction that the public was growing in scope and power raised significant issues about the kind of polity that was emerging, and should emerge, in Britain. These concerns were most obviously apparent in debates about the franchise – debates addressed by generations of historians, but which have been recently restored to historiographical prominence in work on the second and third reform acts.[4] However, discussion over the relationship between the social and the political extended far beyond the question of the suffrage. Within developing understandings of the constitution, 'public opinion' was *both* an essential element of the political system and an expression of social forces. Recent work on the language of 'civil society' has suggested that British usage was more closely tied to the institutions of the polity than the now more familiar continental notion of 'civil society' as a space between the private realm and the state.[5] Scrutiny of the language of 'public opinion' in the second half of the nineteenth century suggests, however, that the continued

---

[3] Simple searching of digitised newspaper sources confirms the frequency of reference to 'public opinion' in the period. In *The Times* alone, search engines suggest 27 153 hits from 1870 to 1914. Compare this with 78 for 'mass opinion' and 1124 for 'popular opinion'.

[4] C. Hall, K. McClelland & J. Rendall, *Defining the Victorian Nation: Class, Race, Gender and the British Reform Act of 1867* (Cambridge, 2000). On 1884–5, M. Roberts, 'Electoral independence and popular politics in later Victorian Britain' (NACBS, 2006) and M. Roberts, *Political Movements in Urban England, 1832–1914* (Basingstoke, 2009).

[5] J. Harris ed., *Civil Society in British History: Ideas, Identities, Institutions* (Oxford, 2003), p. 5.

resonance of the political as a mode of understanding was compatible with an acknowledgement of the impact of economic and social change.

Traditional narratives of this period portray it as a process of democratisation that culminates in the establishment of universal male suffrage in 1918 and the inauguration of genuine universal suffrage in 1928. Of course, before 1918, Britain looked, in comparative perspective or relative to Dahlian conceptions of polyarchal democracy, relatively undemocratic.[6] That said, the virtues, and perhaps more especially the vices, of 'democracy' were certainly much aired in these years. There were certainly those who took Britain to be, or to be becoming, a democracy, but such views were not universally held.[7] Both the second and third reform acts led some to discern the advent of democracy; but, as late as 1914, others emphasised the limitations on participation within the British polity. Contemporaries differed not only in their assessments of Britain *qua* democracy, but also in their understandings of 'democracy' itself. As the reform debates of 1884–5 testify, democracy might be taken as synonymous with direct rule, or equated with rule by the poor, or the many. Importantly, 'democracy' was equally likely to be taken to refer to a social group as to a political system, and contemporaries moved easily between these meanings.[8] Many continued to regard the democratic as but one element within the polity. As with the language of 'public opinion', contemporary usage meshed the social and the political in ways that sit uneasily with their separation in much historiography. In seeking to analyse their changed political world, contemporaries, as in 1884–5, often emphasised the growing capacity of public opinion to mould the developments of formal politics.[9] Debate over the formation and character of 'public opinion' was a primary means by which commentators evaluated the location of political power under the broader franchise of the late nineteenth century.

---

[6] R. A. Dahl, *On Democracy* (Yale, 1998).

[7] This issue is further discussed in J. Thompson, 'Modern liberty redefined' in G. Stedman Jones & G. Claeys, eds., *The Cambridge History of Nineteenth-Century Political Thought* (Cambridge, 2011), pp. 720–47.

[8] See, for instance, the Earl of Carnarvon on the varied meanings of democracy, *Parliamentary Debates*, 3rd ser., CCXC (1884), cols. 386–7.

[9] See Shaw-Lefevre addressing Social Science Congress in Birmingham, *The Times*, 18 Sep. 1884.

In twenty-first-century terms, the electorate and the public are taken
to be coextensive. The nineteenth century, however, inherited an
understanding of the political public which was considerably more
inclusive than the pre-, or indeed post-, 1832 electorate. Whilst successive acts of enfranchisement served to narrow this gap, the extension of
education and growth in literacy helped preserve the broader conception of the public. When discussing parliamentary elections especially,
late Victorians could treat public opinion and the views of the electorate as interchangeable terms, but, generally, the public remained the
more capacious category. Late nineteenth-century politics preserved a
number of means by which non-electors could contribute to shaping
'public opinion', and the constitutional idiom that remained central to
political understandings offered crucial legitimacy to the broader conception of out-of-doors, public opinion. Whilst historians have had
much to say about nineteenth-century constitutionalism, most discussion of the place of 'public opinion' within it has focused upon the
earlier period.[10]

The centrality of the idea of 'public opinion' to nineteenth-century
political debate is matched by its relevance to current historiographical concerns. As Whiggish narratives of democratisation suggest, the
period between the second and fourth reform acts has long been central to accounts of the 'modernisation' of British politics. Historians of
high politics have often focused instead upon the continuities governing 'politics without democracy' in the long nineteenth century.[11] In
recent years, historians of popular politics themselves have increasingly
questioned the organising principles of modernisation narratives. The
challenge has assumed a variety of forms. James Vernon endorsed the
established picture of the growth of party in the era of the secret ballot,
but argued that centralisation tamed popular politics and closed, rather
than opened, the public sphere, whereas Jon Lawrence has powerfully

---

[10] There is an extensive literature on constitutionalism. See, in particular,
     P. Joyce, *Visions of the People: Industrial England and the Question of Class,
     1848–1914* (Cambridge, 1991) and *Democratic Subjects: The Self and the
     Social in Nineteenth-Century England* (Cambridge, 1994); J. Vernon, *Politics
     and the People: A Study in English Political Culture, c. 1815–1867*
     (Cambridge, 1993) and J. Vernon, ed., *Re-reading the Constitution: New
     Narratives in the Political History of England's Long Nineteenth Century*
     (Cambridge, 1996).
[11] M. Bentley, *Politics without Democracy: 1815–1914: Perception and
     Preoccupation in British Government* (London, 1984).

portrayed the limits on party power before 1914 and the enduring dynamism of the localised politics of disruption.[12]

Much of this work has sought to illuminate the discursive field within which popular politics occurred. Whether examining changing references to the 'people' or popular resistance to the claims of 'party', new political historians have sought to excavate the ways in which the contours of political language enabled, and disabled, popular political action.[13] The language of populism was undoubtedly an important component of British political culture, providing a powerful source of rhetorical energy for the likes of Bright and Gladstone. Similarly, quarrels about the place of 'party' in relation to traditions of the open meeting were integral to late Victorian popular politics. Both, however, need to be related to debates about 'public opinion'. Appeals to 'the public' and 'public opinion' were very much part of the arsenal of late Victorian politicians, but, while these terms could be used synonymously with 'the people', their histories and connotations were importantly distinct. Invocation of the public lacked the productivist associations detected by Stedman Jones and Joyce in their accounts of populism.[14] Indeed, the dominant consumerist and intellectualist modes of conceiving of the political public could be quite distant from the radical dichotomy of the idle few and the productive many. However, the emphasis within dominant conceptions of 'public opinion' upon active expression and intensity of belief provided an important bulwark for the legitimacy of open meetings. Equally, the language of 'public opinion' offered significant leverage for those keen to denounce the tyrannical grip of party and the manufacture of opinion through factional organisation. More generally, the language of 'public opinion' provided a crucial means whereby political actors could justify their actions, uphold the importance of their views, and make claims upon the attention of parliament and the executive. As

---

[12] Vernon, *Politics and the People*; J. Lawrence, *Speaking for the People: Party, Language and Popular Politics in England, 1867–1914* (Cambridge, 1998).

[13] On 'the new political history' see D. Wahrman, 'The new political history', *Social History*, 21 (1996), 343–54; L. Black, '"What kind of people are you?" Labour, the people and the "new political history"', in J. T. Callaghan, S. Fielding & S. Ludlam, *Interpreting the Labour Party: Approaches to Labour Politics and History* (Manchester, 2003), pp. 23–38.

[14] G. Stedman Jones, 'Rethinking Chartism', in his *Languages of Class: Studies in English Working Class History, 1832–1982* (Cambridge, 1983), pp. 90–178; Joyce, *Visions of the People*, pp. 56–87.

the political system became more open, invocation of 'public opinion' grew, whereas the resonance of the language of 'the people', while retaining real importance during and beyond this period, especially on the left, was nonetheless arguably in decline as far as its political use was concerned.[15] Individuals, groups and institutions all sought to establish representative status for their views as expressions of 'public opinion'. Charting the discursive dynamics of late nineteenth-century politics requires paying systematic attention to the language of 'public opinion'.

One key dimension of the so-called 'new political history' has been a heightened interest in the politics of gender and the gendering of politics. Feminist historians pioneered the study of the gendered basis of politics and have greatly illuminated the social, ideological and discursive constraints on female participation in public life. Lately, the implications for male politicians of prevailing codes of masculinity have come under increasing scrutiny. As McCormack has recently argued, the narrative of separate spheres that underpins much of this literature has been buttressed by the belated historical reception of Habermas's work on the public sphere, with its emphasis upon the gendered character of public life.[16] Nineteenth-century franchise debates clearly demonstrate the enduring resonance of a masculine conception of the independent political citizen which militated against female enfranchisement. However, this should not simply be equated with female exclusion from contemporary conceptions of the political public. As we shall see, whilst the public was scarcely a gender-blind political imaginary, debate about female membership of the public differed significantly from that over the franchise. Indeed, by the 1900s, some opponents of female enfranchisement even argued that female participation in public life rendered the suffrage superfluous.[17]

---

[15] Detailed support for both these claims is provided in the course of the book. Digitised newspaper databases suggest increased usage of 'public opinion' across the period. Compare the 4902 articles referring to 'public opinion' in *The Times* for 1860–1870 with the 6979 for 1900–1910.

[16] M. McCormack, 'Men, "the public" and political history', in McCormack, ed., *Public Men: Masculinity and Politics in Modern Britain* (Basingstoke, 2007).

[17] See, for instance, A. V. Dicey, *Letters to a Friend on Votes for Women* (London, 1912, 2nd edn), p. 27.

Habermas's work represents the most celebrated analysis of the late nineteenth-century public sphere.[18] Its narrative of the emergence of the bourgeois public sphere has received greater attention from historians than its story of later developments, but its portrayal of social, economic and political pressures deforming the public sphere has been widely echoed in work on the period from 1870 to 1914, most obviously in media history. Habermas offered a general sociological account of the transformation of the public sphere, whereas this book is concerned primarily with the language of 'public opinion' in British political culture. The intellectual history supplied by Habermas is considered in greater detail below, but it is important to recognise the salience of his larger interpretative scheme. Habermas was right to stress the wide-ranging significance of 'public opinion' as a category in the self-understanding of a society. In late nineteenth-century Britain, 'public opinion' was commonly seen as an important economic force, especially in the ordering of industrial relations. The continuing faith invested in the regulatory capacity of a unified, consumerist, yet active, public opinion departs significantly from Habermas's narrative of disillusionment with a fractured passive public, but the capacious conception of society and political economy afforded by his ground-breaking study remains essential in any effort to recover the complex meanings of 'public opinion' in British political culture before 1914.

Media history has been perhaps most sympathetic to Habermas's narrative of the rise and fall of the bourgeois public sphere. It has also paid some attention to ideas of 'public opinion' in these years.[19] Much of this important work, however, has a tendency to equate conceptions of public opinion with attitudes to the press, so underestimating the range of sources in which contemporaries found evidence of 'public opinion'. In its framing intellectual history, much writing about the press adopts a standard narrative of the transition from mid-Victorian rationalistic liberal optimism to fin-de-siècle irrationalist pessimism. Yet, as recent work has begun to show, this approach

[18] J. Habermas, *The Structural Transformation of the Public Sphere: An Inquiry into a Category of Bourgeois Society*, trans. T. Burger (Cambridge, 1989).
[19] A. Jones, *Powers of the Press: Newspapers, Power and the Public in Nineteenth-Century England* (Aldershot, 1996); M. Hampton, *Visions of the Press in Britain, 1850–1950* (Urbana, 2004).

both overestimates the individualism and rationalism of earlier liber-
alisms, and underestimates the resilience of a qualified liberal faith in
public reason.[20]

Indeed, the strange survival of liberal England has been a persistent feature of the recent historiography of late nineteenth- and early
twentieth-century Britain.[21] Whilst disagreement about the origins of
Liberal party decline rumbles on, diagnoses of the fate of liberalism as
an ideology and as a set of norms are increasingly upbeat. Admittedly,
some, particularly those like Vernon who draw upon broadly Foucauldian perspectives, stress the repressive capacities of liberalism, but
relatively few currently dispute the strength of its values. Accounts of
the difficulties of the Liberal party after 1886 – such as those of Parry
and Lawrence – focus upon contemporary perceptions of the Gladstonian party's growing illiberalism, especially its supposedly corrosive
moralism: to some extent, conservative success is presented as stem-
ming from adhering more closely to liberal values than the party that
claimed to embody them.[22]

There remain, however, important differences over how best to characterise the prevailing values of late nineteenth-century political culture. Colin Matthew and Jon Lawrence supply sharply contrasting
accounts of the meanings of the politics of free speech in late Victorian Britain.[23] The legitimacy of centralised party organisation and the
desirability of democracy have been very differently assessed in recent
work on nineteenth-century liberalism.[24] Investigation of the idiom
of 'public opinion' demonstrates notable continuities in the power

---

[20] H. S. Jones, *Victorian Political Thought* (Basingstoke, 2000); M. Freeden,
*Liberal Languages: Ideological Imaginations and Twentieth-Century
Progressive Thought* (Princeton, 2005).

[21] See E. H. H. Green and D. Tanner, eds, *The Strange Survival of Liberal
England: Political Leaders, Moral Values and the Reception of Economic
Debate* (Cambridge, 2007).

[22] Lawrence, *Speaking for the People*; J. Lawrence, 'Class and gender in the
making of urban Toryism, 1880–1914', *English Historical Review*, 108
(1993), 629–52; J. P. Parry, *The Rise and Fall of Liberal Government in
Victorian Britain* (New Haven, 1993).

[23] H. C. G. Matthew, 'Rhetoric and politics in Britain, 1860–1950' in P. J. Waller
(ed.), *Politics and Social Change in Modern Britain: Essays Presented to A. F.
Thompson* (Brighton, 1987), pp. 34–58; Lawrence, *Speaking for the People*.

[24] Parry, *Rise and Fall of Liberal Government*; E. J. Biagini, *Liberty,
Retrenchment and Reform: Popular Liberalism in the Age of Gladstone,
1860–1880* (Cambridge, 1992).

attributed by liberals to intense and reasonable beliefs, whilst also disclosing differing assessments of the representative credentials of various modes of political expression, whether press, platform or petition. In tracing the changing meanings of the language of 'public opinion', we bring the character of late Victorian political culture into much sharper focus.

Changing assessments of the viability and character of Britain's liberal political culture have had important consequences for the historiography of progressivism more generally, and the rise of the Labour party in particular. Many older explanations, most obviously those founded on the emergence of class politics, treated Labour's rise as a step change in the modernisation of British politics, whereby a moribund Liberal party was relegated into obsolescence by rapid economic and social change.[25] Successive waves of revisionist writing have sharply dented many aspects of this picture, revealing both the durability of Britain's liberal political culture and the ambiguities of Labour's relationship to that political culture. Lately, the challenges faced by early Labour politicians seeking to speak for the people have been powerfully anatomised.[26] We lack, however, a comparable study of Labour's discursive relationship to 'the public'. How did Labour politicians and trade unionists seek to represent labour in the polity, given the attractions of free trade and the consumerist tenor of appeals to the public and its interest? Recovering late nineteenth-century debates about the public and its opinion helps us to understand better the character of the early Labour party, and to appreciate more clearly the challenges it faced.

Late Victorian appeals to public opinion were deeply shaped by assumptions associated with liberal political argument. Liberals were not, however, the only group to invoke 'public opinion'. Many studies within intellectual history continue to focus on particular schools, ideologies or traditions, despite much reference to the importance of the argumentative context. Mid-twentieth-century assumptions about

[25] For example, R. McKibbin, *The Evolution of the Labour Party, 1910–1924* (London, 1974). For reviews of trends in Labour party historiography, see D. Tanner, *Political Change and the Labour Party, 1900–1918* (Cambridge, 1990), and 'Class voting and radical politics: the Liberal and Labour parties, 1910–31' in J. Lawrence and M. Taylor (eds.), *Party, State and Society: Electoral Behaviour in Britain since 1820* (Aldershot, 1997), pp. 106–30.

[26] On Labour's relationship to its supposed base, see Lawrence, *Speaking for the People*, esp. pp. 227–64.

the importance of ideology, understood as fairly tightly woven sets of action-oriented ideas, often born of the cold war, have cast a surprisingly long shadow on nineteenth-century studies. Recent studies of ideology have, of course, been a good deal more sophisticated, but, arguably, the danger of rendering earlier debates in overly schematic terms remains.[27] More influential, perhaps, has been the paradigm of the political language, familiar from a number of classics of early modern intellectual history.[28] Here, the desire to eschew anachronism produces greater respect for the terms actually employed by contemporaries than was evident in earlier studies of ideology or unit ideas. However, the metaphor of language, or paradigm, can lead to overly tidy accounts of the relationship between ideas which underestimate the overlaps and exchanges in political vocabulary between distinct positions. Reference will be made here to the 'language' of 'public opinion' to denote the cluster of terms and assumptions associated with the term, but doing so is not to presume that this constituted an entrenched interpretative grid. Rather the intention is to explore the full range of ways in which contemporaries deployed the idea of 'public opinion' in the construction of political arguments. In order to do so, however, we need to say a little more about methodology.

Writing conceptual histories

In seeking to write such a history of 'public opinion', an immediate problem is what kind of conceptual history is being written and why. Recent years have seen a proliferation of methodological discussion about how best to do conceptual history. Much turns on what it is thought conceptual history is for. Some manifestos for the enterprise have stressed the consequences for present-day political theory of grasping the genealogies of the concepts we employ in thinking about

---

[27] Sophisticated treatments include M. Freeden, *Ideologies and Political Theory: A Conceptual Approach* (Oxford, 1996); E. H. H. Green, *Ideologies of Conservatism: Conservative Political Ideas in the Twentieth Century* (Oxford, 2002).

[28] Amidst a vast literature, see, for instance, J. G. A. Pocock, *Virtue, Commerce, and History: Essays on Political Thought and History, Chiefly in the Eighteenth Century* (Cambridge, 1985) and *The Machiavellian Moment: Florentine Political Thought and the Atlantic Republican Tradition* (Princeton, 1975).

politics.[29] In contrast to this, the intention here is more modestly historical. Nor, however, is the primary concern to understand better the place of the idea of public opinion in the classics of late nineteenth-century political thought. The aim is rather to recover the prevalent understandings of public opinion which shaped general use of the term in the period and which were implicated in party doctrine and rhetoric.

Determining the point of writing conceptual history does not, however, explain how to go about doing it. The first example of the genre in English was perhaps Raymond Williams's *Keywords*.[30] This remains the closest Anglophone equivalent to the classics of *Begriffsgeschichte*. It shares their dictionary format, their focus on the years between 1780 and 1850 and some of their theses about the transformative impact of that period. Most work in English has tended to follow the interests of the Cambridge history of political thought and to concentrate on the earlier period. Quentin Skinner's much-reprinted critique of the *Keywords* approach has lost none of its cogency.[31] Williams did fail, especially in the first edition, to distinguish between changes in the criteria for applying a term, changes in the situations deemed to fulfil those criteria and changes in the evaluative force of a term. Change in one of these often leads to change in another, but this is a complex, contingent process whose operation is obscured by Williams's conflation of all of the above under the heading of changes in meaning.

In its original formulations, especially his celebrated essay on meaning and context in the history of ideas, Skinner presented his project in part as a break from an older history of unit ideas.[32] This has sometimes led commentators to regard his approach to intellectual history as antithetical to the kind of conceptual history associated with the German practice of *Begriffsgeschichte*. In recent years, however, Skinner has sought to dispel this view, arguing that there 'ought not in my view to be doubts about the very idea of writing conceptual histories – or

---

[29] J. Farr, 'Understanding conceptual change politically' in T. Ball, J. Farr & R. L. Hanson, eds., *Political Innovation and Conceptual Change* (Cambridge, 1989), pp. 24–49.

[30] R. Williams, *Keywords: A Vocabulary of Culture and Society* (2nd edn, London, 1983).

[31] Q. Skinner, 'Language and political change', in Ball, Farr & Hanson, *Political Innovation*, pp. 6–23.

[32] Q. Skinner, 'Meaning and understanding in the history of ideas', *History and Theory*, 8, 1 (1969), 3–53, repr. in Skinner, *Visions of Politics: Regarding Method*, vol. 1 (Cambridge, 2002), pp. 57–89.

not, at least, if these are histories of how concepts have been put to use over time.' In his Wittgensteinian eagerness not to reify meaning as something other than, or beyond, how words are used, Skinner has suggested that his studies of 'the state' and 'liberty' are accounts of transformations in the 'applications of the terms by which concepts are expressed' rather than histories of alterations in concepts themselves.[33] This book shares Skinner's Wittgensteinian attention to changes in the use of concepts, and his commitment to elucidating the ideational context in which, and rhetorical purpose for which, contemporaries deployed key political terms. It is, however, perfectly Wittgensteinian to regard the history of the use of a concept as precisely a history of that concept, given Wittgenstein's insistence that 'meaning is use'.[34]

Much debate about the viability of conceptual history has turned upon the issue of meaning holism.[35] In practice, few actually argue that holism about meaning makes it impossible to trace changes in the use of a particular concept, and fewer still actually practise intellectual history on this basis. In his critique of Williams's *Keywords*, Skinner notes the 'strongly holistic' implications of change in meaning for a word's relationship to a much wider vocabulary.[36] It is quite clear that any history of the uses of a concept must be sensitive to the intellectual contexts in which that concept is deployed. Martin van Gelderen has rightly noted that questions about the relationship between political concepts and vocabularies can achieve a 'chicken-and-egg' banality.[37] Care must be taken in applying holistic approaches forged in the history of the physical sciences to other realms of discourse. Kuhnian notions of 'paradigms' are too precise to be usefully applied to political and social language. Political and social vocabularies are far more tolerant of contradiction than scientific systems, possess far closer links to the ocean of available words, and are importantly and differently concerned with evaluation and legitimation. Political languages are

---

[33] Q. Skinner, 'Retrospect: studying rhetoric and conceptual change', in his *Visions of Politics*, vol. 1, pp. 178, 179.

[34] L. Wittgenstein, *Philosophical Investigations* (Oxford, 1958).

[35] M. Bevir, *The Logic of the History of Ideas* (Cambridge, 1999).

[36] Q. Skinner, 'Language and social change' in J. Tully, ed., *Meaning and Context: Quentin Skinner and his Critics* (Cambridge, 1988), p. 124.

[37] M. van Gelderen, 'Between Cambridge and Heidelberg: concepts, languages and images in intellectual history' in I. Hampsher-Monk, K. Tilmans & F. van Vree, *History of Concepts: Comparative Perspectives* (Amsterdam, 1998), p. 228.

multiple, overlapping and reliant on moral language and attitudes more generally.

Considerable ink has been spilt on the linked question of the relationship between concepts and words.[38] Are debates about the meaning of 'public opinion' struggles over a shared concept, or instances of the same term being used to refer to different concepts? This is, perhaps, a matter of greater philosophical than historical interest.[39] 'Public opinion' was a privileged term in late Victorian and Edwardian political discourse; understanding why and how contemporaries deployed the term is historically important regardless of whether these are regarded as clashes between different conceptions of a shared concept or of different concepts expressed by the same word. In philosophical terms, both appear possibilities. Even if a strong form of meaning holism were to be accepted, it is far from obvious that this entails that there is no common referent between different theories, given the highly disputed relationship between meaning and reference in the wake of Kripke's work.[40] As David Miller has suggested, it is often possible to re-describe alleged disputes between rival concepts as contrasts between differing conceptions of a shared ideal.[41] Historical investigation may, however, shed light on which appears the more plausible explanation of similarities and differences in contemporary usage. Where historical actors take each other to be referring to the same thing, but to hold different theories about it, and are capable of conducting an argument about it, perhaps we should consider them to be using the same concept. Contesting the definition, scope and evaluative force of a concept does after all require one to talk recognisably about that concept. What, though, of the possibility of terms other than 'public opinion' being used to do the same linguistic work? By the late nineteenth century the term 'public opinion' had been

[38] Skinner, 'Language and social change', pp. 119–21; J. Meadowcroft, *Conceptualizing the State: Innovation and Dispute in British Political Thought, 1880–1914* (Oxford, 1995), pp. 5–6.
[39] For the distinction between concepts and conceptions, see R. Dworkin, *Taking Rights Seriously* (London, 1977). For philosophical reflection on these issues, see C. Swanton, 'On the "essential contestedness" of political concepts', *Ethics*, 95 (1985), pp. 811–27, and A. Mason, *Explaining Political Disagreement* (Cambridge, 1993), pp. 81–7.
[40] The causal theory of reference is developed in S. Kripke, *Naming and Necessity* (Oxford, 1980).
[41] As cited in Mason, *Explaining Political Disagreement*, p. 87.

current for some time. The ubiquity of the term would suggest that its avoidance must have been deliberate and thus unlikely to be taken as equivalent to its use.

It clearly makes a difference, in writing the history of a concept, what sort of concept it is. The genealogies of 'gravity', 'hegemony' and 'unskilled' would look rather different. Three main points must be made about the character of the concept of 'public opinion'. Firstly, it is both a political and a social concept. It is not purely an artefact of political theory, like rights, nor simply a property of society like 'class'. This has important implications for both the sources and the methods by which it can best be studied. It is insufficient to examine solely political texts and images, for ideas of public opinion were informed by more general social and cultural attitudes. Secondly, 'public opinion' possesses many of the characteristics associated with 'essentially contestable' concepts.[42] Views about 'public opinion' entailed various theoretical and evaluative claims which proscribed the possibility of a neutral definition emerging. The subsequent rise of polling might lead one to doubt this statement, but it should rather be taken as the triumph of a particular and debatable conception of 'public opinion' through the authority of positivistic social science. Finally, 'public opinion' is a compound concept, and debates about both the character of the 'public' and the nature of 'opinion' feature in what follows. Particular emphasis is given to changes in the imagined membership of the political 'public', but attention is also paid to developments in political economy which enlarged the perceived role of 'opinion' in the shaping of economic outcomes.

Given the extent to which opinion polling has come to shape notions of 'public opinion', it is worth considering the variety of ways in which the term has been interpreted. In the late nineteenth century, disputes occurred over both the criteria for membership of the public and the application of those criteria. Contemporaries debated what opinion was and to what things it referred. 'Public opinion' could be and

---

[42] For this term see W. B. Gallie, 'Essentially contested concepts', *Proceedings of the Aristotelian Society*, 56 (1956), 167–98, and A. Macintyre, 'The essential contestability of some social concepts', *Ethics*, 84 (1973), 1–9. Strict adherence to meaning holism may not be compatible with the distinction between essentially and non-essentially contestable concepts, but substantive differences in degree, if not kind, would still be present.

was defined in various ways. It could be seen as the aggregate of all relevant views or as the opinion which commanded majority assent. Some insisted that it required a process of deliberation producing a measure of consensus, perhaps even unanimity. The very idea of 'public opinion' could be seen as a reification, or, as Lippman later put it, a 'phantom'.[43] Further complexity resulted from considering the intensity of belief and the scope of collective action required for something to count as 'public opinion'. In general, however, as we shall see, 'public opinion' was a product of deliberative debate, emerging organically from the clash of often strongly held beliefs. Filling in a survey or answering a pollster on the phone would certainly not have satisfied many nineteenth-century thinkers as evidence for the possession of an opinion.

Histories of 'public opinion'

After this general discussion of why and how to write the history of 'public opinion', it is worth looking more closely at the work that has already been done. As Gunn has rightly argued, the history of the historiography of 'public opinion' unsurprisingly registers its intellectual and political context. Work produced in the 1930s sought to chart the views of 'public opinion' extant in the classics of something called the Western philosophical tradition.[44] This could be seen as reflecting concern about both the fragility of democratic values and the growing dominance of statistical accounts of 'public opinion' in the decade of Gallup. The second wave of such work emerged after 1945 and could be construed as similarly preoccupied with the nature of democratic values and the power of polling.[45] This period witnessed the polemical attacks on pollsters of Herbert Blumer[46] and Lindsay Rogers[47] and some more reflective views of the relationship between

---

[43] W. Lippman, *The Phantom Public* (New York, 1925).
[44] See P. A. Palmer, 'The concept of public opinion in political theory', unpublished Ph.D. thesis, Harvard University (1936).
[45] For instance Minar, 'Public opinion in the perspective of political theory'.
[46] H. Blumer, 'Public opinion and public opinion polling', *American Sociological Review*, 13 (1948), 242–9.
[47] L. Rogers, *The Pollsters: Public Opinion, Politics and Democratic Leadership* (New York, 1949).

'classical' and 'empirical' traditions from figures like Lazarsfeld.[48] However, even those who looked sympathetically on the 'classical' tradition did so in order to suggest questions for the present that were taken to be obscured by the claims of polling to deliver a scientific report on the state of public opinion.[49] Little interest was displayed in more historical problems of the place of ideas about public opinion in the politics of the past, and the canon of classic texts was ransacked to provide answers to the allegedly perennial questions of political theory. The 'classical' tradition was essentially constructed in response to the 'empirical' tradition to bolster the claims of political science in a disciplinary war with quantified social psychology. This perhaps helped stifle a more historical approach to the history of 'public opinion'.

In recent years intellectual historians have turned in earnest to public opinion and have mapped much of its development in the late eighteenth and early nineteenth centuries. This expanding body of literature provides an invaluable context for the study of the later period. Particularly suggestive, though importantly contrasting, trajectories of the concept have been plotted by J. A. W. Gunn and John Burrow.

Gunn has provided two main genealogies of 'public opinion'.[50] Unlike Burrow, he does not regard the Scottish enlightenment and its histories of civil society as constituting a turning point in views of the relationship between politics and society. For Gunn the roots of the modern concept of public opinion lie in French satirical polemics inspired by La Bruyère and in British party polemic of the 1730s.[51] The latter has a particular importance in forging the more political idea of public opinion with which he is primarily concerned. Gunn notes the genesis of the 'public' in theatrical audiences and as the tribunal before which reputations were made and unmade.[52] He perhaps

---

[48] P. Lazarsfeld, 'Public opinion and the classical tradition', *Public Opinion Quarterly* 21, 1 (1957), 39–53.

[49] Minar, 'Public opinion in the perspective of political theory', p. 44.

[50] He has also provided a useful account of the fortunes of 'public opinion' in modern political science. See J. A. W. Gunn, '"Public opinion" in modern political science' in J. Farr, J. S. Dryzek & S. T. Leonard, *Political Science in History: Research Programs and Political Traditions* (Cambridge, 1995), pp. 99–122.

[51] J. A. W. Gunn, 'Public opinion' in Ball, Farr & Hanson, *Political Innovation*, p. 249. He reiterates this claim in his '"Public opinion" in modern political science', p. 99.

[52] Gunn, 'Public opinion', p. 249.

overlooks the extent to which this view of 'public opinion' endured into the late nineteenth century. Recent work has been much exercised by the role of melodrama in the popular political imagination, and the performances of Gladstone make clear that politics was an intensely theatrical business long after the time of Beaumarchais.[53]

Gunn draws a broad contrast between the development of 'public opinion' in Britain and France. In Britain he, unlike Kathleen Wilson, sees the 'sense of the people' as embodied by the nation in parliament.[54] There was some recognition of public opinion outdoors when it was expressed at elections, but after the poll it moved firmly within the doors of the Palace of Westminster. The necessity of public borrowing in financing the wars with France did lead to a sense that the state of public credit expressed the opinion of the fiscally defined nation.[55] In general, however, Gunn argues that the existence of an institutional focus for public opinion in parliament blocked the emergence of a more inclusive sense of the people up to the 1780s. In France, however, the very absence of such representation fostered interest in and speculation about the existence and role of public opinion. Rousseau, occasionally seen as introducing the term into England, appears in Gunn's account rather as an important influence in France. While most scholars have stressed Rousseau's authorship of a consensual notion of public opinion, Gunn emphasises his scepticism about current mores and his contention that public opinion was not the agent, but the object, of reform. Gunn's main claim for our purposes is that British notions of public opinion were always vaguer, less concerned with unanimity, less inclined to eulogy or dismissal, and more institutionally situated. Public opinion in France comes across as a form of anti-politics in this account, whereas British ideas were more modestly and comfortably political.

---

[53] On melodrama there is much of interest in J. R. Walkowitz, *City of Dreadful Delight: Narratives of Sexual Danger in Late-Victorian London* (London, 1992). The origins of this burgeoning field perhaps lie in P. Brooks, *The Melodramatic Imagination: Balzac, Henry James, Melodrama, and the Mode of Excess* (New Haven, 1976). For melodramatic politics, see P. Joyce, *Democratic Subjects*, pp. 176–90, 212–14. On Gladstonian melodrama, see Biagini, *Liberty, Retrenchment and Reform*, pp. 369–426, and H. C. G. Matthew, *Gladstone, 1809–1898* (Oxford, 1997).

[54] K. Wilson, *The Sense of the People: Politics, Culture and Imperialism in England, 1715–1785* (Cambridge, 1995), pp. 140–65, 228–35.

[55] Gunn, 'Public opinion', p. 251.

The 1780s witness the revival of sophisticated defences of constitutional monarchy that render public opinion an element in the mixed constitution and defended the existence of a parliamentary opposition. Public opinion in the early nineteenth century was generally affirmed in a Whiggish way as part of a properly balanced constitution. Those who were most troubled by the Tocquevillian fear of the tyranny of the majority were those who adopted his reified notion of the public, like Mill in England or Cooper in the States. The American literature of the 1840s was more impressed by Madison's vision of a 'multiple and shifting majority'. While commentators were always troubled by the vagary of public opinion, it was seen most positively and inclusively in the years up to and around the 1832 reform act. Gunn's more recent emphasis on the openness of the 'public' in this period sits uneasily with his earlier view that it remained limited to the commercial 'middle class'.[56] Writers like Mackinnon undoubtedly presented 'public opinion' as the kind of celebration of 'middle-class' virtues importantly delineated by Dror Wahrman.[57] As we shall see, however, this mixture of inclusiveness and the privileging of middle-class views would be echoed throughout much of the century.

Like many students of public opinion, Gunn has much less to say about the latter period. Public opinion is pretty much confined to elections in Gunn's account. We get little sense of how it was supposed to operate at other times, which issues it was most relevant to, or of how it was supposed to be formed, and by whom. Gunn is keen to argue that Britain, not France, originated the modern political concept of public opinion. However, in doing so, he has perhaps taken the parliamentary preoccupations of the 1730s as too definitive of what 'public opinion' and 'politics' were about.

A very different picture emerges from John Burrow's work. In *Whigs and Liberals* especially he surveyed the tensions in political thought which congregated around the notion of public opinion in the first half of the nineteenth century. His project was, as ever, to understand the more reflective ideas of the educated classes, but it is perhaps fair to say

---

[56] J. A. W. Gunn, *Beyond Liberty and Property: The Process of Self-Recognition in Eighteenth-Century Political Thought* (Kingston, Ont., 1983).

[57] W. A. Mackinnon, *On the Rise, Progress, and Present State of Public Opinion, in Great Britain, and Other Parts of the World* (London, 1828). For the 'middle class' idiom, see D. Wahrman, *Imagining the Middle Class: The Political Representation of Class in Britain, c.1780–1840* (Cambridge, 1995).

that he approaches these mainly through the work of those thinkers who might be expected to have been unduly influential in shaping them. What is perhaps most striking about Burrow's approach is how differently from Gunn he frames the debate about public opinion.

Burrow makes the case that the modern notion of public opinion is a product of the difficulties for political theory created by the conceptual innovations of the Scottish enlightenment.[58] For Burrow, it is the work of Scottish historians of civil society that does most to distil a notion of society to set alongside the traditional idea of the polity. This permits a fan of civilisation like Hume to argue that the form of polity is of little consequence when weighed against the state of society. This marked an obvious departure from and sin against the tenets of classical republicanism which made the exercise of political virtue both the precondition and the fulfilment of liberty. The liberal notion of public opinion was developed in response to those like Hume who would elevate the claims of society over polity and those civic republicans who would raise polity over society. The catalyst for its emergence was the French Revolution and the question of how to avoid such a cataclysm in Britain. To advocates of reform, the Revolution illustrated the dangers of the form of the polity lagging behind the evolution of society, just as the Terror demonstrated the horrors wrought by adherents of virtue using the polity to make war on society. What was required in Britain was adjustment to society, rather than reaction or revolution. Reformers needed an avenue of communication between society and polity to keep the two in step. Public opinion provided just that. This view received an influential formulation in Francis Jeffrey's articles for the *Edinburgh Review* and indeed in the *Review* more generally. Despite a growing distance from popular sentiment, evident in the work of Bagehot, the notion of public opinion preserved its power to mediate between society and polity. It was the progressive quality of public opinion which ensured that there was a rational instrument in society for shaping and guiding the polity.[59]

Burrow suggests that the idea of public opinion as the watchdog of the state and sanction against its abuses declined in the mid-nineteenth century along with the radicalism of which it was part. Similarly, he

---

[58] J. Burrow, *Whigs and Liberals: Continuity and Change in English Political Thought* (Oxford, 1988), pp. 50–76.
[59] ibid., pp. 69–71.

argues that after 1848 it was much more plausible to see public opinion as sluggish and much less plausible to see it as volatile or dangerous.[60] Writers of this period like Mill and Bagehot were thus much occupied with bewailing its stagnancy and its stifling of individuality. While Bagehot saw it as reassuringly bovine, Mill was shrill in his denunciations of its tyranny. After glancing at Morley's anachronistic faith in rational politics, he ends his story with Wallas's 'dismayed' study of the manipulation of electorates by political parties and propaganda. By this stage, one might say, Hume's emphasis on the sovereignty of society over polity has been terrifyingly reversed.[61]

Like Gunn, Burrow has relatively little to say about the later period. Commentators in the 1860s and 1870s less cynical than Bagehot and less fastidious than Mill, scarcely difficult criteria to meet, were often a great deal more sanguine about the operation of 'public opinion'.[62] Burrow's hint about the declining relevance of 'public opinion' as a protection against government abuses does not accord with work emphasising the resilience of popular radicalism, a subject on which he is generally silent.[63] It should be clear too that many of the questions raised earlier about the character of 'public opinion', of how it is formed, where it is found, what it is for, are not dealt with by Burrow, who focuses only on progressiveness and rationality. Nonetheless, Burrow supplies important links between the eighteenth and nineteenth centuries, in particular his emphasis upon the impact of the Scottish enlightenment. Gunn's distinction between a more institutionally rooted Anglo-Saxon conception of public opinion and its more socially based French counterpart does identify an important characteristic of British debates, but this should not be equated with the absence of any sense of either 'society' or of the implications of social change, especially the spread of reading and ideas, for the character and basis of 'public opinion'.

---

[60] ibid., pp. 75–6.
[61] See Wallas on the 'admirable' thought of Hume in G. Wallas, *Human Nature in Politics* (London, 1908), pp. 203–4.
[62] Evidence of this can even be found in such an unpromising source as H. Maine, *Ancient Law* (London, 1861), p. 177.
[63] On this see E. F. Biagini and A. J. Reid, *Currents of Radicalism: Popular Radicalism, Organised Labour and Party Politics in Britain, 1850–1914* (Cambridge, 1991), also Biagini, *Liberty, Retrenchment and Reform*. A rather different note is struck by M. Taylor, *The Decline of British Radicalism, 1847–1860* (Oxford, 1995).

Habermas is best known for his sociological account of the rise and fall of the public sphere, but his intellectual history has also proved both influential and representative. His emphasis upon the rise of a rationalistic, bourgeois conception of 'public opinion' has been widely followed, particularly within literary studies. As Wahrman has shown, this approach can exaggerate the uniformity of ideas about 'public opinion' and neglect the complexities of their political representation. For Habermas, Mill and Tocqueville constitute a significant turning point in liberal views of the public sphere and public opinion.[64] Previous thinkers in the German tradition from Kant to Marx were united by a shared belief in the sovereignty of public opinion based upon a natural order of society which would prevent conflicts of interest from disturbing rational public debate. Where they differed was over the character of that natural order and its relation to capitalist society. Liberals like Mill and Tocqueville doubted the existence of such a natural order. Habermas regards Mill as believing that Chartism showed that class interests could not be excluded from the enlarged public sphere and that the tyranny of the majority had turned public opinion from the defender to the destroyer of political rationality. Liberal thought could only reply to the perversion of public opinion 'from an instrument of liberation into an agent of repression' by finding a source of unpolluted public opinion.[65] This it did by entrusting its formation to the critical discussion of 'a relatively small number of people specially educated for this task'.[66] The rest of the population was to be content with being represented, for 'their judgment must in general be exercised rather upon the characters and talents of the persons whom they appoint to decide these questions for them, than upon the questions themselves'.[67] Thus Mill's public sphere is 'literally declassed and structured into layers of representation'.[68]

'Already a problem for liberalism by the middle of the century, "public opinion" came fully into view as a problematic entity in the final quarter of the nineteenth century.' In this period, Habermas sees public opinion shorn of its normative aspect and reduced to 'an object of

---

[64] For the exposition of Habermas on Mill which follows, see Habermas, *The Structural Transformation of the Public Sphere*, pp. 129–40.

[65] Habermas, *The Structural Transformation of the Public Sphere*, p. 137.

[66] J. S. Mill, 'On liberty', p. 251, in *Collected Works*.

[67] J. S. Mill, 'Appendix', *Dissertations and Discussions* in the *Collected Works* XIX, ed. J. Robson, intro. A. Brady (Toronto, 1977), pp. 648–53.

[68] Habermas, *The Structural Transformation of the Public Sphere*, p. 137.

social-psychological research'. Once Tarde had extracted 'mass opinion' from its functional role it became 'a product of a communication process among masses that is neither bound by the principles of public discussion nor concerned with political domination'.[69] Habermas views Bryce and Dicey as retaining some of this normative dimension while showing traces of the drift to a social-psychological understanding of the term. This left them exposed to critiques such as that of A. C. Bentley, who missed 'a quantitative analysis of public opinion in terms of the different elements of the population'.[70] The new social-scientific approach to public opinion impoverished the concept in two ways. The 'public' became the 'mass' then the 'group', so abstracting the process of opinion formation from social conditions and political context. 'Opinion' was replaced by 'expression' then 'attitude', so including within the pale of public opinion the sort of unreflective and unarticulated prejudices it had been invented to critique.[71]

The existing intellectual history of 'public opinion' in the second half of the nineteenth century tends to focus firmly upon the more systematic writings of British intellectuals and public moralists. It is, though, attentive to ideas in context and to rhetorical nuance in ways not always matched by other kinds of work on political discourse. This study seeks to combine the close contextual reading of intellectual history with the more inclusive conception of political language characteristic of the new political history. Whilst alert to differences in genre and audience, it draws widely upon publications ranging from monographs on political theory to articles in the popular press in order to map the ways in which contemporaries invoked and contested the meaning of public opinion. In charting patterns of use over a significant period, it is necessary both to examine comparable sources over time and to look in depth at particular episodes of contestation and debate. The book therefore combines detailed reconstruction of particular phases of argument, with broader 'text-mining', of both pre- and post-digitisation varieties, to capture the career of 'public opinion' over the period. It seeks to marry extensive and intensive reading of nineteenth- and early twentieth-century discussion of 'public opinion'.

---

[69] ibid., *The Structural Transformation of the Public Sphere*, p. 240.
[70] Cited after P. A. Palmer, 'The concept of public opinion in political theory' in C. F. Wittke, ed., *Essays on History and Political Theory in Honor of Charles Howard McIlwain* (Cambridge, Mass., 1936), pp. 230–57.
[71] Habermas, *The Structural Transformation of the Public Sphere*, p. 241.

At the heart of the book lies the interaction between ideas about the public and public opinion, and ideas about labour. This reflects the character of the public as both a social *and* a political concept. The growth of a labour movement claiming to represent the largest class in society had important implications for inherited unitary, consumerist and intellectualist conceptions of the political public; conversely, the strength of such images of the public and its opinions presented real challenges for a movement and a party seeking to speak for labour. The consequences of the early Labour party's adoption of the older language of interests rather than that of class remain curiously under-explored. Examination of the relationship between ideas of labour and of the public helps us to understand the problems encountered and the choices made by the emergent Labour party in its effort to forge an electoral and political constituency, and hence to illuminate its debt to a broadly liberal political culture which it sought both to salvage and to transcend.

The book begins by tracing how contemporaries constructed the political public. Through careful attention to the nuances of political language, the chapter recovers two key linked conceptions of the political public. The first was deeply indebted to political economy and the market, and eulogised the *consuming* public; the second, related, notion identified the public with the ranks of the literate, of those who participated in the enlarged universe of political discourse made possible by the dissemination of print and education. The composition of the political public was contested throughout these years, but the general trend was towards a more encompassing conception of its membership. This was, not, however, a straightforward linear process, and the language of the public continued to be used to exclude as well as include. Nor, importantly, were all members of the public deemed equally important. The idea that opinions were *weighed* rather than *counted* exercised an enduring influence upon understandings of the emergence and value of public opinion. Reasonable opinions, it was widely argued, should be privileged in the identification of true public opinion. In one influential and symptomatic formulation, reasonableness was upheld, along with volume, persistence and intensity, as a defining characteristic of genuine 'public opinion'.

In a world not dominated by polling, contemporaries discovered 'public opinion' in a variety of locations. Lively disputes occurred over whether political organisations manufactured or collected 'public

opinion'. Such debates often focused upon the legitimacy and openness of public meetings and demonstrations held to advance particular
causes. The 'platform' retained real significance as an expression of
public opinion throughout this period, reflecting a widespread respect
for strongly held convictions. It was far, though, from being the sole
accepted repository of public opinion. The press was commonly considered to reveal much of the movements of the public mind, whether
as mirror or maker of opinion. As is shown in Chapter 2, disputes
over the relationship of the press to public opinion proved persistent,
but for most the press preserved throughout these years an important
role as a barometer of the political mood. Petitions, though less celebrated than press or platform, continued to be regarded as meaningful,
if disputable, tokens of public opinion, as the suffrage debates of the
Edwardian period suggest. Other possible sources of public opinion
existed – most obviously, the pulpit – but conventional understandings of politics laid particular store by the constitutional troika of
press, platform and petition.

In writing about the idea of 'public opinion', most attention has
been devoted to the question of rationality. This issue is addressed in
Chapter 3, which seeks to reconstruct arguments about public opinion that included, but were not necessarily dominated by, the familiar
'classics' of late Victorian and Edwardian political thought. It starts,
conventionally enough, with Mill's *On Liberty*, but contrasts the san-
guinity of its reviewers with the anxiety of its author. Focusing on
a number of debates – ranging from arguments about party organisation to disputes over imperialism – in which the nature of 'public
opinion' was a central concern, it is argued that existing work overstates the speed and finality of the fin-de-siècle decline in the reputation
of public opinion. This reflects in part an exaggerated assessment of
the optimism of earlier conceptions, in part an undue emphasis upon
the canonical over the conventional. More generally, as Wahrman
has noted, much work on 'public opinion' has been overly entranced
by linear rise-and-fall models that smooth out the complex trajectory of nineteenth-century debates.[72] While liberal understandings of
public opinion proved enduringly influential, and not merely on the
left, they never monopolised contemporary debate. However, though

[72] D. Wahrman, 'Public opinion, violence and the limits of constitutional politics'
in Vernon, *Re-reading the Constitution*, pp. 83–122.

conservatives could put greater stress upon the role of instinct and the virtues of the apolitical, they were usually keen to deny that there was any necessary opposition between the reasonable and the traditional.

Existing accounts of the late Victorian loss of faith in 'public opinion' tend to neglect the impact regularly attributed to its verdicts upon industrial disputes. Chapter 4 examines how and why late Victorians came to imbue 'public opinion' with a powerful role in shaping and moralising economic life. It combines close scrutiny of the theoretical consequences of the dissolution of wage-fund theory with an investigation of broader public discussion of industrial bargaining and wage rates. The consumerist connotations of the 'public' delineated in Chapter 1 might appear to suggest that public opinion was regarded as inherently hostile to organised labour, but many commentators argued that the public was becoming increasingly sympathetic to trade unions. Emphasis upon the collective consumer sovereignty of the public could, though, provide a potent rhetorical weapon for opponents of more militant trade union action, as many within the labour movement discovered during the industrial unrest of 1911 to 1914.

The closing chapter deals at length with the relationship between the idea of the labour interest and that of the public, and charts the complex ways in which politicians and trade unions sought to relate labour's interests to prevailing conceptions of the public and its interest. It does so in part by re-examining the interest-based analysis through which labour politicians demanded and justified parliamentary representation for the new party. Advocacy of the labour interest had a clear majoritarian warrant, but all such arguments were liable to charges of sectarianism. Industrial disputes in major industries presented obvious problems for those wishing to defend strikers against allegations of holding the public to ransom. The scale and character of the pre-war labour disputes intensified debates about the respective roles of trade unions and the Labour party, and the relationship between consumers and producers.[73] The powerful notion of the unified *consuming* public could be effectively mobilised against productionist appeals to labour interests. During the labour unrest of 1911–14, disparate voices on the left responded to accusations of robbing the public in a number of ways. Some, notably within the Social

---

[73] This is discussed further in J. Thompson, 'The great labour unrest and political thought in Britain, 1911–1914', *Labour History Review* (forthcoming 2014).

Democratic Federation (SDF), straightforwardly prioritised the productionist claims of strikers over the concerns of the consuming public,
but others, most obviously Ramsay MacDonald and Philip Snowden,
sought to speak for both strikers and the public by blaming price rises
on the monopolistic practices of capitalists. Labour politicians opposed
the sweating of workers to drive down costs, but many argued that
monopoly capitalism enabled employers to exploit consumers through
high prices and thus that public ownership was essential for the protection of both consumption and production.[74] Historians have disagreed markedly over the extent and implications of Labour's support
for free trade. Whilst Edwardian free trade thinking was more flexible
and less laissez-faire than is sometimes suggested, many mainstream
labour politicians retained a concern for the interests of consumers
that struck continental observers as peculiarly English.

The increasing importance attributed to 'public opinion' is a cardinal
feature of late Victorian and Edwardian political culture. The language
of 'public opinion' before 1914 both prefigures and departs from the
concerns of the interwar period recently analysed by historians of
the Labour party and associational culture.[75] However, debates both
before and after the First World War can seem very distant from a contemporary context in which 'public opinion' is often readily equated
with the results of polling. Lamenting the alleged impact of polling
in deadening public debate has become commonplace in recent years.
Even within the polling industry, the rise of the focus group suggests
the desire to secure a more dynamic picture of opinion formation.
The centrality of polling to conceptions of 'public opinion' is neither
inevitable nor inescapable, though many of the more utopian hopes

---

[74] J. Thompson, 'Political economy, the labour movement and the minimum
wage' in E. H. H. Green and D. Tanner, eds., *Strange Survival of Liberal
England: Political Leaders, Moral Values and the Reception of Economic
Debate* (Cambridge, 2007), pp. 62–88.

[75] H. McCarthy, 'Parties, voluntary associations and democratic politics in
interwar Britain, *Historical Journal*, 50 (2007), 891–912, 'Service clubs,
citizenship and equality: gender relations and middle-class associations in
Britain between the wars', *Historical Research*, 81 (2008), 531–52, and
'Democratizing British foreign policy: rethinking the peace ballot, 1934–35',
Journal of British Studies, 49 (2010), 358–87; L. Beers, *Your Britain: Media
and the Making of the Labour Party* (Cambridge, Mass., 2010); J. Lawrence,
'Labour and the politics of class, 1900–1940' in D. Feldman and J. Lawrence,
eds., *Structures and Transformations in Modern British History* (Cambridge,
2011), pp. 237–60.

expressed for the revival of the public sphere – especially through the Internet – have not fared well. Revisiting the history of 'public opinion' both reveals the inadequacy of naïve nostalgia for a more politically engaged past and underlines the poverty of polling-based accounts of the popular will. If the polling industry can appear wilfully ignorant of the historical existence of very different conceptions of 'public opinion', critiques of polling have frequently rested upon a contrast, explicit or implicit, between current trends and a hazily evoked past, in which the latter indicts the failings of the former. Historical reconstruction of a part-familiar, part-distant political culture may help foster more nuanced assessments of our present discontents.

1 | An open demos? The public and the question of membership

In a celebrated essay, Ross McKibbin argued that interwar Conservative electoral hegemony was the product of the prevalent distinction between the public and the working class. He noted that 'the constitutional classes made up civil society; in their own terminology they were "the public", and the public was what remained after the manual working class had been subtracted'.[1] McKibbin's argument has exercised considerable influence, perhaps unsurprisingly given the nature of interwar Britain. This was, after all, the era of the general strike and the challenge of labour. It is thus perhaps not unexpected that Kingsley Martin, the editor of the *New Statesman*, anticipated the McKibbin line in his study of *The British Public and the General Strike*, issued in 1926.[2] The issue is not, however, of relevance only to the interwar period.[3]

In 1914, the new liberal politician L. G. Chiozza Money contributed to a symposium in *Sell's Newspaper World* on the cost of newspapers. The debate was concerned with whether the dependence of newspapers on advertising income compromised their editorial independence. Money suggested that the collusion between newspapers and advertisers had led to an incorrigibly middle-class press. This had unfortunate consequences for the relationship between the 'public' and the 'working class'. As Chiozza Money explained,

---

[1] R. McKibbin, 'Class and conventional wisdom: the Conservative party and the "public" in inter-war Britain' in his *The Ideologies of Class: Social Relations in Britain, 1880–1950* (Oxford, 1990), p. 284; Beers, *Your Britain*.

[2] K. Martin, *The British Public and the General Strike* (London, 1926), p. 48 and *passim*.

[3] McKibbin's view of interwar Britain has been the subject of significant recent discussion. See Beers, *Your Britain*; Lawrence, 'Labour and the politics of class'; H. McCarthy, 'The League of Nations, public ritual and national identity in Britain, c. 1919–56', *History Workshop Journal*, 70 (2010), 109–32.

All our existing, successful newspapers are written for the well-to-do and middle classes, who are always addressed as 'the public', who are told that their class opinion is 'public opinion' and to whom the great mass of the nation – the working classes – are commended in the third person. The leader writer unconsciously addresses the reader as a person belonging to the 'classes' – as a person to whom the majority of advertisers appeal. To such a length is this carried that, when a labour dispute occurs, public opinion is spoken of as something distinguished from, or antagonistic to, working class opinion, although the wage earners form, of course, by far the largest part of the nation.[4]

This chapter addresses the composition of that 'public' whose opinion constituted the rising political force that was 'public opinion'. The interwar respectable 'public' adumbrated by McKibbin rested upon class distinctions, but other forms of exclusion have been found in the category of the 'public' in British political culture.

The faultline of gender has often been taken to be constitutive of the 'public', particularly in work on the early nineteenth century. Feminist historians of the gendering of public life, Habermasian students of the structuring of the public sphere, and Foucauldian analysts of subjectivities – all have shed light upon the degree to which masculinity was a prerequisite for political participation.[5] While these are diverse and complex bodies of work, their arguments often draw upon and link stories about the rise of middle-class domesticity, evangelical religion, and the enduring relevance of republican ideals of masculine virtue and independence.[6] We need to distinguish the question of how far women were actually involved in political life from the related, though distinct, issue of the extent to which contemporary conceptions of the

---

[4] *Sell's World's Press* (1914), 13.
[5] Much of this work is usefully discussed in M. McCormack, 'Men, "the public" and political history'. See also C. Hall, 'Private persons versus public someones: class, gender and politics in England, 1780–1850' in C. Steedman, C. Urwin & V. Walkerdine, eds., *Language, Gender and Childhood* (London, 1985), pp. 10–34; Vernon, *Politics and the People*; P. Joyce, *The Rule of Freedom: Liberalism and the Modern City* (London, 2003).
[6] The key texts here have been L. Davidoff and C. Hall, *Family Fortunes: Men and Women of the English Middle Class, 1780–1850* (London, 1987); B. Hilton, *The Age of Atonement: The Impact of Evangelicalism on Social and Economic Thought, 1795–1865* (Oxford, 1988); Pocock, *The Machiavellian Moment*.

political 'public' did, or did not, include women. The concern here
is essentially with the latter. Gender certainly could play an important part in determining eligibility for membership of the 'public', as
Dror Wahrman has shown for the 1820s.[7] However, the kind of 'public' examined by McKibbin depended upon the *inclusion* of women
for its political salience. The contrast he draws between a disruptive
unionised working class and the respectable public portrays the former
as essentially masculine. The link made between the composition of the
public and the constitution of the Tory electoral majority requires that
women be part of the first since they were so crucial to the second.[8]
It is thus apparent that the political 'public' was not necessarily an
all-male preserve.

The comparison between work on the 1820s and on the 1920s
should not be taken to imply a single shift from a masculine to a uni-
sex political public. As Wahrman makes clear, the concept of 'public
opinion' could follow a more tortuous course than such linear conceptions would predict.[9] The imagined political public was not coextensive
with the electorate. Habermas suggests that developments in communications and society lead to novel conceptions of 'public opinion', but
the relationship between technological and social change and images
of the political public is not so straightforward.[10] The inadequacy of
such a model for tracking the course of 'public opinion' is analogous
to the limitations of materialist accounts of class.[11] The composition
of 'the public' in the past can only be grasped by detailed investigation,
and a tight fit with developments outside of political culture should
not be expected. The 'public' with which we are concerned is that

---

[7] D. Wahrman, '"Middle-class" domesticity goes public: gender, class, and
politics from Queen Caroline to Queen Victoria', *Journal of British Studies*,
32, 4 (1993), 396–432.

[8] An interesting analysis of the Conservative response to female electors is
provided in D. Jarvis, '"Mrs Maggs and Betty": the conservative appeal to
women voters in the 1920s', *Twentieth Century British History*, 5, 2 (1994),
129–52.

[9] Wahrman, 'Public opinion, violence and the limits of constitutional politics',
pp. 108–9, 113.

[10] Habermas, *The Structural Transformation of the Public Sphere*, pp. 89–140.

[11] Fluctuations in the popularity of the language of class are contrasted with the
comparatively steady growth of industry in Wahrman, *Imagining the Middle
Class*. The issue is also examined in J. Thompson, 'After the fall: class and
political language in Britain, 1780–1900', *Historical Journal*, 39, 3 (1996),
785–806.

group whose political views were designated 'public opinion'; the subject matter is the political discourse of 'public opinion', especially in relation to labour issues.

It is important not to assume that class and gender are the only possible criteria for restricting the public. Literacy provides one obvious alternative. Education more generally has often been seen as integral to enlightenment visions of the public.[12] Literacy became increasingly prevalent in this period, and the related expansion of education was frequently assumed to have swelled the public. This argument was often made in relation to the perceived emergence of a more popular press in the 1890s.[13] Respectability, importantly distinct from class, was crucial to the franchise debate which culminated in the reform act of 1867.[14] The gulf between electors and non-voters after 1867 was supposed to mirror that between the 'respectable' and the 'residuum'. It remains to be seen whether the travails of the residuum extended to exclusion from the pale of the public as well as from the body of the electorate.

The rise of the language of the 'residuum' has been strongly linked to antagonism towards Irish migrants.[15] Eulogies to 'English public opinion' or to the 'great British public' were common in these years, as were contrasts with inferior foreign counterparts. In the wake of the boom in studies of national identity in the last two decades, recent years have seen increased scrutiny of ideas about 'national character'. Historians have differed markedly over both the importance and the nature of conceptions of 'national character' in nineteenth-century public life.[16]

---

[12] See the emphasis on informed political debate in R. Chartier, *The Cultural Origins of the French Revolution* (Durham, 1991).

[13] For instance, W. T. Stead, 'The London morning dailies that are and are to be', *Sell's World's Press* (1892), 107.

[14] See Hall, McClelland & Rendall, *Defining the Victorian Nation*.

[15] J. Davis, 'Jennings' buildings and the royal borough' in D. Feldman & G. Stedman Jones, *Metropolis London: Histories and Representations since 1800* (London, 1989), pp. 11–39; J. Davis, 'From "rookeries" to "communities": race, poverty and policing in London, 1850–1985', *History Workshop Journal*, 27 (Spring 1989), 66–85.

[16] P. Mandler, *The English National Character: The History of an Idea from Edmund Burke to Tony Blair* (New Haven, 2006); J. Parry, *The Politics of Patriotism: English Liberalism, National Identity and Europe, 1830–1886* (Cambridge, 2006); H. S. Jones, 'The idea of the "national" in Victorian political thought', *European Journal of Political Theory*, 5 (2006), 12–21.

By the late Victorian era, appeals to 'national character' were common, particularly in the discussion of foreign policy. As we shall see in Chapter 3, debates about the reasonableness of 'public opinion' in Britain could draw upon positive stereotypes about national character. However, the language of 'public opinion' also shared much with more universalist 'civilisational' thinking that emphasised the progressive impact of commercial society and technological progress throughout the developed world. Whereas Teutonist archaeologists of the national character located its origins sometime (when was not always clear) in the distant past, narratives of 'public opinion', even when written by Teutonists, cast its rise as predominantly an eighteenth- and nineteenth- century phenomenon, evident in the growth of the press and the advent of political associations under George III.[17] Peter Mandler has argued that Conservatives were more comfortable inculcating patriotic support for institutions than embracing the more inclusive, even levelling, implications of 'national character'. Others have insisted on the compatibility of the language of 'national character' with inegalitarian objectives.[18] Advocates of franchise extension, such as the radical Joseph Cowen, did try to disarm opposition by insisting that since workmen were Englishmen first and foremost, they could be depended upon to display independence and self-restraint. However, this kind of rhetoric was also used to suggest that it was the English capacity to recognise superior leadership that made further enfranchisement safe.[19] Appeals to 'national character' could thus incorporate a sense of hierarchy.

Part of the attraction of the language of 'public opinion' lay in its capacity to conjoin apparent inclusiveness with a more narrow sense of whose opinions actually counted; but more demotic conceptions

---

[17] J. R. Green, *A Short History of the English People* (London, 1875), pp. 745–6. Freeman was less impressed by the domestic political developments of the eighteenth century, preferring to emphasise later changes in communications and technology: E. A. Freeman, 'Progress in the nineteenth century', *The Chautauquan*, 14 (Jan. 1892), 434. The importance of the Reformation and the seventeenth century in narratives of the constitution could be expressed in terms of 'public opinion', particularly in the context of anti-Catholicism. See J. H. Otway, *Public Opinion: A Lecture* (Dublin, 1854), pp. 23–6.

[18] Mandler, *English National Character*, pp. 61, 106–7, 129; Parry, *Politics of Patriotism*, p. 25.

[19] J. Cowen, speech at Newcastle, 14 Feb. 1885, in E. R. Jones, *The Life and Speeches of Joseph Cowen, MP* (London, 1885), p. 275.

of the political public, pressing the claims of working men, were also advanced. Considerable care is required in interpreting the implied constitution of the public. Investigation must be comparative. Explicit definitions of those included within the scope of the public are relatively scarce. Inferences can be made, however, from comparisons and contrasts involving the public. Late Victorian conceptions of the public cannot, however, be understood solely by examining which groups were excluded from its ranks. Contemporaries considered the process by which the views of individuals became public opinion to be one of weighing rather than counting.[20] This distinction expressed the importance attributed to the intensity with which views were held in determining their contribution to the formation of a public opinion. Some social groups were deemed more influential in the emergence of a public opinion than others. Assumptions about the social centre of gravity of the public were apparent in its various personifications. 'The man on the omnibus' and 'the man in the street' are stereotypes of the public whose currency and use offer valuable insights into popular constructions of the public.

Political activists were eager to speak for the public. In propaganda terms, it was obviously preferable for a demonstration to be labelled an expression of public opinion than an instance of mob disorder. Plebeian politicians had much to gain from appropriating the language of 'public opinion', and much to lose from being portrayed as exterior to the body of the public. The work of Lawrence Goldman on the Social Science Association has helpfully illuminated the efforts of a predominantly middle-class organisation to speak for the public.[21] The Trades Union Congress, influenced in its early days by the model of the Social Science Association, bore a more problematic relationship to prevailing conceptions of the 'public'.[22] The difficulties faced

---

[20] See, for example, A. L. Lowell, *Public Opinion and Popular Government* (London, 1913), pp. 13–14.

[21] L. Goldman, *Science, Reform and Politics in Victorian Britain: The Social Science Association, 1857–1886* (Cambridge, 2002); L. Goldman, 'The Social Science Association: a context for mid-Victorian Liberalism', *English Historical Review*, 101 (Jan. 1986), 95–134.

[22] B. C. Roberts, *The Trades Union Congress, 1868–1921* (London, 1958); W. Hamish Fraser, *Trade Unions and Society: The Struggle for Acceptance, 1850–80* (London, 1974); M. Curthoys, *Governments, Labour, and the Law in Mid-Victorian Britain: The Trade Union Legislation of the 1870s* (Oxford, 2004).

by organisations seeking to articulate a vision of the labour interest, without falling prey to charges of sectionalism, can only be understood in the light of established conventions about the character and composition of the political public.

This book is concerned primarily with the history of political language, rather than with social identities. Since the late 1980s, there has been a massive surge in writing about both identity and consumption in modern Britain – much of it devoted to exploring the relationship between the two. A great deal of this literature has sought to reveal the role of consumption in sustaining such familiar forms of belonging as class, gender or nationhood; but latterly attention has been directed towards identities more intimately related to consumption (smoking, home-decorating), to consumerism as an ideology, and to the congruence of consumerism and citizenship in the politics of 'consumer consciousness'.[23] By the late nineteenth century, the idea of the consuming public was a familiar trope, apparent in discussions of theatre, travel or politics. The manner in which this idiom was deployed both to attack, and to defend, strikers will be examined in a later chapter. Little, however, will be said about the degree to which individuals identified as members of the public.

In his account of interwar Conservative hegemony, Ross McKibbin noted the ease with which middle-class observers spoke or wrote of the public and 'labour' or 'the working class' as mutually

---

[23] M. Hilton, *Smoking in British Popular Culture, 1800–2000: Perfect Pleasures* (Manchester, 2000); D. Cohen, *Household Gods: The British and Their Possessions* (New Haven, 2006); M. Hilton, *Consumerism in Twentieth-Century Britain: The Search for a Historical Movement* (Cambridge, 2003); M. Daunton and M. Hilton, *The Politics of Consumption: Material Culture and Citizenship in Europe and America* (Oxford, 2001); F. Trentmann, 'Civil society, commerce and the "citizen-consumer": popular meanings of free trade in modern Britain' in Trentmann, ed., *Paradoxes of Civil Society: New Perspectives on Modern German and British History* (New York and Oxford, 2000), pp. 306–31; F. Trentmann and V. Taylor, 'From users to consumers: water politics in nineteenth-century London' in F. Trentmann, ed., *The Making of the Consumer: Knowledge, Power and Identity in the Modern World* (Oxford, 2006), pp. 53–79. For a nineteenth-century example of collective action by consumers using the language of the public, see Great Central Gas Consumers Company, *A Letter to the Gas Consumers of the City of London, with an appendix, illustrating the force of public opinion and the advantages of free trade by the rise, progress, proceedings, position and prospects of the Great Central Gas Consumers' Company* (London, 1851).

exclusive.[24] Examples of such language before 1914 are legion. The question remains, though, of whether capitalists or employers were discussed in similar terms. It is suggested below that employers or capitalists and the public were frequently presented as mutually exclusive groups. Now there is clearly a difference between the act of treating a sectional minority, such as employers, as distinct from the public, and that of distinguishing the majoritarian interests of labour from those of the public. However, both employers and employees could be distinguished from the public in the same terms in a single sentence. The category of the public had strong consumerist overtones, and could be contrasted with more productivist collectivities, like capitalists or workers. The distinction between producers and consumers was as significant as that between classes in the construction of the public. Where individuals were located could depend upon in what capacity they were considered.

The second, and related, leading image of the public was cast in essentially intellectualist terms. According to this view, to be part of the public was to be part of the national political conversation. This was very much a reading public, but more active forms of participation, such as attendance at political meetings or involvement in political associations, were often privileged. Intellectualist visions identified the public quite closely with the urban middle classes, but also reflected the growth of literacy and extension of education in the last third of the nineteenth century. It will be argued that these years are marked by a contested expansion of the imagined scope of the public. The key to understanding struggles over the construction of the public lies in the relationship and interaction between consumerist and intellectualist accounts of its composition. These linked conceptions of the public will be considered in turn. We begin, though, with some clichés.

Personifying the public: from the man on the omnibus to the man in the street

The most durable aspect of the nineteenth-century language of 'public opinion' has proven to be its stereotypes. Two in particular have lived on, namely 'the man on the omnibus' (now shortened to bus) and 'the man in the street'. Both still have currency, but their nineteenth- and

---

[24] McKibbin, *Ideologies of Class*, pp. 284–5.

early twentieth-century careers were importantly distinct. 'The man on the omnibus' came into general use earlier, but never attained the currency of 'the man in the street' in its heyday of the 1890s and 1900s. It seems sensible to examine the former first.

'The man on the omnibus' remains a classic mid-Victorianism. The most famous and influential example of its invocation was in Walter Bagehot's *The English Constitution*. In a celebrated passage, Bagehot insisted that

The middle classes – the ordinary majority of educated men – are in the present day the despotic power in England. 'Public opinion', nowadays, 'is the opinion of the bald-headed man at the back of the omnibus.' It is *not* the opinion of the aristocratical classes as such; or of the most educated or refined classes as such; it is simply the opinion of the ordinary mass of educated, but still commonplace mankind.[25]

Nothing could be clearer than Bagehot's identification of 'public opinion' with the views of the middle classes. The coupling of 'man' with 'bald-headed' leaves little doubt about the gender of Bagehot's public. The passenger's lack of hair further suggests that Bagehot's public was as much a dictatorship of the middle-aged as the middle-class. The scene is evidently urban. For mid-century liberals like Bagehot, public opinion, along with liberalism, dwelt in the town rather than the country.[26] The notion of the 'middle classes' employed was fairly broad, not restricted to 'the most educated or refined classes', but it still presumed education at a point when its possession was closely linked to that of wealth.

The question remains, though, why an 'omnibus'? It is important not to exaggerate the significance of any putative answer, but guidance is provided by instances where the personification of the public is located elsewhere. In his discussion of 'Government by journalism' in 1886, the editor and jail inmate W. T. Stead identified the public with 'the man in the train, or the omnibus, or in the restaurant'.[27] Stead's troika affirms the middle-class urban credentials of the public, but, more interestingly, it also reiterates the motif of motion. Trains, omnibuses and travel were often taken as characteristic of

[25] W. Bagehot, *The English Constitution* in *The Collected Works of Walter Bagehot, vol. 5: Political Essays*, ed. N. St John-Stevas (London, 1974), p. 378.

[26] For example, see *Essays on Reform* (London, 1867), pp. 112, 134, 151.

[27] W. T. Stead, 'Government by journalism', *Contemporary Review*, 49 (May 1886), 662.

modernity in this period. Unlike modern-day directors of costume drama, nineteenth-century commentators were frequently struck by the accelerating pace of life, and of political change, in a world dominated by technological innovation. The transport revolution of the age had made the country smaller, and, perhaps, created a national public out of far-flung communities.[28]

It is worth noting, too, that Stead invariably places his representative man in a public space. In discussions of the press, the (male) head of the household, reading his newspaper over breakfast, was often taken to epitomise the public.[29] It might be expected that other Victorian personifications of the public would similarly domesticate the typical opinion-holder. Instead, the man on the omnibus, and, even more, the man in the street, are both *in* public, as well as of the public. 'Public opinion' was to be *public* opinion, forged by discussion. It was a tangible entity, not merely the shadowy summation of individual private views. It may not be fanciful to detect also a sense of the pervasive nature of the public. This is apparent, in precociously acute form, in Mill's meditation on the encroaching ubiquity of 'public opinion' in *On Liberty*.[30]

What is the significance of the descent from the omnibus to the street? Both locations share an unremarkable anonymity, but the street seems more thoroughly public. The street is hardly, of course, a symbol of technological progress. Reference to the man in the street can be found in Greville's *Memoirs* of 1831, but such early instances usually incorporate quotation marks.[31] It was only towards the end of the century that the phrase became widespread. This apotheosis reflects a more sceptical conception of the public, one more readily linked to ideas of the crowd. Views of the crowd were not uniformly derogatory, as the ecstatic descriptions of the London Jubilee crowds of June 1887 testify, but the man in the street was perhaps more susceptible to

---

[28] W. E. H. Lecky, *Democracy and Liberty* (2 vols., London, 1896), I, 210; Freeman, 'Progress in the nineteenth century'; J. Cowen, speech at Newcastle, 15 Nov., 1879 in Jones, *Life and Speeches of Joseph Cowen*, p. 149.

[29] This issue is discussed at greater length in Chapter 2.

[30] J. S. Mill, *On Liberty and Other Writings*, ed. S. Collini (Cambridge, 1989), pp. 66–9.

[31] Entry for 22 March 1831 in C. Greville, *The Greville Memoirs: A Journal of the Reigns of King George IV and King William IV*, ed. H. Reeve (3 vols., London, 1874), II, 131.

feeling, for good or ill, than his predecessor on the bus.[32] The man in
the street was definitely a more democratic individual. Leslie Stephen
made the middle-class character of the man on the omnibus plain in an
article on 'Anonymous Journalism'. Such social precision was unusual,
if unsurprising in the father of Virginia Woolf. Stephen remarked that

> If you want to know what one newspaper will say, ask the first hundred men
> who come out of a club in Pall Mall, and put the opinion of the majority into
> rather smarter language, deck it out with a few antitheses and illustrations,
> and provide it with a short irrelevant preface; – that will be the leading
> article of one newspaper. For another we must go a degree further down,
> and gather our samples in an omnibus; or drop yet another degree, and find
> out what people are saying at the bars of public-houses. But in any case a
> newspaper reflects primarily the sense of that particular spectrum amongst
> which it is intended to circulate.[33]

The man in the street, by virtue of not being on the omnibus, might
be assumed not to be middle class. The inference may be justified,
though the street was perhaps a less socially specific locale than the
omnibus. Reference to 'the man in the street' does not appear to imply
the exclusion of the middle class from the public, though it may signify
a diminished view of their weight in the formation of 'public opinion'.

An obvious continuity is provided by the gender of the stereotype.
The question of women's incorporation in the public will receive full
consideration below. Changing, or in this case unchanging, personifications of the public indicate that, whether gender-exclusive or not,
prevailing conceptions of the political public did not include men and
women on equal terms. Some contemporaries recognised this bias, particularly as female agitation for the suffrage intensified. A rare example
of a man commenting on such gendered language is provided by the
Fabian and free trader Brougham Villiers (F. J. Shaw), who proclaimed
that

> The reader may have noticed that hitherto throughout this book I have
> generally used such terms as 'the *man* in the street,' the 'average *man*,' or
> some other phrase implying the masculine gender, when I have spoken of
> the democratic influence which is fashioning modern politics in the likeness

---

[32] *Daily News*, 22 June 1887; *The Times*, 22 June 1887; *Daily Telegraph*, 22
June 1887.
[33] L. Stephen, 'Anonymous journalism', *Saint Pauls: A Monthly Magazine*, 2
(May 1868), 222.

of itself. I have done this advisedly. All the movements that compete for the support of the democracy to-day – Radicalism, Labourism, Socialism alike – necessarily appeal mainly from their masculine aspect.[34]

Militant suffragists, such as Teresa Billington-Greig, used the more pejorative associations of 'the man in the street' in their analysis of the gendered character of public opposition to female enfranchisement.[35] The journalist J. D. Symon, discussing, significantly, *The Press and its Story*, ended his survey of the work of 'a great newspaper office' with the moment when 'the paper has gone forth to the public, but before it reaches the man in the street or the man at the breakfast-table'.[36] The notion of the newspaper-reading public, it will be argued later, would lead in time to an increasing emphasis on the female presence in the public.[37]

It is important not to exaggerate the size or significance of the shift from the omnibus to the street. In no period was one phrase adopted to the exclusion of the other, though the relative trend is clear. Indeed, 'the man on the omnibus' gained renewed currency with the addition of the word 'Clapham'. This coinage is often attributed to Lord Bowen in the course of a negligence case in 1903. Bowen employed the term as a synonym for 'the reasonable man', and it has continued to serve this function in legal discourse.[38] This usage reflects the sometimes sardonic, but usually appreciative, tenor of nineteenth-century reference to 'the man on the omnibus'. Public transport continued to offer a prime location for representative man into the early twentieth century. Herbert Morrison in 1911 identified the 'dear old British public' with the man on the underground. Cost and competition had replaced the topper with the bowler hat, but Morrison's public man remained a businessman, albeit one ready to consider collectivist measures, and, interestingly, more reasonable than his John Bull predecessor.[39] The man in the street could be less warmly regarded, but his identification

---

[34] B. Villiers (F. J. Shaw), *Modern Democracy: A Study in Tendencies* (London, 1912), p. 212.
[35] T. Billington-Greig, 'The militant policy of women suffragists' in *The Non-Violent Militant: Selected Writings of Teresa Billington-Greig*, ed. C. McPhee & A. FitzGerald (London, 1987), p. 115.
[36] J. D. Symon, *The Press and its Story* (London, 1914), p. 135.
[37] See Chapter 2.
[38] e.g. N. Rees, *Dictionary of Popular Phrases* (London, 1990), p. 158.
[39] *Labour Leader*, 7 April 1911.

with 'public opinion' was also weaker. Not infrequently, the man in the street was taken as a synecdoche for the opinion of the debased 'mass' rather than the more enlightened 'public'.[40]

Both catchphrases have come to be identified with 'average' opinion. It is important, however, not to read nineteenth-century political language through conceptions of 'public opinion' derived from the dominance of opinion polling. Archetypal man, whether on the bus or in the street, was the representative embodiment of 'public opinion' but should not be equated with average, in the sense of mean, opinion. The class bias implicit in the stereotype of the man on the omnibus certainly precludes any identification with an average drawn from the population as a whole. Contemporary notions of 'public opinion', as we shall see in later chapters, tended to regard its formation as due to the weighing rather than counting of opinions, and to emphasise its corporate rather than aggregative character. The language of averages was perhaps in greater evidence in the 1890s and 1900s than earlier in the century, and this does reflect more inclusive and less elitist conceptions of public opinion; but even champions of average opinion, like Harmsworth, recognised the disproportionate role of opinion formers, and much of the discourse of public opinion retained an emphasis upon strongly held, and outwardly expressed, convictions.[41] Where the language of averages was used, it often seems closer to a mode than a mean in its personification of public opinion.

The complexity of the terminology of the man in the street and of reference to the average is evident in an article published in the conservative *Monthly Review* by the unionist free fooder W. R. Malcolm. In making the case for a sanguine appraisal of the socialist threat, Malcolm noted that

The 'essential reasonableness of English public opinion', however, will set a limit to any exaggerated or visionary proposals, for after all it is to the man in the street that the final decision must be referred . . . the man in the street, the average man, is neither profligate nor idle. He is honest and industrious, and endowed with the ordinary qualities which have made our country successful.[42]

The man in the street embodied public opinion, but his location in the class structure was less obvious. Malcolm's remark that 'the man in the

[40] For instance, J. R. MacDonald, *Syndicalism* (London, 1912), p. 19.
[41] *Mitchell's Newspaper Directory* (1905), 9.   [42] ibid., 64.

street . . . will acquiesce in the growing power of trade unions' could be taken to support the view that the working classes were excluded from the ranks of the public.[43] However, Malcolm also noted that 'the man in the street . . . is impressed by the fact that the labourer's normal attitude as regards his employer is more or less antagonism, and in his practical fashion he is willing to consider any means of curing these grievances.'[44] The implication of the last quotation might well be that the man concerned was neither an employer nor a worker. He may be the average man, but he appears to embody a public opinion that operates as the embodiment of a collective hard-working reasonableness rather than as a summation of particular views. This normative dimension was an important aspect of the language of 'public opinion' before 1914. In order to capture more fully the subtle inclusions and exclusions implicit in the political language of public opinion, we need to focus upon two key images: the consuming public, and the thinking public. We start with the former.

The consuming public

In his study of *Trade Unions: Their Origins and Objects, Influence and Efficacy*, issued in 1884, trade unionist William Trant complained that combination amongst workmen was subject to criticisms not faced by other forms of social union. This was hardly a striking observation, but the terms in which it was made repay close attention. Trant wrote that

It is indeed surprising that when the public – or a portion of them – combine as co-operators, so that the tradesmen shall not get too large a profit, no one complains but the shopkeepers; that when capitalists combine to obtain enormous profits at the cost of everybody, nobody grumbles; and it is not until the workmen combine, in order to get increased wages for their labour, that all the world is alarmed, and cries out in despair that the country is going to pieces.[45]

The public, the capitalists and the workmen were treated as distinct, yet the overlap between the first and the last was obvious. Co-operators and trade unionists were scarcely mutually exclusive

---

[43] ibid., 76–7.   [44] ibid., 70.
[45] W. Trant, *Trade Unions: Their Origins and Objects, Influence and Efficacy* (London, 1884), p. 144.

categories. Indeed, they were often seen as almost coextensive. It is clear that Trant's public was a body of consumers, keen to minimise its expenditure. In employing this understanding of 'the public', Trant was perpetuating a standard nineteenth-century trope. This section explores the identification of the public with the body of consumers.

Beatrice and Sidney Webb had little doubt that it was consumption which constituted the public. They argued in *Industrial Democracy* that

> During the last twenty years arbitration has grown in popularity with the public, and each ministry in succession prides itself on having attempted to facilitate its application. Whenever industrial war breaks out, we have, in these days, a widespread feeling among the public that both parties should voluntarily submit to the decision of an impartial arbitrator. But however convenient this solution may be to a *public of consumers*, the two combatants seldom show any alacrity in seeking it, and can rarely be persuaded to agree to refer their quarrel to any outside authority.[46]

For the Webbs, consumption was not simply an activity engaged in by a public otherwise delimited: the public was defined by the act of consumption. Nor was this view a Fabian peculiarity. In a paper given at the 1874 meeting of the National Association for the Promotion of Social Science, A. T. Innes explored the 'severance of interests between trade unions', since 'to each of these unions the members of others are, economically, members of the public, outsiders, and mere consumers, against whom, as well as against capital, the regulations are intended to tell.'[47] R. A. Scott-James in his account of *The Influence of the Press* observed sardonically that 'the capitalist depends no more on the good-will of the consumers – the public – than Rome depended on the faith reposed in it by the masses'.[48]

The distinction between producers and consumers was not the preserve of Fabian theorists. Much important historiography has served to highlight its significance in a variety of contexts. The populist turn in nineteenth-century studies has been concerned to emphasise the identity of the people as the productive nation.[49] Work on tariff reform

---

[46] S. & B. Webb, *Industrial Democracy* (London, 1897), I, 224–5 (my emphasis).
[47] A. T. Innes, 'Trade unionism; its limits and its future', *Transactions of the National Association for the Promotion of Social Science* (1874), 918.
[48] R. A. Scott-James, *The Influence of the Press* (London, 1913), pp. 298–9.
[49] On populism see J. Epstein, 'The populist turn', *Journal of British Studies*, 32, 2 (April 1993), 177–89.

and the fiscal debate has shown the distinction between producers and consumers to be central to Edwardian politics.[50] Most suggestively, the historiography of free trade political culture suggests the potency in Britain of appeals to consumer interests.[51] Popular political argument tended to stress the advantages of free trade to the working-class consumer, most famously through observations about loaf sizes and free breakfasts. Free trade discourse was, of course, both broader and more complex than this; but commemoration of the crusade against the Corn Laws placed the interests of consumers at the heart of popular free trade politics. Free trade became more central to popular politics in the last third of the century than it had actually been in the 1830s and 1840s.[52]

Orthodox political economy in Britain was strongly attached to free trade and to the interests of consumers.[53] The identification of the public with the consumers was conventional within political economy. Chapter 4 addresses the rise of the view that 'public opinion' was an economic force, which did much to regulate industrial disputes and

[50] See, in particular, E. H. H. Green, *The Crisis of Conservatism: The Politics, Economics and Ideology of the British Conservative Party, 1880–1914* (London, 1995).

[51] A. Howe, *Free Trade and Liberal England, 1846–1946* (Oxford, 1997); F. Trentmann, *Free Trade Nation: Commerce, Consumption, and Civil Society in Modern Britain* (Oxford, 2008). See also F. Trentmann, 'The strange death of free trade: the erosion of "liberal consensus" in Great Britain, c. 1903–32' in E. F. Biagini, ed., *Citizenship and Community: Liberals, Radicals and Collective Identities in the British Isles, 1865–1931* (Cambridge, 1996), pp. 219–51; F. Trentmann, 'National identity and consumer politics: free trade and tariff reform' in D. Winch & P. O'Brien, eds., *The Political Economy of British Historical Experience, 1688–1914* (Oxford, 2002), pp. 215–44; F. Trentmann, 'Bread, milk and democracy in modern Britain: material culture and citizenship in Britain and America' in Daunton & Hilton, eds., *The Politics of Consumption*, pp. 129–63; Trentmann, 'Civil society, commerce and the "citizen-consumer"', p. 306.

[52] Biagini, *Liberty, Retrenchment and Reform*, esp. pp. 84–139. See also E. F. Biagini, 'Popular liberals, Gladstonian finance, and the debate on taxation, 1860–1914' in Biagini & Reid, eds., *Currents of Radicalism*, pp. 134–63. The role of organisations like the Cobden Club in fostering this process is examined in Howe, *Free Trade and Liberal England*. For the struggle over Chartism's legacy, see A. Taylor, 'Commemoration, memorialisation and political memory in post-Chartist radicalism: the 1885 Halifax Chartist Reunion in context' in O. Ashton, R. Fyson and S. Roberts, eds., *The Chartist Legacy* (Woodbridge, 1999), esp. pp. 259–61, 267.

[53] It might be suggested that an emphasis on consumption was further encouraged by the development of marginalism in the 1870s.

to preserve economic peace. This view was strongly rooted in a consumerist notion of the public, which provided the common interest that bound the public together and distinguished its interests from those of the producers waging industrial war. The prevalence of consumerist understandings of the public is apparent in debates concerning trade unions and industrial conflicts. The recurrence of strikes and royal commissions provides valuable evidence by which to assess any development over time in the idea of the consuming public.

In the minority report of the Royal Commission of 1867, chiefly written by positivist Frederic Harrison and the Christian socialist Thomas Hughes, consideration was given to the relationship between the interests of trade unions and those of the public. The report argued that accepted views on the matter were mistaken, for

Even on the assumption that the sole object of unionism is to secure the highest wages obtainable, it would be a very shallow conclusion (which is too often drawn) that this is necessarily in antagonism with the public interest. There are people who argue that the interest of the public is to have all products as cheap as possible, and that therefore the larger the profits which are retained by the producers, the worse for the public interest. But this conception of the public as something outside the whole body of producers (who collectively form perhaps nine-tenths of the population) is singularly narrow.[54]

In order to constitute nine-tenths of the population, 'the whole body of producers' must include both employers and employed, as is suggested by the reference to the profits retained by the producers. An account of the public which limited its membership to the remaining tenth of society would indeed be 'singularly narrow', and, perhaps, of limited purchase in the age of Bright. It is possible, of course, that the public, whose interest was 'to have all products as cheap as possible', was a public of consumers, many of whom might also happen to be producers. Support for this interpretation is supplied by Booth's draft report, which refers concisely to 'the general public, the consumers who have to pay a higher price for their commodities than they would otherwise have to'.[55]

[54] *Royal Commission on the Trade Unions*, Parliamentary Papers (1869), Minority report, p. xli.
[55] ibid., draft report by Mr Booth, p. cviii.

This understanding of the public was deployed at the same time by R. H. Hutton in his influential essay on 'The political character of the working classes', in *Essays on Reform*. Hutton addressed the relationship between the old guilds and the new unions in the following terms:

The organization, which, with its good sympathy and its evil of restriction, had characterized the Guilds of former times, has now passed from the whole Trade into the working portion of several of them, acquiring a powerful consistency; and whereas, formerly, each commerce looked on the outside consumer as the enemy, now the master and the public seem combined against the profits of the artisan.[56]

The identification of the public with 'the outside consumer' and the distinction between the public and the producers could not be clearer. This conception of the public is equally apparent, though with a different politics, in the later work of the conservative historical economist, W. J. Cunningham. In *Politics and Economics*, Cunningham lamented the demise of the guilds, remarking that whereas 'the craft guilds were started in the interest of the public and the craft alike, the trades unions were formed for the sake of the workers'.[57]

Invocation of the public as a body of consumers often involved a contrast with some group of producers. This meant, as Hutton suggests, that individuals could be regarded as members of the public when considered as consumers, but excluded from its ranks when viewed as producers. Press and periodical coverage of industrial disputes illuminates this process. Coal miners might be members of the public affected by a railway strike, but not of the public which 'suffered' in the event of a coal dispute. An identical asymmetry holds for the owners of coal mines. Minor disputes in small industries are less revealing, since the exclusion of the participants from the public is less noteworthy where the numbers concerned are small. The focus here, therefore, is on major breakdowns in industrial peace where the forces involved are large. Disputes between miners and owners fulfil this requirement and supply sufficient examples to accommodate comparison through time.

[56] R. H. Hutton, 'The political character of the working classes', *Essays on Reform*, p. 58.
[57] W. J. Cunningham, *Politics and Economics: An Essay on the Principles of Political Economy, Together with a Survey of Recent Legislation* (London, 1885), p. 98.

The struggle of the miners for 'a living wage' in the autumn of 1893 is one of the most celebrated of Victorian strikes. It originated in resistance to wage cuts inspired by falling prices, but came to express more fundamental criticism of the workings of the market. The dispute has also received attention because of the involvement of Rosebery, the foreign secretary, which has been considered a departure from the tradition of government non-intervention in industrial conflicts, if one barely recognised by the Prime Minister of the time.[58] Blanket coverage in the daily press allows the historian to gauge the importance of differing political perspectives in constructions of the public.

Particular interest attaches to the proposal floated during the dispute to prevent future loss of production by the creation of 'a coal trust, to embrace all the collieries of the nation'. *The Times* noted in its leader that this was 'an interesting and striking idea, which, however, the consumer may be pardoned for regarding with suspicion'.[59] The paper elaborated in a subsequent editorial, which noted that

while coalowners and miners habitually differ, and not infrequently fight, upon many things, there is one object which at all times they pursue in common – namely, to see coal at the highest possible price. The interest of the community, however, is directly opposed to that of the coal trade upon this point, and no coal trust can be started with the slightest prospect of success that does not tend to benefit the public as well as the trade.[60]

The equation of the 'public' and the 'community' was absolute, and the interests of consumers foremost. In the larger dispute of 1912, loss of employment was more widespread, but in 1893, at least for the paper of record, it was the inflated cost of coal to the public which was the prime matter of concern.

The tendency to consider the public as a body of consumers is as apparent in the coverage of the plebeian *Reynolds's Newspaper* as in that of the patrician *Times*. There is a certain ambiguity in *Reynolds's* invocation of the public between a consuming public and a public conceived on class lines, whose genealogy is traced in the next section of this chapter. The complexities of the concept of the public in the pages of *Reynolds's* are nicely manifested in 'An appeal to the public' on behalf of the railway workers, which bemoaned that

---

[58] Matthew, *Gladstone*, p. 594.
[59] *The Times*, 20 Sep. 1893.   [60] *The Times*, 25 Sep. 1893.

It must, unfortunately, be admitted that the public in general seldom consider the cause of the workers as particularly appertaining to their own welfare . . . Had the public, on the announcement of the present Coal Strike, come forward and boldly contributed to the men's funds . . . the strike might have been averted. But the people of this country have apparently not yet recognised that by upholding the claims of Labour they are really placing themselves in a better position than heretofore. If they read the Report of the Board of Trade upon the accidents which have occurred on the railways in the last year, they cannot but be convinced. The general public should, therefore, feel greatly indebted to this class of men, who have thus enabled them to rapidly pass from one country to another with such a minimum loss of life.[61]

It is noticeable that the public and the people are used interchangeably, though the workers considered appear somewhat separate from the former. The swift transition from coal miners to railway workers suggests that the exclusion of each from the body of the public is assumed. More surprisingly, the reference to 'the people of this country' does not lead to any consideration of their productivist interests. The benefit of 'upholding the claims of Labour' will be a reduction in the danger of travel for railway passengers rather than an advance in the forward march of labour. 'The general public' seems to operate as a collection of consumers, but one which may also have class overtones.

The public did not, however, receive an entirely bad press from *Reynolds's* during the dispute. 'Northumbrian', a regular column in the paper, argued that the miners 'know full well that it is not the wish of the public that they should work for wages below the possible existence point'. The basis for this statement was that 'when they [the miners] were getting the best standard of wages the consumers cheerfully paid the cost imposed on their fuel'.[62] In general, the paper was concerned to emphasise that the miners and the workers were both victims of the greed of the owners, 'vampires in human form' who, 'like so many leeches, would suck the last drop of blood from the body of their victims.'[63] It backed the eventual intervention of the government, though it felt that this was forced by the support of 'public opinion' for the miners. The paper argued in a leader that

---

[61] *Reynolds's Newspaper*, 10 Sep. 1893.
[62] *Reynolds's Newspaper*, 24 Sep. 1893.
[63] *Reynolds's Newspaper*, 8 Oct. 1893.

Not only have the miners, their wives and children, suffered and even died through starvation, but hundreds and thousands of people in other industries have been compelled either to work less hours or have been thrown out of work altogether. The general public have also suffered by being forced to pay an exorbitant price for coal.[64]

It is noteworthy that the public is distinguished from 'people in other industries' and that the former are considered as consumers, while the latter are treated as producers.

The association of the public with consumption appears clear, but this does not resolve the question of membership in *Reynolds's*. An examination of the idea of the consuming public reveals that apparent contrasts between workers and the public may be contrasts between activities, namely production and consumption, rather than actors. However, the public whose consumption was threatened could be defined in other ways. The public could be considered as producers. One editorial equated 'the weight of public judgement' with the views of the 'average observer' who 'does not deeply interest himself in trade disputes unless it [sic] affects his own particular industry'.[65] In its last editorial on the strike, the paper proudly noted the opposition to the miners of 'the Queen, the clergy, and the wealthy'. The article went on to claim that 'the miner's cause was a just one, and was worthy of the success it has achieved. It won for the toilers the sympathy of the masses, who joined hands in the great war. Despite the lying assertions of the avaricious capitalists, public opinion has not been misled.'[66] *Reynolds's* employment of the term 'public' observed the parameters established by more general use, but gave to it a populist spin, unsurprising in a paper saturated in the language of popular melodrama. Few other newspapers in 1893 compared the owners to the undead.

The daily newspaper most sympathetic to the miners was the *Daily Chronicle*, which energetically encouraged its readers to assist 'these poor creatures'.[67] Its editorials proclaimed a decided debt to the 'ethical conceptions of men like Maurice and Kingsley' and recommended the closing pages of Zola's *Germinal* as an object lesson to the miners'

[64] *Reynolds's Newspaper*, 19 Nov. 1893.
[65] *Reynolds's Newspaper*, 17 Sep. 1893.
[66] *Reynolds's Newspaper*, 26 Nov. 1893.   [67] *Daily Chronicle*, 2 Oct. 1893.

leaders in how to avoid defeat.[68] The interest of the public in the dispute was taken to be that of a consumer, but the question was asked, 'does anyone believe that the public will be better off because the miners get 2s. 11d. instead of 3s. 6d?'[69] In common with other newspapers, the *Chronicle* took the meeting of town mayors, arranged to put pressure on the combatants, 'as representing the neutral though suffering public'.[70] This emphasis upon the representative character of the leaders of local government recurred in 1912, reflecting the prestige and vitality of municipal urban politics, and drawing upon the established notion of a rate-paying public. The neutrality of the public was axiomatic in discussions of the dispute, as was its unity. The 'suffering public' was a public unified by its consuming interest. There was little room for the idea that members of the public might have distinct class interests.

The *Chronicle* addressed 'the newspaper-reading public' in terms which suggest a degree of social distance from the workers.[71] In an interesting editorial, the paper asked

How is it ... that so little sympathy has been extended to the miners ... We cannot help fearing that it is because the public are entertaining a grave misconception as to what the earnings of the miners are ... It is indeed a notable thing that the workpeople who have been thrown out of work by the lock-out in scores of different trades utter no complaint ... We ask the public to take these facts into account.[72]

The mention of workpeople implies a separation from the public in keeping with appealing to readers to 'come to the rescue of these poor creatures'.[73] Opposition to the wages fund was prevalent in the leader columns of the *Chronicle*, and the paper requested that 'the *Pall Mall Gazette* will tell us what the laws of political economy are, as the Professors of the science seem to be at loggerheads about them'. Alarm was expressed, though, at the *Gazette*'s 'pseudo-science', since it might affect those with 'wealth and influence and education ... whose share in creating public opinion is enormous'.[74] The public's centre of gravity was held to lie towards its upper social end.

[68] For Maurice & Kingsley, see *Daily Chronicle*, 21 Oct. 1893, and for Zola, *Daily Chronicle*, 20 Oct. 1893.
[69] *Daily Chronicle*, 28 Sep. 1893.   [70] *Daily Chronicle*, 9 Oct. 1893.
[71] *Daily Chronicle*, 19 Oct. 1893.   [72] *Daily Chronicle*, 19 Sep. 1893.
[73] *Daily Chronicle*, 2 Oct. 1893.   [74] *Daily Chronicle*, 3 Oct. 1893.

The *Pall Mall Gazette* upheld the prestige of political economy, if not of the wages fund, in a manner calculated to outrage the humanitarian sympathies of the *Chronicle*. Its conception of the public was framed very much in terms of consumption. It attacked the 'sympathy' strike, 'where men who have no grievance are brought into the field to support others who have grievances'. Recent events were

a species of strike designed to hit the consumers. 'If our friends' (it is said) 'have to submit to lower wages, you, the public, shall not get any coal. That will make you bring the pressure of opinion to bear upon coal-owners who are trying to cut down our friends' wages.' This is a species of strike which usually fails, as in the present instance, where these strikers are returning to work at the old rate of wages.[75]

It is time to turn now to the larger and more infamous coal dispute of 1912. The focus of the analysis will be on changes from the patterns of 1893.

The miners' strike of 1912 has occupied an important place in the much-studied unrest of 1911–14.[76] It was a national strike which affected large swathes of the British coal industry and resulted in the establishment of a minimum wage structure. The best part of a million men were on strike and the reduction in the supply of coal was more marked than in 1893. Both strikes coincided with periods of Liberal government, but in 1912 the situation was rendered more complex by the existence of the Labour party. The magnitude of the dispute made commentators more likely than in 1893 to argue that the mines were making war not only, or even primarily, upon the owners, but also on the public.[77] Disruption of industry occurred on a significant scale, leading to loss of work and pay. Many individuals thus suffered from more than an increase in the price of coal. The suffering of consumers did not loom so large in the press coverage of 1912 as in that of 1893.

Reporting of the 1912 strike reiterates many of the characteristics of that of 1893. The public is counterpoised to the owners and the miners. Much of the invocation of the public treats its identity and

---

[75] *Pall Mall Gazette*, 29 Sep. 1893.
[76] For the standard account of trade unionism in this period, see H. A. Clegg, A. Fox & A. F. Thompson, *A History of British Trade Unions Since 1889, vol. 2: 1911–1933* (Oxford, 1985). On the government response to the unrest, see J. Morgan, *Conflict and Order: The Police and Labour Disputes in England and Wales, 1900–1939* (Oxford, 1987), ch. 3.
[77] See the letter from R. E. Froude in *The Times*, 12 March 1912.

interests as primarily consumerist. It might be thought that the sheer number of miners involved, particularly once their dependants were added, would complicate the contrast between miners and the public. J. R. Mozley, a correspondent to *The Times*, raised this problem by asking, 'was it not Burke who said that he knew not how to draw up an indictment against a nation? Even so, it is not easy to draw up an indictment against a million workers.'[78] In general, however, the miners are not described as part of the public. Nor were the owners. Sir John Simon in a speech in Manchester neatly summarised conventional wisdom with the statement that 'there were three parties to the dispute – the coalowners, the miners, and the public, including the poorest of the population.'[79] From a differing political perspective, Lyttleton insisted to a Primrose League meeting that the 'third party to great strikes... was the public, the nation'.[80] Considerable emphasis was laid, particularly by those unsympathetic to the miners' claims, on the impact of the strike upon the poorest members of the community. The primacy of the considerations of consumers, and the role of gender, were well captured by the *Daily Chronicle*, which commented that

The Miner's federation... has funds enough to fight a considerable time... And... employers... could afford to let their collieries lie idle for weeks with little net loss... But, again, what of the public? Evidently they would be hurt much sooner, from the poor slum dweller, no longer able to buy coal in her accustomed bucketfulls and pennyworths, to the gigantic iron and steel works compelled to blow out their furnaces. It has been said truly... that all labour disputes injure third parties.[81]

It was, of course, logical to emphasise the actions of women in the consuming public, since so many purchasing decisions were actually made by women. Awareness of women's role as consumers had been fostered by the fiscal controversy. H. W. Massingham edited a volume on *Labour and Protection* that included a chapter on 'The co-operative housewife', which addressed the projected impact of Chamberlain's proposals on the working-class household budget.[82] Political parties

---

[78] *The Times*, 26 Feb. 1912.   [79] Reported in *The Times*, 4 Mar. 1912.
[80] *The Times*, 28 Feb. 1912.   [81] *Daily Chronicle*, 24 Feb. 1912.
[82] R. Nash, 'The co-operative housewife' in H. W. Massingham, ed., *Labour and Protection* (London, 1903), pp. 169–205; E. Rappaport, *Shopping for Pleasure: Women in the Making of London's West End* (Princeton, 2001). On

were unsurprisingly more concerned to appeal to women after 1918, but Edwardian debates about tariff reform and the franchise frequently portrayed women as members of the public.[83]

The category of the 'public' was highly contested, and this is reflected in its invocation by newspapers across the political spectrum. *The Times* regarded the action of the miners as 'individualism in its worst form' and attacked the 'haughty and overbearing position' of the unions.[84] It assured its readers, however, that 'it [the Miner's Federation] will command no sympathy from the general public or from the other classes of workmen who are being thrown out of work and to whom the cost of living... would infallibly rise if the miners had their way'.[85] The paper's use of the term 'general' softens but does not erase the distinction drawn between the public and 'other classes of workmen'. On 14 March, the leader writer predicted that 'the pressure upon the community, the working classes, and the trade union funds becomes more acute and more general'.[86] While the public of *The Times* continued to be conceived as primarily consumers, the divorce implied between it and the working class may not simply be that between consumers and producers. The industrial militancy of the pre-war years, sometimes linked to the bugbear of syndicalism, made labour seem more alien to the *Times*-reading classes. Reference to the 'nation', often paired with the 'public', was more common in 1912 than in 1893, and criticism of the 'selfishness' of the miners in the respectable press was more prevalent. That said, the paper urged the combatants to 'remember the public, and particularly the poorer classes'.[87]

The most popular liberal newspaper of the period was the *Daily News*. Like *The Times*, the *Daily News* argued that 'public opinion' had an important part to play in resolving the dispute. In early March, it ran an editorial claiming that 'the submission of the miners could only be exacted by exhaustion or by the pressure of public opinion, in particular the opinion of the workmen in other industries suspended by

---

gender and free trade, see Trentmann, 'Bread, milk and democracy in modern Britain'.
[83] See 'The thinking public' below.
[84] *The Times*, 25 Mar. 1912; *The Times*, 1 Mar. 1912.
[85] *The Times*, 1 Mar. 1912.   [86] *The Times*, 14 Mar. 1912.
[87] *The Times*, 27 Feb. 1912.

their action'.[88] This inclusive tone characterises liberal invocation of the 'public' during the dispute. The notion that the opinion of the public would determine the outcome of the strike was widely publicised. Eloquent tribute was paid to the indivisible sovereignty of the public by Philip Snowden, writing in the *Daily News*. The future Labour chancellor counselled the miners that

They may have, as one of their leaders is reported to have said, the power to unmake Governments and to shake thrones; but great as is their power, they must not forget that there is a power greater than they – a power against which no class or section can rebel indefinitely with success, and that greater power is public opinion.[89]

It was typical of the *News* to observe that 'the conduct of the owners has been a succession of gross blunders for which the public and not they are called upon to pay'.[90] The eulogy for the consuming interests of the public, 'from the poor slum dweller . . . to the gigantic iron and steel works', offered in the *Daily Chronicle* has already been quoted.[91] In a joint publication, the progressive Cambridge economists Charles Watney and James A. Little considered solutions to *Industrial Warfare* from the perspectives of worker, employer and public, devoting a separate section to each.[92] Their public was dominated by reasonable working-class consumers.

Reynolds's Newspaper was predictably supportive of the miners, though concerned that they might alienate the public by rejecting the government's efforts at conciliation. The paper's cartoons are particularly revealing. In one a stout, prosperous 'John Bull' addresses an eminently respectable miner with the words,

Jack, I admire the brave and honourable fight you have put up, and the splendid restraint you have shown in face of the impudent and contemptible insults of a section of the Tory Press. In this Bill you have got the principle you came out for. Take it, lad, and work it, and fight for every penny of your schedule on the District Boards.[93]

An earlier image portrays a gargantuan coal owner squeezing the life out of a besuited man, 'the consumer', identified with the 'interests of

---

[88] *Daily News*, 6 Mar. 1912.   [89] *Daily News*, 7 Mar. 1912.
[90] *Daily News*, 28 Mar. 1912.   [91] *Daily Chronicle*, 24 Feb. 1912.
[92] C. Watney & J. A. Little, *Industrial Warfare: The Aims and Claims of Capital and Labour* (London, 1912).
[93] *Reynolds's Newspaper*, 31 Mar. 1912.

the state', and doing likewise to a miner, who personifies the 'rights of labour'.[94] In an interesting manifesto on behalf of the Dockers' and General Workers' Union, Ben Tillett extended this rhetorical alliance to embrace other workers and the public. Tillett began,

Dear Sirs and Brothers, The miners have for years fought the question of the abnormal place and the minimum wage; but at all times the coal owners have pleaded poverty, and have set the Press and the public against the Unions and the men; at the same time raising the price of coal and thus pilfering the public they hoodwink ... Another point of great importance to *you and the public* is the fact that millions of tons of small coal is hewn by the toilers without receiving a cent of wages, the toilers being in this case the hewer; one can see how wolfishly the owners and the middlemen fleece the workers.[95]

It should not be assumed that the paper was sponsoring a view of the public as composed exclusively of middle-class consumers. At the start of March, *Reynolds's* asked of the owners, 'Do they not see that the public will not tolerate a prolongation of industrial chaos? All classes are being injured by the prevailing unrest, which to the very poor increases to a tragic extent the stern struggle for existence.'[96] The paper was at its most interesting in its analysis of the advantages of the sectional strike, which created less inconvenience than more general stoppages. This was important since 'the workers in conflict with capital depend so much on the sympathy of the public'.[97] This appears at first to signal a sharp divide between workers and the public. In context, however, it may be that the assumption was that, during a dispute, working-class non-combatants would behave as members of the consuming public rather than identifying with their striking brothers.

This section has sought to delineate the nature of the pervasive equation between public and consumers. The distinction between producers and consumers was a central dichotomy in British political culture. It is arguable that the idea of the consuming public was part of a system of political values which devalued the interests of producers. The unitary consuming public should be located within a free trade culture

---

[94] *Reynolds's Newspaper*, 3 Mar. 1912.
[95] *Reynolds's Newspaper*, 25 Feb. 1912.
[96] *Reynolds's Newspaper*, 3 Mar. 1912.
[97] *Reynolds's Newspaper*, 4 April 1912.

which militated against the politicisation of economic conflict, locating industrial conflict within civil society, and upholding the regulatory function of 'public opinion' itself.[98] Only by recognising the importance of consumption to the identity of the public can we make sense of its invocation. Consider the Christian socialist Percy Dearmer's essay on 'the social work of an undivided church' in a collection entitled *The New Party*. The volume as a whole provided a radical critique of the existing party system. Dearmer's own brand of tractarian radicalism is evident in his proclamation that 'true democracy, which was growing up strong and honest in the trade unionism and local self-government of the Middle Ages, is now taken up, just about where it was left off, by the Labour Party'.[99] Dearmer's enthusiasm for the mediaeval led him to reflect on its beneficial paternalism:

In fact the two classes which are now left to take care of themselves, the public and the workers, were in those days the very classes that were protected: wages were kept up, hours were kept down, work was secured for all the workers, and the production of ... adulterated work ... was made as impossible as our fallen nature will allow.[100]

Dearmer's sharp distinction between the public and the workers can only be understood in the light of his clear understanding of the public as a body of consumers. Lujo Brentano, eulogist of British trade unions, similarly argued that the eschewal of separate strike and benefit funds 'is in the interest of the public as well as in that of the trade unions'.[101] The progressive R. C. K. Ensor made use of this sense of the public

---

[98] The *locus classicus* of the argument that free trade was a structuring doctrine in political debate is R. McKibbin, 'Why was there no Marxism in Britain?', *English Historical Review*, 99 (April 1984), 297–331. For an analogous argument about the sectional neutrality of the tax system, see M. Daunton, *Trusting Leviathan: The Politics of Taxation in Britain, 1799–1914* (Cambridge, 1914). Frank Trentmann questions the extent to which doctrinaire adherence to free trade determined labour thinking in his 'Wealth versus welfare: the British left between free trade and national political economy before the First World War', *Historical Research*, 70 (1997), 70–98. The larger question of Labour views on the relationship between the demands of consumption and production is addressed in Chapter 5. See also Thompson, 'Political economy, the labour movement and the minimum wage'.

[99] P. Dearmer, 'The social work of the undivided church' in A. Reid, ed., *The New Party* (London, 1894), p. 311.

[100] ibid., p. 305.

[101] L. Brentano, *The Relation of Labor to the Law of To-day*, trans. Porter Sherman (New York and London, 1891), p. 124.

in defending, against prevailing sentiments, the efficacy of compulsory arbitration. Ensor's concern for the interests of the consumer was part of a more general scepticism about conventional trade unionism. He reflected that 'the area of the working class benefited is very confined – virtually confined to skilled male workers . . . The residue do not lose only as part of the public during strikes'.[102] The consumerist vision was a powerful element in imaginings of the political 'public' throughout these years. However, it needs to be supplemented by and related to an examination of the 'intellectualist' conception of the public. The next section begins this task.

The thinking public

In *The English Constitution*, Walter Bagehot asserted with characteristic briskness that 'the working classes contribute almost nothing to our corporate public opinion'. This meant that 'their want of influence in Parliament does not impair the coincidence of Parliament with public opinion'. [103] Elsewhere in the book, however, he extolled the advantages of incorporating the intelligence of the artisans within the pale of the constitution.[104] It is apparent, though, that Bagehot identified the public closely with the middle class, and, indeed, with the man on the omnibus, who embodied 'the opinion of the ordinary mass of educated, but still commonplace mankind'.[105] Bagehot's public was certainly literate, and not uninformed; but he was careful not to impose overly stringent intellectual requirements on membership. The public should not be too clever, otherwise England might become France.[106]

This restricted conception of the public is familiar from recent historiography. Studies of the idea of 'public opinion' in the earlier part of the nineteenth century have stressed its roots in the enlightenment vision of a rational deliberative political community.[107] The vast

[102] R. C. K. Ensor, ed., *Modern Socialism* (London, 1904), p. xxxv.
[103] Bagehot, *The English Constitution*, p. 178.
[104] ibid., pp. 183–4.
[105] Bagehot, *Collected Works*, V, p. 378; Otway, *Public Opinion*, p. 10.
[106] W. Bagehot, 'Letters on the French *coup d'état* of 1851', *The Collected Works of Walter Bagehot*, IV (London, 1968), pp. 29–84.
[107] This literature owes its origins to the seminal Habermas, *The Structural Transformation of the Public Sphere*.

majority of this work concerns the period before the reform act of 1832 in which the 'middle-class' public was presumed to have entered into its rightful constitutional inheritance. Dror Wahrman has argued that the reform act created the middle class more than the middle class created the reform act.[108] It is certainly true that late Victorian descriptions of the constitution before 1867, unlike modern histories of the electorate, took 1832 to mark the arrival of the middle classes within its ambit.[109] This raises the obvious question of what happens to the earlier assessment that many members of the public lacked the vote. Considerable light is shed on this issue by the debate about the secret ballot which rumbled on into the 1860s and early 1870s.

The most famous opponent of the secret ballot must be the later Mill. Mill's strenuous assessment of the level of commitment required to exercise the franchise was integral to his preference for open voting. This attachment to activism was combined with a broad conception of the boundaries of the public, apparent in his defence of open voting. In a letter of 1865 to James Beal, he contended that

Voting for a member of parliament is a public & political act, which concerns not solely the elector's individual preferences, but the most important interests of the other electors, of the non-electors, and even of posterity: & my conviction is that in a free country all such acts shd be done in the face & subject to the comments & criticisms of the entire public.[110]

This view was not confined to private communication. In the various editions of the *Principles of Political Economy*, Mill proposed that 'the working classes are now part of the public'.[111] His comment repays further examination.

The use of the word 'now' alerts us to the narrative of historical change that underwrote his statement. Mill rested his claim that the working classes now constituted part of the public on the grounds that

---

[108] Wahrman, *Imagining the Middle Class*.
[109] For representative instances, see H. Cox, *The Reform Bills of 1866 and 1867* (London, 1868), p. 5; *The Times*, 2 Dec., 1884.
[110] Letter to James Beal, 17 April 1865, Avignon, in *The Collected Works of John Stuart Mill*, XVI, ed. J. M. Robson (Toronto, 1972), p. 1033.
[111] Mill, *Collected Works*, III, p. 764.

in all discussions on matters of general interest they, or a portion of them, are now partakers; all who use the press as an instrument may, if it so happens, have them for an audience; the avenues of instruction through which the middle classes acquire such ideas as they have, are accessible to, at least, the operatives in the town.[112]

It is evident that in referring to the working classes Mill was primarily thinking of the urban artisans. This view gains credence from his attributing the growth of 'public spirit' to 'the institutions for lectures and discussions, the collective deliberations... the trade unions, the political agitations'. Mill's was a literate public that embraced all those capable of accessing political discussion and possessing public spirit. His emphasis on the impact of the press is apparent in the argument that the workers might not 'have been as rational and exemplary' in their attitude to the American Civil War 'if the distress had preceded the salutary measure of fiscal emancipation that gave existence to the penny press'.[113] On this understanding, the growth of 'public opinion' related to the rise of civilisation, which Mill had celebrated in one of his most famous early essays.[114] A progressive account of societal development made it possible to argue that the public had expanded beyond the ranks of the middle class without necessarily altering the criteria for membership. The case was famously made by the Mill enthusiast H. T. Buckle in his *History of Civilisation*, in which the 'middle or intellectual' class started rising in the fourteenth century, bringing with it modern civilisation and culminating in the current 'supremacy of public opinion'. Buckle's was a highly intellectualist conception of public opinion, which placed the middle classes at its core; but he was also convinced that the printing press was spreading enlightenment throughout the 'people', so increasing the influence of mind, expanding the public and strengthening its power.[115]

Mill was, of course, not alone in opposing the ballot. The most effective charge against the ballot was thought to be its 'un-English' character, but it was also condemned for excluding the influence of

---

[112] ibid.   [113] ibid., p. 673.
[114] J. S. Mill, 'Civilisation' (1836), *Collected Works*, XVIII, pp. 117–47.
[115] H. T. Buckle, *History of Civilisation*, ed. J. M. Robertson (London, 1904: 1st edn, 1861), pp. 119–20, 281–4; H. T. Buckle, *Miscellaneous and Posthumous Works* (London, 1872), I, pp. 541–2.

'public opinion'. Homersham Cox asserted in his study of *The British Commonwealth* that open voting was to be cherished for exposing the voter to the righteous gaze of the public.[116] This common motif of anti-ballot argument disclosed a capacious conception of the public that embraced the non-voters. While Bagehot favoured the secret ballot as a measure to reduce corruption, he acknowledged that its institution implied abandoning the position that 'the exercise of political rights . . . should be a public act founded on public principles, and intended to exercise at least as much influence through the medium of opinion as through the political machinery'.[117] The most quoted of mid-Victorian histories of the constitution – that of Erskine May – was unambiguous on this point. Erskine May equated the public with 'all free citizens' and distinguished it from the electorate.[118] However, the centre of gravity of May's public remained firmly middle class. England survived the Pittite era due to the Aristotelian sagacity of the middle classes, who 'were with ministers in quelling sedition: but against them when they menaced freedom'.[119]

The controversy over the county franchise in the late 1870s produced a revealing debate over the social distribution of political wisdom, which offers rare insights into views of the nature of political reasoning. The argument was conducted primarily in terms of the relative merits of the 'popular judgement' and that of the 'higher orders'. Gladstone emphasised the moral demands of political reasoning, and insisted on the superior virtue of the masses. He suggested that the great issues in politics, such as the Bulgarian atrocities or the disestablishment of the Irish Church, presented difficulties which were essentially moral. The problem was one of doing right rather than one of knowing right. All men had the innate moral capacity to embrace the just, but the masses were spared the temptations that warped the judgement of the classes.[120]

---

[116] H. Cox, *The British Commonwealth* (London, 1854), pp. 216–17.
[117] W. Bagehot, *The Collected Works of Walter Bagehot, vol. VI: The Political Essays* (London, 1974), p. 400.
[118] T. Erskine May, *The Constitutional History of England since the Accession of George the Third, 1750–1860* (3rd edn, 3 vols., 1871), II, pp. 415–16.
[119] ibid., p. 365.
[120] W. E. Gladstone, *Gleanings of Past Years* (London, 1879), III, 138–171, 176–213.

Discussion within the quarterlies was primarily conducted in terms of the established criteria for membership of the political public. In his debate with Sir James Fitzjames Stephen over the relationship between authority and knowledge, Gladstone applauded the decision of Cornewall Lewis to place '"questions of morality" among those on which the judgement of the public is "more correct" than on "questions of speculation and abstract truth."'[121] Gladstonians leant towards a more inclusive account of the public, but preferred a populist language that upheld the moral goodness of the people. Frederic Harrison, whose paper Gladstone applauded, argued that 'the most important things in politics . . . are – practical sense, generous feeling, quickness to learn, the spirit of trustfulness, and especially freedom from narrow interests'.[122] He also suggested, though, that the healthy state of legislation was 'due in the main to the constant pressure of public opinion leading and yet weighted by popular influence'.[123] This suggests both the inclusiveness of the public, and yet its weighting towards the middle class. Robert Lowe's portrait of 'the thinking and reading public' made apparent the enduring link between the intellectualist conception of the public, and the idolatry of the middle classes.[124] W. R. Greg's anatomy of the opposition to the Bulgarian atrocities similarly contrasted the jingoism of 'Society' and the lower orders, 'in spite of Mr Gladstone's campaign', with the righteous conduct of 'the middle, the intellectual, the commercial classes'.[125]

Conceptions of the public in the 1870s preserved an established concern with the intellectual demands of membership which privileged the literate and the engaged. The spread of enlightenment, however, meant that the conventional criteria appeared more inclusive than they had

---

[121] W. E. Gladstone, 'The influence of authority in matters of opinion' (1877) in Gladstone, *Gleanings*, III, 198.

[122] F. Harrison in 'A modern "symposium": is the popular judgment in politics more just than that of the higher orders?', *Nineteenth Century*, 3 (May 1878), 816.

[123] ibid., 819.

[124] R. Lowe in 'A modern "symposium": is the popular judgment in politics more just than that of the higher orders?', *Nineteenth Century*, 4 (July 1878), 183.

[125] W. R. Greg in 'A modern "symposium": is the popular judgment in politics more just than that of the higher orders?', *Nineteenth Century*, 4 (July 1878), 176, f1.

been in the past.[126] Inclusive conceptions of the public could, though, be married to a fairly elitist account of its formation, in which numbers offered due deference to brains. In 1884, the radical W. E. Forster noted that 'the destinies of England would before long be handed over legally to the householders of all classes. The power would be supposed to rest in them; the power, however, would rest with public opinion, and must, in any circumstances, rest with public opinion and with brains, which were not a matter of equality, quite as much as it ever had'.[127] The emphasis upon public opinion as an urban phenomenon, reflecting the discursive possibilities offered by concentrated populations, also permitted more demotic assessments from within the intellectualist conception. As early as 1843, the Congregationalist minister and historian Robert Vaughan favourably compared the intelligence of artisans with that of college graduates.[128] Such views were not confined to dissenters or to labour activists, though nonconformist distrust of the Anglican elite often manifested itself in less elitist understandings of 'public opinion'. Political intelligence was not simply equated with formal qualifications, or time spent in education. That said, for many commentators the core of the public continued to be middle class.

Disputes about the institutional location of 'public opinion' are addressed fully in Chapter 2, but deserve some attention here for what they imply about the scope of the public.[129] The most important expressions of opinion were generally considered to be the press, the platform, and the petition. Petitioning is perhaps especially indicative of mid-Victorian approaches to the public, though even after 1900 petitions played a sizeable role in the debate over the public's attitude to women's suffrage. The significance of petitioning lies in its accessibility. Any adult capable of writing his or her name could contribute to a petition, and parliament in no way distinguished between the signatures of electors and non-voters, regardless of gender. However, the ability required was not evenly distributed across the social spectrum.

---

[126] J. R. Green offered one version of this narrative in his view that during the second half of the eighteenth century 'public opinion, the general sense of educated Englishmen, had established itself as the dominant element in English government'. Green, *Short History*, p. 765.

[127] Speech at Thornton Mechanics' Institute, reported in *The Times*, 8 Oct, 1884.

[128] R. Vaughan, *The Age of Great Cities* (London, 1843), p. 152.

[129] See Chapter 2.

Nor was there parity between men and women. Estimates of literacy for this period are not unproblematic, but their basis in signatures on marriage registers makes them ideal for assessing the accessibility of petitioning. In 1870 more than 70% of women, and more than 80% of men, were able to sign their names. By 1910 the figure was in excess of 99% in both cases.[130] Petitions also had to follow a particular legal form, which limited access for the poor and the less organised. However, the petition was in principle available to all, and became increasingly so in practice over the course of the nineteenth century.

Radical narratives of constitutional politics focused more upon the platform than the petition. The genre is epitomised by Jephson's two-volume study of *The Platform*.[131] Acclaim for the representative character of the platform was more commonly found on the left than on the right, but was not confined to the margins of politics. Gladstone's appreciative response to Jephson is perhaps unsurprising.[132] More striking, however, is the sympathy towards platform politics expressed in conventional productions of mid-Victorian liberalism like Erskine May's *Constitutional History*.[133] Political meetings were not, of course, necessarily 'open to the public'. Ticketing became increasingly common at the end of the century, particularly at the prestigious gatherings attended by national figures.[134] Despite this, the open meeting retained a special significance, particularly in liberal and radical circles. In the controversy over the Bulgarian atrocities, liberals were swift to seize the banner of the open meeting and to criticise Tory use of ticketing. During the franchise debates of 1884–5, politicians of all stripes tried to uphold the openness of their meetings.[135] Closed

---

[130] G. Sutherland, 'Education' in F. M. L. Thompson, ed., *The Cambridge Social History of Britain 1750–1950, vol. 3: Social Agencies and Institutions* (Cambridge, 1990), p. 123.

[131] H. Jephson, *The Platform: Its Rise and Progress* (2 vols., London, 1892).

[132] W. E. Gladstone, 'The platform, its rise and progress', *Nineteenth Century*, 31 (April 1892), 686–9.

[133] May, *Constitutional History*, II, 270–1.

[134] Vernon, *Politics and the People*, pp. 225–30 emphasises the rise of ticketing as part of the taming of popular politics. A more sceptical view of its prevalence, particularly at the local level, is provided in Lawrence, *Speaking for the People*, pp. 182–4, which, nonetheless, acknowledges its growth at the national level.

[135] The Conservative MP, Marriott, insisted his were 'genuine public meetings', unlike those of Chamberlain: *Parliamentary Debates*, 3rd ser., CCLXXXVI (1884), col. 1358; Salisbury cited the support offered by 'open meetings

meetings were more easily managed than open meetings, but were liable to be disparaged as mere preaching to the converted. The motions carried at open meetings possessed a greater legitimacy. Speeches from differing perspectives may have become less common, but the interaction between speaker and audience, along with contests within the audience, gave them greater status as expressions of 'public opinion'. Respect for open meetings, not confined to liberals, stemmed from an inclusive conception of the limits of the public.

The newspaper-reading public was a potent figure in narratives of Victorian politics. It has been argued that the act of newspaper reading was constitutive of the Victorian public.[136] This view neglects the role of petitions and the platform, and underestimates the importance commonly attributed to intensely held beliefs in the formation of a true public opinion. It is right, though, to note that the press was often considered the best available mirror of the public. Reading a newspaper was frequently taken as both a marker and a source of political intelligence. Criticism of the taxes on knowledge gained much of its resonance from this association between newspaper-reading and the capacity to form genuine opinions. The taxes were swept away by the start of the 1860s. Newspapers were, of course, available to all who could afford them. However, even without the paper duties, the purchase of a daily newspaper was beyond the means of most working-class households, who relied instead upon a Sunday paper, if they bought a newspaper at all. Within labour circles, there was much awareness of the biases of the existing press, particularly in the reporting of industrial conflict, which led to repeated calls for the creation of a Labour press. Speaking at the TUC in 1875, George Howell openly mocked the presumption of newspapers' claims to represent public opinion.[137] Labour activists were more sensitive than most contemporary commentator to the limits of the newspaper-reading classes, though some placed considerable faith in the reformism of the 'thinking and reading public'.[138] Trade unionists, like Joseph Arch, certainly wished to uphold the claims of the unenfranchised in the formation

---

where workmen were represented and voted in large numbers', *Parliamentary Debates*, 3rd ser., CCXC (1884), col. 1372.
[136] Jones, *Powers of the Press*, p. 75.
[137] *TUC Annual Report* (1875), p. 16.
[138] Speech by Ball, *TUC Annual Report* (1880), p. 36.

of public opinion; but the restrictive character of much mainstream intellectualist invocation of the public was evident in the recurrent suspicion in labour ranks that appeals to 'public opinion' were really a cloak for class opinion.[139] However, as support for the establishment of a labour press suggests, many within the movement retained considerable hopes for a reformed and rational 'public opinion' that would embrace the industrial classes.[140]

In his article 'Wanted: a new "Times"', W. T. Stead reflected upon the mid-Victorian status of the 'Thunderer'. He recalled the enormous influence the paper wielded politically as a result of its position as the supposed embodiment of public opinion. He went on to remark on

How small . . . was the 'England', for which the *Times* wrote at the time of the Crimean War . . . The legal nation, as the enfranchised voters may be termed, was a mere handful, and of that handful only a fraction ever saw a daily paper. The great public was outside the pale.[141]

Stead here applied a late nineteenth-century sense of the potential readership of the press to the conditions of forty years earlier. His was a particularly capacious vision of the possibilities of the press. In a piece in the trade magazine *Sell's Newspaper World* for 1892, he claimed that 'there is room for at least two more daily newspapers in London . . . The Education Act has practically created a new reading public, for which the morning daily, as we have it, makes no provision.'[142]

Historians of the press have observed, usually with reference to the 1906 general election, that the attitude of the newspapers was a poor indicator of the views of the electors. The number of regular male readers probably fell short of the size of the electorate.[143] Many contemporaries, however, tended to regard the readership of the press as the larger body. 'A Conservative Journalist' insisted in 1886 that 'there have always been, and will still continue to be, more readers

---

[139] Speech by Arch, *TUC Annual Report* (1884), p. 18. For resentment of an anti-trade union public, see J. S. Murchie, *TUC Annual Report* (1885), p. 11.
[140] *Labour Leader*, 15 Mar. 1912; ibid., 12 April 1912; ibid., 5 Dec. 1912.
[141] W. T. Stead, 'Wanted: a new "Times"' in his *A Journalist on Journalism* (London, 1891), p. 84.
[142] Stead, 'The London morning dailies that are and are to be', 107.
[143] A. J. Lee reflects on press influence in *The Origins of the Popular Press in England, 1855–1914* (London, 1976), p. 212.

than voters'.[144] The idea that the Education Act of 1870 permitted the emergence of the mass press has been subject to much criticism by recent, and not so recent, studies of the nineteenth-century press.[145] It was, however, as Stead's remarks suggest, conventional turn-of-the-century wisdom. The economist Alfred Marshall, in a famous lecture on 'Some aspects of competition', argued that 'for all the great changes which our own age has seen in the relative proportions of different economic forces, there is none so important as the increase in the *area* from which public opinion collects itself, and in the force with which it bears directly upon economic issues'. Marshall went on to add that, while 'the employers... have always had a sympathetic public, the working classes are only now beginning to read newspapers enough to supply an effective national working class opinion', a consequence of 'improvements in their education and their incomes'.[146]

Emphasis upon the impact of the 1870 Act was blind to the vibrant tradition of the popular weekly press. In discussing *The Press and its Story*, the journalist J. D. Symon drew attention to 'the huge budgets of popular news issued weekly for the delectation of the masses'. These papers were 'practically unknown' to the 'educated reader' but represented 'in their quintessence the likings of the lower and the lower-middle classes'. He concluded that 'without these prints... the great body of the public would find Sunday intolerable'.[147] This grasp of the realities of newspaper publishing was, however, fairly rare. The claim that 1870 had fostered a new popular press encouraged the argument that the public was expanding at the close of the century. This growth was not, however, simply about class. Perhaps more fundamentally, it was about gender.

In his remarks upon the results of the Education Act, Stead suggested that 'in the last twenty years the discovery has been made that women can be interested in other things in the papers besides the column

[144] 'A Conservative Journalist', 'Why is the provincial press radical?', *National Review*, 7 (July 1886), 680.
[145] H. Perkin, 'The origins of the popular press', originally in *History Today* (July 1957), reprinted in his *The Structured Crowd: Essays in English Social History* (London, 1981), pp. 47–57.
[146] A. Marshall, 'Some aspects of competition' in A. C. Pigou, ed., *Memorials of Alfred Marshall* (London, 1925), pp. 286–7.
[147] Symon, *The Press and Its Story*, p. 249.

devoted to Births, Marriages and Deaths'.[148] Much of the reaction to the so-called Northcliffe Revolution can only be understood as a response to the perceived feminisation of the newspaper-reading public.[149] Concerns about such changes in the readership of the press need to be related to the broader context of debates about women's relationship to the public.

Parliamentary regulations offered women access to petitions. The peaks in Edwardian petitioning were generated by the dispute over votes for women. By the 1900s, suffragists had been petitioning parliament for forty years, and the history of petitioning by anti-suffragists was only slightly shorter. The submission of petitions signed by women on both sides of the debate reflected and reinvigorated women's claims as members of the public. After 1900 particularly, supporters of women's suffrage made considerable use of public meetings, and of more theatrical devices like processions.[150] Opponents were less comfortable with such incursions into the public sphere, though they did not neglect them completely.[151] The means through which the struggle was conducted tend to suggest that women were considered to be members of the public. A more complex picture is revealed by attention to the content of arguments about women and the vote.

The nineteenth-century debate about women's suffrage is sometimes cast very much in terms of Mill's case in *The Subjection of Women*. Much of the dispute, however, revolved around the narrower question of the rights of female property owners. The resonant cry of 'no taxation without representation' was adopted to advance the claims of propertied women.[152] This approach portrayed the denial of the vote

---

[148] Stead, 'The London morning dailies that are and are to be', 107.

[149] See Chapter 2.

[150] Suffragist use of processions, posters and banners is analysed in L. Tickner, *The Spectacle of Women: Imagery of the Suffrage Campaign 1907–14* (London, 1987). On suffragette use of 'the politics of disruption', see J. Lawrence, 'Contesting the male polity: the suffragettes and the politics of disruption in Edwardian Britain' in A. Vickery, ed., *Women, Privilege, and Power: British Politics, 1750 to the Present* (Stanford, 2001), 201–26. See also B. Griffin, *The politics of Gender in Victorian Britain: Masculinity, Political Culture and the Struggle for Women's Rights* (Cambridge, 2012).

[151] On anti-suffragist attitudes to campaigning, see B. Harrison, *Separate Spheres: The Opposition to Women's Suffrage in Britain* (London, 1978), pp. 156–61.

[152] This slogan was emblazoned on the membership cards for the Reform League reproduced in Vernon, *Politics and the People*, p. 323. See J. Rendall, 'Citizenship, culture and civilisation: the languages of British suffragists, 1866–74' in C. Daly & M. Nolan, eds., *Suffrage and Beyond: International Feminist Perspectives* (Auckland, 1994), pp. 131–3.

to such women as an anomalous departure from the basic and historic principles underpinning the franchise in Britain. Larger questions of female political capacity were often deliberately eschewed. New infusions of male voters into the electorate ensured that the rights of property were displaced from the centre of debate. Changes in the male suffrage also served to reduce the currency of arguments based upon the principle of virtual representation.[153] Nonetheless, ideas of virtual representation continued to play an important role in the opposition to women's suffrage.

The claim that women were virtually represented by male electors could be seen as a subspecies of the more general argument that non-voters were virtually represented by electors. It is useful to examine the case in its heyday before 1867. Opponents of the ballot contended that the influence afforded opinion by open voting ensured that the views of non-voters were incorporated into the electoral process. Voting was a trust, not a right.[154] Independence was required for its just exercise. Property bequeathed independence, but since wives could not own property in their own right independence was not something women could easily attain. It is not coincidental that suffragist efforts in the 1860s were so concerned with the position of women householders. The extension of the franchise in 1867 manifested and reinforced a departure from the idea of the vote as a trust towards the principle of entitlement to the suffrage.[155] Institution of the secret ballot in 1872 and alterations in property law combined with the growth of the electorate to leave the principle of virtual representation increasingly beleaguered. It is important, however, not to exaggerate the news of the death of virtual representation.

It is in fact misleading to see the virtual representation of women as merely an aspect of the virtual representation of the unenfranchised. The idea of 'independence', particularly as embodied in the second reform act, was importantly related to the notion of

---

[153] Anna Clark argues that the second reform act rendered such arguments obsolete, but their repeated emergence in debates about women and the vote suggests otherwise. See A. Clark, 'Gender, class and the constitution: franchise reform in England, 1832–1928' in Vernon, *Re-reading the Constitution*, p. 244.

[154] e.g. Cox, *The British Commonwealth*, pp. 216–20.

[155] On entitlement-based arguments for enfranchising women, see Rendall, 'Citizenship, culture and civilisation', pp. 127–50.

manliness.[156] Women's dependent status was a consequence of their gender which went beyond questions of property ownership. Possession of genuine opinions, as opposed to mere prejudices, required a well-formed character. The evolution of the idea of 'character' in this period was generally towards a more strenuous, manly and masculine ideal, which, arguably, did little to aid attempts to establish that women could hold meaningful political opinions.[157] The prevalence of character discourse in British political culture can be seen as disadvantageous to those who wished to challenge its assumptions about gender. It underpinned the views of opponents of women's suffrage into the Edwardian period.

Virtual representation also licensed the view that women were incorporated in the polity through their participation in the formation of public opinion, and so had no need of the vote. This riposte was reliant upon the notion of the vote as a trust, and its currency diminished correspondingly in the last years of the century. Cathcart Wilson was still able to argue in the Commons debate of 1907 that 'in all matters of legislation the interests of women were already strongly voiced. Were they not already sufficiently heckled at public meetings by women?'[158] Suffragists needed to uphold the ability of women to form political opinions, though this could be linked to the claim that a masculine public neglected women's views.[159] Critiques of the public as a male conspiracy were mostly confined to more radical suffragists, and were comparatively rare before 1900. It was also crucial, if the vote was ever to be won, to demonstrate that women wanted it. Relatively few opponents of women's suffrage (F. E. Smith was one) were prepared to argue publicly that whether women wanted the vote was irrelevant.[160] From the 1870s, it was tacitly granted that women held opinions about the suffrage, and contributed to a 'public opinion' on the issue. In the

[156] K. McClelland, 'Rational and respectable men: gender, the working class and citizenship in Britain, 1850–67' in L. Frader and S. Rose, eds., *Gender and Class in Modern Europe* (Ithaca, NY, 1995), pp. 280–93.

[157] For this shift, and on the idea of 'character' in this period more generally, see S. Collini, 'The idea of character: private habits and public virtues' in his *Public Moralists: Political Thought and Intellectual Life in Britain 1850–1930* (Oxford, 1991), pp. 91–121, esp. 116–17.

[158] *Parliamentary Debates.*, 4th ser., CLXX (1907), col. 1155.

[159] L.S., 'The citizenship of women socially considered', *Westminster Review* (July 1874), reprinted in J. Lewis, ed., *Before the Vote was Won: Arguments For and Against Women's Suffrage* (London, 1987), p. 188.

[160] *Parliamentary Debates*, 5th ser., XIX (1910), col. 58–9.

parliamentary debate of July 1910, Lord Robert Cecil argued that the vote was a small matter compared to 'the power of speaking, of canvassing, of influencing a constituency one way or another, of writing to the newspapers or the magazines – all of which powers women now exercise as well as men'. Women already had 'powers far more considerable and more important to the community' than those conferred by the vote.[161]

Developments in the position of women and changes in the focus of political debate made blunt denials of women's political sagacity less likely to be found plausible. Questions of the state of public opinion, and in particular of whether women wanted the vote, loomed increasingly large in arguments about the suffrage. It became more generally accepted that, as Arabella Shore had argued in 1877, 'conversation, books, journals, joined to all the quickening influences of varied society, are rapidly giving women the power of forming their own opinions'.[162] Women had already received, without much controversy, the municipal vote in 1869. The politics of parishes, school boards and localities could be cast as an extension of the domestic concerns of the home which were presumed to be the proper province of women. However, the end of the century saw social issues assuming an unprecedented prominence in national debate, which made the supposed virtues of the gentler sex appear more relevant to Westminster politics.[163] Arabella Shore anticipated this trend when she noted in 1879 that 'there is much that sensible women can understand and can do in public matters without being at all required to interfere in what is beyond them. In all matters affecting the welfare of the people we have a right to an opinion and we ought to try to have one as far as our knowledge goes.'[164]

Arguments about women's membership of the public were mostly conducted within the terms of the intellectualist conception of the public. Anti-suffragists sometimes compared female political apathy unfavourably to the male appetite for current affairs. In the Commons

---

[161] ibid., col. 102.
[162] A. Shore, 'The present aspect of women's suffrage considered' (1877) in Lewis, ed., *Before the Vote was Won*, p. 300.
[163] J. Harris, 'The transition to high politics in English social policy, 1880–1914' in M. Bentley & J. Stevenson, eds., *High and Low Politics in Modern Britain* (Oxford, 1983), pp. 58–79.
[164] A. Shore, 'What women have a right to' (1879) in Lewis, ed., *Before the Vote was Won*, p. 362.

in 1907, the Conservative member for South East Essex claimed that 'women as a whole did not turn to politics as a subject of thought or discussion', unlike men, who 'read the newspapers and were interested in political discussions'.[165] This indictment could take the form of a contrast between women and the working-class male culture of newspaper-reading, debating societies and public meetings. The leading 'anti' Lord Curzon made this case.[166] It was also possible, as F. E. Smith again demonstrates, to argue that women's political ignorance was linked to their emotional nature, which would introduce a destabilising force into politics.[167] This argument was traditionally framed in terms of fears of religious bigotry, but came to focus more upon the exacerbation of the inherent unsteadiness of democracy.[168] However, the terms of the debate increasingly acknowledged female membership of the public, not least as a consequence of the active efforts of women suffragists.[169]

In his pamphlet on 'Anti-suffrage anxieties', Bertrand Russell suggested that 'the strongest argument against women's suffrage is the argument that all government is based, in the last resort, on *force*'.[170]

---

[165] *Parliamentary Debates*, 4th ser., CLXX (1907), col. 1119.

[166] Harrison, *Separate Spheres*, p. 71.

[167] *Parliamentary Debates*, 5th ser., XIX (1910), col. 67. Later in the debate J. H. M. Kirkwood suggested that 'there is nothing worse than for a country to be involved in a war through hysterical influence' and claimed that 'if we accepted this bill . . . there is every danger . . . of emasculating the nation' (ibid., col. 231). Kettle replied to this point by recalling 'the Boer war agitation, which gave such a magnificent opportunity to masses of the masculine voters in this country to show their absolute freedom from hysteria, their self-restraint, their dignity, and their intellectual balance . . . ' (ibid., cols. 269–70).

[168] For the view that 'they [women] were peculiarly susceptible to priestly influence', see Whitehead's speech, *Parliamentary Debates*, 4th ser., CLXX (1907), col. 1118. For arguments about the fragile democratic equilibrium, see Asquith's remarks about 'that fluid and mobile element [women]' which would 'enormously increase the danger of having fitfulness and capricious movement followed by intervals of indifference', *Parliamentary Debates*, 5th ser., XVII (1910), cols. 250–1.

[169] In the unusually serious debate of 1910, Baker argued that the bill was guilty of 'deliberately ignoring the opinion of the vast majority of electors, and, indeed, of non-electors also, in this country' (*Parliamentary Debates*, 5th ser., XVII (1910), col. 276).

[170] B. Russell, *Anti-Suffragist Anxieties* in *The Collected Papers of Bertrand Russell, vol. 12: Contemplation and Action, 1902–14*, ed. R. A. Rempel, A. Brink & M. Moran (London, 1985), pp. 304–18, at p. 313.

The claim that the physical weakness of women ruled out giving them the vote featured repeatedly in Edwardian parliamentary debates. Its resonance owed much to insecurities about military preparedness in the wake of the Boer War and the Report of the Royal Commission on Physical Degeneracy.[171] The classic reply was to stress that the course of evolution and the fact of progress had banished the era of government by force into the barbarian past.[172] In a civilised modern state, government required an intelligent and virtuous public opinion rather than brute force.

The perceived feminisation of the public was sometimes taken as a cause for cultural pessimism. Ironically, militant Edwardian feminists sometimes shared this sceptical view of the rationality of the public, though they departed from its explanation of this development. Teresa Billington-Greig identified 'public opinion' with the views of 'the man in the street', who personified the 'indifference and carelessness' of an unthinking male public. After her disillusionment with the Pankhurst approach, Billington-Greig became disturbed by the 'popularity of militancy with the Press and the public'. Militancy pandered to an implicitly male public, which 'loves a drama with lust and blood in it'.[173] Vera Collum also blamed the activities of the Women's Social and Political Union (WSPU) on 'the sensation-loving public enjoying the very spectacle it professes to deplore'.[174] Debates about women's position in the polity almost invariably involved disputes about their place in the public.

An important question arises about the terms of women's inclusion in the public. Suffragette autobiographers argued that more strident forms of political expression, such as heckling, traditional amongst men, were not extended to women. Emmeline Pankhurst regretted this departure from 'the time-honoured, almost sacred English privilege of interrupting'. She further argued that 'window-breaking, when Englishmen do it, is regarded as honest expression of political opinion', but 'when English women do it, it is treated as a

---

[171] See G. R. Searle, *The Quest for National Efficiency: A Study in British Politics and Political Thought, 1899–1914* (Oxford, 1971).

[172] For instance, B. Russell, 'Liberalism and women's suffrage', *Contemporary Review*, 94 (July 1908), 11–16.

[173] T. Billington-Greig, *The Militant Suffrage Movement* (London, 1911), reprinted in *The Non-Violent Militant*, p. 190.

[174] Letter in *The Times*, 14 Mar. 1912.

crime'.[175] There was, however, a real tension in militant attitudes to 'the politics of disruption', manifested in Pankhurst's boast that 'we tamed and educated a public that had always been used to violence at elections'.[176] Militants argued that established suffragism had devoted much effort to educating the public, but had paid insufficient attention to arousing it.

Deeply held beliefs were accorded a special significance in Victorian political culture. This was reflected in the value attached to the intensity with which opinions were held in accounts of the emergence of 'public opinion'. In a debate of 1908 on votes for women, Herbert Gladstone gave utterance to the family view that 'members of the House reflect the opinions of the country not only in regard to the numbers out-side, but with regard to the intensity of the feeling in support of a movement'.[177] Such views presented a problem for suffragists keen to display the requisite earnestness, but hedged in by established views of the proper sphere of female political action. One MP conceded in 1908 that 'though we may not agree as to the methods that have been employed, we must all agree that the intensity of [the suffragettes'] feelings has been shown by the willingness of these women to endure hardship.'[178]

It has been persuasively argued that suffragette adoption of 'the politics of disruption' did much to make political violence less acceptable.[179] Tolerance of violence, as opposed to heckling – outside of the hurly-burly of electioneering – was already quite limited. It is important to recognise, however, that the intellectualist conception of the public preserved an attachment to intensity of belief that supported a political culture more unruly than is occasionally implied. Mount-ing levels of militancy alienated many, though Emmeline Pankhurst suggested that it was the disruption of Asquith's golfing that had

[175] E. Pankhurst, *My Own Story* (New York, 1914), p. 119.   [176] ibid., p. 88.
[177] *Parliamentary Debates*, 4th ser., CLXXXV (1908), cols. 242–3.
[178] Pike Pease, ibid., col. 248. See also Sir C. B. McLaren in the 1909 debate, arguing that 'if petitions were to decide questions of this kind there should be no difficulty in getting at least a million signatures of women in support of the Bill. We have to look at the intensity of the agitation outside' (*Parliamentary Debates*, 5th ser., II (1909), col. 1369). The same point was made in characteristically more Hegelian terms by R. B. Haldane in 1910. See *Parliamentary Debates*, 5th ser., XIX (1910), col. 81.
[179] Lawrence, 'Contesting the male polity'.

provoked the greatest indignation.[180] The actions of the suffragettes could be seen as a manifestation of female irrationality, or as incontrovertible evidence of deep convictions. It was typical, however, to argue, as *The Times* did in 1912, that rejection of militancy met with 'the cordial sympathy of the general public'.[181] By 1914, women's position within the public, if not the polity, was more secure than it had been previously.

An interesting comparison to the relationship between women and the political 'public' is provided by the history of the 'residuum'. The term 'residuum' was used by many late nineteenth-century commentators to denote the 'bottom tenth' or, in more contemporary parlance, the 'underclass'.[182] Its inception as a term of social description dates from the publication of Henry Mayhew's *London Labour and the London Poor*. Mayhew did much to establish the image of the 'residuum' as a 'race apart' fundamentally alien to the mainstream of society. He divided humankind into the 'nomadic and the civilised tribes'. The nomads were distinguished by 'greater relative development of the jaws and cheekbones', indicative of their enlarged 'organs subservient to sensation and the animal faculties'. This modish anthropology of 'paupers, beggars, and outcasts' was not always confined by Mayhew to depictions of street folk, but could appear in accounts of carmen, coachmen, watermen and sailors.[183] Throughout its career, the residuum, not unlike the 'underclass', retained an elasticity of reference, which made for much of its popularity.

The second reform act of 1867 has been portrayed as the moment when the male working-class political subject was born.[184] It certainly marked an important moment in the history of the 'residuum'. In an influential speech, John Bright responded to Robert Lowe's attempt to

---

[180] Pankhurst, *My Own Story*, p. 119.
[181] *The Times*, 12 Mar. 1912.
[182] G. Stedman Jones, *Outcast London: A Study in the Relationship between Classes in Victorian Society* (Oxford, 1971); J. Harris, 'Between civic virtue and social Darwinism: the concept of the residuum' in D. Englander and R. O'Day, eds., *Retrieved Riches: Social Investigation in Britain, 1840–1914* (Aldershot, 1995), pp. 67–87. For earlier attitudes to the East End London poor, see J. Marriot, 'Policing the poor: social inquiry and the discovery of the residuum', *Rising East*, 3, 1 (1999), 23–48.
[183] H. Mayhew, *London Labour and the London Poor* (London, 1862), pp. 1–4.
[184] McClelland, 'Rational and respectable men'.

enrol him in the ranks of those who ridiculed the political intelligence of the labouring man. He insisted that his disparaging remarks about 'that class at the very bottom of the scale', quoted by Lowe, applied only to the 'residuum', which he proceeded sharply to distinguish from the respectable working classes. Bright erected a brutal divide between the independent artisans and the dependent poor, urging members to remember that

At this moment in all, or nearly all our boroughs . . . there is a small class which it would be much better for themselves if they were not enfranchised, because they have no independence whatsoever, and it would be much better for the constituency also if they should be excluded, and there is no class so much interested in having that small class excluded as the intelligent and honest working men. I call this class the *residuum*, which there is in almost every constituency, of almost hopeless poverty and dependence.

He then offered an account of the failings of the residuum which merits lengthy quotation.

a class of which there are, unfortunately, too many among us – namely, the excessively poor – many of them intemperate, some of them profligate; some of them, it may be only unfortunate, some of them naturally incapable; but all of them in a condition of dependence, such as to give no reasonable expectation that they would be able to resist the many temptations . . . men would offer them at periods of election to give their votes in a manner not only not consistent with their own opinions and consciences, *if they have any*, but not consistent with the representation of the town or city in which they live.

Bright left his listeners in no confusion on the cardinal issue, reiterating that 'these remarks . . . did not apply to working men paying between 10*l.* and 7*l.* rental but to the small class who are at the bottom of the scale'.[185]

The distinction between the respectable working classes and the residuum forged by Bright was a valuable device for reassuring educated opinion as to the virtues of the former. Bright's emphasis on the dependence of the residuum, and his scepticism over their possession of opinions, reveal the fragility of their claim to membership of the public. In subsequent debate, the term 'residuum' was generally

---

[185] The speech is reported verbatim in *The Times*, 27 Mar. 1867 (my emphasis).

attributed to Bright, and the category remained rooted in the arguments of 1866–7, at least until the social problems of the 1880s. In Mayhew's hands, the residuum was a colourful feature of metropolitan life rather than a constant presence throughout the land, whereas for Bright, the residuum afflicted 'all, or nearly all our boroughs'. In the pages of Matthew Arnold, the entire 'Populace' became 'this vast residuum...marching where it likes, meeting where it likes, bawling what it likes, breaking what it likes'.[186]

Like women, the residuum could be considered the embodiment of dependence. Like women also, it was frequently regarded by liberals as a bulwark of Toryism. The agitation against the Bulgarian atrocities initiated a furious debate about British policy, and over the views of the public. Conservatives were quick to cast the agitation against the atrocities as an uneducated craze.[187] The language of the residuum, however, was primarily adopted by liberals, appalled at popular enthusiasm for the Ottoman Empire. In November 1877, Gladstone observed that 'two new articles, pretty closely associated together, have lately been added to the Tory creed, not by a general council, but by silent consent: faith in the long purse, and faith in what Mr Bright, in one of his many happy phrases, dubbed the *residuum*'.[188] This view of the residuum as susceptible to bribery had been clearly signalled in Bright's speech of 1867. Abjectly dependent, the residuum was as incapable of resisting the indirect bribery of imperial adventures as it was susceptible to the blandishments of unscrupulous electioneers. Despite the institution of the secret ballot, identification of the residuum with poor, biddable voters occurred after both the 1874 and 1880 general elections, when its presence was detected in both rural and urban constituencies. Such fears may have declined somewhat after the passage of the Corrupt and

---

[186] M. Arnold, *Culture and Anarchy: An Essay in Political and Social Criticism*, ed. D. Wilson (Cambridge, 1966), p. 105 (1st edn London, 1869). Arnold is referring here to one of the 'three great classes into which our society is divided' rather than to a group peculiar to London.

[187] In a speech in the Lords on 30 March 1877, Salisbury spoke with distaste of the liberal 'appeal to a grade of opinion lower than that which may be considered as educated'. Quoted in G. Carslake Thompson, *Public Opinion and Lord Beaconsfield, 1875–80* (2 vols., London, 1886), I, 275.

[188] W. E. Gladstone, 'The county franchise and Mr Lowe thereon', *Nineteenth Century*, II (Nov. 1877), 557.

Illegal Practices Act of 1883, though observers were still castigating the willingness of the residuum to sell its votes in 1906.[189]

The 1880s have been seen as a turning point in the history of the 'residuum' during which it becomes conceived as a systemic and threatening social problem rather than a colourful residue of London's past.[190] Revelations about housing in 1883, and the unemployment concerns of 1886–7, clearly helped spawn an increased tendency to analyse the fate of the residuum in terms of the state of its habitations and its tenuous relationship to the job market. The East End of London often loomed large in such accounts, but Hugh P. Tregarthen spoke for many in arguing that 'there is in the metropolis, as in every large town, a residuum'.[191] London supported the largest residuum, but other large towns produced their own reprobates, as did the great cities of the Empire and the New World.[192] Well-established associations with drunkenness and criminality endured. While there was a decline in allegations of electoral corruption, these were merely replaced by the accusation that the residuum constituted a reserve of feckless floating voters, lacking firm convictions, much as Bright had suggested in 1867. Whether it appeared in discussions of dock labour or the travails of electioneering, the residuum operated as an antithesis to the virtues of respectability.[193]

As with the 'public', contemporaries sought to use the 'residuum' to their own political advantage. In 1883, Lord Randolph Churchill castigated Bradlaugh's supporters as the 'residuum' and 'scum'; the following year, when seeking to encapsulate Tory Democracy, he contrasted Disraeli's inclusive vision of the electorate in 1867 with Bright's enormous condescension towards the residuum.[194] During the

---

[189] *The Times*, 17 Feb. 1875; ibid., 25 Aug. 1875; ibid., 4 Jun. 1880; ibid., 29 Aug. 1906.

[190] Stedman Jones, *Outcast London*, p. 283. The picturesque mode of writing about the 'residuum' Stedman Jones identifies with the 1870s did not simply disappear. See, for instance, J. Greenwood, *Odd People in Odd Places, or the Great Residuum* (London, 1883). On these, and other, kinds of encounters, consult S. Koven, *Slumming: Sexual and Social Politics in Victorian London* (Princeton, 2004).

[191] H. P. Tregarthen, 'Pauperism, distress, and the coming winter', *National Review*, 10 (Nov. 1887), 388–9.

[192] E. Hopkins, 'Social wreckage', *Contemporary Review*, 44 (July 1883), 97; *The Times*, 16 Sep. 1886.

[193] *The Times*, 5 Jan. 1892; ibid., 19 Jan. 1898.

[194] *The Times*, 1 May 1883; ibid., 16 Oct. 1884.

suffrage debates of 1884–5, Liberals were charged with endangering the political process by extending the vote to single-room occupiers, who were merely members of the residuum. Demonstrating some flexibility, Bright sought to defuse such claims by denying that the residuum could be defined purely in terms of housing, arguing instead that all classes had their unrespectable residuum.[195] Balfour was predictably sensitive to these linguistic issues, arguing in 1882 that the recipients of bribery were dismissed by Bright as the residuum when he disagreed with them, but embraced as the 'people' when he shared their views. Balfour proved a persistent critic of Gladstonian populism, suggesting to the National Union of Conservative and Constitutional Associations (NUCCA) in 1890 that liberal claims to speak for the people excluded both the professional classes and all those workers who deviated from them, who they termed the residuum.[196] Working men could seek to refocus argument on the immorality of other classes, and the failings of the economic system as a whole.[197] It was, however, precisely the widespread assumption that a residuum existed, and that it had identifiable characteristics, that explained its prominence in social and political debate in the 1880s.

It has been argued that the 1880s saw a shift in the dominant account of the residuum from an emphasis on demoralisation to a stress upon degeneration.[198] The question here, though, is whether such changes affected the relationship of the residuum to the public. Analyses of the residuum often combined explanations based on demoralisation with more degenerationist rhetoric. Regardless of the preferred explanatory mix, the lack of 'character' amongst the residuum was to the fore of the discussion. An article in the *Contemporary Review* described 'the ladies' of the residuum as 'mainly coster-girls, servants out of place from loss of character or from utter laziness'.[199] Samuel Barnett in offering 'a scheme for the unemployed' asserted that 'it is for want of character that so many suffer'. He did so, revealingly, immediately

---

[195] *Parliamentary Debates*, 3rd ser., CCLXXXVI (1884), col. 690.
[196] *The Times*, 26 Apr. 1882; ibid., 12 Jun. 1890.
[197] *The Times*, 14 Oct. 1887.
[198] Stedman Jones, *Outcast London*, pp. 281–315. This view is challenged in E. P. Hennock, 'Poverty and social theory: the experience of the eighteen-eighties', *Social History*, 1 (1976), 67–91. José Harris questions both the significance of the 1880s and the importance of degenerationist concerns in 'Between civic virtue and social Darwinism', p. 77.
[199] Anon., 'The residuum', *Contemporary Review*, 30 (Nov. 1877), 1088.

after arguing that it was 'for want of knowledge' that 'men . . . are in poverty, in misery, and in sin'.[200] The idea of character treated moral and intellectual qualities as almost indistinguishable. Its absence in the residuum rendered them distant from the public. Brooke Lambert, an avowed Christian socialist, suggested that

> those who have worked among the poor of London have long wished that prosperous London could realize how outcast London lived. They are glad that the attention of the public has been aroused, and their only fear is lest the cry should be answered by some sudden act of impulsive generosity, or ill-regulated interference, which would create new evils.[201]

Further insight into the status of the 'residuum' and the limits of the public is provided by the frequent descriptions of London crowds in the 1880s.

The demonstration of the unemployed in February 1885, organised by the Social Democratic Federation, inspired the *Pall Mall Gazette* to remark that 'it would be a great pity . . . if Mr Hyndmann's hysterics were to create a prejudice . . . in public opinion . . . against the cause which he is doing his best to make ridiculous.'[202] The orderliness of the occasion, however, and the evident suffering of the unemployed, provoked more sympathetic comment. The *Daily News* observed that 'nobody who recollects the corn law agitation can fail to contrast the behaviour of crowds of late years with mobs of those days'.[203] Such positive views of collective action were not unusual in a period in which celebration of progress, political and otherwise, was rife. The vocabulary of crowd psychology was yet to enter Britain and assessments of the crowd were more appreciative than they would later become.[204] The relationship, however, between the crowd and the public depended on the social composition of the crowd, as well as the perspective of the observer. Crowd description can thus reveal the conventional boundaries of the public. It was left to the journal of the SDF itself, *Justice*, to identify explicitly the demonstrators with the residuum. In an interesting reversal of conventional attitudes, the paper noted that 'the

[200] S. Barnett, 'A scheme for the unemployed', *Nineteenth Century*, 24 (Nov. 188), 763.
[201] B. Lambert, 'The outcast poor – I. Esau's cry', *Contemporary Review*, 44 (July 1883), 917.
[202] *Pall Mall Gazette*, 17 Feb. 1885.   [203] *Daily News*, 17 Feb. 1885.
[204] See Chapter 3 for a full examination of this.

residuum, as Mr John Bright contemptuously dubbed those working men who have been wise enough to stand outside the lines of party politics, is bestirring itself'. As well as disputing the common view of the residuum as congenitally apolitical and unemployable, *Justice* insisted on referring to 'the public including the unemployed', though the last three words rather signalled the novelty of the definition.[205]

The reporting of the 1885 demonstration was something of a dry run for the more extensive coverage of the 1886 Trafalgar Square riot. The damage to property apparent in 1886 ensured that denunciation of the 'mob' gained a prominence not apparent in the previous year. Through the acres of print devoted to the riots, the distinction between the public and the residuum was made evident. In its first report of the riots, the conservative *Pall Mall Gazette* reflected mordantly on the implications of events for the manliness of the nation. It did so by means of a fashionably Darwinian analogy with the dodo, recalling that

There are no dodos now . . . but *the middle class Englishman* is a biped not altogether dissimilar from his feathered prototype. He has dwelt so long in safety behind his seas and behind his police that the more rugged, self-protecting qualities have died out . . . We are willing to make all excuse for the police. They never thought that an English crowd would deliberately loot jeweller's shops in broad daylight. That is to say, the police, like *the public*, are losing faculties which can only be kept in a state of efficiency by exercise.[206]

The *Echo* underlined the difference between the unemployed and the public by smugly suggesting that 'it may be presumed that those who attended the meeting are not readers of daily newspapers'.[207] This view of the limits of the public was seemingly shared by the socialist H. H. Champion, at least as interviewed in the *Daily Telegraph*. Champion claimed that

Our hold over the people is shown by the ease with which we obtained by far the largest audience in the square. The effect upon public opinion is testified to by the action of a newspaper that pretends to be a Government organ. Last Thursday not a line about our crowded meeting in Holborn Town Hall appeared in its columns. Yesterday it advocated the starting of public works.[208]

---

[205] *Justice*, 28 Feb. 1885.   [206] *Pall Mall Gazette*, 9 Feb. 1886 (my emphasis).
[207] *The Echo*, 12 Feb. 1886.   [208] *Daily Telegraph*, 10 Feb. 1886.

Blame for the violence was generally laid at the door of the SDF. The liberal *Daily News* did so in revealing terms, suggesting that

The riot was the direct consequence of the appeals made by the leaders of the Social Democratic Federation to the excited mob. The unemployed were quiet. They had gathered to show their numbers, to impress the public with the extent of the suffering and distress in the poorer quarters, and there is no reason to believe they had any other object.[209]

It is important to note, however, that the relationship between the unemployed in general and the public was less sharply defined than that between the residuum and the public. The *Daily Telegraph* editorial a few days after the disturbances reflected representatively on this question. It emphasised that

There was never, indeed, any reason to fear that the late deplorable events would alienate the sympathy of the general public from an unfortunate and much-enduring class of their fellow countrymen. They have little difficulty in distinguishing between the labourer and the loafer, and still less in distinguishing the solid body of the working population from the scum of lazy brutality which floats upon its surface, and the mischievous residuum of crime beneath.[210]

Contemplation of the residuum was not confined to the 1880s. The currency of the term was greatly diminished by the demonstration in the First World War that the supposed legions of the unemployable and incapable were nowhere to be found. It has been argued that appraisals of the residuum were much affected by the dock strike of 1889, which fostered a view of the residuum as feckless rather than vicious, and led contemporaries to recast the residuum as 'no longer a political threat – only a social problem'.[211] Fears of the revolutionary potential of the residuum were certainly discouraged by a strike which appeared to demonstrate both the steadiness of casual labour and the power of 'public opinion', although the prior extent of such fears can be overstated. More generally, the politics of the residuum were, as we have seen, a disputed matter. Liberals often considered the submerged tenth not so much a threat to the political order as a mainstay of

---

[209] *Daily News*, 9 Feb. 1886.   [210] *Daily Telegraph*, 11 Feb. 1886.
[211] Stedman Jones, *Outcast London*, p. 321.

Tory reaction. Such views were hardly extinguished by conservative electoral dominance in 'the age of the Cecils'.[212]

This section has investigated intellectualist conceptions of the public. Examination of the relationship of the working class, women and the residuum to the public reveals its complex, shifting and contested boundaries. It also, however, demonstrates the enduring power of a vision of the public which placed the educated middle classes firmly at its centre. The rhetorical constituency of the 'public' certainly expanded in this period, but it is questionable whether this process did much to oust the middle classes from their accustomed position.

Conclusion

Recent years have seen the emergence of a considerable body of work devoted to the history of 'populism' in the long nineteenth century. This literature has been primarily concerned with the role of constitutionalism in the popular politics of the period. The political language of constitutionalism was, however, at least as concerned with the place of out-of-doors 'public opinion' in the polity as with the identity of 'the people'. Historians have generally, if implicitly, treated the two terms as interchangeable in this period. Many instances can certainly be found of their use as synonyms, and differences should not be overplayed. The divergence between the two terms is apparent in those instances where one is consistently preferred to the other. Such cases can suggest their distinct connotations. It was argued above, and the point is developed further in later chapters, that if 'the people' was commonly identified with the productive classes, 'the public' was associated more with the consuming classes. The invocation of the public in the discussion of industrial disputes exemplifies the difference. Similarly, the construction of the engaged literate public rested on the consumption of political intelligence, primarily in the form of newspapers. Discussion of the 'people' was more apt to hymn the inherited consciousness of race and language than the discourse about 'public opinion'. Conceptions of the 'public' emphasised the connections

---

[212] 'The age of the Cecils, like the age of Pitt, has been an age of reaction. Popular interest has been distracted from domestic grievances to foreign and colonial actions', *The Speaker*, 6 September 1902, 592.

between members, but lacked the strongly organic undertow of talk of the people, linked as it often was to the land and the nation.[213]

In a well-known article on working-class housing, published in 1883, Joseph Chamberlain argued that, for existing legislation to yield its full value, 'the government must have the hearty and consistent support of public opinion'. This was not easily secured though, for 'when Property takes alarm, the outcry which it makes is deafening. Personal interests can generally take care of themselves; it is the public good which is so often powerless and voiceless in the presence of the audacity of private wrong.'[214] The opposition between the public interest and private concerns was also apparent in Gladstone's contributions to the debate over the county franchise at the end of the 1870s. In a memorable passage, Gladstone lionised the public. He claimed that

The public, a fine animal, is strong, but sleepy. When he gets active, he gets tired; they tell him he has been excited, and it has been bad for his health; he lays his head upon the pillow; but the interests, ever so anxious lest he should hurt himself by over-assertion, ever wakeful, ever nimble, ever 'redeeming the time,' that is to say, selling it in the best market – they set to, and make a night of it.[215]

There could not be a clearer illustration of the Gladstonian appeal to the masculine active public. Invocations of the public made frequent reference to its gaze, which, if vigilant, would eliminate corruption and preserve the purity of the body politic. This image of the public as the watchdog of the constitution, evident in earlier radical rhetoric, echoed through the century and into the Edwardian debate about plutocracy.

The comparison between the people and the public demonstrates the importance of the idea of unity to the political public. Consumerist idioms of the public rested upon the view that consumers had shared and compatible interests. Discussion of the press, or artistic taste, could acknowledge a variety of publics, but political argument was more strongly attached to the idea of *the* public. In 1866, *The Economist* noted that

---

[213] Vernon, *Politics and the People*, pp. 300–1.
[214] J. Chamberlain, 'Labourers' and artisans' dwellings', *Fortnightly Review*, 34, new ser. (Dec. 1883), 766.
[215] Gladstone, 'The county franchise and Mr Lowe thereon'.

nothing can be more unfortunate than the complete division of the English nation into two bodies of public opinion which we see at present – the one expressed in the press, the other chiefly in the usages of trade unions and of a society which care nothing about the criticism of the society lying side by side with it.[216]

This fear of the fractured public was evident into the early twentieth century and existed in discussions of the economic role of the public.[217]

A complex picture emerges from consideration of the composition of the public. The expansion of the 'democratic imaginary' of the 'public' in these years is clear, but so is the enduring resonance of a more middle-class vision of its constitution. The importance of civic activism in shaping the public is evident throughout the period. In 1885, the conservative journalist H. D. Traill asked the pertinent question, 'What is public opinion?' He insisted that public opinion meant 'the established and effective conviction of the *capable* citizen'. An 'effective' opinion was 'held with sufficient warmth of interest to incite its holder to act, and with sufficient strength of conviction to ensure his acting in a particular way'.[218] The equation of the public with the capable and the identification of 'opinion' with sincerely held views are both apparent in the prevalence of the language of 'character' in these debates. This complex of ideas had important implications, as we have seen, for the relationship of women and the dependent poor to the body of the public.

It is also essential to recognise the resonance of the idea of the public as a collection of consumers. Apparent distinctions between the public and other entities may not mean that the two groups were understood as discrete. It may rather be that different aspects or interests of coextensive or overlapping sets of people are being considered. Images of the consuming public were not, of course, unrelated to intellectualist conceptions of public opinion. As we shall see in later chapters, understanding these complex and interlinked connotations of the political public is crucial to comprehending the invocation of the public in political argument. Interactions between intellectualist and consuming conceptions of the public both reflected and shaped a political culture

---

[216] *The Economist*, 27 Oct. 1866, 1253, which clearly argues that the working class do have opinions.

[217] Marshall, 'Some aspects of competition', pp. 287–8.

[218] H. D. Traill, 'What is public opinion?', *National Review*, 5 (July 1885), 657, 655.

in which consumption and citizenship were not conceived as polar opposites. The possibility existed of combining visions of the suffering 'public', overwhelmed by the ferocity of producer conflict, with domesticated notions of 'public opinion' as the views of the silent majority, as interwar conservatism demonstrated; but before 1914, more active conceptions of the public predominated. In order to recover these, we need to turn to the question of where to find 'public opinion' in a world without opinion polls.

2 | 'The ghost in the machine': Locating public opinion

The Victorian era has rightly been regarded as an age of quantification. Such classically Victorian organisations as the National Association for the Promotion of Social Science displayed a mania for enumeration. Efforts to understand the social world attempted to grasp social reality by counting it. Discussion of 'public opinion' could reflect the attractions of numbering: contemporaries aggregated newspapers by political affiliation, counted signatures on petitions, and estimated the size of demonstrations from the width and density of the procession and the time taken to pass a given point. There were, though, distinct limits to nineteenth-century efforts to quantify public opinion. In part, these were technical: statistical techniques were surprisingly underdeveloped before 1900, with central issues in the relationship between samples and populations unresolved.[1] As recent history of science has shown, however, questions about quantification should not be divorced from the larger intellectual context. Nineteenth-century statistics was deeply concerned with the regularities exhibited by large populations. The holistic turn in late Victorian social and political thought did little to discourage a focus on the totality; advocacy of representative sampling was poorly received at the 1895 meeting of the International Statistic Institute.[2] More importantly, though, capturing 'public opinion' posed challenges that went beyond general doubts about representative sampling – challenges that reflected the particular meanings of 'public opinion' in British political debate.

In an important series of articles, J. R. Seeley sought in 1870 to define 'the English revolution of the nineteenth century'. His account

---

[1] Alain Desrosières, 'The part in relation to the whole: how to generalise? The prehistory of representative sampling' in M. Bulmer, K. Bales & K. K. Sklar, eds., *The Social Survey in Historical Perspective* (Cambridge, 1991), pp. 217–44.
[2] T. Porter, *The Rise of Statistical Thinking* (Princeton, 1986), p. 237.

centred on the rise of public opinion as a political force. In distinguishing between the inchoate mutterings of the eighteenth century and the emergent public opinion of the nineteenth, Seeley gave voice to a general, but often implicit, assumption about the nature of true 'public opinion'. He insisted that 'public opinion . . . is not merely the sum of the opinions of the individuals composing the public'. This was because 'the individuals must be brought into relation with each other, and be formed into some sort of organic whole, before anything worthy to be called a public opinion can spring up among them'.[3] Once brought into such relations, the process by which public opinion emerged from the clash of individual views was widely thought to be one of weighing rather than counting. As W. E. H. Lecky noted in 1896, there were multitudes 'who contribute nothing to . . . public opinion' and act under the direction of others.[4] Such views were not confined to one part of the political spectrum. MacDonald likewise emphasised that 'mathematical thoughts are misleading', since public opinion reflected the intensity as well as the quantity of opinion.[5] Given this deliberative and communal conception, how was 'public opinion' to be established? Or, to put it another way, where was it to be found?

In 1892 William Ewart Gladstone reviewed the radical Henry Jephson's two-volume study of *The Platform: Its Rise and Progress*. Gladstone began by placing Jephson's already expansive narrative in a broader and characteristic chronology. The power of 'the word to prompt and guide the minds of men' was acknowledged, 'as far back as the days of Homer'. Its first and greatest manifestation occurred when 'in the early Christian history, "the world awoke, and found itself Arian"'.[6] In tracing the evolution of the platform in Britain, Gladstone noted that 'it was fully recognised by the Constitution' through the county meeting and the electoral husting. The role of the latter, Gladstone was quick to note, was 'first made classical and famous by Mr Burke at Bristol'.[7] Gladstone claimed that, 'as three F's were the watchword of the Irish tenant . . . three P's have denoted the

---

[3] J. R. Seeley, 'The English revolution of the nineteenth century', *Macmillan's Magazine*, 22 (Aug. & Oct. 1870), 241–51, 347–58, 441–51. The quotations come from 349–50.
[4] Lecky, *Democracy and Liberty*, I, 18.
[5] J. R. MacDonald, *Socialism and Government* (2 vols., London, 1909), I, 166.
[6] Gladstone, 'The platform, its rise and progress', 686.
[7] ibid., 687.

instruments, by which British freedom has been principally developed and confirmed': 'Petition, Press, and Platform'.[8]

The order reflected their successive periods of supremacy. It was the petition which held sway in the aftermath of the first reform act and secured the emancipation of the slaves. Practical difficulties attending the petition and the removal of duties, 'especially the paper duty', then conferred enormous power on the press. 'During the last quarter of a century', or since the second reform act, the platform had attained the greatest power. Gladstone recounted those occasions when press and platform had differed and cast the period since 1886 as the clearest trial of strength between the two. He appealed to the electoral record in which 'no less than twenty seats have been carried over from the side supported by the Press to that espoused by the platform' to justify the conclusion that 'there seems to be some colour given to the opinion that the Platform at its maximum of power is stronger than the Press'.[9] However, the demands of public speaking at a time of 'national fever' distracted from 'study and reflection' and were unsustainable. It was to be expected that 'Press, Petition, and Platform' would resume their accepted roles 'combined as harmoniously as . . . the three Graces' to ensure 'the consolidation and progress of free government'.[10] In upholding this constitutional triptych, Gladstone expounded the conventional wisdom on the loci of 'public opinion'.

It might be argued that the most obvious incarnation of public opinion in this period was parliament, especially the House of Commons. The representative role of the Commons was certainly integral to ideals of parliamentary government, but this very role presumed the existence of a 'public opinion' for the Commons to represent. Publication of parliamentary debates was defended in part as an interface between the public and its representatives. Successive measures of enfranchisement and narratives of constitutional development argued that parliament could lag behind the growth of civilisation and the consequent enlargement of the public. It was widely agreed that Britain was comparatively fortunate in its ability to maintain an intimate relationship between parliamentary and public opinion.[11] Constitutional theory incorporated a notionally inclusive 'public opinion' as a kind of fourth estate.

---

[8] ibid.   [9] ibid., 687–8.   [10] ibid., 689.

[11] See, for instance, W. Bagehot, 'France or England', *The Economist*, 5 Sep. 1863, reprinted in *The Collected Works of Walter Bagehot, vol. 5: Political Essays*, ed. N. St John-Stevas (London, 1974), p. 92.

This public was broader than the electorate and its influence acted as a form of virtual representation.

Many observers argued that the power of the public was growing, and that the Commons was becoming increasingly subservient to outside opinion. This view was commonly linked to the claim that the press and the platform now reflected public opinion more immediately and more accurately than did parliament.[12] None of these alleged trends were universally welcomed. Conservatives especially, but not exclusively, sometimes argued that only parliament was equipped to represent fully the range of interests and opinions within the nation. Criticism of the caucus frequently contrasted the representative conception with the doctrine of delegation that rendered MPs the mouthpiece of vested interests, stifling the genuine debate required to identify the public interest.[13] It was, however, increasingly difficult to deny the importance of public opinion out of doors, or to refuse the established title of press, platform and petition to represent that opinion. Even those ill-disposed to the growth of extra-parliamentary popular politics had to accommodate themselves to its realities, by arguing that the weight of political meetings or press utterance – and thus of 'public opinion' – was on their side.[14] The sway of public opinion was not thought to apply only to politicians. Its beneficial influence as an economic force rested upon and reflected an extra-parliamentary opinion that was crucial to the preservation and restoration of industrial peace.[15]

Contemporaries did not confine their search for public opinion to press, platform and petition. Evidence as to the state of the public mind might be found in a range of sources, from novels to sermons. None, though, could match the salience attributed to press, platform and petition. In recent years, the centrality of religion to understanding Victorian intellectual and political life has been influentially restated.[16]

---

[12] See, for instance, the Commons debate on new procedure rules, *Parliamentary Debates*, 4th ser., CII (1902), especially Dilke's remarks, col. 686.

[13] For example, Joseph Cowen, speaking at North Shields in 1879 on representation and in the Commons in 1882 on the caucus, in Jones, *Life and Speeches of Joseph Cowen*, pp. 144–5, 377.

[14] See below.   [15] See Chapter 4.

[16] See, most especially, Hilton, *Age of Atonement* and J. P. Parry, *Democracy and Religion: Gladstone and the Liberal Party, 1867–1875* (Cambridge, 1986).

Sermons provided an important model for platform speakers, and can be seen as part of the same, often theatrical, culture of public speaking.[17] The relationship between developments in religious thought and attitudes to 'public opinion' is explored at length in the next chapter. That said, readings of political public opinion did not usually accord the same value to the pulpit as to press, platform or petition. There were a number of reasons for this. As even the most outspoken advocates of the need to spiritualise politics admitted, significant misgivings existed towards clerics who turned their pulpits into platforms.[18] Established notions of public opinion set considerable store by the idea of the unitary public, meaning that the machinations of party could seem an obstacle to the emergence of a genuine public opinion. But the often sharp divisions evident in religious life made it yet harder to identify the opinion of the elusive unitary public with the pronouncements of the pulpit. While considerable faith continued to be placed in the capacity of the pulpit for moral reformation, the pulpit did not threaten the status of press, petition and platform as the key constitutional forums for the expression of political public opinion.

In its origins, the terminology of 'public opinion' was liberal, but by the middle of the century it had attained a central position in British political discourse. Conservatives seeking to challenge liberal political dominance had little choice but to argue that 'public opinion' favoured their positions, and to draw upon the evidence of press, platform and petition in doing so. Debates over how best to determine public opinion were complex, varied over time, and cannot be reduced to a simple right–left dichotomy. It is, though, possible to identify some recurring differences in emphasis. Denunciation of demagoguery was never the exclusive preserve of the right, and at both local and national levels conservatives claimed the support of open meetings and so of public opinion. However, conservatives, especially elite politicians, were more likely than their liberal counterparts to question the verdict of the platform, and, in particular, to contrast the wisdom embodied in traditions and institutions with the clamour of manufactured opinion. At times, leading conservatives sought to domesticate 'public opinion'

---

[17] Joe Meisel, *Public Speech and the Culture of Public Life in the Age of Gladstone* (New York, 2001).

[18] See J. Guinness Rogers, 'The pulpit and the press' in T. Vincent Tymms et al., *The Ancient Faith in Modern Light* (Edinburgh, 1897), pp. 351–91.

as the good sense of the people, in ways that anticipated later eulogies of the silent majority.[19] While the press might be attacked for its factionalism, or chastised for its populism, conservatives were more willing to acclaim its value than that of the platform. Disraeli was a pivotal figure in articulating an account of 'public opinion' which embraced the musings of the press while disregarding the utterances of the platform. During the debate over reform in 1867, Disraeli noted that 'there is an influence prevalent in England which exists in no other country, and which forms in a very great degree the character and conduct of the English people, and that is the influence of a free press'. He acclaimed the 'great knowledge... great intelligence, and... high moral feeling' with which 'the press of this country' was conducted.[20] Contrastingly, in 1872, Disraeli attacked Gladstone's susceptibility to the sort of 'inconsiderate multitude' which demanded the abolition of the Lords, and his encouragement of nonconformist public meetings as a counterweight to the opinion of the House of Commons.[21]

Liberals tended to rate the press highly as both mirror and maker of opinion. Regardless of their estimation of its worth, mid-century liberals granted the press great power as the engine and the expression of opinion. Mill's reviewer in the *North British Review* could barely contain his excitement at the rise of 'the Newspaper Press' and celebrated the political intelligence of the 'middle-class' newspaper public.[22] Liberal opinion was, however, happier to put 'public opinion' on the platform than its conservative counterpart. Erskine May argued that it is in the 1770s that 'public meetings... take their place among the institutions of the country' and inaugurate 'a new phase in the development of public opinion'.[23] This widely accepted liberal narrative

---

[19] For an interesting twist on this, see Joseph Chamberlain's appeal to supporters of the South African war, declaring, 'I say it is time your voices were heard, the voices of the great silent majority of the people of this country', from his speech at Birmingham reported in *The Times*, 11 May 1901.

[20] *Selected Speeches of the Late Right Honourable the Earl of Beaconsfield*, ed. T. E. Kebbel (London, 1882), p. 487.

[21] ibid., p. 506.

[22] 'The British press: its growth, liberty and power', *North British Review*, 30 (May 1859), 386, 400.

[23] May, *Constitutional History*, II, 268; J. R. Green argued that 'it is from the quarrels between Wilkes and the House of Commons that we may date the influence of public meetings on English politics', in his *Short History*, p. 751.

linked the emergence of the platform to the rise of the political association, as triumphantly embodied in the form of the Anti-Corn Law
League. Competing accounts memorialised the League differently –
Buckle saw it as merely symptomatic of the general march of mind;
others stressed its role in forming opinion – but its exemplary status
was widely granted.[24] For all liberalism's achievements as a governing
ethos in Victorian Britain, the broader movement was energised by
a sense of distance from established institutions: the Manchester merchant and reformer John Slagg caught this mood well when arguing
that all reform movements were bottom-up expressions of public
opinion to which party leaders belatedly accommodated themselves.[25]
Insistence on the justified power of sincere belief was apparent in the
importance attached to *intensity* of belief in the formation of public
opinion: a tenet that conferred a privileged status upon the public
meeting. As Erskine May explained, 'however forcibly the press might
persuade and convince, it moved men singly in their homes and business: but here were men assembled to bear witness to their *earnestness*:
the scattered forces of public opinion were collected and made known:
a cause was popularised by the sympathies and acclamation of the
multitude'.[26]

The most elaborate portrait of 'public opinion' produced in the last
third of the nineteenth century was that of Carslake Thompson. In his
double-decker on *Public Opinion and Lord Beaconsfield*, Thompson
traced the course of public feeling through the long controversy over
the Eastern Question between 1875 and 1880.[27] He took his evidence
primarily from newspapers and meetings, not omitting other indicators, such as by-elections or letters to the press. Gladstonian liberals
regarded the Bulgarian atrocities agitation as proof that the public
was frequently more moral in its view of international affairs than the
House of Commons. Gladstone's moral populism gained currency and
legitimation from the episode.[28] The impassioned debate about policy

---

[24] Buckle, *History of Civilisation*, p. 155. Robertson stressed the formative role
of the League in his editorial footnote at this point.
[25] John Slagg speaking as Chair of the Executive Committee of the National
Reform Union, reported in *The Times*, 16 Dec. 1875.
[26] May, *Constitutional History*, pp. 270–1 (my emphasis).
[27] Thompson, *Public Opinion and Lord Beaconsfield*.
[28] The classic study remains R. T. Shannon, *Gladstone and the Bulgarian
Agitation, 1872* (London, 1963).

served in many ways to reinforce both liberal and conservative views of the public. It also gave rise to Carslake Thompson's suggestive account of the means of evaluating 'public opinion'.

Thompson argued that 'genuine' public opinion should satisfy four criteria: persistence, volume, earnestness and rationality.[29] Though a strong liberal, Thompson provided a definition agreeable to a broad swathe of the political spectrum. Invocation of 'public opinion' in political argument had to operate within certain parameters to maintain plausibility and rhetorical resonance. Thompson nicely stated the core requirements for a body of belief to constitute a public opinion. What were their implications for locating opinion?

Persistence was an attribute rarely attained by press commentary or platform campaigns. It was often claimed on the right that intense outbursts of public meetings would inevitably fail to meet the prerequisite of persistence. Liberals resisted this view, notably in 1876–80, arguing both that the fire of moral indignation could be sustained, and that conservatives overestimated the value of established views.[30] Volume could be demonstrated by press, platform or petition, but was perhaps most compellingly exhibited by the first of these. Earnestness was most respected by the radical tradition and deeply valued by early Labour politicians like MacDonald.[31] However, as the views of Erskine May and the commemoration of the Anti-Corn Law League suggest, it was more generally prized within liberal political culture and encouraged interest in the acclamation of the platform. The requirement of rationality fostered an emphasis upon sustained debate. Its bearing on the relative merits of the various channels of opinion could be sharply disputed. A widespread presumption existed, at least before the 1880s, that it was best manifested by the press. This came under great strain in the 1890s and after, when many liberals rediscovered the virtues of the public meeting.

Contemporaries urgently debated the relative importance of these criteria. Some, such as rationality and earnestness, were complex attributes, whose assessment was highly contestable. Much turned on complex questions of interpretation, and independent debates about

[29] Thompson, *Public Opinion and Lord Beaconsfield*, I, 32.
[30] Carslake Thompson took this line. See *Public Opinion and Lord Beaconsfield*, I, 38–9.
[31] For further discussion of MacDonald in particular, see Chapter 3. Meisel stresses the importance of earnestness in Victorian public speaking: see *Public Speech and the Culture of Public Life*, p. 116.

the character of the press or the importance of open versus closed meetings. The only way to address these questions adequately is to examine in detail perceptions of press, platform and petition. We begin with the press.

Press

The position of the press as an organ of public opinion had achieved the status of a commonplace by the mid-Victorian era.[32] The importance of the press is unsurprising, but the role attributed to it reflected the particular character of nineteenth-century conceptions of 'public opinion'. As Seeley suggested, publics were created when individuals were 'brought into some kind of organic relation'.[33] It was consequently more common to talk of the opinion of the nation than of larger collective entities.[34] Membership of any public required the existence of some minimal shared interests from which discussion could proceed. 'Public opinion' was in an important sense composed of corporate as much as individual views. Corporate opinions embodied real shared interests and depended for their formation on some display of civic spirit. The language of 'public opinion' retained a normative dimension, reminiscent of Rousseau's general will, in that it was opinions directed towards the common good, as opposed to mere expressions of self-interest, of which true public opinion was held to be composed. Influential liberal narratives of the press encapsulated and expounded these deliberative and collective characteristics of 'public opinion'. Readers interrogated leading articles, and interacted with each other, through the conventionalised discourse of the letters page. Anonymous journalism embodied a collective view of the identity of both the publication and its readership.[35] Opinions were earnestly advocated and independently held.[36]

---

[32] For instance, H. Cox pronounced that 'An English newspaper is certainly a marvellous production', *The British Commonwealth*, pp. 238–9.

[33] Seeley, 'The English revolution of the nineteenth century', 350.

[34] An example of the attribution of a 'public opinion' to a sectional group is Lecky, *Democracy and Liberty*, II, 138.

[35] For perceptive contemporary reflection upon the practice of anonymity, see Symon, *The Press and its Story*, esp. p. 106.

[36] T. H. S. Escott provided an unusually self-conscious celebration of independence. See his *Social Transformation of the Victorian Age: A Survey of Court and Country* (London, 1897), p. 566.

The idea of press independence was, of course, both problematic and contested. As contemporary observers recognised, many newspapers remained intimately connected to political parties; Frederic Harrison suggested that the press 'is really an appendage to the Commons'.[37] It was precisely for this reason, though, that, from the 1850s, *The Times* was conventionally seen as peculiarly representative of public opinion. As *Blackwood's Magazine* noted in 1867, 'there is but one newspaper in existence which so much as affects to go upon the principle of setting its sails to meet the coming breeze . . . all the rest are either the creations of parties . . . or they are purely mercantile speculations'.[38] The importance attached by contemporaries to press independence was closely related to a broader ambivalence about 'party', rooted in critiques of old corruption that championed the willingness of heroic journalists to speak truth unto power.[39] Constitutionalist writing identified the emergence of press independence in the eighteenth century as a crucial bulwark of freedom against executive power.[40]

On the left, criticism of liberal narratives of press independence also focused on economic issues. Trade unionists criticised the capitalist bias that resulted from advertiser power, and offered a starkly interest-based analysis of the newspaper press that rejected pious claims about independence. However, whilst recognising the role of the press in advancing particular interests, the labour movement clung to an essentially optimistic narrative in which the light of publicity would rationalise British political culture. Advocates for a labour press certainly claimed its creation would advance labour interests; but it would do so by enlightening public opinion through telling the truth about British society. Given the movement's self-image – its belief that, as Hardie put it, 'labour is the nation' – advocacy of a labour press may be better seen as consummating than contradicting the ideal of a fearless press, independent of vested interest, and committed to the earnest expression of opinion.

---

[37] See A. Milman, 'Parliamentary procedure versus obstruction', *Quarterly Review*, 178 (Jan. 1894), 488.
[38] G. R. Gleig, 'The government and the press', *Blackwood's Magazine*, 102 (Dec. 1867), 763.
[39] Explored in Lawrence, *Speaking for the People*, passim.
[40] Green, *Short History*, pp. 745–6, 752; Charles Knight, *Charles Knight's School History of England: From the Earliest Period to our Own Times* (London, 1865), p. 602.

The relationship between the press and public opinion could be conceived in a number of ways. Classically, it was argued that readers' choice of newspaper was importantly determined by the paper's politics, and thus that the corporate clash of editorial views paralleled the movement of public opinion at large. Secondarily, though, attention might be focused upon the capacity of newspapers to articulate explicitly the direction of 'public opinion'. Just as with efforts by political associations to speak for the public, such claims were open to dismissal as presumptuous self-promotion. Carslake Thompson subjected the *Daily Telegraph* to sustained criticism for such fakery, insisting that 'we have no means of ascertaining whether... the *Telegraph* was endeavouring to present to its readers a genuine conclusion arrived at from the information to which it had access or whether... it was endeavouring to manufacture the Public Opinion which it loudly asserted already existed, and to claim for a fictitious Public Opinion the right to govern'. However partial Carslake Thompson's charge, the terms in which it was made were highly resonant.[41] In the course of a long-running feud that included a half-hearted fight outside the Beefsteak Club and a mooted duel in Belgium, the radical MP Henry Labouchere attacked Henry Lawson Levy – proprietor of the *Daily Telegraph* – by name for his newspapers' pretensions to speak for the nation. Summing up in the ensuing libel trial, Lord Coleridge argued that the public had a right to know whether the personage behind the 'great trumpet' of the newspaper was 'a giant or a pigmy'.[42]

Recent publications have significantly advanced our understanding of attitudes towards the press in the late nineteenth and early twentieth centuries.[43] However, valuable as this work is, its tight focus on the press can distract from the importance attributed by contemporaries to other conduits of 'public opinion', most notably the platform and the petition. In building on this work, three issues require particular attention. Media historians have offered differing assessments of the degree to which the press was regarded as mirror or maker of 'public opinion'. In either case, of course, the press would provide valuable evidence as to the state of the public mind; only those who regarded the

---

[41] Thompson, *Public Opinion and Lord Beaconsfield*, I, 440.
[42] *The Times*, 29 Mar. 1881.
[43] Jones, *Powers of the Press*; Hampton, *Visions of the Press*.

press as neither mirror nor maker could argue that its contents were worthless as a guide to opinion. In studying attitudes to the press, historians have focused particularly on concerns about working-class reading and responses to the growth of cheaper dailies.[44] However, within political discussion of 'public opinion', another divide loomed equally large: that between 'provincial' and 'London' papers. Here, significant party differences emerge in competing assessments of the geography of political intelligence. It is, though, undeniable that the enhanced commercialisation and capitalisation of the press from the 1890s provoked sharp disagreement amongst contemporaries about the relationship between, and character of, 'public opinion' and the press.

Between 1870 and 1914 commentators devoted considerable attention to the question of whether the press moulded or mirrored opinion. Media historians have approached this question in distinct ways. Jones has argued that the reflective metaphor was particularly prevalent in mid-Victorian Britain, and implied its diminishing relevance in the more party-dominated world of post-1867 politics.[45] In contrast, Hampton argues that, while there was no straightforward or absolute transition, 'educational' views of the press gave way to 'representative' conceptions from the 1880s onwards.[46] As these differences suggest, contemporaries often combined the language of mirroring and making in their discussions of the press. Those who upheld the educative function of the press usually did so with the proviso – also common amongst politicians – that the press could only ripen public opinion by maintaining proximity to it.[47] Similarly, proponents of the mirror metaphor often qualified their position by retaining a leadership role for the press in distilling the public mind, arguing that mirroring occurred at the level of the press as a whole through the operation of a free market in ideas and views.[48] As Hampton suggests, debate intensified in the wake of the late-century popularisation and

---

[44] On working-class reading more broadly, see J. Rose, *The Intellectual Life of the British Working Classes* (New Haven, 2001).

[45] Jones, *Powers of the Press*, p. 90, 143–4.

[46] Hampton, *Visions of the Press*, pp. 9–10, 12, 55.

[47] M. P. Dorman, *The Mind of the Nation: A Study of Political Thought in the Nineteenth Century* (London, 1900), p. 373.

[48] See the views of W. T. Stead, discussed in Chapter 1.

commercialisation of the press.[49] Popularisation was not, however, the only trend: the Edwardian period also saw a flourishing political journalism of ideas aimed at the purportedly opinion-forming political elite. Contemporaries assessed these developments variously. In the political context, especially in relation to labour questions, growing scepticism was evident over the closeness of the fit between a predominantly right-wing press and 'public opinion' in an era of liberal government and labour movement growth.

The beguiling images of mirroring and moulding public opinion were much used by apologists for the press: each encapsulated potent pictures of enlightenment. Their deployment was often tactically motivated: the mirror metaphor countered charges of perverting public taste, the moulding image elevated the power and prestige of the press; but the effectiveness of these rhetorical moves rested upon the resonance of their larger narratives. The ease with which contemporaries moved between the two reflected their shared property of aligning the verdicts of the press with the proper formation of 'public opinion'. Visions of the press as a maker of opinion exercised an obvious appeal for journalists especially, but cooler appraisals were always drawn to the arguably more realistic view of the press as mirror.

The most compelling reason for adopting the mirror metaphor was given by T. H. S. Escott, who noted that 'the average reader chooses his newspaper not because he wants to be converted, but because his self love is flattered by seeing his formed ideas reflected in its columns'.[50] From a notably less radical perspective, James Fitzjames Stephen opined earlier that 'journalists ... are in reality the servants of the public, and the course they take is, and always will be, ultimately determined by the public'.[51] John Morley in 1874 treated as a commonplace the view that 'the press is the more or less flattering mirror of the prevailing doctrines of the day'.[52] In 1902, the trade publication *Sell's World's Press* reiterated the perspective of Alexander Paterson that 'the newspaper is a mirror reflecting the times in

---

[49] Hampton, *Visions of the Press*, p. 43.
[50] Escott, *Social Transformations of the Victorian Age*, p. 382.
[51] J. F. Stephen, 'Journalism', *Cornhill Magazine*, 6 (July 1862), 53.
[52] J. Morley, 'Mr Mill's autobiography', *Fortnightly Review*, 15 new ser. (Jan. 1874), 15.

which it is produced'.[53] This assessment was not confined to liberals and radicals. 'A Conservative Journalist', addressing the question 'Why is the provincial press radical?' in 1886, observed that 'a journal is a reflection of its readers. It is about as good as the public will let it be. It is never worse, either socially or politically. If any journal issues from the press anywhere worse in tone than the public it offers itself to, it dies.'[54]

Kennedy Jones, Alfred Harmsworth's right-hand man, advanced the mirror theory, arguing that 'such power as the daily Press aspired to could only be derived from an accurate reflection of the public mind'.[55] It is perhaps unsurprising that the proponents of the much-criticised 'Northcliffe Revolution' should adopt the view that the press merely mirrored social trends. However, Harmsworth himself revealingly incorporated images of mirroring *and* making in writing for *Mitchell's Newspaper Directory*. While it was the judgement of the public, rather than the depth of the proprietor's pockets, that determined success, in running 'the chief instrument in the formation of public opinion' the staff of a newspaper incurred a heavy responsibility. High-minded critics of the Harmsworth approach deployed the mirror metaphor as an indictment, implicitly contrasting it as an approach with the more strenuous ideal of making. In a series on 'The Harmsworth Brand', occasioned by his purchase of *The Times* in 1908, the liberal *Nation* suggested that Northcliffe's philosophy was that 'the newspaper business is to be run as a great shop is run ... it must constantly seek and follow the public taste in all moods and tenses'.[56] In defending his newspapers in 1905, Harmsworth explicitly mobilised the established rhetoric of independence to reject the charge of caprice, insisting that 'independence and disinterestedness ... have taken the place of servility to political parties, and of subserviency to fleeting phases of popular opinion'.[57]

Hampton links the rise of the representative idiom to increasing disenchantment over the reasonableness of 'public opinion'.[58] Debates over the rationality of public opinion are dealt with in the next chapter,

[53] A. Paterson, 'Two centuries of daily journalism', *Sell's World's Press* (1902), 46.
[54] 'A Conservative Journalist', 'Why is the provincial press radical?', 682.
[55] K. Jones, *Fleet Street and Downing Street* (London, 1919), p. 100.
[56] *The Nation*, 25 July 1908, 599.
[57] *Mitchell's Newspaper Directory* (1905), 9.
[58] Hampton, *Visions of the Press*, pp. 95–6, 101.

but it is worth noting here that the mirror metaphor often continued to be yoked to positive narratives about social progress and the growth of intelligence. In 1887, H. R. Fox Bourne noted that 'the intelligence, as well as the wilfulness, of newspaper readers has weakened the authority of newspaper writers...though he may please himself with the thought that he is, or seems to be, guiding public opinion, the leader writer cannot but be aware that he is generally doing little more than following it'.[59] Frank Taylor in his Oxford prize-winning essay on *The newspaper press* urged that

> there is a tendency, encouraged perhaps by the natural vanity of journalists, to exaggerate the strength of forces external to the public mind. In reality the power of all such forces is slowly declining. Education, especially the education of going to the poll, makes men more self-reliant and less subservient to the voice of the charmer. The mysterious 'majesty of print' is evaporating with every accession to the numbers of those who are capable of forming a judgment of their own.[60]

Taylor portrayed the press as more of a mirror than a maker, but also expressed considerable scepticism about the sensitivity with which newspapers could be said to register shifts in the political mood. Confidence in the intelligence of newspaper readers did not disappear with the arrival of the twentieth century. *Macmillan's Magazine* asked in 1903, 'who can doubt that the intelligent reading of journals is increasing?'[61] The assumption of a critical readership was more compatible with the view that the press reflected opinion than with the idea that it made it.

As the growth of mass daily newspapers suggests, the late nineteenth- and early twentieth-century press was multi-faceted. While commentators increasingly identified the press with the newspaper, weeklies and periodicals retained significance in anatomies of public opinion. Cost and frequency were only two of the dimensions along which variations within the press were charted. Place of publication provided another. Railways made possible the penetration of the London papers into the regions; the invention of the telegraph subsequently enabled the

---

[59] H. R. Fox Bourne, *English Newspapers: Chapters in the History of Journalism* (London, 1887), pp. 387–8.
[60] Taylor, *The Newspaper Press as a Power*, pp. 18–19.
[61] J. G. L., 'The newspaper', *Macmillan's Magazine*, 87 (April 1903), 432.

provincial press to acquire news as quickly as its metropolitan rival.[62] While historians have long scrutinised the divide between metropolitan and provincial newspapers, recent years have seen a powerful reassertion of the political and cultural significance of the regional press. Work on the politics of place and on civic life more generally has recognised the role played by the local press in imagining and contesting the character of urban communities.[63] Both conservatives and liberals had their local papers of choice, but it was liberals who tended to champion the representative importance of the provincial press in general compared to that of metropolitan organs of Fleet Street.

Liberal acclaim for the provincial press in this period was powerfully enunciated in the debate over army purchase in 1871. In a much-cited remark, Gladstone argued that the London press reflected 'the opinion of the clubs rather than the opinion of the great nation'.[64] Liberal emphasis on the representative function of the regional press gained credibility from the realities of newspaper production. London papers were in an important sense no more national than their provincial counterparts, though they were usually less adept at ministering to more local concerns.[65] In the 1880s, the journalists and conservative editors Charles Pebody and Joseph Hatton published popular accounts of journalism that noted the virtues of the provincial press. Hatton remarked that 'the editorial opinion of the country editor is now-a-days a more individual and independent one than that of his London contemporary'.[66] Alexander Paterson claimed in 1902 that 'it has been customary to distinguish between the London and the provincial Press . . . that distinction, which was once very real, cannot be said any longer to exist, save perhaps in the case of one paper, the *Times*'.[67]

---

[62] Lecky, *Democracy and Liberty*, I, 210.
[63] Vernon, *Politics and the People*; Joyce, *Democratic Subjects*; M. Roberts, 'Constructing a Tory world-view: popular politics and the Conservative press in late-Victorian Leeds', *Historical Research*, 79, 203 (2006), 115–43; M. McCormack, ed., *Public Men: Masculinity and Politics in Modern Britain* (Basingstoke, 2007).
[64] *The Times*, 4 Sep. 1871.
[65] G. Bryce, J. Curran & P. Wright, eds., *Newspaper History from the Seventeenth Century to the Present Day* (London, 1978), p. 364.
[66] C. Pebody, *English Journalism, and the Men Who Have Made It* (London, 1882), p. 160; J. Hatton, *Journalistic London: Being a Series of Sketches of the Famous Pens and Papers of the Day* (London, 1882), pp. 36–7.
[67] Paterson, *Sell's World's Press* (1902), 44.

One provincial paper, the *Manchester Guardian*, had a London office from as early as 1868, whereas London papers lacked a foothold in Manchester or Glasgow until the 1900s. Levels of distribution are harder to determine, but disagreement over the comparative significance of regional and London papers is not best understood primarily in terms of disputes about circulation. Nor should it be seen as merely a reflection of the location of electoral constituencies, though party interests obviously coloured debate. Rather, arguments about the relative merits of provincial and metropolitan papers require exploration for the light they shed upon understandings of 'public opinion'.

Liberal insistence upon the merits of the provincial press was not a Gladstonian innovation. The importance attached to the opinion of great commercial cities in *Essays on Reform* extended an older tradition, encompassing Erskine May and Robert Vaughan, of locating opinion in towns.[68] Reform itself strengthened liberal convictions on this issue. Walter Bagehot noted in 1870 that 'the metropolitan press . . . is decidedly and visibly losing influence, vigour, and circulation', arguing that 'power has passed to an electorate which does not take its views from London society, or even from London, – which prefers its own views, its own politics, and, to a growing extent, its own men'.[69] He concluded that 'the fall of the London press and the rise of the provincial press will continue . . . one of its main results must . . . be to make provincial opinion – the opinion of the great trading cities – much more influential than that somewhat over-cautious and feeble but acute set of ideas usually described as "London opinion"'.[70]

Assessments of the geography of opinion did not simply follow party divisions. Journalists, and others, were often moved by more professional criteria for judging the representative power of newspapers. There was, nonetheless, a clear tendency for conservatives to be less enamoured of the provincial press than liberals. Salisbury set the tone for much subsequent commentary. Bemoaning the increasing publicity afforded stump oratory, he suggested that 'it is very possible that to the provincial audiences who hear them they may be not only amusing but instructive. But it is rather hard that the rest of the world

---

[68] See Leslie Stephen in *Essays on Reform* (London, 1867), p. 110. For Erskine May, see the *Constitutional History*, II, 138–9, 184; Vaughan, *The Age of Great Cities*.

[69] W. Bagehot, 'The position of the metropolitan press' in *The Collected Works of Walter Bagehot*, VII, ed. N. St. John-Stevas (London, 1974), pp. 296, 298.

[70] ibid., p. 299.

should be condemned to take them as part of the news of the day'.[71] The agitation against the Bulgarian atrocities further politicised views of the press and consolidated the opposing positions. The *Spectator* was typical of the liberal press in concluding that 'the country papers [are] . . . always first to indicate a change'.[72] Conservative organs were unimpressed by liberal attempts to present the agitation as an expression of 'public opinion'. The *Pall Mall Gazette* was moved to sarcasm by liberal appeals to 'public opinion', observing that 'it [public opinion] lies anywhere except in the regions where men congregate – not in London, not in Middlesex, not in Leeds, not in Worcester: but far away in Scotland, or perhaps in Northumberland'.[73] The paper's contempt was mostly reserved for the 'Celtic fringe', and the existence of urban centres outside of London was accepted, but the metropolitan bias of the *Pall Mall* was clear.

Much debate was generated by the unexpected liberal victory in 1880. Conservative politicians and commentators who had prophesied conservative victory were embarrassed by the liberal success. W. J. Courthope in the *Quarterly Review* felt compelled to argue that 'if the Conservative party has been overthrown by the recent election, so too has been that organised social force which we call public opinion'.[74] His discussion of the press focused solely on the national papers, which he considered unable to reach the least able of electors. Wemyss Reid, editor of the liberal *Leeds Mercury*, took the result to demonstrate that the London press was out of touch with 'public opinion', which was much better represented by the regional papers. Provincial newspapers, disproportionately liberal compared to their London counterparts, had been optimistic about the party's prospects. Reid argued that 'public opinion . . . no longer finds its exclusive or even its authoritative organs in the London press'.[75] Pebody noted that the election 'did much to prove that Mr Gladstone was not so far wrong as his critics supposed at the time'.[76] The electoral success of 1880 provided the suitably moral

---

[71] 'Extra-parliamentary utterances', *Saturday Review*, 5 Dec. 1863, 716.

[72] 'Mr Disraeli and the public', *Spectator*, 22 July 1876.

[73] *Pall Mall Gazette*, 13 Apr. 1878.

[74] W. J. Courthope, 'The Conservative defeat', *Quarterly Review*, 149 (Apr. 1880), 549.

[75] T. Wemyss Reid, 'Public opinion and its leaders', *Fortnightly Review*, 28 new ser. (Aug. 1880), 243–4.

[76] Pebody, *English Journalism*, p. 160.

conclusion to Carslake Thompson's tale of how Beaconsfieldism had sought to flout the will of the public.

Debates over parliamentary reform illustrate party differences over the geography of political intelligence. In the mid 1880s, the issue posed difficulties for both parties. Liberal support for parity between country and borough franchises was hard for conservatives fond of upholding rural virtues to criticise effectively. In 1884, Trevelyan mocked conservatives for denying the significance of liberal meetings in the counties, noting that 'they are exactly the same people, who, till quite recently, were always telling us that the public opinion of the counties was very much more valuable than the public opinion of the towns'.[77] Redistribution was equally awkward, for many liberals were worried by the potential benefits to the opposition of the establishment of one-member constituencies in the counties. Extending the franchise was easily presented as furthering the principle of numbers over that of interests as the basis of representation, so implying the need for more metropolitan seats relative to the periphery. In introducing suffrage reform in 1884, Gladstone attempted to resist these implications by claiming that the concentrated masses and proximity to power of the metropolis gave it a sway that outlying regions could never match.[78] Conservatives were quick to detect a tension between the 'centrifugal theory' and the liberal tendency to suggest that 'they must not look to London for the expression of public opinion'. Conservative criticism took a number of forms: Lowther suggested the centrifugal theory was obsolete 'in these days, not only of railways and newspapers, but also of telegraphs and telephones'; whereas Northcote – in line with most conservatives – made the rather different anti-Gladstonian case that to correspond with political knowledge voting power should reflect proximity to the capital.[79]

The division between county and borough constituencies was distinct from that between the metropolitan and the provincial, but both raised important questions about the geography and character of public opinion. From 1880 onwards, liberal electoral predominance in the boroughs was in decline, and the counties came to loom larger as

[77] Speech given at Snitterfield on 30 Dec. 1885, reported in *The Times*, 31 Dec. 1885.
[78] *Parliamentary Debates*, 3rd ser., CCLXXXVI (1884), col. 130.
[79] H. S. Northcote, *Parliamentary Debates*, 3rd ser., CCLXXXVI (1884), col. 638; Lowther, ibid., col. 692; Northcote, ibid., col. 1900.

a source of liberal members. Recent historiography has revealed a popular urban conservatism which appealed beyond the pineries and vineries of suburbia.[80] However, established liberal assumptions about urban political intelligence persisted. Liberal belief in the moral supremacy of provincial opinion tended to grow, in keeping with electoral realities and the changing nature of the broader party. The growing gap between liberal support in the provincial and metropolitan press after 1886 did little to enamour Fleet Street to liberals. It would be too simple, though, to reduce differing views of the press to mere electoral geography. The relationship between ideas and interests should not be seen as one-way. Liberal emphases upon the claims of provincial opinion and liberal representation in the regions were complementary. Conservative insistence on the weight of London in the distribution of opinion certainly reflected their support in the capital, but also expressed the importance conservatives attributed to the rentier wealth and establishment social capital so evident in the metropole.

Historians of the press have argued that from the 1890s the distinctive variety of the provincial press was increasingly undermined.[81] Some liberal commentators continued to uphold the representative superiority of the provincial newspapers into the 1900s. W. J. Fisher, the former editor of the liberal London *Daily Chronicle*, commended the provincial papers whose 'influence . . . is immeasurably greater than that of the more pretentious London papers'.[82] The right, generally less inclined to eulogise the press, remained convinced of the superiority of metropolitan productions. In 1891, the unionist Earl of Portsmouth commented on the reversal whereby Conservatism was now stronger in the boroughs, Liberalism in the counties. He offered an interpretation clearly based on the primacy of the capital and its press, arguing that 'in London, where there is a competition of other kinds of intellectual excitement, where political leaders are constantly seen, and their

---

[80] J. Lawrence, 'Class and gender in the making of urban Toryism, 1880–1914', *English Historical Review*, 108 (1993), 629–52; A. Windscheffel, *Popular Conservatism in Imperial London, 1868–1906* (Woodbridge, 2007); M. Roberts, '"Villa toryism" and popular Conservatism in Leeds, 1885–1902', *Historical Journal*, 49 (2006), 217–46.

[81] A. Jones, 'Local journalism in Victorian political culture' in L. Brake, A. Jones and L. Madden, eds., *Investigating Victorian Journalism* (London, 1990), p. 67.

[82] W. J. Fisher, 'The Liberal press and the Liberal party', *Nineteenth Century*, 56 (Aug. 1904), 201.

faults and virtues are estimated without the exaggeration that disturbs the provincial mind, political meetings have no undue importance'.[83] T. E. Kebbel's history of Toryism testified that 'Mr Disraeli seems to have thought that the press might come in time to do all the critical and watchful work of Parliament better than Parliament itself'.[84] As a partisan Tory journalist, Kebbel felt no difficulty in stating that 'the extraordinary development of the political press, to which the foremost statesmen of the day are proud to contribute, and which has already eclipsed to some extent the interest of the Parliamentary debates, [has] gone far to justify one part of this conception'.[85] Celebration of the press was thus not confined to liberals, but for Tories it was usually Fleet Street rather than the provinces that merited praise.

The last years of the nineteenth century have attracted enormous attention from students of the press. While much of this writing questions the novelty of developments in the 1880s and 1890s, contemporaries tended to be struck more by the extent and significance of change. In arguing that these years witnessed the gradual replacement of 'educationalist' by 'representative' conceptions of the press, Mark Hampton has contended that a more passive understanding of 'public opinion' emerged, according to which newspapers spoke for those incapable of speaking for themselves.[86] It was suggested earlier that this chronology understates the prevalence of the mirror metaphor in mid-Victorian Britain, and overstates the demise of the idea of the press as a maker of opinion. The latter was powerfully asserted in the wake of press coverage of the South African war, but also recurs amongst labour critiques of press bias against strikers.[87] Developments in the popular press certainly were, as Hampton shows, often cast as representative of broader trends in society, but this relationship was not necessarily one in which the public was perceived as passive or uncritical. As we shall explore further in examining attitudes to the

---

[83] Earl of Portsmouth, 'Executive government and the unionists', *Quarterly Review*, 173 (Oct. 1891), 540.
[84] T. E. Kebbel, *A History of Toryism*, ed. E. J. Feuchtwanger (London, 1972; 1st edn London, 1886), p. 358.
[85] Kebbel, *A History of Toryism*, p. 356.
[86] Hampton, *Visions of the Press*, pp. 9–10, 12, 102.
[87] For labour critiques of press bias, see J. Keir Hardie, 'The socialist daily', *Labour Leader*, 11 Nov. 1910; Clifford Allen, 'The new daily', *Labour Leader*, 18 Aug. 1911; *Labour Leader*, 15 Mar. 1912.

platform and the petition, contemporary observers were far from simply accepting of journalistic aspirations to shape or embody opinion.
As the failure of the tariff reform crusade unfurled, some argued that
a press bought primarily for news and entertainment was a poor guide
to public opinion which, amidst sharp disputes over free trade, votes
for women and Irish home rule, was far from obviously passive.

In a letter to *The Times*, the social democrat H. M. Hyndman considered the meaning of the liberal defeat of 1895. He contrasted liberal
predominance in the press with liberal failure at the polls and asserted

> that the mass of the people, and especially the working classes, are being
> guided less and less in their political action by the writers in the Press;
> and that they form their own judgment with respect to Administrations and
> parties, without paying much attention to the advice of the would-be keepers
> of their political conscience – and votes. In short, I contend that newspapers
> are read nowadays for their news, not their views.[88]

The claim that the press was read for its news, perhaps especially its
sporting news, rather than its views was to become increasingly common in subsequent years. Many observers were struck by the declining
importance of politics in the more commercially successful papers of
the late 1890s.[89] The argument was that this transformation shattered
the political link between the press and the public, for papers no longer
had any incentive to attempt to match the mood of the public in their
editorials. Hyndman, however, was not claiming that the people were
politically apathetic but rather that their increasing self-sufficiency rendered them less malleable by the public press. The existence of this
more positive and recurrent explanation of the discounting of politics
in the press has often been neglected. As we shall see, Hyndman was
notably less sanguine about the populace in the aftermath of the South
African war, but more generous views of the public resurfaced on the
left after 1906. It is important now, however, to examine the response
to Hyndman's rejection of the power of the press to form or to reflect
the public mind.

Most of those who replied to Hyndman did so primarily by suggesting that the balance of newspaper forces was, whatever Hyndman
thought, heavily biased towards the Tories. The liberal journalist John
Bavington Jones spoke for many in arguing that

[88] *The Times*, 31 July 1895.
[89] See Taylor, *The Newspaper Press as a Power*, p. 16.

Anyone who knows anything about the newspaper press at the present time is well aware that there never was a time when the Liberal party had less hold on the newspapers or when the leaders of the Liberal party showed less anxiety to enlist the services of cheap newspapers in support of their cause. In fact, if the public were not already bewildered with the diversity of reasons given for the liberal rout I should be tempted to mention the neglect of the newspaper press as one ... The general public in this busy age forget more in a month than they did formerly in a year, and if the Press ceased publishing views and confined itself to news an election would turn on things which happened yesterday and the day before, while the blunders and blessings of older date would be ignored.[90]

Jones countered Hyndman's account of the state of play in the party press and discerned that newspapers retained a role which rested upon the limitations of the public rather than the more flattering view of the public by which Hyndman explained the irrelevance of the press. In his reply to Hyndman's rejoinder in *The Times*, Jones used newspaper directories to contradict effectively Hyndman's description of press allegiance. He went on to treat the doctrine that 'the Press is discarded as a political guide for the people' as 'ridiculous'.[91] Others, such as the future MP Alan Gardner, emphasised liberal organisational and programmatic weakness rather than press hostility.[92]

   The most interesting intervention came from the American editor St Clair McKelway. McKelway cast the wrangle over the number of liberal and Tory papers as profoundly misconceived. He argued that it was 'independents' who 'hold the balance of power' and thus that, while 'the journalism of ownership' was impotent, that of independence 'was never deservedly more powerful on both sides of the sea'. The kind of fluctuations in the public mood captured by election results could not be reflected by the institutionalised party press, but might be by the more disinterested newspapers. It is worth noting that McKelway contrasted 'the journalism of independence' with that 'of ownership'.[93] Carlyle's celebrated vision of editorial dynasties had given way to an emphasis upon the power of proprietors, which more accurately reflected the realities of the contemporary press in the 1890s.

   If it was plausible to claim in 1895 that press allegiances matched the preferences of the electorate, this was hardly the case in 1906.

[90] *The Times*, 6 Aug. 1895.   [91] *The Times*, 20 Aug. 1895.
[92] *The Times*, 1 Aug. 1895.   [93] *The Times*, 3 Aug. 1895.

Edward Porritt, a lecturer at Harvard, penned an interesting diagnosis of the legacy of 1906 in both the *Atlantic Monthly* and *Sell's* annual for 1910.[94] Porritt offered a comparative analysis of the liberal landslide in England, the Canadian election of 1908 and the 1909 revision of the Dingley tariff in the United States. He argued that in all cases political events had run directly counter to the prognostications of the press.[95] The Scrutator column in *Truth* responded warmly to Porritt's views, but laid greater emphasis upon the loss of faith in the press occasioned by its rapid alterations of view.[96] Such editorial gymnastics did not reflect real changes in 'public opinion'. Scrutator suggested disenchantment with the press was to be welcomed, for 'it is desirable that the public should think for itself, instead of buying its opinions ready-made by wholesale manufacturers'.[97] It was possible to hold that the demise of the political press merely reflected the advent of a more adult and independent public.

Apologists for the 'Northcliffe Revolution' subsequently used 1906 to bolster their view that the press had little importance as a maker of views and acted only as a somewhat belated mirror of opinion. Kennedy Jones noted that 'politics were out of fashion; the people wanted news, not views; good readable matter, not literary thunder-bolts', but cast this shift as the expression of a public opinion increasingly sceptical about 'the majesty of print'. He argued that 'the ferment of political education had worked quickly' and related this to the establishment of universal primary education in 1870.[98] Those who were less committed to the virtues of the new press shared this emphasis upon the impact of the 1870 Education Act, but viewed its results notably less cheerfully.[99]

Leaders in the *Mail* certainly were briefer, but the paper published much in the way of expert commentary and debate. This was in keeping with Kennedy Jones's emphasis upon the declining corporate authority of the newspaper and its replacement by the personal authority of the expert.[100] P. J. Reid, a correspondent of the disenchanted liberal

---

[94] E. Porritt, 'The value of political editorials', *Sell's World's Press* (1910), 508–13.
[95] ibid., 508.   [96] *Truth*, 26 Jan. 1910.   [97] ibid.
[98] Jones, *Fleet Street and Downing Street*, pp. 1, 158.
[99] A reflective *via media* between these positions was mapped out in Scott-James, *The Influence of the Press*, pp. 14–15, 134–5.
[100] Jones, *Fleet Street and Downing Street*, pp. 100–1.

weekly *The Nation*, even noted that 'one of the virtues of the *Daily Mail* [is] that it shows less bias in arranging space for the headlines of the leading political speeches of each of the three parties than most of its morning contemporaries'.[101] Nonetheless, the contention that the post-*Daily Mail* press took politics less seriously commanded considerable support. MacDonald was representative in his view that 'the democratic press finds that the less it says about politics the better. A description of a first-class cricket or football match would get a thousand readers for every ten which a French Revolution would get if it were unattended by horrors and fireworks.'[102]

Prognostications on political reporting were often embedded in larger narratives of cultural change that stressed the rapid pace of modern urban life. 'Scrutator' in *Truth* detailed the changing appearance of newspapers and offered one account of its meaning:

half-penny papers have revolutionised the habit of newspaper reading. Nine-tenths of their 'readers' hardly read them at all. They glance through the paper for headlines that appeal to their taste, and hastily assimilate the scraps that are offered to them in brief paragraphic form. Leading articles are the portions of the paper that are least read, and least of all when they are argumentative or long-winded. Such effect on opinion as a newspaper can produce is now chiefly aimed at by big type and eye-arresting headlines. More than half the papers sold are hastily skimmed on a short railway journey, and thrown aside at the end of it. Writing and reading conducted on these principles can hardly be expected to leave much effect on the public mind, if the public has any mind worthy of the name.[103]

It has been plausibly argued that such stylistic developments were part of a longer story originating in the 1860s, but contemporaries were more struck by the acceleration imparted by the innovations of the 1890s.[104] Much the same was true of worries about the influence of advertisers over the press and fears over contraction of ownership.

Newspapers had always subsidised their cover price through advertising revenue. This process was, however, made more obvious by

---

[101] *The Nation*, 8 Sep. 1908, 805.
[102] J. Ramsay MacDonald, 'The people in power' in S. Coit, ed., *Ethical Democracy: Essays in Social Dynamics* (London, 1900), p. 62.
[103] *Truth*, 26 Jan. 1910.
[104] For a pioneering version of this case, see Perkin, 'The origins of the popular press'.

the arrival of the halfpenny papers. Larger circulations apparently achieved by price cuts seemed to imply a novel level of dependence upon the advertiser. In 1914, *Sell's* organised a symposium on the question, 'Are papers too cheap?' Most of the journalists involved clearly considered the question nonsensical, but some participants were less sanguine. The journalist and novelist Philip Gibbs pronounced that 'every newspaper is competing in the scramble for monster circulations by dragging down its literary quality to the level of the lowest intelligence, which is that of the great uneducated, frivolous sensation-seeking mob'.[105] The popular writer Hall Caine focused more on the danger that the press would lose its vaunted independence if 'the advertisement interests in journalism become paramount'.[106] Such trepidation remained a minority view, but was more common on the left than the right. MacDonald and Lansbury both contributed to the *Sell's* debate. MacDonald spoke for both in arguing that 'our Press is becoming more and more subordinate to advertisers who ... are controlling the editorial side and consequently the free expression of opinion'.[107]

Disapproval of the changing patterns of ownership was more widespread. Concentration of ownership was scarcely unprecedented in Britain, especially amongst provincial papers.[108] Nonetheless, the baronial acquisition of titles by individuals like the Harmsworth brothers strained existing templates. In questions of market contraction, differences of degree could plausibly be cast as differences of kind. The critique of the new proprietor-kings was closely related to more general fears about the rise of trusts and the stifling of competition.[109] Conventional accounts of the press as a mirror of opinion relied upon the operation of a free market in ideas which seemed under threat from the emergent newspaper empires. Opposition to Northcliffism was strengthened both by his elevation to the peerage in 1905 and by his purchase of *The Times* in 1908.

Resistance to the narrowing of ownership was especially pronounced in the labour movement. This was in part because scepticism about the functioning of capitalism, especially the growth of cartels, was

---

[105] 'Are papers too cheap?', *Sell's World's Press* (1914), 16.
[106] ibid., 10.   [107] ibid., 20.
[108] S. Koss, *The Rise and Fall of the Political Press* (2 vols., London, 1976 & 1984), II, 40.
[109] This theme was first seriously broached in H. Pelling, *America and the British Left: From Bright to Bevan* (London, 1956), pp. 53–71.

more common on the left.[110] It was also a consequence of the faith in deliberative politics typical in the Labour party. The importance of a rational 'public opinion', forged by civic activism, was evident in much labour thinking.[111] It accords with Koss's view that 'the emergence of the labour party, wedded to traditional concepts of publicity' helped briefly to revive the political press.[112] The labour movement set great store by the communication of political ideas. The *Pendlebury Pioneer* announced in 1898 that 'this is the day of the Omnipotent Press'.[113] Labour newspapers often retained a high-mindedness that bordered on naivety. This is well exemplified by an optimistic advert for the *Labour Leader*, which urged that 'there is no other paper like it. No police news. No football news. No society news. But it is full of news'.[114] The functions of labour papers were to provide the labour news and the labour views missing from the established press. The latter was made even more difficult to perform by developments in the national media.

MacDonald was troubled by press advertising which ensured that papers 'are too large'. Smaller papers 'would enable independent [i.e. labour] papers to be published'.[115] In an essay on 'The People in Power', MacDonald linked the impact of advertising with the growth of 'the money power'. He offered a lengthy account of his view:

The virtue of a 'cheap press' is only partly realised when the newspaper is sold at a popular price; it is fully experienced when every respectable body of opinion can start its organ and publish its criticisms. But for years the tendency has been to make it almost impossible to start any newspaper unless a man of great wealth or of ample credit is promoter, because the press has been gradually passing out of the control of the reader and has been becoming the organ of the advertiser and the convenience of the capitalist ... The effect of this upon public opinion is very marked already, and the inevitable result will be that the Fourth Estate will be as protected from popular influence, as unanimous in its decisions, as impotent in spreading sound and enlightened opinion as the House of Lords itself.[116]

In an article on the rise of the labour press in 1914, Keighley Snowden attributed the relative weakness of the socialist press in Britain

---

[110] Thompson, 'Political economy, the labour movement and the minimum wage'.

[111] See Chapter 3.   [112] Koss, *The Rise and Fall of the Political Press*, II, 6.

[113] *Pendlebury Pioneer*, Nov. 1898, 1.

[114] *Labour Leader* advertising leaflet, John Johnson collection, Bodleian Library.

[115] *Sell's World's Press* (1914), 20.

[116] MacDonald, 'The people in power', pp. 66–7.

to 'the superior scale of our newspapers, and especially of our great dailies'.[117] Trade unions 'were obsessed with the notion that a newspaper was bought for its opinions, or at least that theirs would be'. Only with Dilnot's editorship of the *Daily Citizen* was a sound journalistic approach taken.[118]

The most obvious feature of the post-Northcliffe press was its enlarged circulation. This should not, of course, be exaggerated. The *Daily Mirror* attained the million mark only occasionally before 1914. It was the interwar period which saw circulations regularly exceeding two million. Reliable circulation figures for the pre-1914 period are notoriously elusive. Newspapers frequently talked up their circulation, and printed many more copies than were ever sold. Contemporaries, however, were widely convinced that the cheap dailies had penetrated areas of society previously unaffected by the newspaper obsession. Two perceived changes in the readership of newspapers need addressing. The first concerns class, the second gender.

Lord Salisbury famously described the *Daily Mail* as written by and for office-boys. While Kennedy Jones was happy to accept this designation, it was hardly an adequate analysis of the readership of the new press.[119] It does, though, well represent conventional wisdom. J. A. Spender's description of the *Mail*'s readership as 'simply middle-class folk who habitually voted Tory' was typical in much contemporary commentary.[120] The new readership was frequently conceived as black-coated workers, who were semi-educated at best, and lacked an appetite for politics. Snobbery, both conventional and inverted, was clearly at play in this verdict. The established relationship between the press and 'public opinion' was threatened by this view of the developments of the 1890s. A large lower-middle-class readership, mostly apathetic politically, could hardly compel its newspapers to maintain an interest in public opinion and made little contribution to opinion itself. Scott-James noted that 'in such a paper it is profitable to advertise pills. But it is not profitable to advertise *ideas*.' This explained the electoral failure of Tariff Reform, 'repeated thousands of times' in 'the most widely circulating papers'.[121]

---

[117] *Sell's World's Press* (1914), 29.   [118] ibid., 30.

[119] Jones, *Fleet Street and Downing Street*, p. 202.

[120] Spender, *Life, Journalism and Politics*, I, 172.

[121] Scott-James, *The Influence of the Press*, pp. 134–5.

Ford Madox Ford insisted in 1907 that 'every journalist knows...that the papers are written with an eye that more often than not is turned to the women'.[122] Kennedy Jones later recalled that 'we [he and Harmsworth] realized that women are by nature more loyal and conservative than men, and that if we had them with us and got a firm footing in their homes, the value of our papers from the advertiser's point of view would be greatly enhanced'.[123] The notion that women were peculiarly susceptible to visual appeals was commonplace within the developing literature on the theory and psychology of advertising. In *The Art of Publicity – and its Application to Business*, Herbert A. Spiers suggested that 'illustrations are generally more for the gentler than the sterner sex...consider for a moment, and you will find that those bills appealing mainly to men are principally lettered only, or the illustration is of the article itself'.[124]

Trepidation at the growth of a new female newspaper readership reflected fear of a literally feminised public. This was often reinforced by worries about a metaphorically feminised 'public opinion' which, it was argued, particularly in the aftermath of the South African war, had become merely a gigantic crowd. The impact of crowd psychology and the spectacle of popular jingoism on views of the rationality of 'public opinion' are addressed later.[125] Here the issue is the perceived relationship between the new press and the war fever of the South African campaign.

J. A. Hobson emphasised the reliance of British papers upon the coverage provided by a small number of South African papers owned by a clique of self-interested financiers.[126] Hobson's attack was highly coloured by anti-Semitism. His complaints about the press were in part a criticism of the contraction in ownership. The connection Hobson saw between a reactionary state and the money power was rooted in

---

[122] Ford Madox Hueffer (later Ford), *The Spirit of the People: An Analysis of the English Mind* (London, 1907), p. 110.

[123] Jones, *Fleet Street and Downing Street*, p. 331.

[124] H. A. Spiers, *The Art of Publicity – and its Application to Business* (London, 1910), p. 56. On supposed female susceptibility to the emotional in advertising, see Sherwin Cody, *How to Do Business by Letter and Advertising* (London, 1911), p. 91. On advertising and politics, see J. Thompson, '"Pictorial lies"? Posters and politics in Britain c.1880–1914', *Past and Present* (Nov. 2007), 177–210.

[125] See Chapter 3.

[126] J. A. Hobson, *The Psychology of Jingoism* (London, 1901), pp. 107–24.

an older radical critique of aristocratic corruption, but with a new emphasis upon financiers and press barons.[127] In his cognate description of *Democracy and Reaction*, L. T. Hobhouse bewailed the false confidence of 'the man in the street' who 'has just got the last news-sheet from his neighbour', but 'has not waited to test or sift it'. A tension existed in such accounts between the view that the press had poisoned the well of 'public opinion' and the belief that newspaper excess mirrored the inadequacies of 'the man in the street... the man in a hurry; the man who has not time to think and will not take the trouble to do so if he has the time'.[128]

Supporters of the South African war were, unsurprisingly, less troubled by its reporting in the press than were opponents. The anti-socialist writer Arthur Shadwell rebuked those who argued proprietors had turned parts of the press into instruments of the mob, insisting that Britain differed from France, since 'in this country it is impossible to carry on a Press propaganda with such a reckless contempt for facts and use of false information; not for want of will but because of the restraint exercised by the stolid and unemotional character of the public'. Shadwell argued that the 'growing intelligence' of readers kept newspapers honest, and counselled that the minority status of pro-Boer views did not make them true.[129]

Others were, however, deeply alienated by press coverage of the conflict. Ramsay MacDonald, in his post-war account of 'What I saw in South Africa', stated that 'it is well known that a nation will not fight except for a cause in which idealism is mingled. The *Daily Mail* supplied the idealism for the South African war by telling lies about the flogging of British women and children'.[130] It was the dishonesty of the press, its supply of what James Bryce called 'perverted news', which caused most dismay in labour circles.[131] The events of the war

---

[127] P. J. Cain, *Hobson and Imperialism: Radicalism, New Liberalism and Finance, 1887–1938* (Oxford, 2002), esp. pp. 81–161.

[128] L. T. Hobhouse, *Democracy and Reaction* (London, 1904), p. 71.

[129] Arthur Shadwell, 'Proprietors and editors', *National Review* (Aug. 1900), 598, 600.

[130] J. Ramsay MacDonald, *What I Saw in South Africa, September and October 1902* (London, 1903).

[131] Bryce wrote to the American E. L. Godkin to say that 'unhappily the press has so hoodwinked the public by supplying perverted news, i.e. by continually repeating falsehoods, and by suppressing the facts which make against Chamberlain's and Milner's policy that the merits of the matter are as little

provided a reference point for future discussions; in 1912 the *Labour Leader* sardonically contrasted government sympathy towards jingo mobs during the South African war with the guns directed at strikers during labour disputes.[132] Within the labour movement, belief in the power of the press to mould opinion in its image, and concern about the tendencies of the existing press, were both strengthened by the South African war. Neither, however, vanquished faith in the potential rationalism of public opinion, especially given correct information by a genuine labour press.[133]

For all his fury at the spectre of jingoism, Bryce's letters during the war anticipate the reaction against jingoism that must come.[134] The liberal landslide of 1906, achieved in the face of pronounced newspaper support for tariff reform, suggested that the public retained a deliberative capacity less apparent in the physical crowd. In its 1908 review of Ross's *Social Psychology*, the liberal weekly *The Nation* noted that 'even the substitution of the yellowest Press for an equally yellow platform... must bring some advance towards rationality'. This revival of the distinction between crowd and public was founded on the fact that 'a Shanghai telegram is less provocative of violent reaction than a Trafalgar Square oration'.[135]

In the years prior to 1914, the press retained a real claim to exhibit the workings of the public mind. Images of the press as both maker and mirror of opinion persisted throughout. While some observers stressed the increasingly representative character of popular journalism, others, not least from within the labour movement, preferred to emphasise the greater capacity of the new press to mould opinion. Contemporary debate was not, however, confined to distinguishing between the press as mirror, and as maker, of opinion. Considerable ink was spilled anatomising the relative significance of different kinds of newspapers. In discussions of politics, particularly after 1906, the evolution of the post-Northcliffe press was commonly considered to have weakened the link between newspapers and public opinion, though this

understood as they were a year ago', 27 Feb. 1901, Godkin Papers, bMS 1083, Houghton Library, Harvard University.
[132] *Labour Leader*, 1 Mar. 1912.   [133] *Labour Leader*, 5 Dec. 1912.
[134] See for instance Bryce to Godkin, 14 Mar. 1900, 'There will doubtless be a reaction, but when?', Godkin papers, bMS 1083, Houghton Library, Harvard University.
[135] 'The mob mind', *The Nation*, 1 Aug. 1908, 631.

could also be seen as a broadening of the definition of politics that mirrored developments in 'public opinion'. It is, however, essential in understanding invocation of 'public opinion' within political argument to recall that the press was not seen as its sole repository. It is time to examine its other loci – starting with the platform.

Platform

By the 1870s, the centrality of the public meeting to constitutionalism increasingly ensured that groups across the political spectrum sought to secure the acclaim of the platform. This section addresses important questions about platform politics and its relationship to ideas about 'public opinion' by attending to the evolving debate about the place of the public meeting in British politics. It focuses in particular on three periods in which the significance and nature of public meetings were widely discussed: the recourse to the mass platform in debating the suffrage question in the 1880s; the struggles over the South African war in 1899–1902; and the Edwardian controversies over fiscal reform and women's suffrage.

The history of public speaking has received considerable attention in recent years. Belchem and Epstein have taken issue with a 'liberal' consensus about continuity in oppositional oratory, which they locate primarily in the work of Joyce and Biagini.[136] Their argument pays careful attention to the politics of public space, and to the accessibility and the structure of meetings. However, their claims about restrictions on access to open spaces, and the reduced accessibility of meetings, have been importantly challenged by Jon Lawrence, who has emphasised the enduring importance of disruption and open meetings in popular politics.[137] The focus here is upon the ways in which public meetings were or were not considered expressions of 'public opinion' rather than upon trends in popular oratory per se. However, narratives of the taming of popular politics in the second half of the nineteenth

---

[136] J. Belchem & J. Epstein, 'The nineteenth-century gentleman leader revisited', *Social History*, 22, 2 (1997), 174–93; Joyce, *Visions of the People*, and *Democratic Subjects*; Biagini, *Liberty, Retrenchment and Reform*.

[137] Lawrence, *Speaking for the People, passim*; J. Lawrence, *Electing our Masters: The Hustings in British Politics from Hogarth to Blair* (Oxford, 2009); J. Lawrence, 'The transformation of British public politics after the First World War', *Past and Present* (Feb. 2006), 185–216.

century have linked the closing of the public sphere to the supposed
hegemony of a literate, masculine, privatised, middle-class conception
of 'public opinion' that militated against the more democratic and
unruly forms of popular politics.[138]

The status of particular meetings as bearers of public opinion was
contested in often complex ways. Nevertheless, the verdicts of open
meetings retained significance as the result of a genuinely accessible
process that could plausibly be presented as spontaneous rather than
fabricated, and thus as a 'true' expression of public opinion. Politicians and commentators of all stripes continued to grade meetings
according to size, so preserving an incentive for the use of open spaces.
As Lawrence has noted, disputes about the legitimacy of street meetings were protracted and involved, but by the 1900s efforts to deny
their legality were found unpersuasive.[139] Established understandings
of 'public opinion' prized the strong feelings that summoned large
assemblies; heckling was widely regarded as indicative of an open
and so representative meeting. 'Organised' and violent disruption,
however, perhaps especially outside the licence of the election campaign, occupied a more ambivalent position: the righteous manifestation of deep feelings could be re-described as the forcible suppression
of freedom of speech. Evaluations of meetings were also shaped by
the debates about the scope of the public already examined: such
assessments, like the visions of the public that informed them, were
often contested. Activists seeking to claim the mantle of 'public opinion' for their meetings highlighted the depth of their convictions, but
they also often sought to defend the respectability of their gatherings, in line with the emphasis on independence and character apparent in discussions of the composition of the political public.[140] Yet
throughout the period public meetings could be persuasively presented
as expressions of an engaged and participatory politics in ways that

---

[138] Vernon, *Politics and the People*.
[139] Lawrence, 'Transformation of British public politics', 189.
[140] See, for instance, Chamberlain attacking Salisbury at Newton: 'He has
derided your demonstrations; he has expressed scorn of these orderly
meetings of the people', *The Times*, 20 Oct. 1884. Commentators could
commend meetings on similar grounds: 'The perfect order which has
prevailed at all the meetings will give the decision of Croydon [in a
by-election] the highest moral value', *The Times*, 26 Mar. 1909.

are hard to reconcile with strong claims about the abolition of public politics.[141]

The permissible scope for violence within the *legitimate* public meeting is an important and difficult question. In revising the traditional emphasis upon the eirenic character of late Victorian and Edwardian English political culture, Lawrence argues that the enduring value attributed to open meetings ensured a previously unrecognised tolerance for disruptive behaviour.[142] Lawrence focuses particularly upon the election meeting, arguing that these provided a space in which the elect, or would-be elect, were expected to meet, and interact with, the public.[143] There is considerable evidence to suggest that both the likelihood and the acceptability of disruption were greatest during elections. What, then, of the public meeting more generally?

Openness was unquestionably an important yardstick for the evaluation of the importance of public meetings. It provided a place for heckling and the struggle for public space. The superiority of the open meeting was not uncontested, but prestige still attended the successful unticketed meeting. The representative value of disruption, however, was undermined if it could be attributed to a rowdy minority. Orderliness could be used – as Chamberlain did at Newton in 1884 – to uphold the significance of public meetings as expressions of public opinion.[144] Highly organised and violent disruption could be described as hooliganism rather than the assertion of public feeling; meetings dominated by violent clashes were not necessarily accorded significance as expressions of public opinion: the tolerance for violence could vary on ideological grounds. In December 1908, Lord Robert Cecil introduced a Public Meetings Bill, inspired, in part, by distaste at suffragette disruption of extra-parliamentary oratory, particularly that of Cabinet ministers. As Lawrence has argued, lib-lab politicians were particularly hostile to what they perceived as 'Britain's disorderly political traditions'.[145] More populist labour politicians, most conspicuously Thorne and Crooks, were concerned that the measure

---

[141] Lawrence, 'Transformation of British public politics'; Thompson, '"Pictorial lies"?'.
[142] Lawrence, *Speaking for the People*, pp. 60, 94, 164, 174–6, 180–2, 184.
[143] Lawrence, *Electing our Masters*.   [144] *The Times*, 20 Oct. 1884.
[145] Lawrence, 'Contesting the male polity'.

would emasculate a robust political culture.[146] MPs generally distinguished between legitimate heckling, and highly systematic attempts to derail meetings; the latter were widely criticised, and seen by some as novelties, dating back only to the 'Boer War'.[147] The value attached to earnest enthusiasm in debates about 'public opinion' was apparent in the distinction drawn between spontaneous interventions and organised intimidation.[148] The enforcement of the 1908 Act suggests a limited support for its use in the electoral context, but also a reluctance to apply to outdoor gatherings in public spaces measures interpreted as narrowly applicable to indoor events: tolerance for violence did in part depend upon the nature of the meeting.[149] While the political resonance of the open meeting derived in part from prevailing conceptions of 'public opinion', it is important to recognise that these could also be used to deprecate organised violence as an attempt to thwart the emergence of public opinion.

Developments in political organisation from the 1870s raised in heightened form long-standing questions about the relationship between the platform and public opinion. While the role of organisation could be castigated as the fabrication of feeling, political associations had a well-established place within liberal constitutionalist discourse, evident in Green's account of the Wilkesite movement, as engines of 'public opinion'.[150] These arguments were, though, less easily applied to the efforts of permanent extra-parliamentary party machinery. Permanence in itself made it harder to present activity as spontaneous, but the elaboration of extensive *party* organisation raised questions of its own. Burke's classic justification of party in terms of shared principles had much in common with liberal celebrations of issue-based association, but appeared more applicable to the horizontal bonds between MPs than to large-scale extra-parliamentary structures. Mid-Victorian liberal thinkers were relatively quiet on the issue of the mass party: Mill devoted little attention to organisation, while

---

[146] *Parliamentary Debates*, 4th ser., CXCVIII (1908), cols. 2331–2, 2334, 2337–8.

[147] See speech by John Ward, *Parliamentary Debates*, 4th ser., CXCVIII (1908), cols. 2329–30.

[148] *Parliamentary Debates*, 4th ser., CXCVIII (1908), col. 2340.

[149] In rejecting an action brought by the Anti-Socialist Union, the magistrate noted that 'I do not think it [the Act] was meant for a meeting on Peckham Rye', *The Times*, 12 June 1909.

[150] Green, *Short History*, p. 751.

Bagehot concentrated on the necessity for a degree of party discipline within the Commons: he objected to Hare's version of proportional voting in part because he deemed it would increase the power of party over the electors.[151] Ghosh's claim that party was 'an all-embracing modality' fails to grapple with the issue of large-scale centralised party machinery, and suffers from an unwillingness to recognise the role contemporaries attributed to non-party manifestations of opinion.[152] It is, then, unsurprising that many politicians in the 1880s sought to discredit platform meetings that opposed their views by portraying them as the product of shadowy organisations.

Late nineteenth-century attitudes to the 'caucus', especially liberal and radical views, have received considerable attention in recent historiography. Lawrence has stressed radical suspicion of the caucus as an exclusionary form of politics that distanced decision making from the people and the locality. Biagini has investigated the rhetoric of the Natural Liberal Federation (NLF), emphasising its self-image as an inclusive parliament of the rank-and-file. While there are certainly differences of emphasis and interpretation between Lawrence and Biagini, these should not be overstated. Both note liberal realism about the uses of organisation. Lawrence acknowledges the tradition of the political committee within radicalism, while Biagini recognises the existence and resonance of anti-caucus arguments. Biagini's NLF apologists did not defend the creation of a party bureaucracy – they denied the NLF was a party machine, insisting instead on its inclusive and participatory character.[153] In doing so, they were assisted by the widespread view, at least amongst liberals, that to be a liberal was to be part of a broad movement rather than a narrow party, united by a creed rather than a doctrine. Speaking at Islington in 1885, Chamberlain drew on established liberal narratives of associational politics, casting the caucus as 'the engine by which public opinion is concentrated'.[154]

Conservatives were quick to use anti-caucus rhetoric as a weapon against public meetings that passed liberal resolutions: Randolph

---

[151] Bagehot, *The English Constitution*.

[152] P. Ghosh, 'Gladstone and Peel' in P. Ghosh and L. Goldman, eds., *Politics and Culture in Victorian Britain* (Oxford, 2006), p. 54.

[153] Lawrence, *Speaking for the People*; E. F. Biagini, *British Democracy and Irish Nationalism 1876–1906* (Cambridge, 2007), p. 185; J. Lawrence, 'Popular radicalism and the socialist revival in Britain', *Journal of British Studies*, 31 (1992), 173.

[154] *The Times*, 18 June 1885.

Churchill contrasted the 'plague-stricken and plague-diffusing' caucus and 'the wholesome oxygen of wide-public discussion', urging that 'we shall let the light of public opinion into the dark corners of the Caucus'. Chamberlain countered with sarcastic reference to 'the meetings of the Constitutional Committees, held in the public-houses . . . recognized as the free and full expression of public opinion'.[155] While anti-caucus language was a persistent feature of British political debate, it was at its most topical in the 1880s.[156] The more general charge of fabrication remained a standard trope of debate about public meetings, contributing to attachment to open meetings and recognition among at least some politicians that their presence at meetings could compromise the non-partisan credentials of platform campaigns.[157] Conservative diatribes against noisy minorities were matched by liberal jeremiads about Tories buying audiences. However, whilst the criterion of spontaneity had implications for the currency of different kinds of meetings as bearers of public opinion, the need to demonstrate earnestness ensured the resilience of the platform as a locus for public opinion throughout the period.

Political congregations took a variety of forms, and a range of terms existed for describing them. Contemporaries could distinguish between 'public meetings' and 'demonstrations', in which the latter were larger and more likely to involve a procession. It would, though, be wrong to overplay this. While Richter suggests that the term 'demonstration' with reference to a political assembly was imported from France in the 1860s, it was actually in use in this sense from the 1830s, and could refer to political dinners of an entirely respectable ilk.[158] Large gatherings that enlisted the full panoply of processions, singing and multiple platforms were more likely to be termed 'demonstrations', but application of the term was not confined to left-wing or plebeian assemblies.

---

[155] Churchill speaking in Birmingham, reported in *The Times*, 18 Oct. 1884; Chamberlain in *Parliamentary Debates*, 3rd ser., CCLXXXVI (1884), col. 952.

[156] J. Owen, 'Triangular contests and caucus rhetoric at the 1885 general election', *Parliamentary History*, 27, 2 (2008), 215–35.

[157] J. Davis, 'Radical clubs and London politics' in G. Stedman Jones and D. Feldman, eds., *Metropolis London: Histories and Representations since 1800* (London, 1989), pp. 103–28.

[158] D. C. Richter, *Riotous Victorians* (London, 1981), p. 87; *The Times*, 22 Feb. 1837; 'Conservative demonstration at Manchester', *The Times*, 12 Aug. 1837. For a later example of a political dinner been referred to in this way, see 'Conservative demonstration at Cambridge', *The Times*, 25 Jan. 1871.

The scale and requisite organisation of the mass meeting made it harder to present as an example of public deliberation; metropolitan radicals, with their deep attachments to the conventions of the mass meeting, were particularly exposed to this difficulty. Yet size mattered in assessments of meetings as expressions of 'public opinion', and processing did not necessarily jeopardise the representative status of a gathering. So, while in late 1877 *The Times* sardonically noted that 'several working men's organisations in the metropolis are, as is usual in times of political excitement, preparing for public "demonstrations"', it nonetheless did so under the banner, 'Public opinion on the war'.[159] In 1884 *The Times* reported the monster meeting for reform in Hyde Park as 'a great and imposing spectacle...It was a demonstration, made by the people and for the people, and it exhibited every sign of spontaneity and enthusiasm.'[160]

The franchise debates of the mid 1880s enunciated some enduring contrasts between liberal and conservative visions of platform politics. Conservatives were increasingly inclined to eulogise metropolitan gatherings; Liberals more apt to celebrate the provincial. At Brechin, Gladstone sought to link liberalism, locality and the land, urging that 'it is to the sober and deliberate manifestation of public opinion throughout the land that we trust... What I see is the fruit of the soil upon which I stand.'[161] In addressing representatives of conservative associations, Northcote nicely encapsulated the Conservative appeal to metropolitan superiority, arguing that this

is no mere gathering of some 1000 or 2000 persons representing some particular constituency. It is a representative meeting of those who are charged to come here on behalf of those metropolitan constituencies, which, whatever Mr Gladstone and his friends may say about them, are at the centre of knowledge and power.[162]

Such claims were not confined to the immediate context of the redistribution debates of 1884–5. Conservatives remained, though, more inclined than liberals to appeal to those who did *not* attend public meetings. 'John Bull Jr.' expressed the strong version of this position in 1901.[163] He asked, 'Who are the people?', and concluded, 'not

---

[159] *The Times*, 20 Dec. 1877.   [160] *The Times*, 22 July 1884.
[161] Jephson, *The Platform*, II, 543.   [162] *The Times*, 29 July 1884.
[163] For an 1891 account of the limitations of public meetings which approvingly cited their supposed unimportance in London, see the unionist Earl of Portsmouth's 'Executive government and the unionists', 540; the former

alone those who shout at public meetings or who vote at elections, but also those intelligent, industrious, and peaceable citizens to whom the whole machinery of politics is fast growing an abomination'.[164] The heyday of this kind of Conservatism was, however, yet to come. As the debates of the mid 1880s suggest, the currency of more activist readings of 'public opinion' empowered platform politics in these years.

The popular debate over the franchise in the mid 1880s demonstrated the extent of Conservative accommodation to platform politics. Descriptions of meetings were, of course, frequently partisan, but the terms in which they operated are revealing. In early 1884, Chamberlain accepted that Conservatives had held more meetings, only to claim that they were unable to carry motions against reform and were held in pubs. The ex-liberal W. T. Marriot responded by stating that it was the Constitutionalists who held 'genuine public meetings'.[165] In August 1884 Salisbury addressed a large conservative meeting at Pomona Gardens in Manchester, arguing that 'I believe that the numbers assembled for the present demonstration exceed anything of which we have had experience before, and that as many as 120,000 tickets have been taken for this demonstration'. Salisbury certainly rejected radical open-air agitation as giving 'no indication whatever of the real opinion of the majority of the constituencies, which is the only opinion for which we care, and by which we are bound', but this should not be confused with wholesale dismissal of the platform or a failure to recognise the symbolic value of open meetings. Salisbury was in fact quick to note that he had received 'communications from every part of the country, from the largest and most populous communities, and from open meetings where workmen were represented and voted in large numbers'.[166] The Tory peer Lord George Hamilton similarly claimed that 'wherever they have been allowed to state their case, and have not had their meetings broken up, they have succeeded in satisfying their audiences'. Conservatives were prepared to defend ticketing as

Gladstonian Earl Grey bemoaned the influence of rowdy meetings in 'In peril from Parliament', *Nineteenth Century*, 28 (Dec. 1890), 1012.

[164] John Bull Jr., 'Parliament and the party-system', *Macmillan's Magazine*, 84 (Oct. 1901), 478.

[165] *Parliamentary Debates*, 3rd ser., CCLXXXVI (1884), col. 952; ibid., col. 1358.

[166] Jephson, *The Platform*, II, 536; *Parliamentary Debates*, 3rd ser., CCXC (1884), col. 468; ibid., col. 1372.

a means of concentrating respectable opinion, and appeals were also made to the evidence of press and petition, but the rhetorical struggles of 1884–5 clearly reveal the resonance of open meetings as an indicator of public opinion.[167]

The controversy surrounding the South African war of 1899–1902 directed renewed attention towards the relationship between public meetings, disruption and public opinion. Liberals and radicals were quick to claim that rowdy demonstrations in favour of the war were organised by shadowy leagues and incited by the press, particularly the local press.[168] Conservatives replied forcibly to such suggestions. Discussion of popular jingoism tended to be initiated by its critics, and so to focus on the more violent instances. This presented an obvious question about to what extent such eruptions were genuine expressions of 'public feeling'. In the Commons debate on disturbances directed against opponents of the war, Balfour reiterated his view that

> There is not the slightest evidence that there has been any organisation of these demonstrations, which are absolutely spontaneous in their char-acter . . . I myself strongly deprecate these demonstrations, and I expect no good of them . . . It must be remembered that public feeling is necessarily deeply stirred at the present time . . . In these circumstances, the tension of public opinion must necessarily be of a kind affording grave anxiety to those responsible for the public peace; and I venture to add that those who call these meetings ought to be careful lest they ask more of human nature than all history shows that human nature is capable of giving.[169]

This was, of course, classic Balfour; elegant and subtle, or convoluted and evasive, according to taste. The invocation of the limits of human nature was especially characteristic.[170] As Jon Lawrence has shown, others in the debate were more robust in their defence of the more rowdy side of jingoism.[171]

---

[167] For Hamilton, see *Parliamentary Debates*, 3rd ser., CCXCIII (1884), col. 1203. For a defence of ticketing along these lines, see Chamberlain's speech at Hanley on 7 Oct. 1884, cited in Jephson, *The Platform*, II, 545–6.

[168] See the debates in the Commons on the disturbances directed against opponents of the war, e.g. Sir R. T. Reid, *Parliamentary Debates*, 4th ser., LXXX (1900), cols. 941–2.

[169] *Parliamentary Debates*, 4th ser., LXXX (1900), cols. 856–7.

[170] See the discussion of Balfour's view of human nature and belief formation in Chapter 3.

[171] Lawrence, *Speaking for the People*, p. 186.

The conservative Bartley objected that 'I have very often seen a great row at meetings'. He urged further that 'we are delighted at this exhibition of feeling' and that 'if the other side excite the public to violence the blame is upon them, and not upon us'.[172] The liberal member Lord Fitzmaurice suggested to the contrary that public opinion would approve of depriving police forces who failed adequately to safeguard freedom of speech of some portion of their grant.[173] Campbell-Bannerman countered Balfour's claim that conservative meetings were routinely disrupted in radical areas. He remarked, 'I can only say that I am not aware that that has occurred at any place except during the excitement of a general election, when meetings are, I believe, in this country, not in mine, broken up by both sides.'[174] C. P. Scott argued that the disturbances constituted an attempt 'to substitute mob violence for reason' and compared 'certain honourable Members' with 'a mob in the street'.[175] There were real limits to the extent to which more bellicose tories could recast disruption as the legitimate expression of platform opinion.

'The Boer War' was often described, by both opponents and supporters, as 'Joe's War'. Chamberlain stoutly defended the war, and its supporters. Replying to an attack on the South Africa League in the Commons, he observed that 'when the honourable member talks about the league or association poisoning the wells of public opinion . . . I call to mind what happened in another country a little while ago, and I think of General Mercier and his Dreyfus syndicate'.[176] He also spoke up for 'the man in the street' in reply to Campbell-Bannerman:

It is true that the leader of the Opposition did say in a speech . . . that the man in the street did not know what the cause of the war was. Well, sir, the man in the street really is wiser than the right honourable gentleman thought him to be. With that great instinct of the British people in all times of crisis, the man in the street has put aside technicalities and legal subtleties and has gone to the root of the question.[177]

It was harder, however, to defend more violent expression of pro-war sentiment in the same fashion. The re-emergence of popular jingoism

---

[172] *Parliamentary Debates*, 4th ser., LXXX (1900), cols. 968–9.
[173] ibid., col. 968.   [174] ibid., col. 980.   [175] ibid., col. 981.
[176] In a speech in the Commons on 19 Oct. 1899, reproduced in *Mr Chamberlain's Speeches*, ed. C. W. Boyd (2 vols., London, 1914), II, p. 15.
[177] ibid., p. 20.

did make conservatives better disposed to popular demonstrations, but the established idea of the platform rendered the re-description of rowdy jingoism as legitimate political expression unpersuasive.

In his great work on *The Government of England*, A. L. Lowell provided a decidedly positive account of the workings of the platform. He recommended Jephson's recognisably radical history as the best work on the subject. In a very nineteenth-century fashion, he argued that the platform had 'entered upon a fresh career' marked by 'the participation of all classes; the organised effort to bring about a definite political change by a legitimate creation of public opinion; and the growing use of public speaking by parliamentary leaders as a regular engine of party warfare'.[178] More interestingly, however, he reflected acutely upon the implications of developments in the press for the relative importance of press and platform opinion:

> Except for a few important utterances, the debates in Parliament are not very widely read; editorials in the press are read solely by the members of one political faith; the remarks of private members to their constituents are published only in the local papers; but public speeches by the chief ministers, and to a lesser extent those by the principal leaders of the Opposition, are printed at great length by the newspapers of both parties, and are read everywhere.[179]

These developments constitute an important backdrop to progressive platform politics in the Edwardian era.

The liberal triumph of 1906 raised serious questions about the representativeness of press opinion. Lowell's suggestion that the platform was now a more powerful force than the press, which also implied its superiority as an indicator of opinion, has already been noted. Edward Porritt made the case for the primacy of the platform at greater length. Porritt argued that 'the platform . . . was never more in service than it has been since the turn of the century'. He observed that 'as in the eighteenth century, political propagandists have adopted the methods of religious preachers', and suggested that such methods were particularly pioneered by the Independent Labour Party (ILP), borrowing from the Salvation Army. The rise of the Labour party, despite press hostility, was another powerful factor in reviving the reputation of the platform,

[178] A. L. Lowell, *The Government of England* (2nd edn, 2 vols., New York, 1912), I, 442.
[179] ibid., I, 446.

at least on the broad left. Porritt made clear his evaluation of the relative performance of platform and press, claiming that 'this open-air propaganda gave the election of 1906 a new significance in the political history of England . . . and accounts in large measure for the extent to which political editorial writing receded into the background'.[180] The columnist on *Truth* who took issue with parts of Porritt's account nonetheless affirmed that 'there is no doubt a good deal in all this'.[181]

Liberal politicians were also prepared to raise the standard of the platform. Winston Churchill, speaking at Birmingham in 1909, counselled that ' . . . the Liberal Party must not allow itself to be overawed by the hostile Press which is ranged against it. Boldly and earnestly occupied, the platform will always beat the Press.'[182] Attempts to explain the growth of the labour movement often addressed the issue of labour meetings. In an alarmist series on 'the socialist movement in Britain' in 1909, *The Times* referred to 'the obscure meetings which are constantly being held all over the country, unreported and unnoticed, but by no means unattended or ineffective'.[183] The difficulties, however, in estimating the circulation of the socialist press could lead contemporaries to exaggerate its impact. *The Times* remarked that 'it is difficult to judge whether the spoken or the written word plays the more influential part in spreading the doctrines of socialism'. It went on to suggest that the two approaches 'supplement each other, and each reaches special classes inaccessible to the other'.[184] Overall, however, it was incessant public speaking that best embodied the peculiar psychology of the socialist, for 'the platform or the pulpit is their natural habitat; they take to it as ducklings take to the pond'.[185] *The Times* concluded the series by arguing that 'the larger public . . . must be approached by the methods adopted by Socialists' and commending the activity of such unpartisan organisations as the Primrose League and the NUCCA. Optimism was expressed about the platform response to socialism, since 'the British public likes to hear both sides of a case, and is generally capable of forming a sound judgment on the merits'.[186]

The most controversial use of the platform in the Edwardian period was that by campaigners for the enfranchisement of women. Suffragette militancy tended to be perceived as stifling rather than

---

[180] Porritt, 'The value of political editorials', 512–13.
[181] *Truth*, 26 Jan. 1910.   [182] *Daily News*, 14 Jan. 1910.
[183] *The Times*, 7 Jan. 1909.   [184] *The Times*, 14 Jan. 1909.
[185] *The Times*, 16 Jan. 1909.   [186] *The Times*, 20 Jan. 1909.

expressing opinion.[187] The scepticism directed by liberal politicians, most infamously Asquith, towards the monster meetings sponsored by suffragists should not distract from the common attribution of representative significance to such demonstrations. As Lisa Tickner has shown, contemporary commentators were in general highly impressed at the display of support generated by the National Union of Women's Suffrage Societies (NUWSS) or the WSPU in 1908.[188] It was the suffragist platform, more than the suffragist press, which commanded the attention of contemporaries.

Suffragette militancy has understandably received the bulk of historiographical interest. The difficulties faced by militants in claiming to speak for the public should by now be apparent. Militancy was, however, primarily intended to evoke rather than express public sympathy, and, of course, to jolt the liberal government into legislative action. More constitutional strategies continued to be pursued throughout the suffragist movement, even after 1912.[189] Such tactics were importantly designed to demonstrate the force of public sympathy for reform and so are of particular interest to the student of 'public opinion'. Suffragists made use of the whole repertoire of nineteenth-century pressure-group devices, partly to show the strength of public feeling, partly to establish their command of political forms and hence their ability to use the vote wisely. It was, after all, hard to argue convincingly that Mrs Pankhurst was lacking in civic virtue. One of the methods adopted by suffragists was the petition.

Petition

The petition completes our study of Gladstone's constitutional trinity of press, platform and petition. There is some truth in the observation that the petition was both the last and least of these. Petitioning loomed larger earlier in the century and was more tainted by association with faddism than either the press or the platform. Petitions

---

[187] A view occasionally expressed in the Commons debate over public meetings in 1908. See *Parliamentary Debates*, 4th ser., CXCVIII (1908), cols. 2229–30.

[188] Tickner, *The Spectacle of*, pp. 87–91.

[189] On overlap between militants and constitutionalists generally, see S. S. Holton, *Feminism and Democracy: Women's Suffrage and Reform Politics in Britain, 1900–1918* (Cambridge, 1986).

retained, however, a genuine role in nineteenth-century politics and in debates about 'public opinion'.

Recent years have seen increased interest in the history of petitioning, particularly in the seventeenth and eighteenth centuries, driven in part by the belated Anglophone interest in the Habermasian public sphere.[190] In nineteenth-century studies, petitions have traditionally supplied evidence of pressure-group activity and have figured prominently in histories of education and temperance. Renewed interest in the meanings of the constitution in nineteenth-century politics has brought with it greater recognition of the enduring appeal of petitioning for a variety of groups, including the chartists. Strikingly, though, our understanding of the overall pattern of petitioning remains that established in the 1950s and 1960s in the pioneering work of Colin Leys and Peter Fraser.[191] It was Leys in particular who supplied the key treatment of the incidence and chronology of petitioning by investigating trends in the number of petitions and the number of signatures over time.

The number of petitions submitted to parliament peaked in 1843, after the procedural reforms sometimes seen as designed to curtail the number of petitions. Petitioning was not an exclusively or essentially radical activity; rather, it was primarily religious issues that inspired nineteenth-century Britons to petition. Bumper crops were recorded in 1860, 1872, 1883 and 1893–4. The first of these was mostly generated by opposition to the church rates, the second and third by the temperance question, and the last by opposition to vivisection. In all cases other issues did produce petitions, but it was religiously fraught questions of moral reform which elicited the bulk of petitioning. It was, these dates suggest, in periods of Liberal government that the

---

[190] See particularly D. Zaret, *Origins of Democratic Culture: Printing, Petitions, and the Public Sphere in Early-Modern England* (Princeton, 2000). For petitioning in the history of political thought, see M. Knight, 'Petitioning and the political theorists: John Locke, Algernon Sidney and London's "Monster" petition of 1680', *Past and Present*, 138 (1993), 94–111.

[191] On pressure groups and petitioning, see, for instance, B. Harrison, *Drink and the Victorians: The Temperance Question in England, 1815–1872* (London, 1971). On nineteenth-century petitioning, see C. Leys, 'Petitioning in the nineteenth and twentieth centuries', *Political Studies*, 3 (1955), 45–64; P. Fraser, 'The growth of ministerial control in the nineteenth-century House of Commons', *English Historical Review* (July 1960), 444–63; P. Fraser, 'Public petitioning and parliament before 1832', *History*, 46 (1961), 195–211.

prospect of such reform loomed largest. Aside from the efflorescence of 1893–4, the trend in the number of petitions was downwards after the middle of the 1880s.

The number of signatures on petitions per session fluctuates more sharply, with a greater distance between the peaks and the mode. Again, though, the trend is broadly downwards, starting in this case from the early 1870s. There are, however, notable booms in the number of signatories as late as 1908 and 1912. The diminishing number of signatures can be related to the average number of signatures per petition. This remained relatively constant from 1860, dipping in the 1890s and early 1900s, but without any huge deviation from the trend. There are, however, sharp increases in the number of signatures per petition in both 1908 and 1912.[192]

The more general decline in the total number of signatures on petitions per session has been taken to correspond to a reduction in religious grievances after 1870. This view, Taylor rightly notes, neglects the salience of religious issues in Edwardian politics, apparent in the controversy over the 1902 Education Act and the revival of the temperance campaign in 1905.[193] Petitioning functioned differently after 1885. It might be suggested that groups well integrated in the party system, such as the nonconformists, especially after 1906, found less use for petitioning than had once been the case. Recourse to petitioning in the twentieth century tended to come from groups who felt distanced from party politics, most famously campaigners against nuclear weapons in 1950–1. The same might, of course, be said of the suffragists responsible for the heavy petitioning of 1908 and 1912, who were rather more fundamentally disenfranchised.

How seriously were petitions taken as expressions of 'public opinion'? Petitioning certainly occupied a central place in Victorian accounts of the constitution. Sheldon Amos was typical in arguing that petitions provided a conduit for communication with 'the public outside the House'.[194] Those, like Joseph Redlich, who emphasised the streamlining of Commons procedure, were rather less well disposed towards petitioning.[195] Miles Taylor argues that petitioning is

---

[192] Leys, 'Petitioning in the nineteenth and twentieth centuries', 54.
[193] Miles Taylor, 'Public petitioning in the nineteenth century: a reinterpretation' (unpublished paper), 3.
[194] S. Amos, *Fifty Years of the Constitution* (London, 1880), pp. 74–5.
[195] J. Reclich, *The Procedure of the House of Commons: A Study of its History and Present Form* (3 vols., 1908), I, 17, *passim*.

best seen as a form of judicial review, designed to offer a degree of
virtual representation and to contribute to the legislative process. He
sees the reforms of the 1830s as intended not simply to curtail petitioning, but to integrate petitioning better into the making of statute
by discouraging petitions which were not relevant to current business.
Taylor contrasts this account of the function of petitioning with the
Victorian emphasis upon the petition as a token of 'public opinion'.[196]
This book is concerned with precisely such Victorian attitudes, but it is
also worth noting that the history of petitioning does reflect its position
as one locus of 'public opinion'. This is particularly apparent in the
Edwardian recourse to petitioning by supporters of female suffrage.

The procedural developments of the 1830s gave rise to the select
committee on public petitions whose sessional reports provide the key
data upon which historians have drawn. These reports, and the accom-
panying appendices reprinting a portion of the session's petitions in
full, shed important light on prevailing conceptions of the role of petitioning. The reports detailed by topic the number of petitions and the
combined number of signatures submitted. The very act of summing
the number of signatures across a number of petitions from a range of
localities reflected a conception of national debate in which the scale of
support mattered. The willingness of the committee to note similarities
of language in petitions suggests both an awareness of the mechanisms
whereby petitioning was co-ordinated nationally, and a discounting of
such activity in relation to apparently more spontaneous local expressions of opinion. In providing a series of updates through the session of
the level of petitioning, the committee displayed a dynamic conception
of the relationship between parliamentary debate and opinion out of
doors. The reports make clear the linkages between different forms of
political communication: petitions frequently emanated from public
meetings throughout the period. Whilst the organisation of the reports
testifies to the enduring importance of mobilising large numbers, they
reveal a more complex relationship than a simple uniform equation
between signatures and support. In a given session, the modal number
of signatures per petition was likely to be one, reflecting the frequency
with which petitions expressed a corporate view.[197] The wording of

---

[196] Taylor, 'Public petitioning in the nineteenth century: a reinterpretation', 1, 5,
9–10.
[197] The modal number of signatures per petition is 1 for the 1870, 1878–9 and
1883 sessions. See Parliamentary Papers, *Reports of the Select Committee on
Public Petitions* (1870); ibid. (1878–9); ibid. (1883).

petitions often stressed the size of the body represented by a small number of signatories; petitions provide telling evidence of the enduring importance of collective views in the late Victorian understanding of the composition of 'public opinion'.[198]

Both the form and the language of petitioning are revealing. The form of petitions was governed by strict rules which, amongst other stipulations, required original signatures and addresses. These restrictions were defended by some as necessary safeguards against fraud, and attacked by others for discriminating against the poor. The combination of inclusiveness (women could sign petitions) and exclusiveness (the requirement to be able to sign your own name and to provide an address) accorded with the definitions of the political public previously discussed. While the Chartist petition of 1848 is much the best-known example, allegations of fraud were not uncommon in later nineteenth-century petitioning.[199] These did not, though, negate the importance of amassing signatures, as Edwardian debates over women's suffrage demonstrate. Petitions had to adopt prescribed language, which could also act as a barrier to entry. However, the rich variety of petitioners reflects the widespread grasp of parliamentary forms apparent in the model Houses of Commons spread throughout Britain. While most petitions focused primarily upon outlining their particular case, some sought to relate their concerns to broader currents of opinion. A petition from Wallingford presented by Dilke in 1870 noted 'with great satisfaction the growth of public opinion' in favour of the ballot. In 1883, the Edinburgh and Leith Grocers petitioned against the Intoxicating Liquors (Off Licences) Bill on a number of grounds, including 'that it is opposed to public opinion'.[200]

While petitions continued to be seen as a vehicle through which public opinion might emerge, their significance was not uncontested. The distinction often made by the Select Committee on Public Petitions, between those petitions that emerged from public meetings and

---

[198] Petition signed by George Sellar on behalf of the Convention of the Royal and Parliamentary Burghs of Scotland, *Reports of the Select Committee on Public Petitions* (1883), p. 15.

[199] For a valuable reconsideration of 1848 and Chartist petitioning more generally, see P. Pickering, 'And your petitioners &c': Chartist petitioning in popular politics 1838–48', *English Historical Review*, 116, 466 (April 2001), 368–88.

[200] *Reports of the Select Committee on Public Petitions* (1870), p. 73; ibid. (1883), p. 22.

those that did not, suggests some of the relevant issues. Signing a petition in a moment while engaged in other activities could be seen as weaker evidence of active engagement than attending a public meeting. Signature collection suited the capacities of the pressure group, particularly those who could make use of local meeting places, like churches or pubs, as politicians were well aware. Spontaneous petitioning in response to proposed legislation, such as the Metropolitan Gas Bill in 1867, was more persuasive than campaigns like those of the Sabbatarians. Petitions without reference to current parliamentary business were open to the charge that they did not reflect a genuine public debate, especially if they were hardy perennials. This was one reason for the muted reception given to petitioning by Sabbatarians and temperance advocates.[201]

The importance accorded petitioning in the Victorian political system has been related to the principle of virtual representation. Virtual representation was, of course, very much a doctrine about 'public opinion'. As we have seen, ideas of virtual representation were very much to the fore in the debate over the ballot. It was often claimed that open voting provided a means by which 'public opinion' could hold voters to account, and thus a form of virtual representation for the disenfranchised of both sexes.[202] Justifications of petitioning operated very similarly. Petitions retained some credibility as tokens of 'public opinion' and so enabled the wider public to affect the parliamentary process. The petition had often been a means by which the politically dispossessed could express their grievances. It is unsurprising that suffragists had recourse to petitioning from the 1870s. The explosion of petitioning in 1908 and 1912 owed much to the suffrage issue and offers an opportunity to gauge the status of the petition on the eve of the First World War.

In the 1908 woman suffrage debate, Cremer noted that in the past seventeen years 198 403 people had signed suffrage petitions, yet there were 10.5 million women in the United Kingdom.[203] The argument that some women did not want the franchise was infuriating to suffragists, who observed that those women would not be compelled to vote if the suffrage was granted, whereas women who wanted the

---

[201] Taylor, 'Public petitioning in the nineteenth century: a reinterpretation', 8.
[202] See Chapter 1.
[203] *Parliamentary Debates*, 4th ser., CLXXXV (1908), col. 271.

vote currently had no such choice. It is striking, however, that as late as 1913 *Votes for Women* continued to cite petitions as an index of support for enfranchisement. It was particularly the petitions of local councils to which appeal was made, though 'processions and demonstrations, larger in size than those in favour of other reforms', took pride of place.[204] There was an obvious division between more and less militant suffragists over the usefulness of petitions. In 1909, *The Vote* commented, with respect to *The Common Cause*, that 'we do not share their touching faith in the efficacy of petitions'.[205] The argument was, however, about the political impact of petitioning, rather than its capacity to express opinion.

Suffragists were perhaps less impressed with petitions than their opponents, because their petitions were smaller, and because petitions required less earnestness and possessed less force than public meetings. Both sides, however, continued to see petitions as significant, though the framing of the debate in terms of what the *majority* of women wanted limited the value of the existing means of making opinions known. More radical liberals and socialists sympathetic to female suffrage may have laid greater stress on the importance of more earnest displays of conviction, but the suffrage debate reveals that petitions remained a locus for public opinion.

Conclusion

Debates over the location of 'public opinion' were complex and multidimensional. Some trends, such as the lessening significance of petitions, are reasonably clear. Other issues, such as the comparative value attributed to press and platform as indicators of opinion, have a more complicated and contested chronology. It is apparent, however, that the constitutional trinity of press, platform and petition endured throughout these years as privileged sites for the expression of opinion. Changes in the character of each of these had implications for their plausibility as mirrors of opinion. The impact of such changes was largely governed by the structure of the prevailing conceptions of 'public opinion'. Criteria for determining whether public declarations of belief amounted to 'public opinion', while contested, were overlapping and widely shared across the political spectrum. Differences

[204] *Votes for Women*, 31 Oct. 1913.   [205] *The Vote*, 1 Sep. 1909.

often arose about the relative importance of agreed criteria. The primary image of 'public opinion' which emerges from these debates is one deeply rooted in an essentially liberal political culture that prized the public declaration of serious, and strongly held, beliefs. Efforts to identify and characterise 'public opinion' allied an attachment to earnestness to related questions about the weight and persistence of opinion. They were also, of course, deeply concerned with the question of the reasonableness of beliefs, and to these debates we turn in the next chapter.

3 | *The mind of the nation? Reason and the public*

The birth of modernism is now traditionally associated with the discovery of the unconscious and the rediscovery of the irrational.[1] The decline of enlightenment optimism into modernist dismay took its toll on conceptions of 'public opinion', consigning faith in the rationality of the public to the dustbin of history along with the idea of progress and the reverential biography. The line of descent is conventionally drawn by joining the dots between the enlightenment, John Stuart Mill and Graham Wallas.[2]

Recent years have seen increased interest in late nineteenth-century debates about 'public opinion', particularly amongst media historians, but these have tended to adopt established narratives about the rise of irrationalist conceptions of 'public opinion' derived from intellectual histories of canonical thinkers, such as that sketched in the later parts of Habermas's study of the structural transformation of the public sphere. Some of these figures, including Mill and Wallas, appear below, but the aim is not simply to revisit their writings, but rather to reconstruct wider debates about the character of public opinion. While more systematic treatises are not ignored, efforts are made to evaluate, rather than assume, their impact on the broader conversation about politics. In order that claims about trends may be tested, careful attention is paid to a series of political arguments, spread through

---

[1] On ideas about the 'unconscious', see Henri Ellenberger, *The Discovery of the Unconscious: The History and Evolution of Dynamic Psychiatry* (London, 1970); D. Rapp, 'The early discovery of Freud by the British general educated public, 1912–1919', *Social History of Medicine*, 3 (1990), 217–43.

[2] For example, Burrow, *Whigs and Liberals* and J. A. W. Gunn, 'Public spirit to public opinion' in *Beyond Liberty and Property: The Process of Self-Recognition in Eighteenth-Century Political Thought* (Kingston, Ont., 1983), pp. 260–315, and his essay on 'Public opinion' in Ball, Farr & Hanson, eds., *Political Innovation*, pp. 247–65.

the period as a whole, which produced discussion about the reason-ableness of British public opinion. Disputes about public reason could reveal differences over its function. Was public opinion a force that should lead politicians, or was it to be shaped by them? Was public opinion best equipped to address a single defining issue, rather than a multiplicity of measures? How far was public opinion able, or required, to address the content of policy, or was its role more to assess men than measures? In examining contemporaries' answers to these questions, it is important not to confuse recognition of the fal-libility of public opinion with the belief that it was inherently or pre-dominantly irrational. Tributes to the reasonableness of public opin-ion, frequently bolstered by complacent assumptions about national character, often hymned not a disembodied abstract rationality but rather an engaged, even shrewd, assessment of the balance of proba-bilities that could be favourably contrasted with more febrile polities abroad.[3]

Developments in the structure of politics in this period fostered a renewal of debates about the rationality of the public. The second reform act was generally understood to have enfranchised the chil-dren of industrial modernity, the urban artisanal working classes. The unfettered popular press produced by the repeal of the stamp duties amplified the verdicts of public opinion to an unprecedented volume. The subsequent emergence of 'party government' was condemned or commended as an efficient translation of public opinion into govern-ment policy which bypassed the traditional mediation of parliamentary debate. Contemporaries were uniformly impressed by the increased impact of public opinion upon the political process. They were, how-ever, less united in their assessment of its consequences.

Liberals were often especially concerned to evaluate the changing character of political culture. Liberal politics had emerged in the early nineteenth century, pledged to address and to educate the concerns of the people through an understanding of the constitution in which the fourth estate of 'public opinion' occupied a prominent place.[4] This vision of politics was exhibited in Erskine May's *Constitutional History*, where political progress was identified with the growth of

[3] Mandler, *English National Character*.
[4] On this consult Parry, *The Rise and Fall of Liberal Government*.

towns and the ensuing production of political intelligence.[5] 'Public opinion' was closely associated in this account with the mercantile middle classes, whose enfranchisement in 1832 had led to that oft-celebrated triumph of reason, the repeal of the Corn Laws in 1846.[6] Many mid-century liberals took political economy as a model of political reasoning, and located political intelligence in the mind of the enterprising burgher.[7] They valued a 'public opinion' that was attached to a science of politics whose cardinal tenet was the validity of free trade.[8]

Increasingly intimate relations between high and low politics in the last third of the century had serious implications for established liberalism. The rise of legislative liberalism and the growing necessity of programmatic appeals in the last years of the century registered the increasing precision and insistence of public expectations and challenged inherited liberal accounts of the relationship between public opinion and political conduct. Changes in the social composition of the electorate and the operation of the constitution required liberals to reconsider the influence and character of an increasingly visible 'public opinion'.

'Public opinion' was a concept whose centrality to early nineteenth-century liberal politics can be contrasted with its relative absence from traditional conservative visions of the polity. The history of the idea of 'public opinion' has been written almost entirely through the study of liberal writers.[9] This approach neglects the invocations of 'public opinion' evident in late nineteenth-century conservative politics that were explored in Chapter 2. As was noted there, conservatives on occasion mobilised a domesticated conception of 'public opinion' as the good sense of the people that anticipated subsequent advocacy of the 'silent majority'. This line of argument has been seen as Burkean, though

[5] May, *Constitutional History*, 138–9, 184.
[6] ibid., 340–1, and A. Todd, *On Parliamentary Government* (2nd edn, London, 1887), p. 413. On 1832 and its impact on the idea of 'the middle class', see Wahrman, *Imagining the Middle Class*.
[7] H. J. Hanham, ed., *The Nineteenth-Century Constitution 1815–1914: Documents and Commentary* (London, 1969), p. 3.
[8] Earl Grey, *Parliamentary Government Considered with Reference to a Reform of Parliament* (London, 1858), pp. 163–4.
[9] This is in part a product of the fact that the literature which touches upon the history of 'public opinion' is sometimes in fact about liberalism, e.g. Burrow, *Whigs and Liberals*. This is not, however, always true, e.g. Gunn, 'Public opinion'.

it is important to recognise the Burke of *Thoughts on the Present Discontents*, where he lambasts the House of Commons for voting thanks 'when the public opinion calls on them for impeachment', as well as the now more familiar Burke of *Reflections on the Revolution in France*. It is also important to recall that citations of Burke were for much of the nineteenth century more common amongst liberals than Conservatives, and that Burke could be cast in many guises: Fitzjames Stephen found him to be from 'first to last a utilitarian of the strongest kind'.[10] Twentieth-century Tory mythologies are a poor guide both to Burke, and to Burke's afterlives in the nineteenth century. While at times Salisbury clothed approval of the good sense of the people in the language of 'public opinion', as we saw in Chapter 2 he also appealed to much more determinate and deliberative understandings of public opinion.[11] Conversely, liberals could combine an appreciation of the articulate public with a distrust of abstraction, an approach well epitomised by Walter Bagehot.[12] In order to reconstruct the career of 'public opinion' in later nineteenth-century Britain, we need to reappraise mid-century views of the public and its reasonableness. These are helpfully clarified by revisiting the debate about the secret ballot.

As demands for the ballot re-emerged in the 1850s, they were forcefully contested by defenders of open voting, amongst them John Stuart Mill, who had jettisoned his earlier support for the ballot sometime around 1850.[13] As was noted in Chapter 1, advocates of open voting commonly cited openness to public opinion as one of its more conspicuous virtues. Public opinion merited virtual representation through open voting, and fostered honesty amongst the electors.[14] In *Thoughts on Parliamentary Reform* (1859) – parts of which were reproduced in the relevant chapter of *Considerations on Representative Government* – Mill distinguished between the criteria that needed to be met to deserve the franchise, and the less exacting standard that sufficed

---

[10] J. F. Stephen, *Horae Sabbaticae* (2nd ser., London, 1892), p. 115.
[11] Jephson, *The Platform*, II, 542.
[12] S. Collini, D. Winch & J. Burrow, *That Noble Science of Politics: A Study in Nineteenth-Century Intellectual History* (Cambridge, 1983), pp. 178–80.
[13] On Mill and the ballot, see B. L. Kinzer, 'J. S. Mill and the secret ballot', *Historical Reflections/Réflexions historiques*, 5 (1978), 19–39, revised as 'Mill and the secret ballot' in his *J. S. Mill Revisited: Biographical and Political Explorations* (Basingstoke, 2007), pp. 146–63; and G. McNiece, 'Shelley, John Stuart Mill, and the secret ballot', *Mill Newsletter*, 8 (1973), 2–7.
[14] Cox, *The British Commonwealth*, pp. 216–17.

to exercise an influence upon the voters. He argued that 'this indirect influence of those who have not the suffrage over those who have' developed progressively, so allowing the franchise to be peacefully and incrementally extended. Mill insisted, however, that the value of scrutiny was not dependent upon the wisdom of the public, or upon submission to its wishes, for 'to be under the eyes of others – to have to defend oneself to others – is never more important than to those who act in opposition to the opinion of others'. The clash of views benefited the dissenter, as 'nothing has so steadying an influence, as working against pressure'.[15] Mill's notably strenuous ideal of political participation was highly apparent in his mature writings on the ballot.[16]

Proponents of the ballot emphasised the role of coercion rather than public opinion in shaping voter behaviour, much as Mill once had. It was, though, difficult for the friends of the ballot to refute aspects of the case for open voting, for these appealed to widely resonant political values. The claim, for instance, made with great force by Mill, that the genuine possession of an opinion required the willingness to defend it in public, had broad resonance.[17] The argument that the abolition of open voting would encourage lying was felt to be a powerful one, and led to the charges that the ballot was un-English and unmanly.[18] Debates about the method of voting demonstrate the popularity of an expressive conception of public opinion in which the formation of opinion was closely associated with the possession of character.[19]

Even amongst defenders of open voting, Mill's was an especially exacting conception of the duties of the elector. He was far from unusual in emphasising the dangers of selfishly elevating personal preferences over public interests, and in stressing publicity as a remedy. His argument, though, that the value of exposure to public opinion

[15] J. S. Mill, *Thoughts on Parliamentary Reform* (London, 1859), 42–3.
[16] On this aspect of Mill, see Collini, *Public Moralists*, pp. 121–70; B. L. Kinzer, A. P. Robson and J. M. Robson, *A Moralist In and Out of Parliament: John Stuart Mill at Westminster, 1865–1868* (Toronto, 1992), pp. 218–96. Also valuable is E. F. Biagini, 'Liberalism and direct democracy: John Stuart Mill and the model of ancient Athens' in Biagini, ed., *Citizenship and Community*, pp. 21–45.
[17] Mill to James Beal, 17 April 1865, *Collected Works*, XVI, 1033–4.
[18] B. L. Kinzer, *The Ballot Question in Nineteenth-Century English Politics* (New York, 1982).
[19] S. Collini, 'The idea of character'. On the importance of expression, see F. Harrison, *Order and Progress* (London, 1875), pp. 96–9.

did not depend upon its being right or upon conformity to it was more distinctive. Like his claim that those unwilling to face the rigours of open voting lacked conviction and thus undermined their right to vote at all, it reflected his stern insistence upon the necessity of political virtue for the preservation of freedom and the proper cultivation of the self. This intense attachment to an agonistic model of politics helps us to understand something of the response to *On Liberty*. Reviewers did not recognise Mill's vision of an England rendered uniform by the weight of public opinion upon the atomised individual. Its fearfulness was seen as overly fastidious or even mildly hysterical. Erskine May contrasted British freedom with American servitude to majority opinion and took Mill's eulogy to liberty as evidence of its security in Britain rather than as an attack on its erosion.[20] Even Mill's disciples, such as Morley, argued that the eloquence of *On Liberty* had made its message into a social fact.[21] It was further claimed that Mill failed to appreciate the particular characteristics of British society. Tocqueville had emphasised the role of associational life in filling the void left by the demise of the corporate structures of the ancien regime and strengthening individuals in their views against the dictates of public opinion.[22] Britain was seen as the home of voluntary association and so inoculated against Tocquevillian oppression. Mill's failure to take proper account of associations could be taken as evidence of a carping attitude towards Britain and its institutions.

The reception of *On Liberty* indicates the prevalence of positive conceptions of public opinion in mid-Victorian Britain.[23] Mill's reviewers refused to accept that public opinion was as uniform or as dull as *On Liberty* suggested. Historians who see Mill as a transitional figure tend to link the trepidation expressed in his most famous work with the views of Walter Bagehot.[24] Bagehot's characteristic celebration of 'animated moderation' combined an appreciation of the value of shared beliefs for ensuring stability with recognition of the crucial role

---

[20] May, *Constitutional History*, II, 382–3.
[21] J. Morley, 'The death of Mr Mill', *Fortnightly*, 13 new ser. (June 1873), 669–76.
[22] L. Siedentop, *Tocqueville* (Oxford, 1994), pp. 82–3.
[23] On mid-Victorian optimism, see Parry, *The Politics of Patriotism*, pp. 43, 59, 85, 98, 237.
[24] Burrow, *Whigs and Liberals*.

of discussion in fostering progress.[25] There are some difficulties in reconstructing his vision of 'public opinion', not least an occasional unsteadiness about the composition of the deferring mass that is mesmerised by the theatre of the dignified parts of the constitution.[26] His general position is, however, clear. As we have seen, Bagehot's conception of the public privileged the middle class, and his portrait of 'public opinion', however sardonic, was one in which the political virtues of English middle-class opinion vastly exceeded its faults, as comparisons with abroad, notably France, powerfully demonstrated. The underlying assumptions about collective psychology with which Bagehot operated were made explicit in *Physics and Politics*. While Bagehot confined progress to a 'few nations, and those of European origin', his account of the impact of government by discussion, fortified by a teleological conception of evolution, was firmly progressive, inculcating 'animated moderation' but also, helpfully, reducing the birth rate.

Physics and Politics drew extensively upon the burgeoning literature applying evolutionary ideas, often comparatively, to explain continuity and change in different societies and polities. Bagehot's own analysis was very much framed in terms of 'national character', and reflected a representatively high assessment of the English aptitude for political society. Ideas about public opinion could be closely bound up with convictions about national character, but they were also strongly linked to 'civilisational' discourses rooted in enlightenment thinking. The languages of civilisation and national character were both chiefly deployed as collective categories. Discussion of the reasonableness of public opinion was deeply concerned with the social processes through which shared views coalesced, but was also importantly informed by ideas about individual reason. We need to examine differing conceptions of individual psychology before returning to ideas about the relationship between individual and collective opinions.

The established creed of associationism remained influential in mid-nineteenth-century understandings of the workings of the mind.[27]

---

[25] W. Bagehot, *Physics and Politics; or Thoughts on the Application of 'Natural Selection' and 'Inheritance' to Political Society* (London, 1872), p. 200; Collini, Winch & Burrow, *That Noble Science*, pp. 286–8.

[26] See his introduction to W. Bagehot, *The English Constitution* (2nd edn, London, 1872).

[27] On the enduring significance of associationism, note remarks in Collini, 'The idea of character', pp. 98–9.

Rooted in Lockean epistemology, associationism regarded the mind as a *tabula rasa* upon which experience wrote. It could underpin a stark form of environmentalism in which the formation of good habits was essential. The impact of evolutionary ideas in the third quarter of the century was to insert an emphasis upon instincts which could produce a more sceptical view of the human capacity for rational thought. As Bagehot, however, exemplifies, evolutionary doctrines in this period were at least as coloured by Lamarck as by Darwin.[28] Lamarck's doctrine of the inheritance of acquired characteristics suggested a more positive view of human rationality and its likely progress. More generally, contemporaries frequently treated evolutionary ideas as part of a larger historical turn in thinking about society and politics, which was commonly taken to distinguish the ideas of the nineteenth from those of the eighteenth century. This often imparted a progressive spin to conceptions of both individual and collective reason. Similar tendencies were very much apparent within subsequent idealist doctrines, despite the obvious philosophical differences. Idealists emphasised their more communitarian view of personhood, and sharply rejected 'materialism'; but their denial of dualism often issued in a spiritualised, teleological account of evolution in which, as Henry Jones put it, 'the struggle between man and his surroundings is unequal, and must end in the victory of spirit'.[29]

As Stefan Collini canonically noted, much Victorian discussion of individual psychology was conducted through the prism of 'character', especially in the second half of the century.[30] The language of character was strongly shaped by the tension between associationist psychology and older traditions of moral psychology, informed by religious concerns, which privileged the exercise of free will. In his *Logic*, Mill presented character as the means by which free will could be preserved in his apparently necessitarian scheme, arguing that the independent causal power of character supplied the basis of true freedom, concluding that 'none but a person of confirmed virtue is completely free'.[31]

---

[28] Bagehot, *Physics and Politics*.

[29] H. Jones, 'The social organism' in D. Boucher, ed., *The British Idealists* (Cambridge, 1997), p. 13.

[30] H. S. Jones emphasises that the language of character already had wide currency in the 1850s in his *Victorian Political Thought*, p. 32.

[31] J. S. Mill, *A System of Logic, Ratiocinative and Inductive: Being a Connected View of the Principles of Evidence, and the Methods of Scientific Investigation* (1843), p. 841.

Invocation of 'character' should not be seen as a blithe dismissal of the impact of the environment; indeed, it could express anxiety about the power of association to produce damaging habits. Champions of 'character' frequently emphasised the importance of education in developing appropriate predispositions. As we saw in a previous chapter, members of the 'residuum' were commonly represented in political debate as characterless, and thus unable to contribute towards the proper formation of 'public opinion'. The relationship between social stratum and character was, though, highly contested. Critics of aristocracy, for instance, were quick to insist that a lack of character was scarcely the preserve of the poor. However socially distributed, the language of character supplied a check on interpretations that emphasised the onerous burdens of heredity and instinct, much as it had earlier been used to save notions of free will from the spectre of determinism.

The language of character was evidently shaped in part by religious concerns. Religion supplied its own rich vocabulary for the analysis of moral psychology, chief amongst which was the category of conscience. The evangelical revival hymned the authority of conscience, and much nineteenth-century moral philosophy responded to Butler's analysis of its operation. Mill, while thoroughly hostile to intuitionism, argued that the cultivation of conscience was entirely compatible with utilitarian ethics.[32] In contrast, Maurice argued that utilitarianism, unlike conscience, could not capture our sense of what we ought to do. Maurice saw conscience as prior to, and more reliable than, opinion. It would, however, be misleading to present 'conscience' and 'opinion' as polar opposites: widespread invocation of the former fostered a positive conception of the latter. The more naturalised approaches to religious thinking popularised by Butler proved lastingly influential, and his probabilism rendered conscience and opinion more closely intertwined. 'Conscience' was primarily a *moral* category, but, as much recent work has insisted, few in the nineteenth century saw a sharp divide between morals and politics: Gladstone's appeal to the superior judgement of the masses rested on a moralised view of politics which, while particularly fervent in his instance, resonated across the political spectrum.

The idea of conscience was a persistent feature of nineteenth-century conceptions of moral psychology that was not reliant upon the

---

[32] J. S. Mill, *Utilitarianism* (London, 1863), p. 42.

particular theological underpinnings supplied by the age of atonement. In his ruminations on 'Bishop Butler and the *Zeit-Geist*', Matthew Arnold bemoaned, not unconventionally, the Bishop's failure to found his psychology upon a 'natural history' of the mind. While Arnold's appraisal reflected the impact of evolutionary and incarnationalist perspectives, it preserved an important place for conscience, now rooted in man's instinct to live and in experience's testament to the reality of solidarity. Indeed, for all his insistence on Butler's eighteenth-century limitations, Arnold suggested his account of conscience 'corresponds in a general way with the facts of which we are all conscious'.[33]

The advent of incarnationalism has been powerfully depicted as marking the demise of dualism in the face of a new conception of time and the reintegration of humanity into the natural world.[34] The death of dualism was repeatedly announced in the late nineteenth century, but its import was variously understood. Adherence to evolution did not necessarily entail adopting the same mode of explanation for natural and moral phenomena. Incarnationalism, immanentism and idealism denied dualism by spiritualising nature rather than naturalising spirit. Evolutionary language often burnished teleological depictions of man's higher nature. The 'unthinking Kantianism of Victorian moral commonplaces' to which Stefan Collini has drawn our attention needs to be set alongside the late nineteenth-century emergence of a thinking Kantianism.[35]

While the arrival of incarnationalism has been situated in the third quarter of the century, it was in the late 1880s and early 1890s that its most canonical texts appeared.[36] The replacement of the atonement by the incarnation at the heart of Christian belief encouraged more positive estimates of human nature and greater faith in social activism as the means to build the kingdom of God on Earth. The language of character was, if anything, strengthened by these developments. The Reverend J. E. Hand's incarnationalist collection of essays, *Good Citizenship*, insisted that 'the driving-wheel of all human machinery is CHARACTER'.[37] This stress on character was accompanied by the conviction that 'public opinion' was the instrument through which

[33] M. Arnold, 'Bishop Butler and the *Zeit-Geist*' in *Last Essays on Church and Religion* (London, 1903), pp. 45–107.
[34] Hilton, *Age of Atonement*, pp. 187–8.
[35] ibid., p. 98.   [36] ibid., p. 6 and *passim*.
[37] Rev. J. E. Hand, ed., *Good Citizenship* (London, 1899), p. xxiii.

society could be reformed. Hand declared that in order to advance reform 'what is first needed is an intelligent citizenship to appeal to, a public opinion based on sound knowledge, on careful study, and on high moral principle'.[38] Changes in religious culture thus supported a continued emphasis upon public opinion and offered succour for those who wished to believe in its reasonableness.

Convictions about moral psychology crucially underpinned views of individual rationality in nineteenth-century Britain. Debates about the reasonableness of 'public opinion', however, cannot be reduced to ideas about individuals. 'Public opinion' was a composite force, emerging from a process of deliberation and discussion, to which collective, as well as individual, views contributed. The political public was, as we have seen, sharply distinguished from the mob, though this distinction would come under considerable pressure later on in the century, as this chapter details. While the crowd could be seen as volatile, or as sullenly inarticulate, the political public was constituted through speaking and writing.[39]

Much recent work in intellectual history has undermined the traditional emphasis on the individualism, even atomism, of nineteenth-century liberalism, restoring a sense of the importance of sociability and community to liberals.[40] As we have seen, political associations and collective action were widely applauded by late nineteenth-century liberals. Even those working with more individualist premises were often confident of the rationality of many forms of collaboration, while many liberals anchored positive images of collective political actors in more communitarian tenets.[41] Both liberal Anglicanism and Conservatism fostered an appreciation of the virtues of institutions, and of corporate actors. As we have seen, late nineteenth-century conceptions of 'public opinion' were apt to emphasise the importance of weighing rather than counting opinions, and to privilege earnestly held and persistent views.[42] These normative elements of the idea of '*public* opinion' had important implications for debates about rationality,

---

[38] ibid., pp. xxiv–xxv.
[39] Gareth Stedman Jones, 'The redemptive power of violence? Carlyle, Marx and Dickens', *History Workshop Journal*, 65, 1 (2008), 1–22.
[40] The relevant literature is discussed in Thompson, 'Modern liberty redefined'.
[41] On the former, see R. Tuck, *Free Riding* (Cambridge, Mass., 2008); on the latter, Biagini, ed., *Citizenship and Community*.
[42] Lowell, *Public Opinion and Popular Government*, pp. 13–14.

building in an emphasis upon the reasonableness that was required for a body of views to constitute genuine public opinion. They embodied a widely shared ideal of the deliberative processes through which true public opinion emerged.

The nature of 'public opinion' was extensively discussed in this period. Contrasting characterisations were offered, and commentary was informed by complex developments in British political culture. Conservatives were happier upholding the value of fixed beliefs and the wisdom of institutions than their liberal counterparts. A focus on particular moments of contestation reveals the rich texture of late nineteenth- and early twentieth-century views of public opinion, which is not well captured by simple narratives about the rise and fall of its reputation. The rest of this chapter addresses a series of contexts in which the relationship between reason and the public came to the fore, ranging from the caucus debates of the 1880s to the South African war. It starts with debates about the franchise.

Franchise debates and public reason

The essential background to the debate about the public was the growth of the electorate. The franchise debates of the 1860s saw considerable reflection upon the nature of public opinion. The classic case for extending the franchise was the collective work, *Essays on Reform*, which featured many of the arguments that became standard justifications for granting the vote to urban working-class men. This volume has been discussed with regard to attitudes towards democracy, and its advanced liberal contributors certainly addressed the performance of democratic polities at length, responding in part to Robert Lowe's attacks on reform that sought to frame the debate in those terms. However, the essayists were more generally concerned to assess the arguments for a more open and inclusive political system, and in doing so they had much to say about the character of 'public opinion', a subject many of them, not least James Bryce and Albert Venn Dicey, would continue to discuss in the years to come. As well as providing insights into the advanced attitudes of the 1860s, *Essays on Reform* had an important legacy for debates about public opinion in the next two decades.

While many of the contributors to *Essays on Reform* profoundly admired Mill, their assessment of 'public opinion' was notably more optimistic. Lord Houghton's belief that 'the Custom of the country [was] amenable to every modification that public opinion and the sense of right may introduce' was echoed by other essayists.[43] Leslie Stephen confidently disposed of worries about corruption by arguing that 'if there is an effective control by public opinion, the work of the country is somehow done'.[44] The essayists had inherited the positive view of the city apparent in earlier writers like Mackinnon and Vaughan.[45] They were particularly outraged at the electoral weight still conferred upon small boroughs. Stephen suggested that these boroughs had 'no convictions and no public opinion of their own' and that 'when the public is thoroughly excited by some great question of war or internal policy, the members of small boroughs are comparatively sheltered'.[46] He was joined in this view by Kinnear and Ruston.[47]

The essayists were not in complete agreement and it is significant that Dicey's contribution was perhaps the least radical.[48] More typical, however, was Bernard Cracroft's declaration that 'public opinion has reformed the squire and the peer, not exclusion from Parliamentary power, and public opinion may be left to reform those working men who may happen to be drunken now'.[49] This exemplifies the un-Millian view of the benign influence of the majority in social affairs espoused by the majority of the essayists. The contributors to *Essays on Reform* were radical by the standards of 1867, and some of them became less radical over time. But the arguments they employed were widely canvassed in ensuing decades.

The debate over the county franchise initiated in the 1870s both reiterated and extended the concerns of the 1860s. The essayists of 1867 contrasted the virtues of larger urban constituencies with the vices of the smaller boroughs. Mid-century liberalism tended to view agricultural labourers as unpromisingly deferential. By the 1870s, however, many liberals were convinced that the modernisation of the countryside had led to an increase in the political intelligence of the agricultural classes, apparent in their new-found capacity for combination, paralleling earlier trends in the cities. Amongst liberals, the most prominent critic of this perspective was Robert Lowe. His opposition

---

[43] *Essays on Reform* (London, 1967), p. 65.   [44] ibid., p. 89.
[45] W. A. Mackinnon, *On the Rise, Progress, and Present State of Public Opinion*; Vaughan, *The Age of Great Cities*.
[46] *Essays on Reform*, pp. 110–11.   [47] ibid., pp. 131, 151, 296–7.
[48] ibid., p. 81.   [49] ibid., p. 187.

gave rise to an exchange with Gladstone in the periodical press that manifested contrasting liberal views of political reasoning and public opinion.[50]

Lowe argued that politics was a science and the views of the ignorant were of no value in making political decisions.[51] He took the success of the Anti-Corn Law League to epitomise the virtues of sound public opinion.[52] For Lowe, the League had triumphed by steadfast adherence to economic truth. Its middle-class composition reflected the intellectual demands of political economy. Political economy provided the architecture of his thought and politics was to him essentially the application of economic doctrine. Lowe was a fierce enemy of induction and defended classical economics against the revisionism of the late 1860s and early 1870s.[53] Knowledge of this science was a prerequisite for political insight firmly denied to the great unwashed.

Gladstone shared Lowe's admiration for classical economics. His remarks at the Political Economy Club dinner to celebrate the hundredth anniversary of the *Wealth of Nations* testified to his respect for Smith's legacy.[54] The broader vision of politics, however, which he developed in the 1870s focused rather more upon questions of foreign policy and the constitution. In part, this reflected his belief that the truths of political economy were incontestable and thus, in some sense, apolitical. Issues like Bulgaria and Ireland demanded moral virtue rather than intellectual stature. The masses were uncorrupted and so better able to feel appropriately about such matters.[55]

---

[50] The debate about the social location of political wisdom became conjoined with that over the county franchise. The former comprised 'a modern "symposium"' in *Nineteenth Century*, 3 (May 1878), 797–822 and (June 1878), 174–92. Participants included Lord Arthur Russell, R. H. Hutton, Grant Duff, Frederic Harrison, W. R. Gregg, Robert Lowe and W. E. Gladstone.

[51] Lowe in 'A modern "symposium": is the popular judgment more just than that of the higher orders?', 182–3.

[52] R. Lowe, 'A new reform bill', *Fortnightly Review*, 22 new ser. (Oct. 1877), 449.

[53] R. Lowe, 'Recent attacks on political economy', *Nineteenth Century*, 4 (Nov. 1878), 858–68.

[54] *Revised Report of the Proceedings at the Dinner of 31st May, 1876, Held in Celebration of the Hundredth Year of the Publication of the 'Wealth of Nations'* (London, 1876), p. 46.

[55] Gladstone, *Gleanings*, III, 204, 210.

Lowe was a Lockean empiricist for whom the potent deductions of political economy rested upon a hypothesis about human motivation subject to the experimental validation typical of the natural sciences.[56] In contrast, Gladstone was committed to the belief that there were a priori truths in religion and morals. His epistemology was founded upon his religious convictions. Empiricism did not provide a sufficiently robust account of our knowledge of self-evident religious truths such as the existence and goodness of the Creator. The great political questions upon which public opinion spoke primarily required simply the undistracted exercise of our moral intuitions.[57]

Gladstone did not take the *vox populi* to be irrational. He argued forcibly that the enlargement of the electorate would increase the demand for retrenchment and advance the pursuit of sound financial policies by the administration. He retained a highly moralistic vision of political economy in which fiscal fairness and economic laissez-faire were happily conjoined.[58] The collective self-help which Gladstone continued to regard as typical of trade unionism was a legitimate application of Smithian political economy. It would consequently be mistaken to interpret Gladstone's moral populism as simply an elevation of the claims of feeling over those of reason. It might perhaps be more accurate to suggest that Gladstone discerned an identity between reason and feeling which Lowe regarded as illusory.

As we have seen, Conservatives were prepared to defend their own positions in the franchise and redistribution debates of the 1880s through citations of 'public opinion'. Salisbury sought to castigate liberal gatherings by portraying them as expressions of a clamorous 'mass opinion' in contrast to the true public opinion that gathered to hear conservatives speak.[59] Salisbury's relationship to late nineteenth-century conservatism was not straightforward, and his early publications especially can be read as unusually stark in their economistic interpretations of human motivations. He did, though, retain many of the stock assumptions of his party, even if the justifications for these were for him more hard-headed and less sacramental than for

[56] Lowe, 'A new reform bill', 449.
[57] B. Hilton, 'Gladstone's theological politics' in M. Bentley and H. Stevenson, eds., *High and Low Politics in Modern Britain* (Oxford, 1983), pp. 28–57.
[58] See Matthew, 'Disraeli, Gladstone, and the policy of mid-Victorian budgets'.
[59] For example the speech by Salisbury quoted in Jephson, *The Platform*, II, 532.

some of his colleagues.[60] His approach to 'public opinion' certainly exemplified larger patterns of conservative discourse. As Paul Smith has noted, in his famously vitriolic articles in the *Quarterly Review* in the 1860s Salisbury actually argued that the power of the landed interest needs checking by the vigilance of an 'active public opinion'. He continued to deploy the language of public opinion throughout his career.

In his speeches of 1879–80, Salisbury revealingly developed his account of 'true' public opinion. 'Mass opinion' was characterised by remarkable apathy interrupted by violent spasms of excitement. 'Public opinion' proper crystallised from a process of protracted debate and was to be sharply distinguished from the rantings of mass demonstrations.[61] Salisbury identified 'true' national opinion with those whose opinions were sincere, steady and disinterested, which he contrasted with the sentimental whims of a sect. He worried in his *Quarterly* articles about Liberalism's hold over 'the class by whom public opinion is manufactured – the journalists, the literary men, the professors, the advanced thinkers of the party'.[62] His fear was, however, as much about the fabrication as the manufacture of public opinion, as his litany of malefactors suggests. Like others on the right, Salisbury was willing to denounce the Commons as the servile instrument of the caucus, but this should not be equated with contempt for the public.[63] The growing emphasis he placed on the Lords' referendal function reflected both hostility towards the increasing radicalism of Gladstone's policy and heightened apprehension over the alliance between demagoguery and general opinion which made the former possible.[64] Its justification rested, though, on the argument that mandates required confirmation, since the Commons was *not* representative of public opinion.

---

[60] P. Smith, ed., *Lord Salisbury on Politics: A Selection of his Articles in the Quarterly Review, 1860–1883* (Cambridge, 1972), pp. 21–2.

[61] For an earlier instance of this, see 'The budget and the reform bill', *Quarterly Review* (1860) in Smith, ed., *Lord Salisbury on Politics*, pp. 134–5.

[62] 'The Conservative surrender', *Quarterly Review* (1867), reprinted in Smith, ed., *Lord Salisbury on Politics*, p. 289.

[63] Speech quoted in Jephson, *The Platform*, II, 532.

[64] On the mandate, see C. C. Weston, *The House of Lords and Ideological Politics: Lord Salisbury's Referendal Theory and the Conservative Party, 1846–1922* (Philadelphia, 1995).

At points, Salisbury insisted that 'the nation can speak only at the polling booth'.[65] His conception of true public opinion set greater store by the quiet wisdom of the politically unexcitable than more activist and liberal visions were apt to do. In developing his account of the electoral mandate, Salisbury recognised that it was often far from clear on precisely what question elections turned, and that shifts in opinion could render mandates obsolete.[66] In the argument over the Lords' rejection of the Home Rule Bill in 1893, conservatives had to find alternatives to the ballot box to justify their actions. The tactical demands of defending the Lords' referendal function required a degree of flexibility in identifying vessels of public opinion. By the 1880s, conservatives, including Salisbury, were willing to draw upon the familiar repertoire of press, platform and petition in seeking to attach the weight of public opinion to their positions.

It is the materialist and determinist aspects of Salisbury's writing of the 1860s that have attracted most coverage.[67] As Michael Bentley has noted, however, it is important not to rely solely upon this, admittedly highly quotable, material.[68] Attention to his deployment of 'public opinion' reveals the limits of Salisbury's materialism. His public opinion was national in its scope; its formation registered the just influence of enduring interests and institutions. Individual opinions did not contribute equally to the emergence of the public view: the chattering classes and the dumb masses were both suspect. True public opinion embodied the steady preferences of the nation rather than the whims of the faddish intelligentsia.

The franchise debates of the 1860s and 1880s disclose differing conceptions of 'public opinion'. Amongst leading politicians, Salisbury, Lowe and Gladstone each offered distinct accounts of the nature and formation of public opinion. Views varied about the exact role public opinion should play within the model of parliamentary politics. Yet, these discussions also suggest the prevalence of a positive conception of the reasonableness of public opinion. Further light can be shed on

---

[65] Speech quoted in Jephson, *The Platform*, II, 532.
[66] On the debate about mandates, see P. Kelvin, 'The development and use of the concept of electoral mandate in British politics, 1867–1911', unpublished Ph.D. thesis, University of London (1977).
[67] See, for instance, 'The House of Commons', *Quarterly Review* (1864), reprinted in Smith, ed., *Lord Salisbury on Politics*, pp. 173–4.
[68] M. Bentley, *Lord Salisbury's World: Conservative Environments in Late-Victorian Britain* (Cambridge, 2001), pp. 89, 126.

attitudes to public opinion by examining in greater detail the debates about the caucus touched upon in the last chapter.

Party organisation, one-man rule and the character of the public

The charge of 'Americanisation' was already in use at the start of our period, as evidenced by the parliamentary debates about the secret ballot in 1871.[69] It was within this emerging tradition that 'caucus' was deployed as a term of abuse designed to conjure up the corrupt demi-monde of bosses, rings and wire-pullers widely associated with the United States.[70] As Biagini has stressed, many within the NLF saw it as Athenian rather than American in inspiration; T. H. S. Escott rebutted the caucus accusation with the ringing declaration that 'what is called the caucus is the practical expression of the principle that the popular will is the basis of political power'.[71] While anti-caucus language persisted, the trepidations of the 1880s and early 1890s about developments in political organisation could seem overblown to later observers. In his introduction to Ostrogorski's *Democracy and the Organisation of Political Parties*, James Bryce suggested that its portrait of the horrors of the caucus expressed the obsolete fears of an earlier period.[72] By 1908, A. L. Lowell felt able to entitle a chapter of *The Government of England* 'The rise and fall of the caucus'.[73]

The debate about the caucus in its classical phase incorporated a variety of arguments embracing a range of issues beyond the character of public opinion. Recently, it has been chiefly scrutinised by historians in search of popular attitudes to party. Contemporaries analysed the impact of the caucus in terms of the prospects for 'party government', often arguing that the new organisations would transform MPs

---

[69] *Parliamentary Debates*, 3rd ser., CCVII (1871), col. 1244.
[70] The account in Pelling, *America and the British Left* remains helpful.
[71] J. Chamberlain et al., *The Radical Programme (1885)*, ed. D. A. Hamer (Brighton, 1971), pp. lviii–lix.
[72] J. Bryce, 'Preface' to M. Ostrogorski, *Democracy and the Organisation of Political Parties* (2 vols., London, 1899), pp. xliii, xlvii.
[73] Lowell, *The Government of England*, I, esp. 545–8.

from representatives to delegates.[74] For such opponents, the caucus threatened a fundamental alteration in the polity. Frequently drawing upon Burke's words to the Bristol electors, these critics argued that the primary duty of the representative was to safeguard interests rather than to transmit opinions.[75] Within the Burkean doctrine of representation, it was national rather than local interests that were uppermost, and one complaint against the caucus was precisely that it led MPs to uphold narrow local concerns over the broader national interest. This argument about the incompatibility of the caucus with representative government could lead to a desire for parliament to assert its position against the claims of out-of-doors pressure, founded upon the belief that the proper role of public opinion lay in the selection of men rather than measures. However, even in Burke's canonical formulations, opinion was entitled to a respectful hearing, and those who presented the caucus as a threat to the deliberative function of parliament were not committed to denying its reasonableness. Perhaps more importantly, criticism of the caucus was not confined to its impact on the role of the MP.

As recent historiography has made clear, the caucus was often condemned as the nadir of party government.[76] It was accused of acting as a secret committee – a mere clique – that excluded broader opinion and rejected proper scrutiny. This charge was made by radicals in the 1870s, but was also evident in Randolph Churchill's talk of letting 'the light of public opinion into the dark corners of the Caucus' in 1884.[77] In this view, the private deformations of party organisation could be contrasted to the wholesomeness of public opinion. It was arguably this strand of criticism which, particularly after the publication of James Bryce's *The American Commonwealth*, was the more influential.[78]

[74] For example C. B. Roylance-Kent, 'The future of party government', *Macmillan's Magazine*, 68 (June 1893), 105, and L. J. Jennings, 'Parliamentary and election prospects', *Quarterly Review*, 174 (Jan. 1892), 269–70.

[75] 'Speech at the conclusion of the poll 3 Nov. 1774' in W. M. Elofson & J. A. Woods, eds., *The Writings and Speeches of Edmund Burke, vol. 3: Party, Parliament, and the American War, 1774–1780* (Oxford, 1996), pp. 68–70; 'Speech at Bristol previous to election 6 Sep. 1780', ibid., pp. 623–6, 637.

[76] For a later example of the contemporary argument, see L. Courtney, 'The decline of parliament', *Monthly Review*, 11 (Dec. 1904), 18.

[77] Lloyd Jones, *Industrial Review*, 31 August 1878; 'Gracchus', *Reynolds's Weekly*, 1 September 1878; Churchill speaking in Birmingham, reported in *The Times*, 18 Oct. 1884.

[78] J. Bryce, *The American Commonwealth* (3 vols., London, 1888).

In practice, it was of course possible to interpret organisational change in a variety of ways. Political committees were scarcely novel, and even radicals had frequently accepted their necessity. In the case of Birmingham itself, the inclusive character of new organisation created difficulties for efforts to portray it as the advent of full-blown machine politics at their most corrupt.[79] Candidates without independent means had little choice but to rely on some external financial source; this presented obvious problems for attempts to reconcile labour representation with the rhetoric of independence.[80] One response to this was to claim that trade union support reflected integration in a larger political movement, in contrast to the party games of the caucus, and thus again to present the caucus as stifling rather than amplifying public opinion.[81]

The publication of James Bryce's massive study of *The American Commonwealth* was a literary event attracting an impressive number of notices. Its reception supplies insights into attitudes to the relationship between party and the public. Regarded as an instant classic, the work was even likened to Tocqueville's *Democracy in America* and went through multiple editions.[82] Bryce combined the immediacy of the travelogue with an encyclopaedic thoroughness. The observation of one modern scholar that Bryce's chief gift was 'an infinite capacity for taking trains' is not without force.[83] However, while Bryce's vast opus owed much to his sheer doggedness, it also benefited from a friendliness and lack of snobbery which distinguished him from many British visitors and endeared him to his American hosts.

Bryce sought to avoid contemporary politics and produce a work founded upon solid research. He was careful to avoid the Irish question, which divided him from some of his closest friends. His book, though, reflected the 1880s controversies over the caucus. Bryce provided the first substantial account of the mechanics of urban electoral politics in the States to achieve wide currency in Britain. It was not an

---

[79] For acceptance of the Birmingham caucus as an encapsulation of local liberal opinion, see G. J. Howell, 'The caucus system and the liberal party', *New Quarterly Magazine*, 10 (Oct. 1878), 579–90.

[80] On this see Lawrence, *Speaking for the People*.

[81] *Industrial Review*, 31 Aug. 1878. The question of the relationship between the labour interest and public opinion is explored at length in Chapter 5.

[82] One friendly contemporary certainly felt the comparison with Tocqueville was overblown: A. V. Dicey to E. L. Godkin, 5 Nov. 1896, Godkin Papers, bMS 1083, Houghton Library, Harvard University.

[83] Collini, Winch & Burrow, *That Noble Science*, p. 243.

edifying portrait. It must be remembered, however, that Bryce repeatedly insisted on the soundness of American public opinion and on occasion privately contrasted its healthiness to the infirmities of its British counterpart.[84]

Modern historians have remarked upon the contrast between Bryce's dazzling depiction of a man forming his opinion between breakfast and arrival at work and his bland approval of the vigorous tone of American opinion in general.[85] Bryce essentially retained throughout his life the optimism about public rationality evident in his contribution to *Essays on Reform*. He was profoundly depressed during the Boer War by the public's refusal to hear the truth and its addiction to the lies of the 'creature' Chamberlain.[86] It is striking, however, that even at moments of blackest despair Bryce proclaimed that a reaction must come.[87] The triumph of 1906 revived a faith in 'public opinion' which survived the Great War to emerge in a deep commitment to the ideals of the League of Nations.[88]

Bryce responded to the Tocquevillian vision of oppressive majoritarianism by distinguishing between the tyranny of the majority and the fatalism of the multitude. Bryce identified the former with legal coercion and equated the latter with social conformity.[89] This was a fundamental departure from Tocqueville's understanding of the tyranny of the majority.[90] As we have seen, Mill's sensitivity to the sociological perspicacity of Tocqueville's thought was not widely

---

[84] He describes public opinion as 'a sort of atmosphere, fresh, keen, and full of sunlight . . . and this sunlight kills many of those noxious germs which are hatched where politicians congregate' in *The American Commonwealth*, II, 355. 'You are doubtless right in thinking that both your political system and your political class are worse than ours. But I am not sure that the bulk of the nation and its public opinion are not sounder in sense and conscience than ours have lately shown themselves', Bryce to Godkin, 15 June 1900, Godkin papers.

[85] H. Tulloch, *James Bryce's American Commonwealth – the Anglo-American Background* (Woodbridge, 1988), p. 139.

[86] 'No such creature as Chamberlain has ever led this country since the days of the Stuarts: you can judge by his success how demoralised England has become', Bryce to Godkin, 31 Mar. 1900, Godkin papers.

[87] 'Of course there will be a reaction, but probably not soon enough to prevent this profligate ministry from getting another large majority at next general election', ibid.

[88] J. Bryce, *Modern Democracies* (2 vols., London, 1921).

[89] Bryce, *The American Commonwealth*, III, pp. 120–44.

[90] Noted in Tulloch, *James Bryce's American Commonwealth*, p. 145.

shared by Anglophone critics. This myopia was apparent in the reception given to Bryce's suggested distinction between the tyranny of the majority and the fatalism of the multitude.

E. A. Freeman noted approvingly that Bryce 'explains the very secondary sense in which only a majority can be said to practice tyranny.'[91] The *Westminster Review* stressed that 'the charge [of majority tyranny] is at present by no means well founded, though undoubtedly there was much reason for it half a century ago'.[92] In a characteristically pugnacious review Goldwin Smith took the un-Brycean line that 'Mr Schnadhorst is already a "boss" full blown and on the grandest scale.' He followed this, however, by affirming that 'Mr Bryce is happily right in thinking that the tyranny of democratic majority, which De Tocqueville denounced in ever-memorable words and Dickens satirized, is in great measure a thing of the past'.[93] Even the *Quarterly Review*, in the course of a forceful attack on universal suffrage, agreed that 'the degradation of American politics, in those parts of the country where it exists, is in defiance of public opinion, and not in consequence of it'.[94]

Some reviewers reconciled Bryce and Tocqueville by suggesting that the maturation of democracy in the United States had erased any semblance of majority tyranny that might previously have existed. The only notice by a future President proposed that 'even what Mr Bryce says of American public opinion in his very suggestive and valuable fourth part will doubtless be true only so long as our country is new'.[95] This emphasis upon the beneficial passage of time both implied and reflected confidence in the soundness of public opinion in the older Anglo-Saxon polity. Various reviewers commended Bryce's demonstration that, as Freeman put it, 'the people of the United States are still, after all changes, an English people'.[96] Bryce was careful not to conflate political forms and cultures. Differences in social

[91] *Manchester Guardian*, 26 Feb. 1889.
[92] 'Mr Bryce's American commonwealth', *Westminster Review*, 131 (Mar. 1889), 402.
[93] G. Smith, 'The American commonwealth', *Macmillan's Magazine*, 59 (Feb. 1889), 245, 252.
[94] E. J. Phelps, 'The American commonwealth and its lessons', *Quarterly Review*, 169 (July 1889), 277.
[95] W. Wilson, 'Bryce's American Commonwealth', *Political Science Quarterly*, 4 (1889), 156.
[96] *Manchester Guardian*, 26 Feb. 1889.

arrangements could negate apparent similarity in political structures. Richard Hofstadter located the origin of Turner's frontier thesis in Bryce's account of the American West. In contrast, Hugh Tulloch contended that Hofstadter's reading of Bryce fails to do justice to the significance Bryce, as a follower of Freeman, attributed to the robust spirit of Anglo-Saxon independence apparent on both sides of the Atlantic.[97]

It might be argued that this is a false antithesis. Paolo Pombeni has drawn attention to the approach to comparative politics presented in the *Quarterly* essays of 1905.[98] There Bryce sketched a methodology attentive to both social and environmental constraints on the evolution of political forms and institutions.[99] Dicey was troubled by the awkward paradox that 'while [Bryce] gives us pictures of profound political immorality and triumphant corruption, he is, nevertheless, convinced that public opinion is on the whole wholesome and upright'.[100] His was, however, one of the few contemporary reviews to make what has become a common criticism of the Bryce thesis. Bryce reconciled his account of the political system with his evaluation of American mores through the claim that 'in America the political life of the country is not the main or central channel of its life, but seems a kind of side channel encumbered by weeds and bushes'.[101] This diminished status was a consequence of the material position of a young, prosperous and relatively unpopulated country. An acceptance of his picture of Anglo-Saxon public opinion in America married to an emphasis on the peculiarities of America implied that Britain would avoid the debasement of politics apparent in the States. It is sometimes suggested that the impact of Bryce's book was simply to foster trepidation over the future of British party politics. Yet *The American Commonwealth* amounted to a forceful explanation of why the British future could not be foretold from a dissection of the American present. Furthermore,

---

[97] Tulloch, *James Bryce's American Commonwealth*, p. 2. Burrow argues that Tulloch overstates Freeman's influence on Bryce; see his 'Some British views of the US Constitution', in R. C. Simmons, ed., *The United States Constitution: The First 200 Years* (Manchester, 1989), p. 134.

[98] P. Pombeni, 'Starting in reason, ending in passion: Bryce, Lowell, Ostrogorski and the problem of democracy', *Historical Journal*, 37, 2 (1994), 319–20.

[99] J. Bryce, 'The study of popular governments', *Quarterly Review*, 203 (July 1905), 179–80.

[100] A. V. Dicey, 'Bryce's American Commonwealth', *Edinburgh Review*, 169 (April 1889), 505.

[101] J. Bryce, 'Some aspects of American public life', *Fortnightly Review*, 32 new ser. (Nov. 1882), 642.

Bryce provided a defence of American public opinion which distanced it from the party system and provided a model by which to defend developments in British public opinion and party politics.

The 'caucus' was not the only political trend in the 1880s provoking debate about the character of 'public opinion'. As Bryce noted, in the first half of the decade especially there was much trepidation about the supposed emergence of 'one-man rule', anticipating later discussions of Britain as an elective dictatorship. It was argued that Cabinet government as immortalised by Bagehot had been superseded by the dominance of the Premier and that this was a consequence of the extension of the suffrage.[102] The need to make a national appeal and to mobilise the newly enfranchised produced an enhanced emphasis upon the party leader which the likes of Gladstone and Disraeli were well qualified to satisfy. The importance of the charismatic tribune was further increased by the advent of the telegraph and the development of the press.[103] This provided the leadership with a network of power which was independent of the mechanism of the caucus. These tendencies could be seen as compatible or cognate, but the decision of the National Liberal Federation to abandon Chamberlain in 1886 suggested that the leadership retained its old form in a newly democratic guise.

Fears over the emergence of one-man rule embraced a variety of views of the state of public opinion. Some viewed it as a result of the unformed nature of public opinion, whether due to apathy, ignorance, or some combination of the two.[104] Others saw it rather as a reflection of the increasingly binary division of an enlarged electorate whose whims permitted executive tyranny because of changes in parliamentary procedure.[105] The power of the Premier was linked to the alternating fortunes of the parties which gave rise to the phrase 'the

---

[102] For useful comment on the transition, see A. H. Hawkins, '"Parliamentary government" and Victorian political parties, c. 1830–1880', *English Historical Review*, 104 (July 1989), 638–69. For earlier ideas about the role of members, see P. M. Gurowich, 'Party and independence in the early and mid-Victorian House of Commons: aspects of political theory and practice, 1832–1868, considered with special reference to the period 1852–1868', unpublished Ph.D. thesis, University of Cambridge (1986).

[103] Matthew, 'Rhetoric and politics in Britain'.

[104] For example, Jennings, 'Parliamentary and election prospects', 284.

[105] This process could be related to the third reform act. See T. E. Kebbel, 'Is the party system breaking up?', *Nineteenth Century*, 45 (Mar. 1899), 506–7.

swing of the pendulum'. It was sometimes suggested that the oscilla-
tions of party politics illustrated the suggestible and inconstant quality
of the popular mind.[106] Such complaints continued, however, to distinguish between the vicissitudes of the electorate and the character
of the public, favouring a more positive reading of the latter than the
former.[107]

Intense discussion of one-man rule was a relatively brief affair,
reflecting electoral fluctuations between the second and third reform
acts. The radical Arthur Crump noted in 1885 that one-man rule was
'very much the fashion'.[108] As Bryce later observed, this modishness
did not endure. The legislation of 1884–5 ushered in an era of comparative electoral stability. Lamentations about the prevalence of one-man
rule are a recurring feature of British politics whose currency is most
closely related to the personal dominance of the sitting Prime Minister.
Powerful leaders with a large personal constituency from Disraeli and
Gladstone to Thatcher and Blair have occasioned references to elective
dictatorship markedly absent during the sojourn of figures as varied as
Salisbury, Asquith and Major.

The trajectory of the debates about political organisation is evident
in the reception of Ostrogorski's *Democracy and the Organization of
Political Parties* published in 1902. In an important study, Gaetano
Quagliariello makes clear the continental, and specifically French, origins of Ostrogorski's thought and the lack of attention given to his
work in the Anglophone world. American scholars responded to his
chapters on the United States but their British counterparts mostly
ignored the work.[109] This is perhaps unsurprising. Bryce's introduction to Ostrogorski's book questioned its key arguments, and his allies,
particularly Lowell, took issue with what they regarded as the anachronistic intellectualism of Ostrogorski's denunciation of the caucus.[110]

---

[106] John Bull Jr., 'Parliament and the party system', 471–80.

[107] For instance, A. Milman, 'The peril of parliament', *Quarterly Review*, 178
    (Jan. 1894), 278.

[108] A. Crump, *A Short Enquiry into the Formation of Political Opinion from the
    Reign of the Great Families to the Advent of Democracy* (London, 1885),
    p. 162.

[109] G. Quagliariello, *Politics without Parties: Moisei Ostrogorski and the
    Debate on Political Parties on the Eve of the Twentieth Century* (Aldershot,
    1996); on French origins, p. 2; on reception, p. 101.

[110] See Lowell, *The Government of England*, I, esp. 544–5.

Those commentators who made use of Ostrogorski's work tended to be confirmed sceptics about the existing party and electoral system. Leonard Courtney, whom Wallas termed the 'last survivor in public life of the personal disciples of Mill', recommended the book as 'a monument of years of careful and acute study', but this was an unusual view.[111] Neither the extent of caucus power identified by Ostrogorski nor his parallels with the United States proved particularly persuasive to British readers.

In noting the capacity of an independent 'public opinion' to moderate the excesses of the new party organizations, Bryce offered an optimistic assessment that was widely echoed, particularly after the decline of the more feverish jeremiads of the 1880s. In its early phase, opposition to the caucus had most frequently centred upon its unrepresentative nature. Developments in the 1890s raised further questions about the impact of the new machinery at a national level. The adoption of the Newcastle programme as official liberal policy at the 1892 election focused concern upon the issue of programmatic politics.[112] In the ensuing debate over the legitimacy and meaning of such systematic appeals, the character of public opinion was much canvassed.

The rise of the programme has often been related to the fragmentation of the liberal party in its late Gladstone period.[113] The litany of pledges submitted to the electorate is linked to the proliferation of single-issue groups and the absence of an overarching vision or an overwhelming cause around which the movement could coalesce. This approach roots the emergence of the programme firmly within radicalism, primarily in its Chamberlainite form. While it is important not to overstate the salience of programmatic appeals in politics before 1914, their existence certainly provoked a considerable response.

In line with attacks on the caucus, assailants of programmatic politics claimed it was transforming parliamentary candidates into mere instruments of party machinery. This could be presented as a regrettable undermining of localism, and as further evidence of the power of the wire-puller. Such charges were, of course, strongly contested,

---

[111] Wallas, *Human Nature*, p. 217; Courtney, 'The decline of parliament', 18.
[112] For instance Jennings, 'Parliamentary and election prospects', 269–70.
[113] See the works of D. A. Hamer, especially *Liberal Politics in the Age of Gladstone and Rosebery* (Oxford, 1972).

as Biagini has shown.[114] Debate also focused on the implications of programmatic politics for elections: in particular the consequences of asking electors to evaluate a shopping list of proposed measures rather than assess the candidates or adjudicate on a defining moral issue. The production of a list of promises might be taken to imply that the electorate was balkanised into disparate groups, or it might be defended as due recognition of the multifariousness and complexity of politics. It was certainly the case that attempts were made to argue for the internal coherence of consolidated proposals. Indeed, for its radical champions, programmatic politics embodied a more elevated conception of the capacities of the elector.[115]

The most tireless defender of programmatic politics was perhaps T. H. S. Escott, whose devotion to Joseph Chamberlain manifested itself in prodigious efforts as editor of the *Radical Programme* of 1885. Escott had a talent for making radical arguments through established motifs of political discourse. He piously cited Burke's remark that 'when the people had a feeling they were commonly in the right, although sometimes they mistook the physician' in his trailer article for the *Radical Programme* published in the *Fortnightly*.[116] His defence of the caucus combined Tocquevillian reverence for free combination with a traditional radical emphasis on the link between taxation and representation. He announced that 'ours is the age of association, and the Caucus is simply an association of ratepayers, who are parliamentary electors, to secure a parliamentary representative who is fairly in accord with their views'. He insisted that 'the Caucus is public opinion – not its manufactory, but its expression'.[117] Escott recognised 'the convictions, prejudices and sentiments into which public opinion can be analysed' and in his account of the modern stage noted that 'the peculiar influence of dramatic representations depends upon the contagious sympathy of a crowd'.[118] He did not, however, extend this view of the theatrical crowd to the political public, and reassured those who feared the democratic debasement of parliament

---

[114] Biagini, *British Democracy and Irish Nationalism*, p. 185.

[115] T. H. S. Escott, 'The future of the radical party', *Fortnightly Review* (July 1883), quoting Chamberlain's Bingley Hall speech in Chamberlain et al., *The Radical Programme (1885)*, ed. Hamer, p. lviii.

[116] Hamer, ed., *The Radical Programme*, p. lviii.

[117] Escott, *England*, pp. 354–6.   [118] ibid., p. 549.

that 'great . . . even in social matters, is the educating force of public opinion'.[119]

Opponents of programmatic politics liked to figure the Newcastle programme as a compendium of Gladstonian bribes designed to distract the electorate from the real issues. The Conservative MP and journalist L. J. Jennings combined an attack on the caucus with an analysis of the failings of programmes. 'The famous Newcastle Programme' was described as 'give all comers whatever they may ask for . . . [and] intended to provide something for every taste, but which, on the face of it, could not possibly be carried'. Programmatic politics and one-man rule were mutually reinforcing since 'for the preparation of a "programme" there is no one in the present day to equal Mr Gladstone', and Gladstonian dominance ensured that 'discussion is not required, and indeed, at the formal meetings of the party, nothing of the kind is tolerated'. The wire-pullers protected one-man rule, as 'no time for deliberation was conceded, no voice was permitted to be raised in criticism. This is the Radical caucus in all its glory.'[120]

Underpinning these highly partisan critiques of programmatic politics lay the charge of sectionalism. This could take the familiar form of the accusation that programmes amounted to bribery and marked the advent of confiscatory class politics. More generally, the atomism of the programme could be cast as a divisive failure to address the public as a whole that served to confuse debate and obstruct the emergence of a mature and focused public opinion. Criticism of the programme did not depend upon the belief that electors were unable to formulate opinions on a variety of topics, though it was often argued that issues were better dealt with in series rather than in parallel. The heyday of discussion of the programme was the first half of the 1890s, but the state of the debate on the eve of the twentieth century is well captured in the reception of W. E. H. Lecky's massive study of *Democracy and Liberty*.[121]

These stout volumes attracted a more considerable response than has been recognised. The preface to the *Review of Reviews*' 'Index to the Periodicals of 1896' noted that 'Mr Balfour's "Foundations of Belief," and Mr Lecky's "Democracy and Liberty" have still been favourite

---

[119] Hamer, ed., *The Radical Programme*, p. lx.
[120] Jennings, 'Parliamentary and electoral prospects', 269–70.
[121] Lecky, *Democracy and Liberty*.

subjects of criticism' and placed them before any other books in its list of popular topics.[122] Lecky's status as a historian and political commentator ensured that his melancholic indictment of most aspects of contemporary politics was widely discussed. His restatement of a classic mid-nineteenth-century liberal view of the public under the conditions of emergent democracy provoked a series of valuable reflections on the nature of public opinion.

Whilst receptive to *On Liberty*'s assault on the tyranny of the majority, Lecky's portrait of majority tyranny did not really embrace the more sociological dimensions of Mill's thought.[123] Lecky adumbrated the traditional liberal view of the single-issue crusade according to which 'the strength of public opinion . . . needed to carry a great organic change in Britain can never be simultaneously evoked on two totally different questions'.[124] The established identification of 'the middle class' with 'public opinion' was presented in stark form. Lecky argued that 'the world has not seen a better constitution than that England enjoyed between the Reform Bill of 1832 and the Reform Bill of 1867'. The virtue of 1832 lay in its realisation that 'the middle class, which now became the most powerful in the political system, was one which could be excellently trusted with a controlling power'. Lecky proceeded to eulogise the middle class in Aristotelian terms for 'its political independence, its caution, its solid practical intelligence, its steady industry, its high moral average'.[125] The early Victorian political system was built upon the fact that 'the constituencies at this time coincided very substantially with the area of public opinion'. Lecky explained that this was because 'the public opinion of a nation is something quite different from the votes that can be extracted from all the multitudes who compose it', for 'there are multitudes in every nation who contribute nothing to its public opinion'.[126] His nostalgia extended to opposition to the ballot, since 'It obscures the moral weight of an election, by making it impossible to estimate the real force of opinion, knowledge, and character that is thrown on either side'.[127]

Lecky nicely exemplifies the canonical liberal conception of the public. His was an essentially middle-class conception of 'public opinion', within which, however, as more populist critics noted, there was some

---

[122] *Index to the Periodicals of 1896* (London, 1897), p. iii.
[123] Lecky, *Democracy and Liberty*, I, 64.   [124] ibid., 14.
[125] ibid., 17–18.   [126] ibid., 18.   [127] ibid., 74.

room for '[t]he skilled artisans [who] are among the most intelligent and orderly classes in the nation'.[128] At times, he claimed that 'public opinion' should be confined to the estimation of 'the characters and motives of public men'.[129] His belief, however, that 'public opinion' could speak on single issues was apparent in his discussion of Catholic emancipation and perhaps in his willingness to embrace the referendum. It is revealing that he limited the uses of the referendum to 'rare and grave occasions' in 'home politics'.[130]

Lecky was impressed, though insufficiently for some of his reviewers, by the progress of the press. He linked firmly the possession of literacy with the capacity to form opinions. '[G]enuine opinion being overlaid and crushed by great multitudes of ignorant voters', he concluded that 'In our day, the press is becoming far more than the House of Commons the representative of the real public opinion of the nation'.[131] Lecky remained convinced, however, that while it was important to read newspapers, it was even more important not to read only newspapers, for 'an immense proportion of those who have learnt to read, never read anything but a party newspaper – very probably a newspaper specially intended to inflame or to mislead them – and the half-educated mind is specially open to political utopias and fanaticisms'.[132]

Much of the reaction to Lecky's book followed the obvious lines of party politics. Morley savaged the work in the pages of the *Fortnightly*, describing one passage as 'a mere bit of thoughtlessness' before asking 'what is the use of a man being a thinker, if he will not think?'[133] *Blackwood's Magazine* was rather more impressed and commended the work's 'judicial moderation'.[134] Some common ground does, however, emerge.

The most popular tone amongst the reviewers was one of 'disappointment'.[135] It was generally thought that Lecky had succumbed to the temptations of playing Cassandra. Many critics were

---

[128] 'Democracy and liberty', *London Quarterly Review*, 27 new ser. (Oct. 1896), 157.
[129] Lecky, *Democracy and Liberty*, I, 193.
[130] ibid., 242.   [131] ibid., 210.   [132] ibid., 264.
[133] J. Morley, 'Mr Lecky on democracy', *Nineteenth Century*, 39 (May 1896), 706.
[134] H. Cowell, 'Lecky's "Democracy and Liberty"', *Blackwood's Magazine*, 159 (May 1896), 749.
[135] The word can be found in the first few paragraphs of four early reviews.

keen to defend the democracy against his strictures. Both the *Fort-nightly* and the *Review of Reviews* stressed that Lecky had wholly ignored the sphere of local government, in which civic virtue was so plentifully displayed.[136] It is striking that Lecky's democratic critics rarely took issue with his characterisation of 'public opinion'. The observation in the *London Quarterly Review* that 'public opinion' was as capricious before 1867 as after was uncharacteristic.[137] More typical was the *Review of Reviews*, which noted Lecky's view that much of the electorate 'contribute nothing to public opinion' without comment before arguing that 'the majority is always ignorant, but the advantage of democracy is that it gives a free field to an intelligent and enlightened citizen'.[138] Some conservatives predictably shared Lecky's nostalgia for the period when 'the multitudes who have no opinions were excluded from votes'.[139] Defenders of the democracy suggested that the test Lecky set for popular opinion was too strenuous. Voters did not need to be able to formulate opinions on particular technical issues merely to 'be intelligent, honest, patriotic, and have an eye for the men most likely to serve the country well', and 'we must not forget the great change which the school-master and the Press have wrought'.[140]

More radical reviewers made two linked objections to Lecky's account of the relationship between rationality and social class. A number of critics noted that Lecky himself acknowledged that 'the skilled artisans are amongst the most intelligent and orderly classes in the nation', and the Irish positivist S. H. Swinny contrasted the wisdom of the worker with the learned ignorance of the university graduate.[141] It was Morley who forcibly noted that 'the broken loafer', for whom Lecky reserved his most caustic denunciation, was known by 'any electioneering agent of either party' to be 'in nine cases out of ten . . . the ardent supporter of Church and Queen'.[142] The debate around Lecky's work, which rumbled on through 1897 and 1898, confirms the resilience of the established liberal conception of

---

[136] Morley, 'Mr Lecky on democracy', 706, and 'The book of the month', *Review of Reviews*, 12 (April 1896), 372.
[137] 'Democracy and liberty', 143.
[138] 'The book of the month', 368, 370.
[139] Cowell, 'Lecky's "Democracy and Liberty"', 750.
[140] 'Democracy and liberty', 143–4.
[141] ibid., 157, and S. H. Swinny, 'Lecky's liberty and democracy', *Positivist Review*, 4 (Aug. 1896), 164.
[142] Morley, 'Mr Lecky on democracy', 707.

enlightened opinion. Almost immediately, however, this understanding was placed under immense pressure. It is time to consider its fate, and that of the idea of public opinion more generally, in the early years of the twentieth century, as the political temperature rose markedly, both at home and abroad.

Crowd psychology, war and the public mind

Historians dating the strange death of the liberal public have recurred repeatedly to the impact of popular enthusiasm for the Boer War. There is much to be said for this view. Liberal intellectuals were appalled by the jingo excesses of Mafeking night and the Tory campaign of 1900. J. A. Hobson produced a justly famous account of the psychology of jingoism, L. T. Hobhouse analysed the ousting of John Bull by the imperialist man in the street and Bertrand Russell replied to anti-suffragists with a litany of *male* political irrationality in which the South African war loomed large.[143] The new scepticism received its most sustained exposition in Graham Wallas's classic *Human Nature in Politics*. No attempt will be made here to deny the shock of the war for many on the left. The accepted view will, however, be both qualified and developed. The history of 'public opinion' should not be written as the search for the moment when faith was lost, as though the career of the concept was comparable to the spiritual autobiography of a godless Victorian. The secular trend in the reputation of 'public opinion' across the divide of 1900 was unquestionably downwards, but this was not a steady, linear or indivisible process. More and less optimistic views of 'public opinion' could coincide and phases of pessimism could be and were succeeded by bouts of cheerfulness.

It is not clear, for instance, that widespread rejoicing over an imperialist war permanently transformed progressive conceptions of the public. There is substantial evidence that the liberal landslide of 1906 and the subsequent reforms revived, at least in part, the reputation of the public. Perhaps more importantly, the history of 'public opinion' in these years has been dominated by the perspective of liberal intellectuals. Others, liberal imperialists for instance, shared their conception of

---

[143] Hobson, *The Psychology of Jingoism*; Hobhouse, *Democracy and Reaction*; Russell, *Anti-Suffragist Anxieties*.

the public, while regarding its appreciation of British victories rather differently. Alternative conceptions of public opinion were available: conservatives could view the solidarities of popular patriotism in a rather more favourable light; labour activists might conceive political reaction as the treason of the clerks.

The rhetoric of 'public opinion' traditionally contrasted the public and the crowd. As we have seen, established understandings of 'public opinion' embraced strongly held beliefs and the verdict of the open meeting, but there were always limits on the scope for disorderly conduct if the platform were to signify effectively as a bearer of opinion. 'Public opinion' was taken to be formed by reasonable discussion distributed across both space and time. 'The crowd' was an unreasonable swarm of individuals united both spatially and temporally. The dichotomy came under great pressure with the rise of crowd psychology and the events of the Boer War.

The distinction between public and crowd received cogent contemporary development in the hands of the French social psychologist Gabriel Tarde. Tarde was best known in his lifetime and later for his early study of the *Laws of Imitation*, which made a lasting impression upon A. V. Dicey.[144] His mature essays, however, departed significantly from the crowd psychology of his first productions. Inspired by the gulf he perceived between the Dreyfusard public of newspaper readers and the anti-Dreyfusard crowds, Tarde distinguished between the rationality of the former and the emotionalism of the latter. In doing so, Tarde was explicitly attacking the views of Gustave Le Bon, the most celebrated of crowd psychologists, and author of the cross-channel best-seller *The Crowd*, translated into English in 1896. After adumbrating the differences between crowd and public, Tarde announced, 'I therefore cannot agree with that vigorous writer, Dr Le Bon, that our age is the "era of crowds." It is the era of the public or of publics, and that is a very different thing.'[145]

One important aspect of the distinction was the question of membership. Whereas the individual swept up in one of Le Bon's crowds was immersed in a single mass, individuals could simultaneously belong to several Tardean publics. Tarde's essay on the public and the crowd

---

[144] Dicey to Bryce, 11 Oct. 1917, Bryce Papers, Bodleian Library.
[145] G. Tarde, 'The public and the crowd' in *Gabriel Tarde: On Communication and Social Influence: Selected Papers*, ed. T. N. Clark (London, 1969), p. 281.

remained, however, untranslated and, unlike his earlier work, was not cited in the original French. Britons at the turn of the century, caught up in what the *Westminster Review*'s notice of *The Crowd* called 'the present age of transition', were more inclined to argue that theirs was indeed an age of crowds, and not an era of publics.[146] Furthermore, it became more common to deny the difference between crowds and publics, and to view the great British public as one great big crowd.

In 1898 the barrister Marcus R. P. Dorman published *Ignorance: A Study of the Causes and Defects of Popular Thought*. Dorman was impressed by the amount of ignorance in popular thought and produced a sequel entitled *The Mind of the Nation*, which concluded that if the nation had ever possessed a mind, it had now lost it.[147] The character of Dorman's work was well captured by *The Observer*'s recommendation of *Ignorance* as 'though philosophical, not too profound'.[148] He had an eye for the modish target, epitomised by the mocking reference to fashionable idealism implied in entitling a portrait of cultural debasement *The Mind of the Nation*. The chorus of approval elicited by *Ignorance* was in large part due to the resonance of its analysis of political developments. Dorman exemplifies a broader tendency to view the close of the nineteenth century as an age of crowds in which intellectual debate was being replaced by advertising. The following extract finds Dorman striking an unusually resonant note:

Any printer of posters will tell us that the first essential is to 'catch the eye' of the passer-by, and to do this the bill must stand out from the board. We are all posters and all engaged in endeavouring to catch the eye of the crowd . . . But when we have accomplished this, what is the use of being stared at? No one but a professional beauty or a young actor derives satisfaction from that.[149]

The link made in this passage between the dominance of the crowd and the reign of the advert was by no means unique to Dorman. The idealist D. G. Richie noted that 'the political and moral consequences of advertising would . . . be too long a story to begin now; to have named it

---

[146] *Westminster Review* (Sep. 1897), 350.
[147] Dorman, *The Mind of the Nation*.   [148] *The Observer*, 9 Oct. 1898.
[149] M. R. P. Dorman, *Ignorance: A Study of the Causes and Effects of Popular Thought* (London, 1898), p. 100.

may suffice'.[150] Bold, large-scale posters were often taken to epitomise the excesses and power of advertising, though they also had their defenders. In the political realm, the poster seemed symptomatic of the undue intrusion of commercial practices into the public sphere.[151] The consequence of this constant visibility was, as Masterman put it, that 'the Crowd may be stampeded by constant repetition of the same thing, by pictorial illustration from which it cannot escape'.[152] It was Hobson in *The Psychology of Jingoism* who provided perhaps the most caustic account of how the techniques of advertising enabled the mass press to delude a nation which had become a mere mob. He noted that 'many persons are convinced that there was a Boer Conspiracy, and can even tell you what it was and what it aimed at, in the same manner as they are convinced that Colman's is the best mustard, and Bryant and May's the best matches'.[153]

The idea that this was 'an age of crowds' was clearly in part a sociological thesis about modernity. Growing urbanisation and technological innovation were thought to subject individuals to more information and to surround them more constantly with other people. There was, of course, a large dose of crude stereotyping in this account. The spread of suburbia did not obviously foster community, and improvements in communications tended to reduce the need for face-to-face contact. Masterman later advanced this view of town life and, despite real imaginative sympathy, reproduced many of its prejudices, arguing that 'whole peoples... are reared in a Crowd, labour in a Crowd, in a Crowd take their enjoyments, die in a Crowd, and in a Crowd are buried at the end'.[154]

The more sociological dimensions of the crowd idiom must be considered in tandem with the psychological aspects. Crowd psychology developed rapidly on the Continent in the 1890s and travelled to England through the early work of Tarde and, especially, Gustave Le Bon's study of *The Crowd*.[155] Crowd psychologists aimed to transcend the atomism of conventional psychology by producing an account of

[150] D. G. Ritchie, 'The rights of minorities' in D. Boucher, ed., *The British Idealists* (Cambridge, 1997), pp. 148–9.
[151] Thompson, '"Pictorial lies?"'.
[152] C. F. G. Masterman, *The Condition of England*, ed. & intro. J. T. Boulton (London, 1960), p. 101.
[153] Hobson, *The Psychology of Jingoism*, p. 100.
[154] Masterman, *The Condition of England*, p. 94.
[155] G. Le Bon, *The Crowd: A Study of the Popular Mind* (London, 1896).

collective behaviour which incorporated the tendency for individuals to behave differently in group situations. The archetypal group was taken to be the crowd, understood primarily in terms of the physical proximity of its members. It was not, of course, self-evident that such gatherings should be seen as typifying collective action. Crowd psychologists tended, however, to view the crowd as the model for all forms of collective action and to regard all forms of association as more or less crowd-like. Theirs was not an especially flattering picture of the crowd. Crowds were seen as emotional, unreasoning, and feminised.[156]

In order to understand how such a picture of crowd behaviour could appear plausible, it is necessary to examine more closely the structure of Le Bon's argument. *The Crowd* provided an approach to collective action which was found attractive by a variety of cultural commentators, especially in the wake of the Boer War. Martin Conway based much of his collection of essays, *The Crowd in Peace and War*, upon Le Bon's nostrums.[157] J. A. Hobson reviewed Le Bon sympathetically in the South Place Ethical Society house magazine, *Ethical World*.[158] The *Westminster Review* summarised Le Bon's case with revealing economy. 'Crowds,' it wrote, 'like women, always rush to extremes, and, of all crowds, Latin crowds are the most feminine, and in this we have the key to much French history.'[159] Le Bon's racialism chimed nicely with prevailing prejudices.[160] As the *Westminster* noted, 'the Anglo-Saxon system, on the other hand, has the author's undivided approval'.[161] This approval was extended equally to political arrangements and racial personality. *The Speaker* suggested that Le Bon was too strongly influenced by the proclivities of the French. The Boer War discouraged such complacency.

L. T. Hobhouse noted in 1904 that the Edwardian 'man-in-the-street' possessed 'the character and tone which the proud and slow-going John Bull of old days was wont to attribute to his volatile

---

[156] On crowd psychology, see especially S. Barrows, *Distorting Mirrors: Visions of the Crowd in Late Nineteenth-Century France* (New Haven, 1981) and R. A. Nye, *The Origins of Crowd Psychology: Gustave Le Bon and the Crisis of Mass Democracy in the Third Republic* (London, 1975).

[157] M. Conway, *The Crowd in Peace and War* (London, 1915), some articles previously published in *Nineteenth Century* (1905–8).

[158] *Ethical World*, 9 Dec. 1899.   [159] *Westminster Review* (Sep. 1897), 351.

[160] For example, 'The moral of M. Le Bon's fascinating book is that we Anglo-Saxons have a great deal to be thankful for', *The Spectator*, 5 Nov. 1898, 652.

[161] *Westminster Review* (Sep. 1897), 350.

and emotional neighbours who made revolutions and cut off the heads of kings'.[162] This was very much a view of 'public opinion' as a massive instance of crowd psychology. It was Le Bon to whom Hobhouse, like his comrade-in-arms Hobson, looked for his account of the crowd. A chief inspiration for *The Crowd* was Hippolyte Taine's account of the French Revolution, which painted a vivid portrait of the Parisian mob. Le Bon claimed, however, that an assembly of educated men could and would behave like a crowd. His arguments about collective behaviour affirmed that congregation unleashed primal forces whose sovereignty was not dependent on the intellectual or class background of the participants. This made his work more palatable to Hobson, Hobhouse and other moral populists of the left. Hobson was horrified at the bloodlust of the educated during the Boer War. Le Bon provided a means by which to counter those who located jingoism solely in the masses and to explain what Hobson regarded as an almost universal reversion to barbarism.

Although crowd psychology affected the views of political thinkers as different as Hobson and Conway, some currents of political thought were not seduced by its scientific credentials. Notwithstanding the impact of Mendelian genetics upon Lamarckian doctrines, evolutionary theory itself was far from clearly committed to a social Darwinist emphasis upon instinct and conflict. William Clarke was not alone in arguing that science supported a much more positive view of co-operation than that of the crowd psychologists.[163] British idealists preserved a more positive view of collectivities and often transferred the characteristics of the established liberal notion of 'public opinion' onto the term 'general will'.[164] Members of the progressive left like MacDonald showed signs of succumbing to scepticism about group action, but distrusted the kind of denigration of the masses indulged in by conservative crowd theorists. Syndicalists stressed the rationality exhibited by certain forms of collective action, such as strikes, while some militant socialists embraced the role of instinct as a spur to action. J. M. McLachan provides a good example

---

[162] Hobhouse, *Democracy and Reaction*, pp. 69–71.

[163] J. Thompson, 'Democracy, monism and the common good: rethinking William Clarke's political religion', *History of European Ideas*, 38 (2012), 239.

[164] See, for instance, B. Bosanquet, 'The reality of the general will' in Boucher, ed., *The British Idealists*, pp. 131–2.

of the latter tendency.[165] It was not, however, confined to those who identified with the Labour party. The romantic Tory Stephen Reynolds linked his jointly written account of a working-class view of politics to the ideas of Henri Bergson and emphasised the value of weighing things up rather than reasoning them out.[166]

Dissension from the conclusions of crowd psychology could also stem from a wider acquaintance with developments in social psychology. It is striking that the most psychologically inclined of all British political thinkers was singularly unconvinced by the claims of crowd psychology. In *Human Nature in Politics*, Graham Wallas rejected the crowd metaphor as an adequate means of understanding collective action. He noted that 'London in the twentieth century is very unlike Paris in the eighteenth century... if only because it is very difficult for any considerable portion of the citizens to be gathered under circumstances likely to produce the special Psychology of the Crowd.' His judgement was influenced by the consideration that 'the facts vary greatly among different races, and the exaggeration which one seems to notice when reading the French sociologists on this point may be due to their observations having been made among a Latin and not a Northern race'.[167]

Wallas refused wholly to equate the public with the crowd, even in *Human Nature*. He was more forthright in defending this distinction in his 1914 book on *The Great Society*, where he stressed that problem-solving was a rather basic human drive and that consequently reason and instinct could not be strictly separated.[168] Interestingly, Stephen Reynolds observed that 'Mr Graham Wallas does not, as a factor in modern electioneering, attach much importance to the distinctive psychology of the crowd' before claiming that 'shortly before the polling... the psychology of the electorate changes from a collection of individuals to a psychology, if not of the crowd, at all events of public excitement'. Reynolds went on, however, to remark that 'the critical day tends to draw nearer and nearer to the polling-day' and 'the people are capable of voting far more reasonably than they are allowed to do; and in proportion'.[169] The distinction between

---

[165] See D. Tanner, 'Ideological debate in Edwardian Labour politics: radicalism, revisionism and socialism' in Biagini & Reid, eds., *Currents of Radicalism*, pp. 271–94.

[166] Reynolds et al., *Seems so!*, p. xxvi.   [167] Wallas, *Human Nature*, pp. 54–5.

[168] G. Wallas, *The Great Society: A Psychological Analysis* (London, 1914).

[169] Reynolds et al., *Seems so!*, p. 152.

crowd and public thus resurfaced, if in weaker form, in the unlike-
liest of locations. It was the Boer War which did most to make the
identification of public and crowd appear temporarily convincing. This
requires further consideration.

The enthusiasm aroused by the Boer War troubled progressives for
a variety of reasons. Britain was engaged in what many on the left
regarded as an imperialist war against precisely the sort of small
nation struggling to be free to which British liberalism had traditionally pledged support. The famous victories, most obviously Mafeking, which halted or reversed the early run of defeats were greeted
by widespread and occasionally violent rejoicing. Unlike the jingoes
of the late 1870s, the warmongers of the late 1890s were not offset
by a large-scale movement of resistance. The camaraderie apparent
amongst pro-Boers, nicely exemplified by the *Manchester Guardian*
circle, gained much of its intensity from their sense of marginalism
and adversity.[170]

The disruption of pro-Boer meetings and the blatant nationalism
of the popular press deeply disillusioned anti-war liberals. Opponents
of the war found it hard to hold even private meetings, except in
strongholds of radical politics, and had no appreciable impact on the
broader public. The conservative banker G. T. C. Bartley remarked in
the Commons debate on 'disturbances directed against opponents of
the war in South Africa' in March 1900 that 'it is amusing to some
of us who have fought a good many contested elections to hear what
has been going on this evening'.[171] It was generally accepted by non-
Unionists in the debate that public opinion was strongly in favour
of the war, but the government's failure to protect the right of free
speech in ticketed meetings was deplored. Public anger at 'pro-Boer'
sentiments ran high and moved C. P. Scott, member for Leigh and
editor of the *Manchester Guardian*, to describe the disturbances as 'an
attempt ... to substitute mob violence for reason and humanity'. The
crushing Tory victory in the Khaki election of October 1900 merely
seemed to confirm the public's identification with such lawlessness.

The stance of the press was a cause of perhaps even greater anguish.
Hobson's *The Psychology of Jingoism* fairly vibrates with anger at

---

[170] On the *Manchester Guardian* circle, see M. Hampton, 'The press, patriotism,
and public discussion: C. P. Scott, the *Manchester Guardian* and the Boer
War, 1899–1902', *Historical Journal*, 44 (2001), 177–97.

[171] *Parliamentary Debates*, 4th ser., LXXX (1900), cols. 968–9.

the lies perpetrated by a plutocratic press. In the case of Hobson and others, anti-Semitism sharpened their hostility to a press which fed the public an unrelieved diet of distortions and untruths. The freedom and honesty of the press were mainstays of the inherited notion of 'public opinion', and even after 1886 the press had not been so uniformly Tory. Radical condemnation of the press saw it as both mirror and moulder of public opinion, but the novel power of the press baron under oligarchic conditions meant that the press was able to shape public opinion more aggressively than ever before. Liberals were, however, appalled by the gullibility of a public which appeared to care so little for the unpleasant truth from which it could not entirely hide. James Bryce wrote to his American friend and editor of *The Nation*, E. L. Godkin, to observe that 'the most singular phenomenon of the last six months has been the indifference of the people to the discovery of truth'.[172] The people had the demagogue they deserved, for 'no such creature as Chamberlain has ever led this country since the days of the Stuarts'.[173] His eminence owed much to 'the zeal of the Chamberlain press', who supported 'the music hall hero'.[174]

The Boer War divided the left. Robert Blatchford and George Bernard Shaw supported it; J. A. Hobson and J. R. MacDonald opposed it. MacDonald wrote later that 'it is well known that a nation will not fight except for a cause in which idealism is mingled. The *Daily Mail* supplied the idealism for the South African War by telling lies about the flogging of British women and children'.[175] It is notable that MacDonald placed the blame for popular jingoism upon the distortions of the press, which misled the better feelings of the public.

The importance attached by MacDonald to the influence of a rational public opinion was apparent in his claim in the *Socialist Review* that the power of socialism lay in 'public opinion, not in strikes'.[176] MacDonald's opposition to syndicalist strategy rested on this view, for by the time the state of opinion made a general strike possible, public opinion would already have secured the desired goals. Duncan Tanner once observed that MacDonald was perhaps more of a rationalist than the new liberals.[177] His first book, on *Socialism and Society*, contained

---

[172] Bryce to Godkin, n.d., Godkin Papers.
[173] Bryce to Godkin, 31 Mar. 1900, Godkin Papers.
[174] Bryce to Godkin, 17 Feb. 1900, Godkin Papers.
[175] *Labour Leader*, 15 Aug. 1914.
[176] J. R. MacDonald, 'Outlook', *Socialist Review*, 15 (Oct.–Dec. 1919), 320.
[177] Tanner, 'Ideological debate in Edwardian Labour politics: radicalism, revisionism and socialism', p. 277.

the ringing anti-Marxian statement that 'socialism . . . is inevitable only if we are to develop on rational lines; it is inevitable, not because men are exploited or because the fabric of capitalism must collapse under its own weight, but because men are rational'.[178] In labour circles, such rationalism was by no means unique to MacDonald. Arthur Henderson wrote that 'there is no success which will stand the wear and tear of life, other than the success of converting public opinion to socialism', with the firm expectation that this would ensue given the reasonableness of the public.[179] MacDonald's extensive writings, however, offer particular insights into labour ideas about 'public opinion'.

MacDonald was clearly affected by the work of Le Bon. In his criticism of syndicalism, MacDonald noted that

> Le Bon pointed out in his *Psychology of the Crowd* that the mind of a mass of people was different not only in weight but also in quality from the mind of an individual. Now the Syndicalist lays the greatest stress upon solidarity. He suspects the individual; he trusts the mass.[180]

It is apparent from his remarks here and elsewhere where MacDonald's sympathy lay. References to the crowd are frequent and invariably derogatory in MacDonald's work. He defines 'the general crowd' to which 'the elector' belongs as 'the most primitive and least rational of all associations'.[181] His debt to crowd theory is evident in a passage in his description of parliament 'as more amenable to the appeals which make the judgements of crowds so true on matters of sentiment or of principle, but so unfortunate on matters of detail and administration'.[182]

The 'mass' or 'masses' fare little better. It is important to note, however, that, at least before the anxiety of *Parliament and Democracy* (1920), MacDonald was careful to make clear that in using the term 'mass' he did 'not mean the poor only . . . but all who are moved by interest or habit, and whose minds can think of nothing existing except the *status quo*'.[183] MacDonald had seen from the Boer War that 'there

---

[178] J. R. MacDonald, *Socialism and Society* (London, 1905), p. 92.
[179] Cited in Tanner, 'Ideological debate in Edwardian Labour politics: radicalism, revisionism and socialism', p. 281.
[180] MacDonald, *Syndicalism*, p. 11. This work was based on six articles in the *Daily Chronicle* in May 1912.
[181] J. R. MacDonald, *Parliament and Democracy* (London, 1920), p. 4.
[182] MacDonald, *Socialism and Government*, II, 30.   [183] ibid., 61–2.

is as much political incapacity, as much moral obliquity, amongst the well-to-do in Britain to-day as amongst the poor'.[184]

The public to which MacDonald appealed was an inclusive body. He contrasted the way 'the Socialist appeals to the whole body of public opinion' with 'the Syndicalist [who] considers the working class only'.[185] This understanding of public opinion was often expressed in terms of 'the general will' and founded upon the view that society possessed a governing intelligence irreducible to its various component functions. It had much in common with the idealist framework erected by Bernard Bosanquet. Bosanquet contrasted the vulnerabilities of 'public opinion' with the competence of a less tangible concept of the general will, but in doing so provided a version of the latter not dissimilar to the more active, corporatist interpretation of the former.[186] MacDonald's tendency to equate the 'general will' with 'public opinion' illustrates the proximity of the two concepts. He wrote that

This General Will is not the agreement of electors upon programmes. It is not the will of individuals. Society as a whole has inherited habits, modes of thought, axioms of conduct, traditions both of thought and activity; it has accumulated within itself certain forces and tendencies just as a living organism has ... Its strength, its enlightenment, its willingness, determine the rapidity and direction of progress. Politicians have a glimmering of its power and its independence when they speak of public opinion as something which controls them.[187]

MacDonald himself set great store by the corporate and participatory aspects of 'public opinion'. His hostility to proportional representation was justified in terms of its individualist failure to represent real associative life. He argued that 'mathematical thoughts are misleading, for the public opinion behind Parliament is only partly a question of the number of votes, it is also partly a question of the intensity of the voters' will'.[188] The importance he attributed, in traditional radical fashion, to civic activism is made evident on numerous occasions. He insisted that an opinion

should have to stand the test of public criticism and be so acceptable as to gain not only a following, but a following which considers it to be of

---

[184] ibid., I, 53.   [185] *Syndicalism*, p. 5.
[186] Bosanquet, 'The reality of the general will', pp. 135–7.
[187] *Socialism and Government*, I, 89–90.   [188] ibid., 166.

sufficient importance to bring it into the arena of politics in one or other of the several ways in which this can be done. It should also have to win a place in that arena and establish itself in relation to other opinions there at the same time. This is necessary in order that legislative acts may reflect the General Will.[189]

The vagaries of the established political structure supported this by allowing 'for an element in public opinion which is of great political importance, but which cannot be valued by mechanical means: viz., the activity of the will, as well as the mass of the will, of electoral groups'.[190]

A sizeable portion of the political nation was, of course, blissfully free of the agonies suffered by opponents of the Boer War. As the October 1900 election testified, British success was greeted with considerable popular enthusiasm. The renewed emphasis upon the virtue of patriotism evident in the last years of the nineteenth century was only intensified by the difficult experience of the South African war. Patriotic revival was accompanied by an emphasis upon the value of instinct, especially the martial instinct which radicals so despised. Tories were less optimistic about 'public opinion' and worried that the clamour of democracy drowned out the still small voice of national common sense. More hysterical figures like Arnold White, the Tory journalist and advocate of national efficiency, were overwhelmed by the failings of the demos, but preserved a basic confidence in the good instincts of the people. White often argued that the electorate had been debased, but concentrated his fire upon the category of the demos rather than the public. He attached much of the blame for the short-lived character of the national efficiency campaign, generated by poor military performance in South Africa, to the machinations of the press. White demonstrates, however, that it was possible for tories to interpret jingoism as evidence of the survival of patriotic good sense rather than the degeneration of the public.[191]

One of the ironies of the impact of the Boer War was that while the left was often keen to base foreign policy on public opinion, the right was traditionally more doubtful. It was an accepted axiom of much conservative thought that the arcane mysteries of diplomacy could only be conducted in secret and that an ill-informed public

---

[189] ibid., 131–2.   [190] ibid., 135.
[191] A. White, *Efficiency and Empire*, ed. G. R. Searle (Brighton, 1973, first published 1901), p. 44.

could contribute little to the formulation of foreign policy. Journalists like Frederick Greenwood were quick to lambast the sentimentalism apparent in demands for action in Armenia.[192] It was undeniable, however, that the popular press had played an important role in the campaign for naval expansion waged by the nationalist right in the 1880s. Greenwood himself recognised this, and in an article on the duties of the patriotic editor in wartime Vice-Admiral Colomb conferred much of the credit for the repair of the naval situation in the 1880s on 'independent and patriotic editors'.[193] The more nationalist right was 'delighted at the exhibition of feeling throughout the country' during the South African conflict and argued that 'if the other side excite the public to violence the blame is upon them, and not upon us'.[194] Some conservatives were less impressed, however, by the various manifestations of popular patriotism. Owen M. Green noted in the *Monthly Review* that 'as the war dragged on the abuse of our opponents happily became less because it was checked by the popular admiration aroused by the game resistance of the Boers'.[195] It is important not to suggest that widespread enthusiasm during the war reconciled the right to the influence of the populace over foreign policy. Similarly, it would be mistaken to overestimate the impact of jingoism on conservative views of the public.

The historiography of the age of transformation has been powerfully shaped by narratives about class and empire. The rise of the Labour party and the demise of the Liberal party have traditionally been explained in terms of the rise of class politics.[196] Tory dominance before 1906 and after 1918 has often been linked to the emergence of middle-class consciousness and to their successful appropriation of the language of patriotism. The increased currency of appeals to collective identities, whether economic or ethnic, is sometimes taken to indicate

---

[192] F. Greenwood, 'Sentiment in politics', *Cosmopolis*, 4 (Nov. 1896), 340–54.

[193] F. Greenwood, 'Public opinion in public affairs', *Macmillan's Magazine*, 79 (Jan. 1899), 162 and Admiral P. H. Colomb, 'The patriotic editor in war', *National Review*, 29 (April 1897), 254.

[194] *Parliamentary Debates*, 4th ser., LXXX (1900), col. 969.

[195] O. M. Green, 'The people and modern journalism', *Monthly Review*, 10 (Feb. 1903), 85.

[196] The literature on these topics is enormous. Perhaps the most influential rendition of the class explanation of Labour success is that of Ross McKibbin. See R. McKibbin, *Evolution of the Labour Party*, *Ideologies of Class* and *Classes and Cultures: England 1918–1951* (Oxford, 1998). His most recent assessment, which modifies some earlier positions, is in *Parties and People: England 1914–1951* (Oxford, 2010).

a reduction in the rationality of political culture.[197] More plausibly, it is suggested that contemporaries interpreted the potency of collective appeals as indicative of the limited role of individual reason in politics and the fractured character of the public. The perceived importance of class could be taken to imply the absence of a single, unitary public and the obsolescence of a politics built upon debate over particular issues. Such fears are certainly apparent in Lowell's treatise on *The Government of England* or Dicey's study of *Law and Public Opinion in England*.[198] These kinds of accounts tended to depict the Labour party as both the manifestation and the maker of class politics. More progressive commentators, like Hobhouse or Hobson, cast the Tory party in a similar role as both the exploiters and the engineers of a new nationalism in which the rational formation of public opinion was replaced by tribal invocations of Englishness. There are problems, however, with this picture of the idea of 'public opinion' in the Edwardian era.

Historians have come to lay considerably less emphasis on the explanatory power of class in understanding Edwardian politics. It was similarly far from obvious to contemporaries that class was established as the basis of party politics. Card-carrying Tories were perhaps most inclined to see class as crucial, but the success of the Conservative party in wining votes, and the electoral appeal of Unionism, suggested the limits of a class analysis. Progressives were confronted before 1903 with what they regarded as an efflorescence of imperialist sentiment. Their three successive election victories might be taken to reveal the compatibility of liberalism with class politics under democratic conditions. Alternatively, they might be viewed as evidence of the continuing viability of the radical crusade of the people against the peers. The modest progress made by the nascent Labour party in these years did not compel contemporaries to view politics in primarily class terms. As we have seen, and will explore further in Chapter 5, it is indeed unclear that the Labour movement is best understood as the champion of a class politics fundamentally at variance with established liberal and radical conceptions of the public.

Much recent work has focused on the difficult task facing labour politicians attempting to mediate between the claims of class and

---

[197] See Matthew, 'Rhetoric and politics in Britain'.
[198] For instance, Lowell, *The Government of England*, I, 453.

locality.[199] Through the close of the nineteenth century and after, the labour movement shared with particular intensity the wider radical distrust of cliques and parties. This suspicion stemmed from a democratic enthusiasm for debate. Commitment to the politics of locality and the representation of real communities reinforced hostility to nationalised machine politics. It might be thought that the evolution of a national party structure in the Edwardian period signalled the end of radical fondness for open-platform politics. Attention should be paid, however, to the way figures like MacDonald emphasised the devolution of decision-making in the Labour party.[200] The desire to sustain the politics of locality could be accompanied by a desire to preserve or perhaps restore an open inclusive politics founded on an enlightened public opinion. Such sentiments are much to the fore in the writings of MacDonald. Other labour commentators could present existing invocations of 'public opinion' as deeply middle-class, but were keen to view industrial action as collectively rational, and often to redeem a more inclusive sense of public opinion.

Histories of the concept of 'public opinion' have leant towards an understanding of 'public opinion' primarily in relation to politics, especially electoral politics. It is striking, however, that discussion of 'public opinion' frequently addressed its influence upon the economy. This debate is the subject of Chapter 4, but it is important to note that reference to the role of 'public opinion' in regulating industrial disputes was usually positive. It was generally anticipated that 'public opinion' would adjudicate fairly and efficiently between the warring parties of capital and labour. This optimism depended upon confidence in the justice of the public and a degree of faith in its rationality. The enthusiasm for publishing statistical information so characteristic of officials in the Board of Trade rested upon the belief that an educated public would reach an appropriate opinion on, for instance, the merits of a particular wage claim. This concept of 'public opinion' as an economic force was embraced by commentators across the political spectrum but held a special attraction for liberals, radicals and the left.

---

[199] See especially Lawrence, *Speaking for the People*, esp. pp. 227–64. For a good example of the spatial turn in political history, see Windscheffel, *Popular Conservatism in Imperial London*.

[200] MacDonald, *Socialism and Government*, II, 26.

As I argued in Chapter 1, the nineteenth-century public was very much a community of consumers. If 'the people' was often identified with the producing classes, 'the public' comprised the consuming classes. There was, of course, overlap between the two categories, but their connotations were importantly different. The 'public opinion' which was to settle industrial disputes was very much that of the consuming nation. The mechanism by which its beneficial influence was exercised was never clearly specified and generally remained clouded in obscurity. It should not be assumed, though, that the public's capacity to regulate rationally industrial affairs was simply an extension of the rationality presumed more generally in economists' accounts. However the public exercised its sway, it was not through the individual buying decisions of consumers.

The sense of 'public opinion' invoked in economic debate was akin to that adopted in earlier political discussions. Some liberal commentators feared that the forces of capital and labour would develop the power to shape views possessed by political parties and so extinguish enlightened public opinion.[201] The analysis of the growth of monopoly offered by Marshall is not dissimilar to the account of the collapse of the public sphere in the second half of Habermas's *The Structural Transformation of the Public Sphere*. Whereas it was thought possible to provide the necessary data for informed public debate about industrial relations, for other kinds of questions, diplomatic for instance, such publicity might not be possible. The role of the government as a neutral umpire in industrial disputes ensured a supply of accurate information which the activities of a partisan press could not replicate. Industrial affairs were not central to party politics and did not usually inspire the kind of journalism spawned by foreign wars or general elections. There remains an element of paradox in the enthusiasm with which certain commentators acclaimed the impact of public opinion on economic life and bemoaned its irrational influence upon politicians. It is apparent from the invocation of 'public opinion' in economic debate that considerable faith still existed in the reasonableness and justice of the public when it was not overwhelmed by the power of party and press.

---

[201] For instance, Marshall, 'Some aspects of competition' (1890), pp. 287–8.

4 | *Political economy and the idea of 'public opinion'*

On 26 September 1889, *The Times* reflected upon the debate surrounding the recent London dock strike. Under the headline 'Public Sympathy v. Political Economy' its commentator remarked that 'when a dispute of this kind arose a generation ago, the majority of people were found complacently quoting certain well-worn formulas about demand and supply, or dwelling with emphasis upon the strictness of the analogy between labour and other commodities...But we have changed all that. During the recent strike I do not remember to have seen a single invocation of the once revered laws of demand and supply'.[1] In the third article the contributor criticised the influence of 'public sympathy in its new *rôle* of arbiter of commercial disputes and regulator of social action'.[2] The case was encapsulated in the first sentence of the first article: 'The most remarkable peculiarity of the recent strike as compared with previous movements of a similar kind is the substitution of appeals to public sympathy for appeals to the laws of political economy.'[3]

These articles, reprinted two months later in the *Journal* of the Royal Statistical Society, not only capture a belief prevalent at the start of the 1890s, but correctly diagnose and date its novelty.[4] They are, as we shall see, also revealing in their account of the character and composition of the public whose sentimentality they bemoan. Their greatest peculiarity lies in the dismal view they take of the consequences of public opinion's 'new role' as 'arbiter of commercial disputes'.[5] For contemporaries displayed a widespread faith in the power of public opinion to regulate justly the economy and to preserve industrial peace.

An important shift occurred between the 1870s and the 1890s in both popular and academic perceptions of the process of collective

---

[1] *The Times*, 26 Sep. 1889.
[2] *The Times*, 9 Oct. 1889.   [3] *The Times*, 26 Sep. 1889.
[4] *Journal of the Royal Statistical Society* (Dec. 1889), 595–604.
[5] *The Times*, 9 Oct. 1889.

bargaining and wage resolution. The dissolution of the doctrine of the wages fund radically disrupted the prevailing account of the emergence of a stable wage rate. Despite the construction of marginal productivity theory in the 1890s, no compelling theoretical account of imperfect competition existed before the work of Hicks and others in the 1920s and 1930s. Amongst economists, there was rather an enduring emphasis upon the indeterminacy of the wage rate. For the wider public, there was a growing sense that trade unions could affect collective bargaining and that economists could not predict its outcome. This theoretical vacuum at both popular and academic levels led to the adoption of ad hoc explanations which were reliant upon an institutional account of the bargaining process. The most popular solution which emerged to the problem of indeterminacy was the invocation of public opinion as the umpire in the industrial struggle. Economists and commentators across the political spectrum regarded public opinion as the referee of last resort.

The rise and fall of the wage-fund doctrine is an important part of the story. The doctrine had peculiar significance as a readily understood portion of political economy. Its authority was frequently invoked by those anxious to cast aspersions on the role of trade unions, and it defined public attitudes to the wages question into the 1870s. The theory's collapse has been much investigated as a problem in the retrospective history of economic analysis. Such accounts have often breached the canons of internalist explanation in their efforts to understand why the attacks of the late 1860s succeeded where other equally coherent rebuttals had failed.[6] My concern is with more popular understanding of the theory and its implications. This perspective leads to a different focus from that offered in some conventional histories of economic theory. Mill's recantation was a significant development and recent work has, if anything, served to heighten our sense of his significance in shaping popular political economy.[7] Other influences were, however, at work. The importance of empirical studies of work and wages in establishing the existence of a secular rise in remuneration over the

[6] John Vint, *Capital and Wages: A Lakatosian History of the Wages Fund Doctrine* (Aldershot, 1994).
[7] For instance, E. F. Biagini, 'British trade unions and popular political economy, 1860–1880', *Historical Journal*, 30, 4 (1987), 811–40. On the late Mill and his circle, see especially J. Lipkes, *Politics, Religion and Classical Economy in Britain: John Stuart Mill and his Followers* (Basingstoke, 1999).

nineteenth century and in linking it to productivity gains should not be overlooked.[8] After Mill's apostasy the development of popular and technical economic thought more clearly reflected distinct patterns of influence. The crucial problem in understanding this process is the nature of the 'crisis' of economic thought in the 1870s and of its resolution. In tracing the evolution of non-technical economic thinking, the relative impact of positivism and marginalism will be very different from that observable at the level of high theory.

The wage-fund doctrine proposed that a fixed sum of circulating capital existed out of which workers were paid. Wages could be established by dividing this stock by the number of workers. In its more stylised Ricardian form, there was little room for variation in levels of remuneration. The governing assumption was of harvest time in an overwhelmingly agricultural economy. Labourers had to be sustained before they gathered the harvest, and this could only happen if their wages were advanced out of capital. The agrarian premise explains both the insistence that capital must precede labour and the implied uniformity of wages. The wages fund was part of a classical synthesis designed to explain long-term macroeconomic trends. The Ricardian theory of rent, the Malthusian population principle, and the associated fear of a stationary state linked together. Malthusianism proclaimed that an increase in the size of the wages fund would merely induce a corresponding rise in the number of workers. The Ricardian theory of rent with its assumptions about diminishing returns precluded any possibility of a sustained growth of capital. The stationary state was thus inescapable.

The character of the classical wage theory is evident from Mill's *Principles* of 1848. Mill insists that 'Wages cannot rise, but by an increase of the aggregate fund employed in hiring labourers, or the diminution of the number of competitors for hire.'[9] His chapter on the stationary state shows he was hardly complacent about the prospects for the former. The passages on population show that the latter was likewise not to be anticipated in the shorter term. Mill was, though, more optimistic about the possibility of labourers altering their reproductive behaviour. He was convinced, especially in later editions, that

[8] R. Petridis, 'Brassey's law and the economy of high wages in nineteenth-century economics', *History of Political Economy*, 24, 4 (1996), 583–606.
[9] J. S. Mill, *Principles of Political Economy, with Some of their Applications to Social Philosophy* (2 vols., London, 1848).

public opinion could be brought to see the accuracy of Malthus's views and that this would contain population growth.[10] Mill echoed an argument of Ricardo's that the notion of a living wage was culturally determined. This meant that labourers would secure different remuneration and exhibit different reproductive behaviour according to whether they set their collective minimum wage higher or lower.

Classical economics supplied a number of justifications for trade unions. Adam Smith remarked on the tendency of masters to combine to depress wages and the corresponding necessity for labourers to combine to secure market rates. In addition he allowed that where low wages impaired worker efficiency, trade unions could achieve a rise in wages that would be sustained by productivity gains. This was an important argument which, it will be seen, was capable of being greatly extended.[11] Smith had also devoted considerable attention to the source and nature of variations in wages. He recognised that the assumption of perfect competition was not fully applicable to the labour market. Mill's later ruminations on the inexplicably high fees commanded by professionals similarly acknowledged that in some areas the cake of custom remained unbroken.[12]

Malthusianism was clearly on the retreat by the 1850s and 1860s, and by then as few anticipated the arrival of the stationary state as had earlier believed in its avoidability. Shorn of the stationary-state argument and the Malthusian premise, the wage-fund doctrine became a claim about the primacy of capital and the inability of trade unions to influence wage levels. The only possible source of an increase in wages was the growth of capital. This is not to suggest that an emphasis on labour's status as a *commodity* subject to the laws of supply and demand offered no room for trade unions and their apologists to defend the principle of combination. Eugenio Biagini has thoroughly investigated the use made by trade unions of classical arguments.[13] But outside the labour movement, the wages fund retained considerable purchase.

John Vint has drawn a striking picture of the theoretical achievements made possible by the doctrine. It is arguable, though, that it

[10] J. S. Mill, *Principles of Political Economy* (8th edn, 2 vols., London, 1878), I, 461–2.
[11] Thompson, 'Political economy, the labour movement and the minimum wage'.
[12] Mill, *Principles of Political Economy* (8th edn), I, 487.
[13] Biagini, 'British trade unions and popular political economy'.

is mainly in the discussion of the 1860s, which eventuated in Mill's recantation, that such theoretical innovation can be found in the various attempts to sink or save the doctrine.[14] There is a tradition amongst historians of economic thought that the wages fund was actually a good theory of capital disguised as a bad theory of wages.[15] The argument is that the emphasis on the primacy of capital in wage-fund theory anticipates the view of the Austrian school that in a *growing* economy wages are in part paid out of past product and thus that 'the stock-of-goods-in-the-pipelines has real significance for the functioning of the system'.[16] It is not, however, solely in such rarefied realms that we shall find the key to the lay appeal of the short-term understanding of the wage-fund theory, though it is important that Fawcett, Mill and others continued to propagate the doctrine right up to the 1878 edition of the *Principles*.

The stubborn refusal to acknowledge that the men could ever win a strike, complained of by Frederic Harrison in 1865 and continually apparent in the employers' evidence to the Royal Commission, suggests some of the sources of the wage-fund theory's appeal.[17] While the vulgar notion of the wages fund was seductively simple, it was also materially convenient for those who were not subject to its strictures. Furthermore, it partook of the authority of political economy, which was perhaps at its peak in the 1850s and 1860s. The emphasis on supply and demand incorporated labour within the conventional understanding of pricing and accorded with the basic assumption of commercial society. Nonetheless, the resilience of wage-fund theory should not be exaggerated, for while the doctrine did not finally leave the stage of public discourse till the end of the 1880s, it was clearly shuffling towards the exit from the end of the 1870s.

Mill had defended the doctrine against the criticisms of Longe but finally capitulated in a *Fortnightly* review of the work of Thornton.[18] It has been noted that he renounced a doctrine far cruder than anything he had actually promulgated. He was persuaded by the argument that

---

[14] Vint, *Capital and Wages*, pp. 124–76.
[15] M. Blaug, *Economic Theory in Retrospect* (3rd edn, Cambridge, 1978), p. 196.
[16] E. Bohm-Bawerk, *Positive Theory of Capital* (London, 1889).
[17] F. Harrison, 'The limits of political economy', *Fortnightly Review*, 1 (Aug. 1865), 356–76.
[18] J. S. Mill, 'Thornton on labour and its claims', *Fortnightly Review*, 5 new ser. (May 1869), 505–18 and (June 1869), 680–700.

there was no fixed fund out of which labour was paid. The agrarian assumptions underpinning the theory were clearly no longer applicable. Thornton's claim that workers were paid out of the value of the goods they produced seemed more plausible. It was similarly evident that a great deal depended on how much employers choose to pay themselves and on how circulating and fixed capital related. Neither of these was determinate. Edgeworth once described economists as somewhat indeterminate in their use of indeterminacy. The wages fund was a prime example of this, but it became increasingly obvious that the epicycles necessary to save the doctrine required rendered it not so much indeterminate as tautologous.

Biagini has noted that it is only in the late 1870s that trade unionists and working-class newspapers begin to make use of the recantation.[19] In order to understand the popular reception of its academic rejection it is necessary to begin with the state and status of political economy in the decade of the English *Methodenstreit*.

The 1870s witnessed a fierce debate about the methodological character and epistemological status of economic knowledge. The pages of the *Fortnightly* in particular resounded to various assaults on the verities of orthodox classical political economy. The dinner held in 1876 by the Political Economy Club to commemorate the hundredth anniversary of the publication of the *Wealth of Nations* sheds light on the state of the debate.[20] The Belgian historical economist Laveleye offered an account of Adam Smith's project diametrically opposed to the deductive Smith invoked by Robert Lowe.[21] Nonetheless, faith in the structure of classical political economy, especially with regard to the great principle of free trade, was much in evidence. The coverage of the dinner suggests some of the speakers were considerably more sanguine than many thought appropriate.

The proceedings of the commemorative dinner end with a digest of 'public opinion' drawn from a handful of contemporary newspapers.[22]

[19] Biagini, 'British trade unions and popular political economy', 824–6.
[20] D. Winch, *Wealth and Life: Essays on the Intellectual History of Political Economy in Britain, 1848–1914* (Cambridge, 2009).
[21] *Revised Report of the Proceedings at the Dinner of 31st May, 1876, Held in Celebration of the Hundredth Year of the Publication of the "'Wealth of Nations'"*, p. 20.
[22] ibid., p. 65. The publications included were *The Economist*, the *Daily News*, *Capital and Labour* and the *Pall Mall Gazette*. Most of the articles are approving and the excerpts from the *Pall Mall* do not reflect its acerbity.

The picture is selective. Jevons reflected in his *Fortnightly* article on 'the future of political economy' that 'some of the newspapers hinted in reference to the centenary dinner that the political economists had better be celebrating the obsequies of their science than its jubilee'. He went on to remark that 'the *Pall Mall Gazette* especially thought that Mr Lowe's task was to explain the decline, not the consummation, of economical science'.[23] Jevons detected a widespread disenchantment with the claims of political economy and identified it especially with advanced liberalism. For Jevons this opposition clearly stemmed from a historically induced relativism which in the 1870s was more radical than conservative in its political thrust.

The impact of the historical method on late nineteenth-century political economy has been much discussed.[24] It has particular significance to an argument about the shift from political economy to public opinion as the primary mode of explaining wage rates. Historical economists in both Britain and Germany were especially concerned with wages and trade unions. Investigations of wages were often designed to prove that Ricardian (and later Marxian) predictions of immiseration were historically inaccurate. Examinations of trade unions were frequently intended to demonstrate their role in raising wages and to reveal the necessity of a historical and institutional approach to economic understanding. The centrality of trade unions to historical economics was matched by the centrality of the historical method to the economics of trade unions. In the theoretical vacuum produced by the fall of the wages fund, recourse to history was a common response amongst economic writers faced with the problems posed by trade unions. It is in considerations of collective bargaining and imperfect competition that the extent of the concessions made to the historical method by orthodox political economy become apparent. To gauge the impact of the historical method on late nineteenth-century political economy, we need to examine the place of trade unions in the historical economics of the 1870s.

---

[23] W. S. Jevons, 'The future of political economy', *Fortnightly Review*, 20 new ser. (Nov. 1876), 619.

[24] See for example G. M. Koot, *English Historical Economics, 1870–1926: The Rise of Economic History and Neo-mercantilism* (Cambridge, 1987), and Collini, Winch J. Burrow, *That Noble Science*.

The most influential work about trade unions produced by a historical economist was perhaps Brentano's *On the History and Development of Gilds, and the Origin of Trade-Unions*, published in 1870.[25] This greatly influenced Schulze-Gaevernitz's later *Social Peace* and largely held the field as a history of trade unionism prior to the Webbs' book of 1894.[26] Jevons, who counselled that Brentano's view on legislation should be read '*cum grano*', thought that his history was 'excellent'.[27] The appreciative reception of Brentano's work is important because it did much to impart a favourable teleology to contemporary accounts of the evolution of trade unions. Brentano portrayed trade unions as analogous to guilds but characteristic of a more advanced stage of industrial development. Both were a response to the rise of disorganisation and class conflict in previously harmonious societies. Guilds originated in the family and merely extended the scope of the recognised community. Trade unions had emerged from the ravages of industrialisation with its concomitant class antagonisms. They were destined, though, to establish the rule of conciliation and thus restore the harmonious community of producers which had existed prior to the guilds' decline into sectional selfishness. However, unlike guilds, trade unions would not degenerate into sectarianism but would instead establish the end of history. Trade unions were a panacea in Brentano for the ills of industrial society. Importantly, they were also peculiarly English. Brentano went to great lengths to stress the precocious Englishness of trade unions and began his book by declaring 'most emphatically' that England was the 'birthplace of guilds' and hence of trade unions.[28] His Whiggishness is deeply apparent in his emphasis on the continuity in origin, intention and ritual between trade unions and guilds. The peroration to his book seamlessly wove

---

[25] L. Brentano, *On the History and Development of Gilds, and the Origin of Trade-Unions* (London, 1870).

[26] G. von Schulze-Gaevernitz, *Social Peace: A Study of the Trade Union Movement in England*, trans. C. M. Wicksteed (London, 1893), and S. & B. Webb, *The History of Trade Unionism* (London, 1894). On Brentano and his school, see J. Thompson, '"A nearly related people": German views of the British labour market, 1870–1900' in D. Winch & P. K. O'Brien, eds., *The Political Economy of British Historical Experience, 1688–1914* (Oxford, 2002), pp. 93–119.

[27] W. S. Jevons, *The State in Relation to Labour* (London, 1882), p. 90.

[28] Brentano, *On the History and Development of Gilds*, p. ix.

together political and economic firsts in tribute to the precocity of English development.[29]

Brentano's work was a curious combination of stage theory, economic determinism and Whiggish insistence on continuity. There was a strong dose of Hegelianism in his story of how the thesis (factory owners) calls forth the antithesis (trade unions), which later produces a synthesis through conciliation in the community of producers. Jevons's distinction between Brentano's political proposals and his history obscures how much politics there was in the history. When orthodox economists like Marshall or Jevons borrowed this history, they were importing and indeed building on a very particular and very progressive view of the past and meaning of trade unionism. This is not to claim that Marshall and Jevons propagated a view of trade unions directly akin to that of Brentano. It is, however, to note some of the assumptions implicit in the synoptic histories of combination they relied upon in trying to make sense of how the labour market worked.

Brentano provided the classic radical historicist account of trade unionism. His book was, however, but one part of the challenge mounted in the 1870s to the universalist assumptions of classical political economy. It is deleterious to an understanding of this assault to divorce the attacks launched by card-carrying historical economists from the criticisms made by positivist social thinkers. Many of the arguments were similar and there was a considerable degree of mutual appreciation. The historicist challenge fostered an increased appreciation of the anomalies and imperfections of the labour market and encouraged an increased emphasis upon collective social action of the kind typified by trade unions. It also, however, produced a more concrete attack on classical theory through the historical study of work and wages.

The most generally admired treatise produced by a historical economist prior to Ashley's economic history was probably Thorold Rogers's *Six Centuries of Work and Wages*.[30] This massive work combined the long-term perspective favoured by those most influenced by the historical method with a statistical enthusiasm widespread in

---

[29] ibid., p. 134.
[30] J. E. Thorold Rogers, *Six Centuries of Work and Wages* (London, 1884).

Victorian England.[31] It served to refute the more dismal assumptions
about wages popularly associated with the prophecies of Malthus. The
mounting numerical evidence of improvements in remuneration cast
increasing doubt on the stationary-state contentions of classical wage-
fund theory. This was, however, less important than the support given
by historical and comparative studies of remuneration to Smith's argument linking wages and productivity. If Rogers provided the strongest
historical support for high-wage theory, it was Brassey's best-seller
On Work and Wages which cemented the comparative case.[32] His
figures were cited and amplified in reviews and newspapers by positivist defenders of trade unionism such as Harrison and Beesly.[33] As
professional railway contractor to the world and amateur economist
and statistician, Brassey's contribution nicely illustrates the confluence
between empirical and theoretical, popular and specialist economic
writing in this period.

Petridis has explored the response by orthodox economists to the
results produced by Brassey and to his proposed law that real labour
costs are geographically invariant. He notes that it was not until the
work of Hobson that the limitations of Brassey's putative law were
properly exposed.[34] Hobson distinguished carefully between the case
for the so-called law and that for the wages–productivity link. It
is worth noting, however, that the evidence for the latter was also
somewhat less than overwhelming. The appeal of high-wages theory
requires further explanation. Hobson observed that there must be a
physical limit to the gains in productivity produced by better pay.
Many previous writers had, however, been prepared to treat the productivity argument for high wages as almost infinitely extendible. This
was, at least in part, because much of the case for the efficacy of better
wages was about mental rather than physical improvements in human
capital. This amelioration was often linked as both symptom and cause
to the process of unionisation. It is here that historical accounts of

---

[31] On statistical enthusiasm, see J. Thompson, 'Printed statistics and the public
    sphere: numeracy, electoral politics and the visual culture of numbers,
    1880–1914' in T. Crook and G. O'Hara, eds., *Statistics and the Public Sphere:
    Numbers and the People in Modern Britain, c. 1800–2000* (Abingdon, 2011),
    pp. 121–43.
[32] T. Brassey, *On Work and Wages* (London, 1872).
[33] F. Harrison, 'Mr Brassey on work and wages', *Fortnightly Review*, 12 new ser.
    (Sep. 1872), 268–86.
[34] Petridis, 'Brassey's law and the economy of high wages', 600–1.

societal evolution and empirical studies of remuneration combined to undermine the assumptions behind wage-fund theories.

Marshall once privately described trade unions as 'a greater glory to England than her wealth'.[35] On other occasions he was, of course, less complimentary, and he had a taste for hyperbole as a letter writer absent from his cautious public pronouncements. It is important to define the nature of Marshall's approval of unions. He was an ardent fan of the older trade unionism and deeply impressed by its capacity for encouraging thrift, foresight and organisation amongst workmen.[36] The beneficial influence of combination was summed up for Marshall in its capacity to raise the *intelligence* of the workman. The education offered by the trade union was peculiarly apt for teaching the workman to appreciate the difficulties and skills of the employer. It was this increased *intelligence* which afforded the probability of productivity gains. Marshall exhibited a marked faith in the power of the education provided by craft unions to improve human capital and indeed human nature.[37] In many of these sentiments, the Marshall of the 1870s was entirely typical of his time.

He was also influenced by historical accounts. In the chapter of the *Principles* on earnings of labour, Marshall remarks that Brentano 'was the first to call attention to several of the points discussed in this chapter'.[38] The analysis of the emergence of guilds in the historical section of *Economics of Industry* and the hopes continually held out for conciliation owe much to Brentano. It is important, however, in tracing the origins of faith in public opinion as an economic regulator to recall that the legacy of historical economics went beyond acting as a solvent on wage-fund theory.

The heart of the historical critique of orthodox political economy was the claim that custom rather than competition informed the behaviour of economic agents.[39] This was sometimes advanced as an argument about the distant past but in its more typical and stronger form it held that classical assumptions about self-interest were only

---

[35] Letter to Caird (5 Dec. 1897), Pigou, ed., *Memorials*, p. 400.
[36] Letter to Caird (22 Oct. 1897), Pigou, ed., *Memorials*, p. 398.
[37] A. Marshall, 'A fair rate of wages', preface to L. Price, *Industrial Peace* (1887), reprinted in Pigou, ed., *Memorials*, p. 225.
[38] Marshall included this comment even in the last edition of the *Principles*. See A. Marshall, *Principles of Economics: An Introductory Volume* (8th edn, London, 1920), p. 569.
[39] On this see Collini, Winch & Burrow, *That Noble Science*, p. 260.

true of the time that had produced them and were only true then because they were the customary. It was further observed that the classical edifice rested on a methodological individualism which had grave difficulties in accounting for institutions and collective action. In an age of monopolies and state intervention, it was clear to historical economists that the conditions postulated by Ricardian political economy had vanished and that the present was better understood through the study of much earlier periods.[40]

The argument that the economic actions of agents could not be explained if regarded as motivated purely by utility-maximising rationality was, of course, also at the core of the influential positivist assault on conventional economics.[41] To a significant extent, positivists and historical economists could be seen as waging the same war against *homo economicus*. It is importantly true, however, that there were subtle differences between the use made by historical economists of the idea of custom and the deployment by positivists of their preferred term of *public opinion*. The notion of custom adopted by historical economists and anthropologists tended to emphasise its timeless lack of self-consciousness.[42] In the hands of the positivist, public opinion was characterised more by acute self-consciousness and interventionism. It was essentially an aspect of modernity and, as such, distinguished from the sleepy antiquity studied by historical economists and ruled by custom. This distinction is crucial to grasping the response of conventional economics to the denial of the primacy of self-interest and the existence of perfect competition.

Orthodox economic thought did not, of course, adopt most of these positions intact. Marginalism indeed can be seen as *more* individualist in its approach and universalist in its ambition than its classical

---

[40] A general account of the emphasis on the rise of monopolies in historical economics is provided in Green, *The Crisis of Conservatism*, pp. 159–84.

[41] Most famously, F. Harrison's articles in the *Fortnightly*. See 'The limits of political economy' and 'The good and evil of trade unionism', *Fortnightly Review*, 3 (Nov. 1865), 33–54.

[42] For anthropologists on custom, consult J. W. Burrow, *Evolution and Society: A Study in Victorian Social Theory* (Cambridge, 1966) and '"The village community" and the uses of history in late nineteenth-century England' in N. McKendrick, ed., *Historical Perspectives: Studies in English Thought and Society in Honour of J. H. Plumb* (London, 1974), pp. 255–84. See also G. W. Stocking, *Victorian Anthropology* (New York, 1987).

predecessor.[43] Marshallian orthodoxy granted historical economics its own fiefdom of economic history, thus rendering it both independent and irrelevant. It was difficult, however, to argue convincingly that the labour market operated according to the tenets of perfect competition. The 'growth of monopoly' and the emergence of collective bargaining clearly posed immense difficulties for such an account. Theoretical innovations in the analysis of bilateral monopoly revealed the essential indeterminacy of the wage bargain.[44] It was thus increasingly difficult to exorcise the ghost of custom from the machine of economic analysis.

Conventional economists responded in a variety of ways to this impasse. Jevons declared as early as 1882 that economics could offer no help in explaining short-term movements in wage rates.[45] This was, however, a greater concession than he perhaps realised and not one often made by others. Economists in fact continued to discuss strikes and wages with ever greater frequency. Generally keen to demonstrate the relevance of their subject, they perhaps had little choice.

The most common reply to the twin challenge of indeterminacy and custom was to invoke the deity worshipped by positivism, namely public opinion. In doing this, orthodox economists were not simply capitulating. Schulze-Gaevernitz noted that public opinion never became as central to orthodox economics as it was to positivist social philosophy.[46] Furthermore, the public to whom academic economists appealed differed markedly in composition and character from that of the positivists. It is true, however, that the new emphasis on the regulatory capacity of public opinion registers the growing prevalence of holistic modes of thought and thus qualifies the *increasing* individualism Harris takes to characterise neo-classicism.

We have examined the influence of positivism and historicism on the position of trade unions in consensual orthodox economics. It is now time to consider more explicitly the impact of marginalism. It has been conventional to relate the emergence of the marginal paradigm within economics to the process of professionalisation.[47]

[43] As suggested by J. Harris, *Private Lives, Public Spirit: Britain 1870–1914* (Oxford, 1993), p. 224.

[44] F. Y. Edgeworth, *Mathematical Psychics: An Essay on the Application of Mathematics to the Moral Sciences* (1881), pp. 29–30, 44–5.

[45] Jevons, *The State in Relation to Labour*, p. 155.

[46] Schulze-Gaevernitz, *Social Peace*, p. 257.

[47] J. Maloney, *Marshall, Orthodoxy and the Professionalisation of Economics* (Cambridge, 1985).

This approach attributes coherence, clarity and inevitability to processes better seen as complex, gradual and ambiguous. The early contents of the *Economic Review* or the *Economic Journal* do not support a high estimation of their role in either the genesis of neo-classicism or the incipient professionalisation of the discipline. Lively economic debate continued in the pages of the great nineteenth-century reviews. It is true, nonetheless, that work deemed of first-rate importance *within* the field was more likely than before to appear in periodicals read mostly by other economists. This tendency had important ramifications for the capacity of economists to act as political commentators whilst retaining their economic credentials. In assessing the significance of marginalism, it is important to relate an increase in professional authority to the consequent loss of cultural centrality.

The most far-reaching of the innovations of neo-classical economics was its redefinition of the notion of value. It was the notion of the marginal increment which permitted the mathematical treatment so important to economics' claim to scientific status and authority. However, marginalism promised more than mathematisation. It promised a widening of the scope of theory which ran directly counter to the relativist caveats of historicist critics. The principle of substitution made possible an integrated account of the derived demand for factors. It seemed plausible that marginalism could provide a unified analysis of the price mechanism for allocating scarce resources, whether goods, capital or labour. This ambition issued in the elaboration of the marginal productivity theory of distribution in the 1890s.[48] It was argued that the derived demand for factors could be considered in terms of their marginal productivity, just as demand for goods could be understood with regard to their marginal value. A vibrant debate in the pages of the *Quarterly Journal of Economics* united a fledgling Anglo-American academic community in the construction of a newly comprehensive account of distribution.

The arrival of the *Quarterly Journal of Economics* and the emergence of a scholarly community make plain the contribution of marginalism to the birth of the profession. It is important, though, to establish the limitations of the new economics. Marginalism provided a powerful theory of demand but had much less to say about supply. A

---

[48] On this process see S. Gordon, 'The wages fund controversy: the second round', *History of Political Economy*, 5, 1 (1973), 14–35.

microeconomic focus on the revealed preferences of consumers placed many of the traditional macroeconomic concerns of the discipline out of conceptual reach. In particular, the kind of macroeconomic questions about the aggregate level of remuneration to which wage-fund theory was a response were left conspicuously hanging. Marshall was aware of these shortcomings and sought to combine the best of the neo-classical account of supply with the new theory of demand.[49] He was reliant, however, on the twin assumptions of perfect competition and stasis. He recognised the need for a dynamic consideration of the impact of trade unions but perpetually postponed its adumbration for the promised second volume of the *Principles*.[50]

Petridis has presented the treatment of trade unions by British economists in this period as one of malign neglect.[51] L. L. Price appears as the one figure to face up to the challenge of understanding collective bargaining. Petridis underestimates, however, the prevalence of belief in the indeterminacy of wage bargains under the increasingly common conditions of bilateral monopoly. Jevons and Edgeworth provided mathematical demonstrations of such indeterminacy which were widely thought to be authoritative.[52] Petridis exaggerates the extent to which economists ignored trade unions. Textbook accounts of the principles of the discipline did tend to marginalise institutions of imperfect competition, but elsewhere economists displayed an awareness of the problems of bilateral monopoly and made rudimentary attempts to gauge the factors determining the result of the wage bargain. Such efforts reveal the impact of Marshall. They also display a considerable willingness to appeal to public opinion to explain remuneration.

In his presidential address to the Economic Science and Statistics section of the British Association in 1890, Marshall chose to dilate upon 'some aspects of competition'.[53] The concluding section of his

---

[49] Note Marshall's letter to Clark of 2 July 1900 in which he remarks that 'the von Thunen doctrine' (or marginal productivity theory) 'covers only a very small part of the real difficulties of the wages problem', reprinted in Pigou, ed., *Memorials*, p. 413.

[50] A. Petridis, 'The trade unions in the Principles: the ethical versus the practical in Marshall's economics', *Economie Appliquée*, 43, 1 (1990), 161–86.

[51] A. Petridis, 'The economic analysis of trade unions by British economists, 1870–1930', unpublished Ph.D. thesis, Duke University (1974).

[52] Edgeworth, *Mathematical Psychics*, pp. 44–5, and Jevons, *The State in Relation to Labour*, pp. 153–5.

[53] Marshall, 'Some aspects of competition'.

talk was devoted to 'the growing importance of public opinion as an economic force'. Marshall was quick to chide socialists for their exaggeration of the power of public opinion to regulate competition. He went on, however, to note that 'yet, unquestionably, the economists of to-day do go beyond those of earlier generations in believing that the desire of men for the approval of their own conscience and for the esteem of others is an economic force of the first order of importance, and that the strength of public opinion is steadily increasing with the increase and diffusion of knowledge, and with the constant tendency of what had been regarded as private and personal issues to become public and national'.[54] The influence of opinion was not primarily through legislation since 'there are many matters in which public opinion can exercise its influence more quickly and effectively by a direct route than by the indirect route of first altering the law'. He proceeded to argue that 'for all the great changes which our age has seen in the relative proportions of different economic forces, there is none so important as the increase in the *area* from which public opinion collects itself, and in the force which it bears directly upon economic issues'.[55]

Marshall attributed an important role to public opinion. It is significant that he stressed its direct influence rather than the socialist insistence on its statutory embodiment. Trade unions were central to his account of the operation of opinion. Increased federation of employers and employees meant that 'affairs which would only be of local interest are discussed over the whole kingdom'. Furthermore, 'many turbulent little quarrels... are now displaced by a few great strikes; as to which public opinion is on the alert' so that 'each side strives to put itself right with the public'. Marshall argued that the employed had benefited from improvements in communications and that the growth of newspapers for the working classes had brought a more inclusive public into existence. He was personally persuaded that 'in all this the good predominates over the evil' but was concerned to establish that 'in the scientific problem of estimating the forces by which wages are adjusted, a larger place has to be allowed now than formerly to the power of combination, and to the power of *public opinion* in judging, and criticizing, and aiding that combination; and that all these changes tend to strengthen the side of the employees, and to help them to get a substantial... increase of real wages; which they may... so use as

[54] ibid., p. 285.   [55] ibid., p. 286.

to increase their efficiency, and therefore to increase still further the wages which they are capable of earning.'[56]

The democratic impulse in Marshall's advocacy of public opinion should not be exaggerated. He spoke of it as the opinion of the 'average man; that is, of an average member of one of *those classes of society that is* [sic] *not directly and immediately concerned in the question at issue*'. This should not be taken to refer to all those not actually personally involved in a dispute. Marshall went on to provide a classic liberal warning about the consequences of the fracturing of the unitary public. 'In an industrial conflict each side cares for the opinion of the public at large . . . But . . . there is some fear that, when party discipline becomes better organised, those on either side will *again* get to care less for any public opinion save that of their own side . . . there may be no great tendency towards agreement between the two sides as to what are reasonable demands.'[57] The use of the word 'again' was crucial here, for Marshall was anticipating the return to a quasi-feudal society bereft of progressive intelligence. This was a very concrete image, for it was essentially Marshall's view of Britain before free trade.

The most significant aspect of the Marshallian public was that it was a public of consumers. He was particularly horrified by the prospect of a mercantilist guild of producers holding this consumerist public to ransom. He was careful in the *Elements of Economics of Industry* to remark that 'it is true now, as it was at the time of the old Gilds, that . . . the interests of the public are apt to be sacrificed most, when peace reigns in a trade, and employers and employed are agreeing'.[58] Marshall did, of course, acknowledge that most consumers were also producers but, should these roles contradict, the former always took precedence. The primacy of consumption was implicit in the marginalist focus on utility but it was also and more importantly integral to the rhetoric of free trade. Free trade was a liberal creed of sufficient sanctity for Marshall to enter public controversy in its defence.[59] The power of the language of free trade had always derived in part from its appeal to the community of consumers against the selfish interests

---

[56] ibid., pp. 286–7.   [57] ibid., pp. 287–8 (my emphasis).
[58] A. Marshall, *Elements of the Economics of Industry: Being the First Volume of the Elements of Industry* (London, 1892), p. 403.
[59] In the economists' letter to *The Times*, 15 Aug. 1903.

of sectional producers, especially landlords.[60] It provided a powerful tradition of equating consumption with membership of the public.

Marshall discerned the growth of combination and regarded its continuation as inevitable. He was not despairing, however, for its effects 'contain much good as well as much evil'.[61] Nor did the new industrial democracy undermine the importance of competition. Indeed, Marshall succeeded in regarding the spread of unions as heightening the need for a clearer understanding of normal competition. In noting the declining force in many trades of 'direct outside competition', Marshall appealed to public opinion to preserve the reign of competition. Public opinion emerges as a secularised providence whose moral suasion guaranteed the social justice of a reformed market. This faith is most apparent in the conclusion to 'Some aspects of competition', where Marshall divides up the younger economists according to their attitude to competition:

some would not be sorry to see small firms displaced by large, large funds by Trusts, and Trusts by Government departments[;] others, in whom the Anglo-Saxon spirit is stronger, regard these tendencies with very mixed feelings, and are prepared to exert themselves to the utmost to keep Government management within narrow limits . . . In order to preserve what is essential in the benefits of free competition, they are willing to have a great extension of public control over private and semi-public undertakings; but, *above all*, they look to the extension of the *new force of public opinion* as a means of eliminating much of the evil effects of competition, while retaining its good effects.[62]

The extent of Marshall's influence has received thorough examination in recent years.[63] Less attention has been devoted to his moralism. It should be clear, however, from consideration of his use of 'public opinion' that the distinction between his economics and his moralism cannot be credibly sustained.[64] In this, Marshall was both

---

[60] On the evolution of free trade thinking see Howe, *Free Trade and Liberal England*, and Trentmann, *Free Trade Nation*.

[61] Marshall, 'Some aspects of competition', p. 287.

[62] ibid., p. 290 (my emphasis).

[63] See especially Maloney, *Marshall, Orthodoxy and the Professionalisation of Economics*.

[64] The classic lament for the stifling of Marshall's economics by his moralism is that of J. Maynard Keynes: 'Marshall was too anxious to do good' in his *Essays in Biography* (London, 1951), p. 175. Keynes's judgement became conjoined with that of T. Parsons, 'Economics and sociology: Marshall in

typical and influential. This is not to neglect the impact of his revision of wage-fund doctrine. In his article on wages for the co-operative society yearbook, in his participation in the Industrial Remuneration Conference of 1885 and in his evidence before the Royal Commission on Gold and Silver of 1887, Marshall expressed, sometimes indirectly, his opposition to the wage-fund theory.[65] He made it clear that within certain parameters the division of income between employers and employed was a function of comparative bargaining strength. Furthermore, as was suggested earlier, Marshall took very seriously the contentions of high-wage theory. This technical framework commanded great respect. It did, however, also imply the need for an evolved theory of collective bargaining. Marshall never provided this but instead offered an analysis of the realities of imperfect competition which made repeated and insistent reference to the sovereignty of public opinion. It was an account which coincided with that of many of his colleagues.

This becomes immediately apparent through an investigation of the views of the Jevonian and enthusiastic bimetallist H. S. Foxwell. Foxwell produced a pioneering analysis of the roots of unemployment in a lecture on 'Irregularity of employment and fluctuations in prices' published both on its own and in a book in 1886.[66] He emphasised the role of price changes in causing irregularity of employment and advocated bimetallism as a solution to the deflationary instability consequent upon the rise in the value of gold since the 1870s.[67] The place of Foxwell's work in the emerging analysis of unemployment has been well treated.[68] Less attention, however, has been given to his account of the role of 'public opinion'.

relation to the thought of his time', *Quarterly Journal of Economics*, 46 (1931–2), 316–47.

[65] A. Marshall, 'How far do remediable causes influence prejudicially (a) the continuity of employment, (b) the rates of wages?' in the *Industrial Remuneration Conference: The Report of the Proceedings and Papers* (1885), pp. 173–83, 'Theories and facts about wages' in the *Annual of the Wholesale Co-operative Society* (1885), and 'Memoranda and evidence before the Gold and Silver Commission' in the *Official Papers* (1926), pp. 17–197.

[66] H. S. Foxwell, *Irregularity of Employment and Fluctuation of Prices* (Edinburgh, 1886), also published in J. Oliphant ed., *The Claims of Labour* (Edinburgh, 1886).

[67] ibid., p. 24.

[68] J. Harris, *Unemployment and Politics: A Study in English Social Policy, 1886–1914* (Oxford, 1972).

An important strand of Foxwell's work was the argument that the governing power of the public would encourage the stability without which regular employment was impossible. His concern with employment lent predictable urgency to his efforts to refute the socialists. The beneficial influence of public opinion was crucial because it showed that capitalist society could moderate its own excesses. Foxwell followed Rae in criticising socialists for identifying capitalism with the fraudulent world of finance in which 'personal relations, old commercial traditions and public opinion count for less... than the smaller and more local markets'. 'Even on the Stock Exchange', however, 'the power of speculators to injure the public... is generally overrated'. There was little, for Foxwell, which could gainsay the power of public opinion.[69]

Like Marshall, Foxwell regarded the state as 'the ultimate and supreme expression of public opinion', but, also like Marshall, he preferred the direct exercise of public opinion to its promulgation by the state. Regarding the state as the embodiment of opinion tended to denude it of importance and even at times to signal its conquest by civil society. Foxwell suggested that

it would be a mistake to burden the State too much with the duty of direct control. All that is necessary is that the control should be exerted in the public interest, with due intelligence and with practical efficiency. These conditions secured, the more we can decentralise control the better. It may be applied by voluntary associations, by trade organisations, or by municipal authority; perhaps best and most effectively of all, by *educated* public opinion.[70]

He went beyond Marshall in his enthusiasm for vertical organisation by trade along the lines of 'what the gilds did for the mediaeval industries'.[71] Foxwell was less anxious than Marshall about the prospect of a confiscatory alliance of producers because, unlike Marshall, he took unemployment seriously and because he had, if anything, even more confidence in the governing force of opinion.[72]

'Socialists and progressive reformers alike have insisted on the necessity of control. But as public opinion gathers strength, it becomes

[69] Foxwell, *Irregularity of Employment*, p. 60.
[70] ibid., p. 73 (my emphasis).   [71] ibid., p. 77.
[72] On Marshall's complacency about unemployment consult R. C. Matthew, 'Marshall and the labour market' in J. Whitaker, ed., *Centenary Essays on Alfred Marshall* (Cambridge, 1990), pp. 14–43.

evident that one of the best forms of control is that secured by publicity.'[73] Foxwell counselled that 'if the state instead of trying in a clumsy way to remove abuses, would content itself with publishing the facts, public opinion would deal with them much more effectively'.[74] The primary purpose of state intervention was to furnish public opinion with the requisite information. While the reign of public opinion rendered collectivism unnecessary, it also made democracy compatible with good government and refuted its conservative opponents. Foxwell noted:

It has been well remarked by a critic of Sir Henry Maine's *Popular Government*, that the essence of democracy is not so much government by the many, which is impossible, as publicity, which makes public opinion effective, and public interests supreme. Nothing is more certain than that, with the advance of democracy, publicity must become the order of the day. Publicity and organisation, no doubt; but publicity, I think, even more than organisation. It is the necessary protection against fraud, against falsification, against oppression; the first condition of self-help as well as of intelligent charity. It is even more indispensable as the exterminator of corruption.[75]

The last was especially important because the American example had been so often taken to prove the inextricable link between democratic institutions and the corruption of public life. It is revealing that Foxwell contrasts the rule of opinion with government by the many. The distinction lay not only in the difference between government and influence but also in that between the educated and the many. For Foxwell, 'public opinion' was coextensive with '*civilised* opinion'. The 'light of civilised opinion' would eliminate 'the worst abuses of modern society', which were dependent on the cloak of secrecy. Foxwell could become positively messianic in his hostility to secrecy:

Imagine the result in such cases as those of sweating, falsification, and unhealthy conditions of employment, if the law of libel permitted the publication of the facts and names, and the products were traced and identified. There is enough common humanity in the English *consumer* to ensure the commercial ruin of men to whom such malpractices were brought home. The fault is not with public morality. Moral opinion cannot operate till there is cognisance of the facts. Secrecy has crept into and corrupted trade, just as it has complicated and confused transactions in land. In both cases

---

[73] Foxwell, *Irregularity of Employment*, p. 87.
[74] ibid., p. 85.   [75] ibid., p. 89.

it is as foreign to old English practice as it is to natural healthy instincts. In this as in other matters, we are likely to revert to the more popular habits of an earlier period. The age of secrecy is gone.[76]

Here again moral and consumer opinion are treated as identical. Foxwell was lauding the influence of a community of educated consumers. He was, of course, advancing a relatively inclusive notion of this public which incorporated the views of the employed. 'The crowd was becoming articulate' and its 'moral fashion now rules affairs'. Foxwell hoped that 'it is not yet idle to appeal to the old romantic *noblesse oblige*' but was reassured that 'if ever it should be, we can at any rate rely on the very effective *publicité oblige*'.[77]

For Foxwell as for Marshall, the increasing influence of public opinion and the rise of combination were closely linked. In a paper on the 'growth of monopoly' read to the British Association, Foxwell postulated that 'no class gains more by the rise of these huge firms than the *employees*'. He argued that 'the larger the firm the more effective is the public opinion of the employed', for the more dependent the employer was on their loyalty. Furthermore, 'the master lives in the face of the public' and 'pays the penalty of greatness in his exposure to criticism'. Sweating was thus confined to small workshops, since 'the public opinion of the employed, and the honour of the employer' were sufficient to regulate larger establishments.[78] In general, 'with due publicity, self-help would be far easier, and public opinion would come in to aid the right, and would largely dispense with the need for direct legal control'.[79]

Foxwell and Marshall differed in their beliefs and allegiances. Neither was, however, heavily inclined to historicist analysis. Langford Price was trained by Marshall but moved increasingly towards historical studies and disagreed sharply with the establishment over free trade. Furthermore, he retained throughout his career a serious interest in labour economics. He provided an unusually clear account of the factors determining bargaining strength in industrial disputes considered in terms of bilateral monopoly. 'Public opinion' occupied a central place in Price's portrayal of the bargaining process.

---

[76] ibid., pp. 88–9 (my emphasis).   [77] ibid., p. 90.
[78] H. S. Foxwell, 'The growth of monopoly, and its bearings on the functions of the state', published in *Papers on Current Finance* (London, 1919), p. 271.
[79] ibid., p. 275.

In an address on 'the relations between industrial conciliation and social reform' given to Section F of the British Association in 1889, Price outlined the implications of the new recognition of the legitimacy of trade unions amongst economists and society at large. He argued that

> it implies that employers are more disposed to meet on terms of equality representatives of working-men. It implies that public opinion – a force for good or for evil, the potency of which, if once thoroughly awakened, it is impossible to deny – will sanction, will encourage, and will exercise some moral compulsion to bring about, that meeting. And it also implies that trade unions, occupying a position of acknowledged importance and responsibility, will become more sensible of the duties of that position, will be more ready to abandon an attitude of determined hostility, more disposed to court publicity and to enlist public support and sympathy, more inclined to oppose argument to argument rather than force to force, and to convince public opinion that the strength of the argument, not merely of the force, lies on their side. And here, once again, public opinion cannot fail to exercise some moral compulsion. It may be weak, it may be strong, but it will, beyond a doubt, increase with succeeding years.[80]

The influence of public opinion may have been increasing but was hardly new. In a paper on 'the positions and prospects of industrial conciliation' Price remarked of the dock strike that 'it was no new thing in industrial quarrels for public sympathy to be aroused; and there are few, if any contests where public opinion is not a factor to be considered in favour of one side or the other'.[81]

The consensus within economics about the importance of public opinion is further confirmed by an examination of the views of J. Shield Nicholson. A devoted Smithian, Nicholson was a popular speaker who was frequently invited to address Chambers of Commerce throughout Scotland. His topical lecture on 'strikes and a living wage' in 1893 provides a telling illustration of the importance he attributed to public opinion.

Nicholson's concern was, as always, that strikes should be conducted and resolved 'on business principles'. This required 'not more

---

[80] L. L. Price, 'The relations between industrial conciliation and social reform' reprinted in the *Journal of the Royal Statistical Society*, 53 (June 1890), 295–6.
[81] L. L. Price, 'The position and prospects of industrial conciliation', *Journal of the Royal Statistical Society*, 53 (Sep. 1890), 430.

legislation, but more light'. He went on to develop this theme along what will now be familiar lines:

It is quite true that a board of conciliation or of arbitration cannot enforce its recommendations; but it can throw light upon the subject in dispute, and point out what is for the interest of both parties. And there can be no doubt that the pressure of public opinion would be brought to bear upon the side of justice. The great difficulty now, in bringing public opinion to bear, is that the facts are not known. But if the question had been thoroughly argued by a board of conciliation, and if the contentious matter had been submitted to qualified arbitrators, public opinion would declare strongly against the side that rejected the decision. It is not necessary for the public to know the details, or even the main facts of the case; it is enough if they accept the statement of the arbitrators. Some people profess to think little of the force of public opinion; they want written laws, courts, and penalties to remedy every abuse. But if they would reflect, at every turn of their lives they are more or less under public opinion, and as a matter of fact their conduct is moulded much more by public opinion than by law.[82]

Nicholson sheds an interesting light on the question of the assumed membership of the public. In attacking trade unions for aspiring to operate like trusts, he tried to unsettle the conventional contrast between the people and the public, but in terms which merely under-lined its ubiquity.

Trade Unionists ... wish to act in the style of trusts and syndicates, and to create monopolies. Fortunately, experience shows they are not likely to succeed; if they did succeed, they could only injure the public, and by their own showing at least two-thirds of the public are the working classes themselves. And that is one of the very simple things that is [sic] constantly overlooked. We hear the leaders say to the men: You must make the public feel your power; you must put Glasgow in darkness, and bring London to the verge of starvation. But the public that will suffer are the working classes themselves.[83]

Public opinion was not banished from theoretical discussion before the First World War. Pigou's ground-breaking analysis of collective bargaining in the *Principles and Methods of Industrial Peace* made an important contribution to both imperfect competition theory and

---

[82] J. S. Nicholson, 'Strikes and a living wage' in his *Strikes and Social Problems* (London, 1896), pp. 7–8.
[83] ibid., pp. 12–13.

welfare economics. Its references to public opinion suggest the influence of Pigou's teacher and mentor Alfred Marshall. Pigou was concerned that 'at present... one set of newspapers almost invariably takes the side of the employers and another that of the employed, with the result that the general public is too confused and divided to bring effective pressure to bear upon either'. This was, however, immediately followed by the observation that 'the history of the dock strike... shows that... when it is in any measure united... the moral force of its opinion is very great'. Both remarks come from a section in which Pigou prefers the publication of official reports to elicit the '*sanction of opinion*' over more direct or compulsory intervention.[84]

Given the widespread appeal to 'public opinion' in economic theory the *Times* leader writer's opposition between 'political economy' and 'public sympathy' was misleading. Much of the impetus for the increased reliance on 'public opinion' in accounting for the course of industrial life emerged from within political economy rather than constituting a departure from its teachings. It is true, however, that more technical developments in marginal productivity theory, which denied both public opinion and trade unions an influence on distribution, were casualties of the increasing distance between academic innovation and popular consciousness. It is also true, though, as Marshall recognised, that such work in fact had little to say about the role of collective actors or the realities of imperfect competition.

It is not possible to recapture the role of 'public opinion' in popular political economy solely by attention to academic economics. A broader intellectual context is required that embraces wider currents in social and political thought. This is also true, however, of the attempt to understand developments *within* economics. The emphasis here on positivism and historiography reflects this belief. Political economy still possessed considerable prestige in the second half of the nineteenth century and popular debate cannot be understood except in relation to theoretical developments. Even in the 1890s technical and popular economics were scarcely insulated from each other and can be found happily cohabiting in the pages of periodicals like the *Economic Journal* and *Economic Review*. Amateur economists, usually businessmen or financiers, were frequent contributors to such publications and

---

[84] A. C. Pigou, *Principles and Methods of Industrial Peace* (London, 1905), p. 187.

reinforced the strongly practical cast of much economic discussion. More technical developments exercised a significant influence upon popular political economy. There were, however, others, some of which operated in reaction to political economy, and these will be examined next. It is important to recall, though, that some of these, for instance idealism, were also part of the context in which technical economists thought.

It has already been remarked that the observable increase in wages over the century tended to undermine the credibility of wage-fund theory. This corrosion affected both the longer- and shorter-term versions of the doctrine. Debate raged over whether the history of wages contradicted the view that unions could produce a sustainable increase in remuneration. The evidence before various royal commissions indicated a widespread acknowledgement that some highly unionised trades had witnessed impressive improvements in pay. It was less clear, however, which way, if any, the causal connection between combination and wage rises ran. Sceptics often noted the enormous increase during the previous half-century in the remuneration of domestic servants. The Webbs were keen to parry this objection and noted that the absolute necessity of staff in middle-class homes conjoined with the asset-specificity of domestic employment to place the servant in an unusually powerful bargaining position.[85] In general, however, there is little doubt that it became increasingly plausible and common to link strong unions to improvements in pay.

Economic developments undercut more than just wage-fund theory. The close of the nineteenth century was a period of acute concern about the state of the British economy. Agricultural depression from the 1870s coincided with the loss of export markets to rapidly industrialising rivals. Faith in free trade, invariably regarded as the central tenet of conventional political economy, was shaken. The 'discovery' of poverty in the 1880s led to a re-evaluation of a previously widespread confidence in the distributive justice of the market. Increased levels of industrial federation rendered assumptions about the reign of competition distinctly less convincing. Most importantly, the growing acceptance of the possibility and presence of unemployment was difficult to reconcile with the self-regulating economy presumed by economists. Orthodox political economy was revealed as

[85] S. & B. Webb, *Industrial Democracy*, II, 674–5.

unable to account for or ameliorate the most visible social problem of the time. This could not help but diminish the belief that industrial phenomena such as disputes accorded with the presumptions of political economy.[86]

This economic background provides the context for a relative loss of confidence in the claims of political economy. It cannot, however, explain the *content* of the emerging account of collective bargaining. In particular, it cannot account for the prevalent belief that public opinion would justly and pacifically regulate the course of industrial life. This can only be understood through a rather fuller recovery of the intellectual context of popular discussion of trade unions.

A growing belief that the level of wages was not rigidly prescribed by the laws of supply and demand was increasingly accompanied by a rejection of the claim that the market produced a just rate of wages. This is apparent in the campaign for a 'living wage' which gathered strength in the 1890s. The difficulty was in finding a mechanism which would explain how wage disputes were settled and ideally also ensure that they were resolved fairly. It was this need that 'public opinion' answered. There was, however, something mildly implausible about conferring such an adjudicatory capacity on public opinion and especially in so confidently assuming that its influence would be beneficial. The prevalence of such a view further illustrates the argument of this book that historians have underestimated the survival of positive conceptions of the public into the early twentieth century. It remains in this chapter, however, to explain and document the influence attributed to the socio-political concept of 'public opinion' in ordering commercial and industrial affairs.

The crucial intellectual context for these changes in popular political economy was the rise of more organic and holistic modes of thinking about the newly significant category of society. There were many sources for this increased emphasis on the social.[87] The point that

---

[86] A good summary of these trends and perceptions can be found in Green, *The Crisis of Conservatism*, pp. 27–59.

[87] Important accounts of these developments can be found in J. Harris, *Private Lives, Public Spirit* and 'Political thought and the welfare state 1880–1940: an intellectual framework for British social policy', *Past and Present*, 135 (May 1992), 116–41. See also S. Collini, *Liberalism and Sociology: L. T. Hobhouse and Political Argument in England, 1880–1914* (Cambridge, 1979), M. Freeden, *The New Liberalism: An Ideology of Social Reform* (Oxford, 1978),

requires emphasis is that this heightened awareness of society also led to a denial of the autonomy of the economy and an insistence on the primacy of moral forces in determining the behaviour of economic agents. It became increasingly plausible to attribute to 'public opinion' a role in regulating the economy and thus to claim that, while the economy narrowly conceived was not self-regulating, society might be. This appeal to 'public opinion' was not confined to commentators on the left, but it was perhaps most congenial to liberals and free traders. Conservative historical economists like Cunningham were sometimes less keen to adopt the idiom than their more orthodox colleagues.[88] This was, in part, because, like the socialists, they were more comfortable with a significant enhancement of the role of the state than free trade economists who preferred to trust in the spontaneous play of public opinion. The example of Price indicates, however, that this should be seen as a difference of emphasis rather than a sharp distinction.

The shift in the intellectual climate towards 'popular Platonism' should not be seen as unambiguous or too tightly related to a particular set of doctrines.[89] Serious idealists often did incorporate trade unions into their holistic model of society, but this did not necessarily imply much sympathy for their sectional activities.[90] That said, an emphasis on the moral suasion of the public rather than direct intervention was in keeping with the idealist creed. Belief in the influence of opinion on the economy could coincide with a variety of degrees of sympathy for the actions of trade unions. Idealism was merely part

G. Jones, *Social Darwinism and English Thought* (Brighton, 1980), Searle, *The Quest for National Efficiency*, and P. J. Nicholson, *The Political Philosophy of the British Idealists* (Cambridge, 1990).

[88] Cunningham did have positive things to say about public opinion but was more prepared to see it act through the state. This preference emerges in his support for compulsory arbitration. See Cunningham, *Politics and Economics*, pp. 236–7. Historical economists like Cunningham and Fabians like the Webbs were united in both their attachment to the state and their distaste for the consumerism of much of the rhetoric of public opinion.

[89] On 'the spell of Plato' consult J. Harris, 'Platonism, positivism and progressivism: aspects of British sociological thought in the early twentieth century' in Biagini, ed., *Citizenship and Community*, pp. 343–60.

[90] For instance, B. Bosanquet, *The Philosophical Theory of the State* (London, 1899).

of a wider reorientation in which biological evolutionary metaphors played a significant part.[91]

Recurring to the articles in the *Times* with which we began, it is now possible to see them as a rearguard attempt to defend the sovereignty of an old-fashioned conception of political economy in the face of the observable and applauded influence of public opinion. The decision to refer to public *sympathy* rather than the more common *opinion* reveals a hostility to what the writer clearly regards as the impulsive and sentimental interference of those not directly involved. It was obvious to the *Times* that dockers were 'as little entitled to public sympathy as any class ... can be' for they constituted a 'disclassed residuum ... as nearly as possible valueless to the community'. This assault on the residuum placed them squarely outside the community and, likewise, the public. The public was to be found 'at dinner tables or on the top of the omnibus' and was clearly predominantly middle-class. While 'public sentiment was dead against the Trafalgar Square meetings, ... it ran strongly in favour of the dockers', though it obviously excluded the classes involved in either instance. The public favoured the dockers because their strike 'operated at the East End, where the public did not see it very closely'.[92]

More interesting perhaps than the articles themselves was the correspondence they occasioned. Some respondents lauded the author's vigorous condemnation of the foolishness of the public. Their proposed solution was, however, not reliance upon the laws of political economy but rather the further intervention of opinion. One letter writer counselled readers that

[t]he real lesson of value which the London strike has for us will only become generally apparent when the thoughtful part of the public shall have perceived that the lowest and most ignorant section of our people do not know what their self-interest really is, and, thus perceiving, will gradually bring to bear the all-powerful pressure of public opinion upon capitalists and employers of labour, upon the true 'captains of industry' as Carlyle called them, in order to obtain from them that they shall take the leadership of their own men into their own hands, and out of those of demagogues,

---

[91] On the balance and relationship between Darwinian and idealist influences see Freeden, *The New Liberalism*.
[92] *The Times*, 26 Sep. 1889.

socialistic agitators, and irresponsible chatterers – that they shall be true masters to their men, when, perhaps, the men shall become true servants to their masters.[93]

Those moved to write more positively about the strike espoused a similar confidence in public opinion, observing that 'those who have sympathised with the strikers are now turning their attention to improving the position of those who cannot benefit by the late struggle, and thoughtful, organised effort will surely do much good'. It is striking that such correspondents were distinctly unimpressed by the *Times*'s eulogy to the laws of political economy. M. M. S. remarked that 'admitting all we owe to the older and still revered writers on political economy, very many modifications of their theories have been found necessary, and, however unassailable they might be, without taking into account human feeling, more modern thinkers find that no question even of work and wages can be decided without the influence of sentiment of some kind being taken more or less into consideration'.[94]

The dock strike emerges as a pivotal demonstration of the power of public opinion. It was easier to commend the influence of the public on disputes involving unskilled than skilled labour. The latter had often developed complex systems of wage adjustment that limited the value of non-expert comment. It is notable, however, that even Robert Spence Watson, the doyen of the joint board, while deprecating the importance of outside opinion, insisted that 'enlightened public opinion in favour of industrial peace ... will have great and proper influence'.[95] The great dock strike appeared to provide a vivid illustration of the potency of public opinion, allied to the determination of the men, in securing a wage rise in an industry traditionally regarded as irredeemably casual. Sydney Buxton's introduction to Llewellyn Smith and Vaughan Nash's history of the strike remarked with relish that the 'extraordinary public sympathy evoked on the side of the strikers, was a novel and most satisfactory feature of the time'.[96] Schulze-Gaevernitz's account of the origins of *Social Peace* made increasing mention of public opinion as it entered the 1890s and considered the legacy of the dockers' dispute. He argued that 'the success of the dockers was the signal for a movement which ran through the whole

---

[93] *The Times*, 14 Oct. 1889.   [94] ibid.   [95] *The Times*, 5 Oct. 1889.
[96] Introduction to H. Llewellyn Smith and Vaughan Nash, *The Story of the Dockers' Strike, Told by Two East Londoners* (London, 1890), p. 7.

army of unskilled labour . . . like the dockers, they owe their success to the fact that the solidarity of the working classes has become effective, and to the sympathetic attitude of public opinion'.[97] John Saville has depicted public opinion as merely initially sympathetic to the strikers and stressed instead the hardening of attitudes in its aftermath.[98] This reading is overly dependent on equating 'public opinion' with *Times* editorials but also neglects the more interesting legacy of the strike in reinforcing the belief that public sympathy mattered in industrial disputes.

Disenchantment with wage-fund theory was important in the popular as well as the professional case. Eugenio Biagini has examined the reception of Mill's recantation amongst trade union leaders and labour journalists and dates its advent as a rhetorical slogan to the late 1870s.[99] *The Bee-Hive* first dismissed the doctrine in 1874, but employers' periodicals were noticeably more reluctant to acknowledge that anything had changed. *Capital and Labour* remained staunchly committed to wage-fund theory throughout its existence.[100] There is evidence, however, that less partisan opinion was distancing itself from the doctrine by the close of the 1870s. In a distressed presidential address on the state of political economy in 1878, Bonamy Price warned the National Association for the Promotion of Social Science of the unfortunate inclination of economics 'to give a scientific form to its teachings'. He illustrated by recalling that 'a wage fund of the most definite amount, incapable of all expansion, was announced as the law of their labour and the condemner of their conduct to men on strike, who nevertheless, on previous occasions, by striking had extorted the payment of higher wages'. Bonamy Price's admission was rare amongst the enthusiasts of the Social Science Association. It is noteworthy, however, that doubts about wage-fund theory had afflicted such a bastion of classical political economy before the end of the 1870s.[101]

---

[97] Schulze-Gaevernitz, *Social Peace*, p. 273.

[98] J. Saville, 'Trade unions and free labour: the background to the Taff Vale decision' in A. Briggs and J. Saville, eds., *Essays in Labour History* (London, 1960), pp. 317–51.

[99] Biagini, 'British trade unions and popular political economy'.

[100] *The Bee-Hive*, 3 Jan. 1874.

[101] *Transactions of the National Association for the Promotion of Social Science* (1879), 121.

The proceedings of the Industrial Remuneration Conference indicate that defenders of the wages fund could still be found in 1885.[102] In tracing ideas about public opinion as an economic force, the evidence and reports produced by the various royal commissions on labour are particularly useful. There was much empirical debate in the proceedings of the 1867 Commission over the impact of trade unions on wage rates but there was little explicit dissension from the tenets of wage-fund theory and scarce reference to 'public opinion'. The union boycott of the 1874 Commission ensured that it would be dominated by employers wishfully asserting the primacy of political economy. It was observed previously that Marshall's evidence to the Gold and Silver Commission of 1887 rested on a rejection of the inherited notion of the wages fund. In his remarks to the Commission on the Aged Poor in 1893, Marshall was characteristically concerned to refute the appeals to wage-fund theory made by trade unionists in advocating the eight-hour day. Marshall claimed that 'many of the working men believe that they can raise the aggregate of wages by merely diminishing the supply of work; they believe that there is . . . a sort of work fund, and that if one man is allowed to work overtime he takes away from one of his neighbours a certain amount of work that that person might have done'.[103] Such arguments remind us of the element of opportunism in political appeals to economics, but the sparsity and lack of resonance of the trade union case underline the eclipse of wage-fund theory by the early 1890s. This is apparent in the reports and recommendations of the 1891–4 Commission on labour.

The majority report, in which Marshall had a hand, was a forthright expression of the position of post-wage-fund labour economics. Much was made of the prevalence of wage boards and sliding scales but the report insisted that even in their absence 'the wage rate is settled, partly by *custom*, partly by the comparative amount of the demand for and supply of labour, partly by occasional temporary combinations on the part of the workmen to make a particular demand'.[104] Custom was the term used in this instance but more often the Commissioners invoked the assistance of public opinion. In preferring mediation over arbitration, they suggested that 'some outside agency . . . might

[102] For example, *Industrial Remuneration Conference*, p. 393.
[103] A. Marshall, *Official Papers*, ed. J. M. Keynes (London, 1926), p. 227.
[104] *Report of the Royal Commission on Labour*, Parliamentary Papers, XXXV (1894), p. 47.

sometimes make and even publish recommendations as to the course which should be followed' and so facilitate 'what may be termed arbitration by public opinion'.[105] In summarising the present industrial situation the report noted with relief that 'formal collective agreements between the representatives of great associations' were 'enforceable by public opinion'.[106] The 'concluding observations' to the majority report's recommendations nicely capture the centrality of public opinion to its case:

A more cordial understanding, and one based on a better knowledge of the relations between employers and employed, is growing up. This better knowledge is passing outside the ranks of the combatants themselves, and is tending to spread throughout the nation; and the public opinion thus developed re-acts upon special industrial disputes and operates to bring about a pacific solution of them.[107]

The importance of opinion outside the ranks of the productive classes is evident in this quote. Those commissioners who advocated making collective agreements legally binding did so in part because 'the judgement would be promoted by a competent authority, would be made publicly, have tangible results, and thus greatly help to form public opinion.'[108] An emphasis on the impact of public opinion is also apparent in some of the evidence before the Royal Commission on Trade Disputes and Trade Combinations of 1903–6. The employer Sir Benjamin Browne, whose answers were not unsympathetic to trade unions, bewailed the baleful influence of public opinion in fostering militancy:

Strikes are very much fostered by the action of outsiders and by an unhappy public opinion, which is very often and very wrongly in their favour, and of course the highest opinion in the country is that of Parliament, and to legislate to facilitate strikes is to make workmen more and more look upon strikes as the proper and right way of settling their disputes, and that applies to employers also, whereas in my mind we more and more find that the disputes can be settled without stoppages at all.[109]

---

[105] ibid., p. 49.   [106] ibid., p. 54.   [107] ibid., p. 113.

[108] 'Observations appended to the Report by the Chairman, Mr David Dale, Sir Michael E. Hicks-Beach, Mr Leonard H. Courtney, Sir Frederick Pollock, Mr Thos. H. Ismay, Mr George Livesey, and Mr William Tunstill', p. 118.

[109] *Evidence to the Royal Commission on Trade Disputes and Trade Combinations*, Parliamentary Papers, LVI (1906), p. 183.

Such sentiments were, however, less pervasive than the more positive conception of the influence of public opinion which has been explored in this chapter. It could be argued that commentators lauded the moral suasion of public opinion when they were confident that it would support their interests. Thus, the Labour Correspondent of the Board of Trade observed in 1889 that

> if it were always easily possible to determine on what side right lies in such struggles, a powerful public opinion might do much to limit the number and duration of trade disputes. Unfortunately, however, public opinion has generally been too one-sided to act as a mediatorial agency on all occasions, for it has generally assumed, without due inquiry, that the workmen were in the wrong.[110]

The contrast with Sir Benjamin Browne's subsequent remark is obvious. It is striking, however, that they were in accord over the importance of the public's judgement. Nor is it in fact the case that attitudes to public opinion were simply determined by the calculation of whether it was likely to work in one's favour or not. This is made clear by the debates on conciliation bills and other trade union legislation in parliament between 1896 and 1906. The belief that public opinion would act justly was widespread in the Commons even amongst employers who might have reason to resent its intrusion. It was undoubtedly a view which appealed most but not exclusively to liberals. This was, of course, unsurprising given the liberal provenance of positive conceptions of the public. The debates make clear the resilience and resonance of a traditionally liberal appreciation of public opinion. The focus in what follows will be on the debates surrounding the conciliation bills of 1895 and 1896.

Speakers on both sides of the House were quick to cite the beneficial effect of public opinion in arguing for the extension of conciliation. The Tory democrat Alfred Rollitt proposed the second reading of his Board of Conciliation Bill with a paean to the 'extremely useful and able work' done by conciliation boards, in which he stressed that 'it was essential that there should be a body which, by eliciting the facts, would inform public opinion accurately, and so bring to bear upon the settlement of the dispute a force which none could ultimately resist'.[111]

---

[110] *Report on the Strikes and Lock-outs of 1888*, Parliamentary Papers, LXX (1889), p. 17.
[111] *Parliamentary Debates*, 4th ser., XXXVII (1896), col. 647.

Rollitt emerges, however, as a relatively tepid advocate of efforts to develop the guiding force of opinion. The conservative Francis Sharp Powell stated during the second reading of the government's conciliation bill that 'public opinion was prompt to pronounce upon one side or the other in these trade disputes, and that the side upon which public opinion pronounced must succeed'.[112] In a debate on the liberal bill of the previous year, Pease had assured the House that 'there was nothing which terminated a strike so quickly as public opinion'.[113] Donald Crawford, MP for Lanarkshire North East, remarked in the following year that 'the force of public opinion in these cases was one of the most important elements in the question', while the coal owner James Joicey reiterated that 'public opinion was a most important matter in connection with these disputes'.[114] It was generally agreed that public opinion would swiftly settle disputes and that, duly educated, it would do so fairly. Bryce provided the most emphatic version of the 'public opinion' argument in his contention that the board should produce reports *ex parte*, for 'as soon as the Report was published, public opinion would be so strong against the recalcitrant side that they would be compelled to consider their position'.[115]

It was perhaps the Trades Disputes Act of 1906 which most clearly enacted the principles inherent in the new emphasis on 'public opinion' as the regulator of economic life.[116] The Act was essentially an extension of the precepts guiding the Conciliation Act of ten years earlier. As the chapter has sought to demonstrate, a full understanding of this legislation requires the recovery of the intellectual context in which such a faith in the economic impact of public opinion could seem plausible. It remains, however, to examine in detail the engagement of trade unionists and labour activists with the idea of 'public opinion' in an era in which its power was widely seen as growing in both scope and intensity.

[112] *Parliamentary Debates*, 4th ser., XLII (1896), col. 436.
[113] *Parliamentary Debates*, 4th ser., XXXI (1895), col. 398.
[114] For Crawford & Joicey, see *Parliamentary Debates*, 4th ser., XXXIV (1895), col. 841.
[115] *Parliamentary Debates*, 4th ser., XLII (1896), col. 429.
[116] J. Thompson, 'The genesis of the 1906 Trades Disputes Act: liberalism, trade unions and the law', *Twentieth Century British History*, 9, 2 (1998), 175–200.

5 | Representing labour: The Labour movement, politics and the public

This chapter examines the relationship between attempts to represent labour and the idea of the 'public'. It develops the themes raised in Chapter 1 by scrutinising the efforts of those who sought to speak for labour to define the labour interest, and the relationship between labour's emerging identity and its conception of the public. It thus builds upon work examining popular attitudes to party and the importance of independence in the politics of the period.[1] The chapter focuses upon both labour politicians and trade unionists in order to assess the scope of the labour movement in these years. It is argued that labour's identity was very much that of a movement, rather than a party.[2] This self-perception in part derived from and related to the existing self-image of radical liberalism. It helps explain and contextualise the wealth of anti-party rhetoric in labour circles now restored to historiographical prominence. The idea of the labour interest as beyond or outside politics provided a recurring sense of distance from party and from much of conventional politics. The chapter's first major task is thus to establish the boundaries of the labour interest before 1914.

The second major theme of the chapter is the relationship between the idea of the labour interest and the category of the public. Here, again, it is labour perceptions that constitute the object of study. How did the labour movement, in both the parliamentary and industrial spheres, seek to represent the relationship between itself and the public? The growth and history of labour representation at Westminster provides one dimension of this struggle. Equally important, and closely related, however, were efforts to speak for labour's interests during periods of industrial strife. Many labour activists combined scepticism

---

[1] See especially Lawrence, *Speaking for the People*.
[2] A point suggested in J. Thompson, 'A people's voice?', *History Workshop Journal*, 47 (1999), 283–4.

towards a consumerist, even middle-class, public, with a measure of faith in the reformist credentials of a broader thinking and reading public. The rise of trusts, large-scale industrial unrest and syndicalist advocacy of productionism, heavily publicised by the established media, brought the relationship between labour and the consuming public into sharper focus, especially after 1910. Syndicalists were chastised by mainstream labour figures for ignoring the interests of the working class as consumers. Yet the assumption of the daily newspapers that the public was hostile to the strikes was also challenged on the grounds that the vast majority of the public was working-class. While the left, most obviously industrial unionists but also populists like Blatchford, sought to emphasise the productionist interests of the workers rather than the capitalist concerns of consumers, more liberal Labour politicians stressed the interests of workers as consumers and attacked the coal owners in 1912 for passing on wage increases to the public. It was very difficult for a fledgling Labour party to articulate its productionist concerns within a liberal free trade political culture, particularly when many in the party owed a considerable debt to that culture.

The chapter begins with Labour's own self-image. It examines changing rhetorics, of labour representation in particular, to elucidate the meaning of the labour interest before 1914. Attention is paid to arguments about the status of brain workers, views of the co-operative movement and the status of the TUC as a labour parliament. As throughout this study, the emphasis is upon moments of contestation and the shape of ensuing debate rather than the views of individual thinkers or schools. Discussion of labour representation, however, stretched throughout this period, and provides a useful barometer of change over time.

Imagining the labour interest

The institutional embodiment of the labour interest in these years was widely assumed to be the Trades Union Congress. In its initial incarnation from 1868, the TUC was designed in part to act as a plebeian equivalent to the National Association for the Promotion of Social Science. The Social Science Association was a mid-Victorian forum for the discussion of social issues, intended as a means of both educating and representing public opinion upon key questions. Significant political figures were regular attenders at its gatherings, and its debates were copiously reported in the national and regional press. Papers were given and followed by lengthy periods of discussion.[3] Trade unionism was a recurrent topic of debate, but by the late 1860s trade unionists themselves were increasingly unhappy with the terms in which it was discussed, and felt marginalised in these debates. Early trade union gatherings included elaborate debates on formal papers, not unlike the structure of NAPSS meetings. In this short-lived form, the TUC sought to persuade the Royal Commission on the labour laws that, in the words of George Potter, 'they [the TUC] were right and that the public were wrong'.[4]

Soon, however, the TUC evolved into a meeting of trade unionists which increasingly cast itself as a representative assembly of the labour interest. In adopting this position, the TUC was not simply portraying itself as a pressure group rather than an educator of the public. It increasingly sought to act as a kind of labour parliament, and to encourage others to see it in these terms. In doing so, it certainly aimed to represent the labour interest, but also to enlighten outsiders through the extensive coverage its debates received. Papers were no longer given, but elaborate arguments, not merely in the presidents' introductory address, littered the debates, very much on the Westminster model. The character of TUC debate must be understood in relation to the popularity of model parliaments and debating societies in late Victorian political culture remarked upon by Matthew.[5] This notion of the TUC as a labour parliament merits further scrutiny.

In 1881, William Crawford, from the chair, described Congress as a 'Labour Parliament'.[6] The report of the Parliamentary Committee in 1892 referred to the TUC as 'this Labour Parliament', and lauded 'the confidence . . . already won from the general public'.[7] This notion of the Congress's dignity shaped the regulation of debate. In 1907, the president A. H. Gill censured a delegate for his language on the

---

[3] Goldman, *Science, Reform and Politics in Victorian Britain*, and 'The Social Science Association.

[4] *TUC Annual Report, 1871*, pp. 11–12.

[5] Matthew, 'Rhetoric and politics in Britain', and McKibbin, 'Why was there no Marxism in Britain?' in *Ideologies of Class*, pp. 21–3.

[6] *TUC Annual Report, 1881*, p. 6.   [7] *TUC Annual Report, 1892*, p. 25.

grounds that, 'the terms are not Parliamentary; you will not use them'.[8] By 1912 there was an air of stating the obvious about the Mayor of Newport's declaration that 'I fully recognise the great importance of this large industrial assembly'. He went on to note, 'It is well and truly entitled to the name of the Great Parliament of Labour. (Cheers.)'.[9]

This description of the TUC as a labour parliament secured considerable, though not universal, assent outside the ranks of labour. It was noted by some that trade unionists remained a minority of workers, though the movement was growing significantly throughout the period. Trade unionists could cast themselves as the leaders of labour, and as the pick of workers, most endowed with foresight, character and organisational prowess. The Royal Commissions of the period, along with the operations of the labour department of the Board of Trade, increasingly utilised the testimony and expertise of trade unionists. It is important to evaluate the significance and implications of the TUC's purported role as a parliament of labour.

The claim that the TUC amounted to a labour parliament cast the labour interest as both unified and various. A parliament of labour, replete with majority votes and procedural wrangles, implied the existence of a variety of interests that required mediation through the democratic process. Yet the TUC was also keen to present labour as a unified interest, speaking with one voice, namely that of the TUC. Over time the parliamentary committee secured greater control over Congress. The tradition of electing a local president was abandoned, and voting after 1895 reflected union membership, cementing the power of coal and cotton within the union movement. Events in 1895 reflected concerns about ILP infiltration and the complex requirements of 'independence', but also embodied a notion of representation which set greater store by numerical strength than did the parliamentary system.[10] It had implications for arguments about labour representation in parliament. Debates within the TUC on this question require consideration.

From its earliest days, motions were debated at the TUC demanding labour representation in the Commons. Walton's 1872 motion insisted that 'working men [were] best qualified to give expression to the wants and wishes of the working classes', so that 'the interests

---

[8] *TUC Annual Report, 1907*, p. 145.	[9] *TUC Annual Report, 1912*, p. 44.
[10] On 1895, see Lawrence, *Speaking for the People*, pp. 215, 252–3.

of labour may have the same attention in the House of Commons as . . . the other interests represented there'.[11] The appeal was not for a specific body of principles to be represented in the Commons but rather for the labour interest to be represented. This could only be done, it was argued, by working men. Established theories of representation regarded members of parliament as representative not merely of their constituents but of the nation as a whole. The language of interests, rooted in eighteenth-century traditions of country politics, ran counter to such views, regarding members as representative of those interests, whether of the railways or the City, from which they sprang and to which they were beholden.[12] This notion of direct representation challenged the credentials of indirect or virtual representation. In its strong form, the argument implied real scepticism towards liberal conceptions of representative government.

Appeals for labour representation faced indictment as mere class representation. The doctrine of interests insisted, however, that class representation was inherent in the composition of the Commons. So Potter and Kane suggested in 1874 when moving the motion that 'as all interests are represented in the House of Commons, except the great interest of labour . . . the time has arrived . . . to secure direct representation of labour in Parliament'.[13] The difficulties involved in this position are apparent in Broadhurst's argument in 1875 that 'they did not desire class representation – (hear, hear). They simply wished to protest against class exclusion'.[14] This was a popular if problematic position, reflected in the demand of these years for a labour presence in parliament rather than representation concomitant with numerical weight in the population as a whole.

Broadhurst was keen to distinguish labour representation from politics. Enduring attachment to Liberal and Unionist politics within the labour movement underpinned this position, which militated against the creation of a Labour party. In 1885, Broadhurst rebutted understandable criticism of his support for liberal measures by claiming that 'he had never imported politics into his actions; his whole course had been based upon the rights of labour'.[15] Fenwick similarly asked,

---

[11] *TUC Annual Report, 1872*, p. 36.
[12] See J. Harris, 'Labour's political and social thought' in D. Tanner, P. Thane & N. Tiratsoo, *Labour's First Century* (2000), pp. 8–9.
[13] *TUC Annual Report, 1874*, p. 28.
[14] *TUC Annual Report, 1875*, p. 18.   [15] *TUC Annual Report, 1885*, p. 24.

'were there not already enough and to spare of political parties in the country?'[16] The birth of the parliamentary Labour party clearly involved a rethinking of the value of party in representing the labour interest. This process was, of course, bound up with strategic considerations, and with the need to defend the legal position of trade unions. Before 1914, however, the importance of labour representation endured. The identity of Labour expressed in labourism will be examined further in discussion of the political Labour party before 1914. We need now to explore more fully the concept of direct representation.

The repeated efforts in parliament to legislate on accidents to workmen provided a series of opportunities for labour spokesmen to speak for the labour interest. One interesting aspect of these debates is the parliamentary response to such claims. Gladstone spoke for many in asserting that 'the working men of this country were happily, to a certain extent, directly represented in that House'. He acknowledged that 'they were morally and indirectly represented to a much larger extent by the intelligence and philanthropy of many Members, among whom were many great employers of labour', but noted that 'their direct representation being small, it was natural that they should view, partly, indeed, with confidence, and partly, also, with jealousy, a reference of the Bill to a Committee upstairs'.[17] During the debates of the 1880s and 1890s on employers' liability and workmen's compensation, special significance could be accorded to those who, in the words of Colonel Denny, 'directly represented labour'.[18] Deference to the views of labour members was not general, nor was acknowledgment of their distinctive relationship to the issues, but in practice direct representation was often taken to be a reality. The advent of Labour as a parliamentary force increased members' readiness to confer a special legitimacy on the views of labour representatives, as evidenced by discussions of labour unrest after 1910.

The debates of the early Labour party constitute a significant arena in which the movement sought to define its scope. Generations of historians have discussed the formation of a parliamentary party, and the intention here is not simply to revisit these arguments. Instead, the aim

[16] *TUC Annual Report, 1887*, p. 31.
[17] *Parliamentary Debates*, 3rd ser., vol. CCXLIV, cols. 1785–6.
[18] *Parliamentary Debates*, 4th ser., L (1897), cols. 88–9.

is to discern the conception of labour, and its interest, evident in these discussions. Some participants in the debates, notably John Burns, were clearly uncomfortable with the thrust towards independent organisation associated particularly with Keir Hardie. Burns complained at the Labour Representation Committee meeting of 1900 about the obsession with 'working-class boots, working-class trains, working-class houses, and working-class margarine', arguing that 'they ... should consider parties and policies apart from all class organisations'.[19] More socialist participants repeatedly urged the need for the party to adopt an explicitly socialist platform rather than focus upon Labour representation. It was, however, labour representation which provided what unity the movement possessed, and which served as the most popular definition of the new organisation's purpose.

The object of the 1900 gathering was a resolution 'in favour of working-class opinion being represented in the Commons by men sympathetic with the aims and demands of the Labour movement'. Early articulations of this need continued to emphasise that 'every interest was represented and protected in that House but the interest of labour'.[20] W. J. Davis stressed in 1902 that 'in the ranks of labour are men of exceptional ability', suggesting that it was the exclusion of labour representatives by the established parties which required correction by independent organisation. In these early days, anti-party aspirations mingled with support for labour representation which, it was hoped, announced the supersession of mere party politics. Davis yearned for 'a State such as Macaulay says existed in Rome:– "Then none was for a Party; then all were for the State; then the great man helped the poor, and the poor man loved the great"'. These sentiments should not be dismissed as mere collaborationism, for Davis added the caveat that, unlike direct Labour representatives, Chamberlain lacked the 'practical knowledge' without which none could voice 'the true conditions of Labour'.[21]

It was 'practical knowledge' that lay at the heart of the labour interest. As R. W. Jones of the upholsterers argued in 1900, 'however sympathetic a man might be with their aims, if he had not actually been a worker he could not understand the needs and aspirations of

---

[19] *Labour Representation Committee* (1900), p. 11.   [20] ibid., pp. 8, 10.
[21] *Labour Representation Committee* (1902), pp. 17, 19.

the working classes'.[22] There were groups, notably the Fabians, who failed this test, but whose revisionist socialism permitted their inclusion in the party. But the movement's conception of the labour interest remained strongly rooted in the experience of manual labour. It was, as noted in 1902, 'the general interests of the wage-earners' which required representation. There was here an insistence on the irrelevance of sectional distinctions, explicit in the claim that 'it is the wage-earner, and not only the miner, the engineer, or the railway servant who needs representation'.[23] This was not, of course, always evident in the actual composition of the party, or the TUC, but it was central to the construction of the labour interest. Groups like the unionised shop assistants who were not traditionally regarded as workers had to adopt the terminology of labourism. W. C. Anderson argued that, though 'in the eyes of the law the shop assistant was not a worker', actually 'the shop assistants desired to rank with the wage-earners of the land'.[24] Key architects of the new party, especially Hardie, were wont to define its constituency as not so much workers, as industrial workers, identified as 'the democracy'. After the 1906 general election, Ramsay MacDonald rejoiced that 'they had a voice given out from the democracy that at any rate, in some instances, seemed as if it came from the heavens itself'.[25]

The importance attached to waged industrial work in labour's self-image is apparent in relations between trade unionists and socialist forces. There were, clearly, significant ideological differences between these groups, but the constant recourse to talk of 'labour' by trade unionists is striking. The cotton leader, T. Ashton, contended in 1903: 'If the Trade Unionists and workers generally would only ally themselves to the movement and go upon Trade Unionist lines, and keep clear of all "isms," except Labourism and Trade Unionism, he believed there was a great prospect of getting Labour members into Parliament'.[26] The sensitivities manifest in such remarks were well understood by Hardie, who replied by urging, 'Let them have done with Liberalism and Toryism and every other "ism" that was not

[22] *Labour Representation Committee* (1900), pp. 10–11.
[23] *Labour Representation Committee* (1902), p. 11.
[24] *Labour Representation Committee* (1906), p. 61.
[25] *Labour Representation Committee* (1906), p. 69.
[26] *Labour Representation Committee* (1903), p. 19.

Labourism'.[27] As late as 1913, Tom Shaw was insisting that 'labour was a term as high and holy in the truest sense as socialism ever was'.[28]

The tensions inherent in this understanding of the labour interest became acute in discussions of the role of brain workers in the movement. In the atmosphere of heightened unrest after 1911, this question recurred in the pages of the ILP's *Labour Leader*. Clifford Allan, later an important labour editor, urged that 'so far as our own movement is concerned, we are running the risk of dividing our members into political parties according to class, so that the Socialist who works with his hands belongs to the Labour party, and the Socialist who works with his brain to the Liberal party'[29]. Ellen Wilkinson attacked 'the Philistines who think that it is only labour spent on material things that is useful'.[30] This comment produced pained rejoinders from labouring readers of the paper who felt patronised by middle-class socialists.[31] Collaboration across class lines was clearly difficult at times for those on the left. Very occasionally, correspondents of the paper suggested that the middle classes were members of the working class too, but the prevalent conception of labour after 1900 militated against this view.[32]

This chapter is concerned primarily with Labour's attempts to advance its interests in the face of claims that it was guilty of placing sectional concerns above the interests of the public as a whole. This has required some investigation of the self-image of the Labour movement. Further light can be shed on this question, and a start made on the larger project of relating it to the dominant conception of the public, by examining attitudes to the co-operative movement within labour circles.

Co-operation was, unquestionably, a central part of labour culture throughout these years, and beyond. It was, however, the section of the labour movement least interested in labour representation. This is not to deny the political valence of co-operative retailing, but rather to distinguish this from the engagement with formal politics characteristic of other parts of the movement. Some work on co-operative culture has argued for the survival, especially evident at times of

---

[27] ibid., p. 31.   [28] *Labour Representation Committee* (1913), p. 101.
[29] *Labour Leader*, 5 Jan. 1912.
[30] *Labour Leader*, 15 Mar. 1912.   [31] *Labour Leader*, 22 Mar. 1912.
[32] *Labour Leader*, article by Alan Gordon, 1 Dec. 1911.

crisis, of the demand for fair and customary prices rather than accepting the dictates of the market.[33] Others have emphasised the novelty of wartime consumer activism and rejected the distinction between moral and political economy.[34] Certainly a critique of the market was evident in the charge after the 1912 coal strike that owners were exploiting the public, and in the persistent hostility in labour circles towards trusts and that classic eighteenth-century bugbear, the middleman. However, the consumerist conception of the public owed much to the political culture of the market. The politics of consumerism registered a tension between an appeal to 'fairness' and an inextricable involvement in market relations. It is the implications for a 'productionist' labour interest of the consumerist overtones of the language of the public which form the central concern of this chapter. This was a period in which mass labour action had serious implications for consumers, forcing labour to reconsider its understanding of the relationship between producers and consumers.

The Co-operative movement remained closely attached to liberalism before 1914, though an increased socialist presence is discernible.[35] Entry into formal politics only came in 1917. It is notable, however, that Labour party conferences indicate that many continued to hope that co-operators would come within the embrace of the party. In 1903, the co-operative society of Workington became 'the first representative of the third great section of the Labour movement that has declared for Labour representation'. Hope was expressed that this was 'the beginning of many similar affiliations'.[36] Fabians and new liberals sympathetic to labour had repeatedly urged the importance of co-operation for labour's vision of social transformation. In her celebrated study of the co-operative movement, Beatrice Potter argued that 'Against the frauds of the individual trader the wage-earner as a Trade Unionist has no defence.' Shrewdly noting that 'a Trade Union among the workers directly fosters the growth of the capitalist trust by uniting the employers', she stressed the value of 'the democratic form of

---

[33] B. Waites, 'The government of the home front and the "moral economy" of the working class' in P. H. Liddle, ed., *Home Fires and Foreign Fields* (London, 1985), pp. 175–94.

[34] Trentmann, *Free Trade Nation, passim.*

[35] Peter Gurney, *Co-operative Culture and the Politics of Consumption in England, 1870–1930* (Manchester, 1996), p. 191.

[36] *Labour Representation Committee* (1904), pp. 16–17.

Co-operation in protecting the public from that modern development of unrestrained competition – the capitalist trust'.[37]

At the 1910 party conference, R. Davies of the municipal employees claimed that 'labour was as much socialist as it was trade union-ist, and as much Co-operative as either of the others'. The labour unrest of 1911–14, and the ensuing appeals against unions on behalf of the 'public', reinvigorated concern with reorganising consumption in terms of co-operation, especially through theories of Guild Socialism. Disappointment at the failure of the co-operative movement to do more than pass motions supportive of trade union action led to a pro-posal at the 1914 party conference urging trade unionists to join Co-operative societies and redirect their policy. Some hoped that allying production and consumption through the trade union and co-operative movement would short-circuit interest group conflicts. Beatrice Potter summarised this argument well, suggesting that 'if the issues between the producer and consumer of commodities or services were uncompli-cated by the unknown profits and losses of individual capitalists and brain-workers, public opinion would be a final and irresistible court of appeal'.[38]

Sympathy towards co-operators, and their moralised vision of con-sumption, was combined, somewhat uneasily, with a conception of labour that privileged production. Widespread adherence to a kind of labour theory of value, particularly amongst trade unionists, reinforced this productionist emphasis. It is important that from its inception, as detailed below, the Labour party sought to speak for and represent the consumptionist needs of the public. Guild socialism provided the most developed attempt to reconcile these concerns, but they were also reg-istered in broader discussions of the politics of industrial war.[39] The movement's complex response to the settlement of the 1912 coal dis-pute cannot be understood without an awareness of notions of the fair price, institutionalised in co-operative culture. It is time to examine how labour related its self-identity to conceptions of the 'public', con-ceptions infused with a consumerist undertow and central to the free trade political culture to which many in labour were strongly attached.

[37] B. Potter, *The Co-operative Movement in Great Britain* (Aldershot, 1987, reprint; 1st edn London, 1893), pp. 198–9.
[38] ibid., p. 219.
[39] Thompson, 'The great labour unrest and political thought in Britain'.

Labour and 'the public'

Progressive concern with the growth of trusts has been well documented in the history of early twentieth-century America. Some time
ago, Henry Pelling drew attention to the existence of similar sentiments
in Edwardian Britain.[40] Observers of British political economy from
the 1880s onwards had become increasingly struck by the development
of monopoly capitalism. The early history of the Labour party provides considerable evidence of worries about the emergence of trusts.
A motion at the 1901 party conference recognised that 'the inevitable
tendency of privately-owned capital is towards combination to monopolies known as Trusts', and argued that these were 'disastrous to the
welfare of the consuming public, inimical to the social and political
welfare of the people, and especially injurious to the industrial liberty
and economic conditions of the workers'.[41] Hostility to monopolists,
and to their capacity to hold consumers to ransom, was a long-standing
element of radical politics in Britain. Trepidation at the advent of
monopoly trusts helped invigorate labour's concern for the consuming
public after 1900. It was, however, industrial disputes which placed
the relationship between labour and the public at the core of political
argument.

Labour's attitude to the public as consumers became a matter of
particular concern after 1910, but it was not only industrial disputes
which raised such concerns. The debate over employers' liability and
workmen's compensation sheds valuable light on the question. This
issue was repeatedly debated in parliament and at the TUC throughout
the 1880s and 1890s. Developments in the common law had created a
doctrine of common employment whereby employers were not liable
for injuries received by workers due to the actions of fellow employees.
Members of the general public were, however, entitled to recompense.
This seemed particularly unjust where workers were in no way cog-
nisant of the behaviour of their colleagues. The labour movement was
determined to alter the law so as to make employers liable for accidents to workmen, arguing that this would improve safety and reduce
injuries. Views varied within parliament, but discussion of the issue

---

[40] Pelling, *America and the British Left*, pp. 66–7.
[41] *Labour Representation Committee* (1901), p. 20.

frequently addressed the differing legal position of workers and outsiders. It was perfectly possible to distinguish between workers and
the outside public without generalising about the relationship between
labour and the public. Often, however, the arguments were posed in
terms which revealed the precarious position of workers as members
of the public. In the discussions of 1880, Alexander MacDonald suggested that the abolition of common employment would ensure that
'the working men of England would be placed on an equality with the
remainder of the public'.[42] During the same debate Broadhurst repu-
diated 'any attempt to place the working man in a different position to
the general public'.[43] It was, however, in arguments about where the
cost of compensating workers would fall that appeals to the consuming
public were most evident.

Members of parliament differed about whether the abolition of common employment, or the institution of a right to compensation, would
hit profits, reduce wages or raise prices. In response to Asquith's liability bill of 1893, the Earl of Dudley argued that if employers insured
against accidents 'the doctrine of common employment with its possible hardships would be swept away at the cost of a small tax on the
public as consumers'.[44] Similarly during the debates over Chamberlain's compensation bill of 1897, the Bishop of Winchester observed
that 'he was one of those who did believe in the principle of throwing
the cost of all accidents primarily on the trades concerned, and then,
ultimately and indirectly, upon the public at large'.[45] Clearly workers were both producers and consumers, but the distinction between
labour and the public tended to mask this fact. Drage was unusual
in noting that if the money did not come out of workmen's 'pockets
either as wage-earners or consumers, it would be found by them as
tax-payers'.[46]

After a debate in 1893 over employer liability, Alfred Rollitt moved
a motion requesting a select committee on strikes, lock-outs and boards
of conciliation. His motion was a response to the prospect of a national
coal dispute. Rollitt argued that 'the Motion was justified by the
national character and consequences of the dispute now pending, a

[42] *Parliamentary Debates*, 3rd ser., CCLII (1880), col. 1110.
[43] ibid., col. 1118.
[44] *Parliamentary Debates*, 4th ser., XIX (1893), col. 64.
[45] *Parliamentary Debates*, 4th ser., LI (1897), col. 1428.
[46] *Parliamentary Debates*, 4th ser., XLVIII (1897), col. 1456.

dispute which affected the whole body of the people... and which most seriously affected every consumer of one of the necessaries of life'. Rollitt's characteristic solution, discussed in Chapter 4, was 'to elicit the facts in order that public opinion, if there was no other remedy, could make itself felt, and exercise a force upon the parties to which they must submit'.[47]

Faith in the moral sway of public opinion in trade disputes was challenged by the scale and ferocity of industrial conflict after 1910. Concern for the public was also heightened. A series of nation-wide battles occurred in major industries. The supply of coal, a necessity for both industry and the home consumer, was threatened by the dispute of March 1912, which followed hard upon the railway strike of August 1911, which generated fears over the nation's food supply. The conception of the public invoked in 1912, discussed in Chapter 1, cast its interests in consumerist terms rather than simply contrasting middle- and working-class interests. However, this emphasis was highly problematic for a labour movement keen to defend the actions of strikers. Within parliament, the interests of the public were forcefully upheld against the claims of labour. Viscount Helmsley asserted that 'the rights of the community... are far greater than the rights of any body of men to strike, and they are rights which we in this House are bound to consider and bound to give effect to'.[48] Austen Chamberlain argued that public opinion had turned against the miners because their 'claim has been pressed, with all the methods and sacrifices of war, not against employers who have withstood it, but against the masses of the public who are the victims'.[49] During the railway dispute of 1911, Chamberlain had similarly asserted that 'our primary concern is the protection of the public'.[50] This view was echoed from the government benches by the Home Secretary, Winston Churchill, who argued, in the face of criticism of his use of troops, that 'it was not a question of taking sides with capital against labour, or with the companies against their employees. We took sides only with the public'.[51]

[47] *Parliamentary Debates*, 4th ser., XVIII (1893), col. 647.
[48] *Parliamentary Debates*, 5th ser., XXXV (1912), col. 2107. On the language of 'community', consult S. Yeo, ed., *New Views of Co-operation* (London, 1988).
[49] *Parliamentary Debates*, 5th ser., XXXV (1912), col. 2177.
[50] *Parliamentary Debates*, 5th ser., XXIV (1911), col. 2300.
[51] *Parliamentary Debates*, 5th ser., XXIV (1911), col. 2328.

Such claims placed Labour in a difficult position. How did the fledgling party respond?

Constant appeals to the interests of the public from critics of the railwaymen angered labour members, already enraged by the hypocrisy of belligerent Unionists justifying the use of troops against strikers. Hardie was sceptical that 'all this was being done in the interests of the suffering poor'. After all, 'When millions of these same poor were dying of starvation from lack of employment, there was no tremendous zeal then to protect them or to provide food for them.'[52] There were, however, grave dangers attached to appearing to disregard the interests of the public, and Labour, as a party strongly committed to free trade, was more mindful of the concerns of consumers than its reputation would suggest. MacDonald counselled, in language made familiar by Chamberlain and Churchill, that 'when there is a dispute, when there is unrest, public interest is bound to suffer, and this House is the custodian of the public interest'.[53] He was arguing for a sympathetic approach to the grievances of railwaymen, but the terms in which he did so are highly revealing.

The railway dispute of 1911 was a relatively brief affair. More protracted, and painful, was the titanic struggle in the coal industry the following year. Here too the interests of the public were often urged, leading one parliamentarian to observe that 'The interests of the consumer are important; but we can not entirely ignore the producer, as our opponents would have us do.'[54] Hardie and MacDonald, as the foremost labour members, were again prominent in parliamentary debate. MacDonald's arguments in particular repay close attention. Labour called for a debate over industrial unrest in order to argue for nationalisation as the only true solution. MacDonald attacked the role of monopolists, claiming that 'the rise in prices was simply due to the operation of a coal ring in London'. Tariff reform would only exacerbate such problems, for it would 'multiply the cases where such monopolies could be created, and consequently increase the opportunities for exploiting the people'. Wage rises were necessary, but not at the expense of the consuming public. MacDonald explained that 'When we raise wages we do not mean that the consumer should

---

[52] *Parliamentary Debates*, 5th ser., XXIV (1911), cols. 2336–7.
[53] *Parliamentary Debates*, 5th ser., XXXI (1911), col. 1223.
[54] *Parliamentary Debates*, 5th ser., XXXIV (1912), col. 761.

pay those wages except in certain circumstances. If the consumer is
not paying enough to bear a decent wage he ought to pay enough.'
As in 1911, MacDonald had no quarrel with the view that during
a struggle between capital and labour 'This House...must represent
the third party, the general public'. Furthermore, 'we cannot allow an
increase of wages to be merely the means of a further exploitation of
the general public'. For 'We are not going to improve matters by anything which merely means robbing Peter to pay Paul, especially when
Peter and Paul are the same person. Accordingly, we are opposed to
all those extraordinary propositions for increasing the cost of living
in order to improve the conditions of the people, known as Tariff
Reform.'[55]

Given MacDonald's reformist rationalism, his position might be
regarded as unrepresentative of labour argument. However, in a debate
on profit-sharing in 1912, Hardie too advocated the cause of the public. Hardie's fundamental criticism of profit-sharing was that 'It still
leaves profits to be obtained by competition.' This left open the 'possibility of sweating the public'. Allied in 'a great trust like the Sugar
Trust of America, or the Cotton Trust of this country', workers and
employers would agree on a 'joint scheme under which profits would
be considerably enhanced and shared out between the workers and
the employers, but the extra profits would come from the public...a
condition of things which the public could not long be expected to
tolerate.' It was nationalisation, most obviously of the railways, which
would solve these problems, in part by amplifying the power of public
opinion. For 'At the present time the tide of public opinion dashes
itself in vain against the rocks of the directors', whereas 'a question
discussed here in the full publicity of the public and with the weight
of public opinion behind it will stand a much better chance of finding a fair solution than is the case...when the railways are privately
owned'. Problems of supply cease under socialism as 'the people who
are producers, being also consumers, will want the best supply obtainable, both in quality and in quantity'.[56]

Hardie and MacDonald were not alone amongst labour representatives in seeking to speak for the public. It was the Labour party which
insisted on debating the price of coal in the Commons in late March

---

[55] *Parliamentary Debates*, 5th ser., XXXIV (1912), cols. 49–54.
[56] *Parliamentary Debates*, 5th ser., XXXIV (1912), cols. 154–60.

1912. The motion was introduced by Thomas Richardson in terms
that deserve full quotation:

That this House regrets the action recently taken by owners and middlemen
in raising the price of coal to consumers for no other reason than to take
advantage of a national crisis for securing inflated profits at the expense of
the general community, and considers that this exploitation of the public is a
motive inducing sections of the employers to resist the reasonable demands of
the workmen; and, further, this House is of opinion that a Committee should
be appointed to consider and report how in future the general community
can be protected against such action.[57]

Richardson approved of MacDonald's view that 'we cannot allow an
increase in wages to be merely a means of the further exploitation of
the general public', but went further, protesting 'against the system of
exploitation of the British public even in the absence of any increase
of the wages of the people of the country'. He was careful to emphasise the difficulties of 'small consumers' and 'people whose income
is precarious'. Richardson observed that 'During the present serious
industrial dispute strong indictments have been levelled against the
miners on the score of selfishness.'[58] He proceeded to 'claim on behalf
of the party with which I am associated that when in this House or in
the country we discuss industrial and economic questions, our outlook
is not confined to the interests of the wage-earning sections of the community'. Price hikes proved that 'as a result of the growing power of
the modern capitalist the general public are being compelled to face the
fact that they are just as effectively exploited, and are largely as helpless
to protect themselves as others against the almost unlimited power of
capitalism as we find it to-day'.[59] In his speech, Richardson contrasts
workmen and the public, and includes 'small consumers' amongst the
latter. The inclusive but consumerist connotations of the 'public' were
apparent in John Hodge's speech in support of the motion. Hodge suggested that 'we might have condemned the coal owners and middlemen
for their exploitation . . . of the public during the present strike'. The
real victims of price rises were 'the poor people who have to buy their
coal in small quantities'.[60]

The Labour party in parliament evidently sought to articulate the
interests of the consuming public. It is essential to investigate the

---

[57] *Parliamentary Debates*, 5th ser., XXXV (1912), col. 1993.
[58] ibid., cols. 1993–4.   [59] ibid., cols. 1994–5.   [60] ibid., cols. 1997.

response of the movement outside the gilded world of Westminster. Discussion of the public was common in the pages of the *Labour Leader*. Articles on railway nationalisation almost invariably argued that nationalisation would spare the suffering public the combined burden of 'the disadvantages of competition and the disadvantages of monopoly'.[61] Editorials attacked the railway companies over the August 1911 settlement, arguing that profits would be obtained by 'sweating the public'.[62] The 'merciless robbery' inflicted upon the public by coal owners in 1912 supplied a powerful 'argument for the public ownership of the coal supply'.[63] By February 1913, a leader of the co-operative movement urged that 'we are getting into the habit of looking at all problems from the wage-earners' and employers' view points only, and we are in danger of forgetting the very elementary fact that we are all consumers'.[64]

It is important to recognise the diversity of views within the labour movement on questions of consumer politics. In an article of October 1913, Hardie asked 'what the "public" has done to aid in finding a solution to the industrial problem to entitle it to be taken into consideration?' and insisted that 'if the present fever of unrest ... is putting the "public" to inconvenience, and causing it to begin to think how to protect itself, that is one more point to the credit of the strike'.[65] These sentiments provoked a swift and forceful response from Philip Snowden. Snowden wrote that

Mr Hardie expresses a scornful contempt for the 'public'. This is the public, which, he tells us in a previous paragraph, subscribed £15,000 for the miners' strike when the miners' funds were gone. And who is this general public, 'who has done nothing to find a solution of the industrial problem that entitles it to be taken into consideration'? I will tell Mr Hardie who that 'public' is. To the extent of four fifths of its members it consists of the working men and women who are ... the ... victims of industrial disputes, over which they have no control.[66]

This exchange illustrates the differing views of strikes taken by the two labour parliamentarians. Hardie's reply to Snowden is highly revealing. He observed that 'I am glad to have the "public" defined', for 'if it be true that it consists – to the extent of four-fifths of its numbers – of

---

[61] *Labour Leader*, 20 Jan. 1911.   [62] *Labour Leader*, 25 Aug. 1911.
[63] *Labour Leader*, 19 Jan. 1912.   [64] *Labour Leader*, 13 Feb. 1913.
[65] *Labour Leader*, 2 Oct. 1913.   [66] *Labour Leader*, 9 Oct. 1913.

the working men and women of the country, then I am glad to have disposed of a bogey which was beginning to do service in some unexpected quarters'.[67]

The scope of the public was always contested. Hardie's confusion reflects, in part, the influence of notions of the thinking public, which, while not simply excluding labour, imparted a middle-class inflection to talk of the public. Many labour politicians, most obviously MacDonald, celebrated a conception of public opinion in which the population as a whole was united by the formation of a general will. Hardie's inability here to conceive of working people as members of the public illustrates the sharp division between the productionist accent of 'labour' and the consumerist connotations of the 'public'.

It was possible to counter those who ranged the interest of the public against strikers in a number of ways. We have seen mainstream labour attempting in parliament to speak for the interests of the public, and to argue that socialism would unite producers and consumers in a democratic commonwealth dominated by the reign of 'public opinion'. This perspective is evident in the *Labour Leader* response to syndicalism. As we have seen, the paper reminded its readers in February 1913 that 'we are all consumers'.[68] Fenner Brockway made the argument explicit in an article in which he urged that 'syndicalism overlooks the consumer'. It was true that while, under syndicalism, 'the producers who would own and control industry would also be consumers, it would be as producers that they would perform this function'.[69] How did syndicalists respond to this argument?

In a letter to the *Labour Leader*, Gaylord Wilshire remarked that 'it seems to the Syndicalist that one of the things that will pass away with it [the Capitalist State] is the power of the consumer to dominate the producer'.[70] The syndicalist reply to talk of the public was to privilege the productionist interests of its working-class members over their interests as consumers. When asking in 1910, 'Who are the Public?', the *Industrial Syndicalist* answered, 'does not the Public consist of 85 per cent of the workers, and the balance of those who live upon the workers? Therefore, every properly-conducted struggle of the whole of the workers, or a section thereof, is truly in the interests of the

[67] *Labour Leader*, 23 Oct. 1913.   [68] *Labour Leader*, 13 Feb. 1913.
[69] *Labour Leader*, 12 Mar. 1914.   [70] *Labour Leader*, 19 Mar. 1914.

Public itself'.[71] This lack of interest in questions of consumption was also apparent in the columns of *Justice*. The paper opined that the 'vast mass is the true public', and emphasised that 'for this vast mass of – for the most part – sober and honest, labouring men and women, working in field, factory, workshop, school and office, the Constitution is framed'. So far, so *Labour Leader*, but differences became evident in the *Justice* view of strikes:

A strike for better material conditions, even if it is declared on behalf of one small trade, is in effect an action on behalf of the general public – that is, the many millions of citizens who possess no property, or next to none. Every uplift in the material condition of a section of the labouring public is a gain for the whole; for it means less suffering, less sickness, and less crime in that social area. The true public are recognising this elementary fact.[72]

Robert Blatchford's *Clarion* took a starkly productionist line during the coal strike. Its leader column commented that

High-falutin speeches and articles about the injury to the public, the danger to the Empire, the damage to trade, and the sufferings of the poor might be more reasonably addressed to the rich employer than the poor collier. The public, and the Empire, and commerce, and the poor have got the sacred right of contract and the divine law of supply and demand on which the structure of Britain's greatness rests. Let them make the most of those blessings. They have nothing to do with the collier.[73]

There was thus a range of views on the left about the position of the public during strikes. These do roughly correlate with the degree of emphasis placed on strike action, but support for strikes could coincide with concern at the capacity of trusts to exploit the public.

This discussion would be incomplete without some attention to the views of trade unionists. Local groups of trade unionists expressed their attitude towards invocation of the 'public' against strikers by passing motions. The No 6 branch of the National Amalgamated Furnishing Trades Association resolved that

Arising out of the attempt of certain capitalist newspapers to affect indignation in the name of the general public at the attitude of the miners in

---

[71] *Industrial Syndicalist* (Oct. 1910), p. 4.
[72] *Justice*, 6 July 1912.   [73] *Clarion*, 23 Feb. 1912.

their present struggle, this meeting of Wood Carvers, composed as it is of members of the general public, here places on record its entire satisfaction at the manly stand which the miners are making and, furthermore, pledges itself willing to endure such inconveniences as are inseparable from such a glorious struggle until we can rejoice with them in a decisive victory for the principle of a minimum wage.[74]

Trade union newspapers likewise challenged those who claimed to represent 'public opinion' against strikers. In an angry editorial, the *Railway Review* asked, 'are railwaymen not also of that public of which the weal is so much vaunted?'[75] During the 1912 coal dispute it published a lengthy piece by J. W. Frost, under the title 'Pro Bono Publico'. Frost observed that 'pulpit, press and platform . . . all unite in one solemn affirmation: whatever the rights or wrongs, the faults, the follies, or the heroisms of our 30 millions of workers, it is the public who in the final issue are to be protected by the strong arm of the State. Who, then, are the public?'

Frost answered his question by arguing that 'the public is a charmed circle, or shall we say a series of concentric circles, and even the out-ermost one an income-taxable area'. As suggested in Chapter 1, a conception of the public which placed the middle class at its core retained its resonance throughout this period. It was not, however, uncontested. Frost went on to ask 'how the public can be contradis-tinguished from the majority of its members, or by what confusion of thought the state is to be opposed to those millions of productive and distributive workers upon whom the very existence of the state depends'. Public interest 'must ultimately rest, not on abject servi-tude, but on the quantity and quality of its self-respecting manhood'. Aware of the consumerist overtones of the 'public', Frost challenged its implicit denial of productionist concerns. He argued that

By some process of muddled thinking the windy orator declares John Smith the consumer and member of the community to be in need of armed 'protection', while John Smith, the obstinate striker, deserves to be shot. Or Tom Brown, the miner, is asked to curse Smith, the railway servant, because of the inconvenience he suffers from Smith's being on strike. Yet Brown, or any wage-earning consumer, knows how soon the tables may be turned . . . Surely, the public interest is the interest of all the people, not

[74] Reported in *Justice*, 13 Apr. 1910.   [75] *Railway Review*, 6 Oct. 1911.

the vulgar and sordid 'interests' of a few thousand parasites who bleed and exploit the people.[76]

It is useful to compare the views expounded in the *Railway Review* with the less radical, and staunchly free trade, positions taken in the *Cotton Factory Times*.

The editorial line of the *Cotton Factory Times* combined sensitivity towards 'public opinion' with contempt for workers who relied more upon its generosity than upon their own powers of organisation. Thus, in 1889, cardroom operatives were encouraged 'to wait patiently the result of a claim which is not ... in any way denied, relying upon the good sense of the public to assist, by their counsel and advice, in the equitable solution of their case'.[77] However, Manchester gas stokers were told 'they must now prepare to fight their own battles, at least until public opinion again takes them in hand for a hobby'. The paper stressed that 'trade unions have been born, have thrived, and become powerful, in opposition to public opinion', which 'is generally supposed to consist of the views of employers, shopkeepers, professional men and clerks, and what are called the educated classes generally'.[78] Such comments remind us that intellectualist, middle-class conceptions of 'public opinion' retained real currency.

As we have already seen, however, more inclusive visions of the public coexisted and interacted with this more elitist approach. In a lecture to operatives in the aftermath of the Manningham strike of 1891, Byles noted that 'public opinion had been divided as to the merits of the case of the workpeople. The labouring classes to a man sympathised with the hands, while the upper classes applauded the directors'. The complex mixture of populist inclusiveness and class feeling, characteristic of the *Cotton Factory Times*, was well captured by Byles's next observation that 'it was always an alarming feature when it was found that public opinion was ruled by social rank'.[79] This broader conception of the public was further apparent in an appeal 'to the public', issued by the Oldham Engineers and Steam Engine Makers' Society, which began 'Friends and fellow-workmen' and urged that 'we are not only fighting our own battle, but the battle of every working man in this country, seeing that we are virtually

[76] *Railway Review*, 22 Mar. 1912.   [77] *Cotton Factory Times*, 5 July 1889.
[78] *Cotton Factory Times*, 13 Dec. 1889.
[79] *Cotton Factory Times*, 8 May 1891.

fighting for a shortening of the hours of labour, in which all must eventually participate'.[80]

The paper's response to the miner's strike of 1912 is suggestive. A series of articles by 'Old Stager' described 'the whole thing' as a 'game of bluff in which the public, and especially the poorer classes, are the sufferers'.[81] In an editorial on 1 March, the paper opined that 'it is not the poor or the workers generally who grudge the collier his due recompense', prophesying that 'the public as a whole will become very angry, and properly so, if the business of the country is tied up... because of the cupidity and stupidity of a few plutocrats'.[82] Considerable suffering occurred in the Lancashire cotton trade during the dispute, and this was extensively documented by the *Cotton Factory Times*. By 5 April, the paper sighed that 'if the strike is ended... it will come as a great relief to everybody'. It was careful 'not [to] imply that other workers blame the miners for going on strike', but proposed that 'their best policy will be to resume work with as little delay as possible'.[83]

Speaking for the public?

This chapter has explored labour's complex attempts to relate its self-conception to the category of the public. This was a project, replete with tensions, through which very different understandings of the relationship between consumers and producers were expressed and defended. Arguments for labour representation in parliament were frequently founded upon an interest-based analysis of politics. The claim was not that 'labour' was an interest, along with that of the 'public', which required representation in parliament, so much as an implicit scepticism about the sense in which the public, as opposed to the City or railway directors, was an interest group represented in parliament. It was industrial conflict, especially nationwide strikes affecting essential commodities after 1910, which pushed relations between labour and the public to the centre of political debate. Labour sought not merely to redefine the public interest, but to represent the consuming public, and ally its concerns with established labour arguments for public ownership of industry.

[80] *Cotton Factory Times*, 22 Mar. 1891.
[81] *Cotton Factory Times*, 1 Mar. 1912.   [82] ibid.
[83] *Cotton Factory Times*, 5 Apr. 1912.

Some writing on later labour history, preoccupied with the gender gap in voting, has cast Labour as a productionist party uncomfortable with the consumerist interests of women.[84] This analysis suggests that the rhetorical relationship between 'labour' and the 'public' was highly gendered. The consuming public is seen as feminised, and distinguished from the masculine world of labour. As was argued in Chapter 1, however, it is far from clear that the 'public' was feminised before 1914. Male politicians in parliament such as Major Morrison-Bell were happy to 'speak...purely as a member of the ordinary public', and personifications of the public, whether the man on the omnibus or the man in the railway carriage, remained firmly male.[85] Periods of scepticism about the rationality of 'public opinion', especially around 1900, fostered feminised conceptions of the public, but this was not typical of appeals to the public interest in the face of labour unrest after 1910. Examples can be found of writers who cast the distinction between production and consumption in gendered terms. Fenner Brockway argued that

As our spheres vary, so our interests vary. The man who toils in the workshop from morning to night is primarily interested as a producer. He strikes for a higher wage with little thought of the increased cost in living which the concession of higher wages must mean so long as employers are allowed to place the burden on the purchasing public. The woman who toils in the home from morning to night is primarily interested as a consumer.[86]

The field of consumption could be seen as a female preserve. Separation of production and consumption facilitated their portrayal through gendered language. Ideas of the suffering, silent and put-upon public could be conveyed through its feminisation. But, at least before 1914, such instances were rare. Many services were primarily used by men, and views of consumption incorporated the demands of industrial purchases. There is no doubt that the potency of appeals to the consuming public created problems for labour, but these should not be seen primarily in gendered terms. The fiscal controversy produced many representations of the value of free trade to consumers, some

[84] For instance, A. Black & S. Brooke, 'The Labour Party, women, and the problem of gender, 1951–1966', *Journal of British Studies*, 36, 4 (1997), 419–52.

[85] *Parliamentary Debates*, 5th ser., XXXI (1911), col. 1298.

[86] *Labour Leader*, 12 Mar. 1914.

of which appealed to women as consumers, but many of which did not.[87] It was, however, through invoking the interests of consumers that many aimed to undercut the claims of labour. Labour's responses indicate the difficulties involved in speaking for a 'sectional' interest, and for the public. It is notable, though, that many within Labour sought both to redefine the public interest, and to represent the consuming public, as befitted a party strongly attached to free trade. Labour's relationship to the 'public' was certainly problematic, but its response to the challenge was more creative, and more complex, than has been recognised. Crude criticism of labour's inability to articulate consumer concerns underestimates its rhetorical difficulties, but, more importantly, it neglects the movement's real efforts to speak for both the people, and the public.

[87] Thompson, '"Pictorial lies"?'.

Conclusion

'Public opinion' and political culture in Britain, 1867–1914

This book has sought to provide a thick conceptual history of 'public opinion' between 1870 and 1914. In the last thirty years, intellectual history has focused primarily upon locating the ideas of individual thinkers in their proper context, or upon the development of schools of thought. Recent years have seen the halting advance of a 'conceptual history', which has claimed distinctness from an older history of 'unit-ideas', still reeling from a now much-discussed methodological assault.[1] Different political creeds rely upon a common stock of concepts, which have particular histories, imparting distinctive associations and resonances. Political thought and argument demand recourse to concepts whose meaning, reference and valence, while not fixed, are equally not open to arbitrary redefinition.[2] This book has aimed to do justice both to the weight of conceptual inheritance and to the creativity of political discussion in the past. It has, however, been argued that a liberal consensus existed around the term 'public opinion', which gave the concept its shape in an era characterised by widespread and significant political engagement.

The structure of the idea of 'public opinion' was well expressed in the work of Carslake Thompson. Thompson summarised the criteria for a political mood to constitute 'public opinion' as volume, persistence, rationality and earnestness. The first two are familiar to early twenty-first-century readers, though 'persistence' is perhaps less prized by the polling industry. The latter two requirements are, however, more alien. In explicit rejection of a positivistic approach to

---

[1] This literature is very well known. It includes Q. Skinner, 'Meaning and understanding in the history of ideas', and 'Some problems in the analysis of political thought and action', *Political Theory*, 2 (1974), 277–303. The debate occasioned by Skinner's work is best approached through Tully, ed., *Meaning and Context*.

[2] For an approach to the history of ideology that emphasises the role of political concepts, see Freeden, *Ideologies and Political Theory*.

the assessment of 'public opinion', Thompson insisted that 'there are qualitative elements which must be regarded too'. He observed that 'We recognise that a few men who hold a definite opinion *earnestly* and on *rational grounds* will outweigh a greater number who merely entertain a slight preference which they cannot explain for something vague and general'.[3] As a statement about the place of 'public opinion' in the political argument of the period, this was broadly correct. Public opinion was as much a normative as a descriptive category. Earnestness and rationality were highly valued in an engaged political culture, which endured into the Edwardian years. Conceptions of 'public opinion' manifested this preoccupation with public spirit and intense convictions, which lent the term its honorific connotations.

The implications of this complex of ideas for the constitution of the public were explored in Chapter 1. Contemporaries did on occasion, usually in discussing elections, equate the public with the voters, but the dominant account of the public extended its embrace beyond the electorate throughout this period. The public was frequently conceived, particularly in discussions of labour questions, as a body of consumers. This conception was illuminated through an examination of the public discourse surrounding major industrial disputes in the period. The public were also, crucially, consumers of ideas, particularly those circulated in the discursive free market of the Victorian press. Members of the public were not, however, to be passive consumers of ideas, but rather active participants in an engaged debate. The formulation of views on such matters as the 1893 coal lock-out was a duty rather than a right. Demands for rationality and earnestness in opinion-holders were demands for the display of 'character'. The importance of character is very apparent in debates about the composition of the public.

It was both possible and plausible, given the prevalent account of 'public opinion', to hold that artisans were members of the public. This view, found in explicit form in the first edition of Mill's *Principles*, was reinforced by the political debates over reform in the 1860s.[4] Emphasis upon the public as a community of consumers made it hard

---

[3] Thompson, *Public Opinion and Lord Beaconsfield*, I, 32.
[4] J. S. Mill, *Principles of Political Economy* in *The Collected Works of John Stuart Mill*, III, ed. J. M. Robson, intro. V. W. Brady (Toronto, 1977), p. 764.

to defend the productivist interests of labour by reference to those of the public, but this did not leave the artisanal classes outside its scope. The 'mind' of the public continued to be found amongst the educated middle classes, but its heart could be identified, in Gladstonian terms, with the moral sense of the people. Women's position in the public was, unsurprisingly, more precarious than that of men. Nonetheless, women, especially middle-class women, were increasingly included in the public in these years. Their position can be contrasted with that of the characterless poor, the 'residuum', whose exclusion from the ranks of the public was clear, consistent and enduring.

The status of working-class men and women makes clear that the composition of the public was never uncontested. Dispute centred more perhaps upon the implications of a shared set of requirements than upon the requirements themselves. The end of the period sees the advent of more capacious and more neutral conceptions of the limits of the public, though this development only really comes in the interwar era of more domesticated politics and the advent of opinion polling.[5] Expansion does roughly characterise the career of the 'public' in the long nineteenth century, but, as the case of the residuum demonstrates, the process had its limits. While periods of contraction in the size of the public are hard to find, expansion did not necessarily disrupt the identification of 'public opinion' with middle-class views. The Edwardian period, in the aftermath of the Boer War, did, however, witness a shift in stereotypes of the public, apparent in the growth of reference to 'the man in the street'.

Invocation of 'public opinion' presented the obvious difficulty of how so elusive an entity is to be identified. Late nineteenth-century 'public opinion' was the organic product of reasonable debate in which individual and corporate opinions were weighed rather than counted. This made it peculiarly resistant to the Victorian enthusiasm for quantification. Attempts to locate and interpret 'public opinion' exhibited a constitutionalist concern for the pronouncements of press, platform and petition. Interest focused primarily upon the first two of these. The development of the press was integral to narratives of the emergence of a political public.[6] Histories of the platform were, however, no less important to accounts of 'public opinion'. Constitutionalist emphasis

---

[5] Lawrence, *Electing our Masters*.
[6] A point made in Jones, *Powers of the Press*, p. 75.

upon the power of the platform rested upon its efficacy as a means of demonstrating intense convictions. The platform was dependent upon the press for its capacity to reach a wider audience, but the press could not match its capacity to crystallise the public mind.

Evaluation of the respective merits of press and platform as mirrors of opinion was shown to be highly contested, often on party lines. Celebration of the platform was more common on the left. A variety of attitudes was detected towards the press, particularly over the relative significance of its provincial and metropolitan branches. Liberals, and radicals, were more enamoured of provincial newspapers than their Conservative counterparts. This distinction became more pronounced as the century wore on. Faith in the press as the embodiment of 'public opinion' survived the protracted rise of the new journalism, and was less vulnerable to the 'Northcliffe Revolution' than is sometimes implied. The failure of tariff reform, however, and the consequent electoral success of the Liberal party, did suggest that the press was of limited worth as a mirror of opinion. Earlier general elections, notably in 1880, had encouraged liberals and radicals to uphold the supremacy of the platform, particularly in its Gladstonian incarnation. Arguments about the comparative importance of press and platform reveal the ambiguities inherent in a concept of 'public opinion' which valued both the rationality and the intensity of beliefs, and was committed to an organic model of deliberative politics.

The search for 'public opinion' in an era without polling reveals the hegemony of the constitutionalist triptych of press, platform and petition. The extensive literature on constitutionalism can be usefully supplemented by consideration of the understanding of society manifested in discourses about the press and platform.[7] The free market in ideas supposedly provided by the press was crucial to the emergence of the 'public opinion' on which constitutional politics depended. This was frequently felt, particularly on the left, to be threatened by contractions in press ownership, and by the advent of a new mass press. Dismay at developments in the popular media often manifested a deep distrust of the feminisation of the newspaper-reading public.

---

[7] See, for instance, Joyce, *Visions of the People* and *Democratic Subjects*; Vernon, *Politics and the People*; Vernon, ed., *Re-reading the Constitution*.

Constitutionalism can be better understood in the light of arguments about political communication and the production of public opinion.

The existing historiography has probably given most attention to debates about the rationality of the public. Chapter 3 argued against a catastrophist view of the reputation of the public, denying that the 1850s or the 1900s initiated the fall of 'public opinion' from its heyday in the early nineteenth century. The reception of Mill's *On Liberty* indicates greater faith in the reasonableness of 'public opinion' at the start of the 1860s than during the previous decade. Debates over the caucus and programmatic politics were used to establish the resilience of more positive views of the reasonableness of the public. Popular enthusiasm for the Boer War certainly dented liberal confidence in the public in the early 1900s. It is important, however, to recall that liberal prospects began to improve as early as 1902, and culminated in the triumph of 1906, in which the electorate proved its adherence to the rational creed of free trade. Conservative conceptions of the public, more tolerant of the role of emotion and committed to the war, did not suffer a comparable crisis of confidence in the public.

The history of 'public opinion' as a political concept has received some scholarly attention. There has, however, been little written about its role in political economy.[8] Yet a broad consensus, embracing a number of political perspectives and apparent both in popular debate and expert discussion, regarded 'public opinion' as a powerful economic force, whose beneficent sway preserved, or if necessary restored, economic peace. The collapse of the wage-fund theory left economists with little by way of a convincing means of explaining how wage rates emerged. This gap was increasingly filled by the claim that 'public opinion', conceived very much in consumerist terms, justly determined the outcome of industrial disputes and preserved peaceful relations between employers and employed. The analysis was similarly apparent at a more popular level in press reporting, parliamentary debates and evidence to royal commissions. Coverage of the coal strike in 1912 reverted to the paradoxical view that a clearly stated judgement by

---

[8] An exception to this is the remarks in J. K. Whitaker, 'Some neglected aspects of Alfred Marshall's economic and social thought', *History of Political Economy*, 9, 2 (1977), 171–5.

public opinion could terminate the dispute. Mainstream labour politicians, like Snowden and MacDonald, displayed enormous faith in the opinion of a broadly defined public to regulate civil and economic life. MacDonald especially was true to his progressivist background in equating true 'public opinion' with the 'general will' of society.[9] Such idealist overtones are apparent in much discussion of 'public opinion', particularly in its civic role as industrial umpire.

This book has tried to demonstrate the possibilities of a broadly conceived conceptual history that takes seriously forms of discourse still often neglected by much intellectual history. The attraction of linear narratives, usually involving some combination of a rise and a fall, has been resisted, as such approaches cannot do justice to the elusive trajectory of 'public opinion' in this period. A complex and variegated picture has resulted. The now familiar theme of the survival of liberal political culture into the twentieth century has received further support.[10] It has, however, been argued that while the mantle of 'public opinion' provided a prize worth fighting for, it was one for which all could not compete equally. The gendering of 'public opinion', equally evident in Gladstone's lionising of the masculine public and in fin-de-siècle fears of its feminisation, presented obstacles to female political activism apparent in the response to the suffragettes. The necessity of 'character' amongst members of the public distanced them from the benighted ranks of the residuum. The traditional heroes (and villains) of labour history, the unionised male working class, had relatively strong claims to membership of the public. There were, however, difficulties in defending the productivist interests of labour when those of the public were often interpreted in consumerist terms.

The importance of the distinction between producers and consumers in understanding the political culture of the period has become increasingly clear.[11] Attention to populism has demonstrated the

---

[9] For example, MacDonald, *Socialism and Government*, pp. 89–90.

[10] On this large theme, see Biagini & Reid, eds., *Currents of Radicalism*; Biagini, *Citizenship and Community*; Harris, *Private Lives, Public Spirit*, pp. 220–51; Collini, *Public Moralists*; S. Pedersen & P. Mandler, eds., *After the Victorians: Private Conscience and Public Duty in Modern Britain: Essays in Memory of John Clive* (London, 1994).

[11] See especially, Howe, *Free Trade and Liberal England*; Green, *The Crisis of Conservatism*; Trentmann, *Free Trade Nation*.

resonance of appeals to the productive nation, but more consumerist political idioms have received less scrutiny.[12] Excavation of the consumerist associations of the language of 'public opinion' has also served to demonstrate its importance to understandings of the economy. Existing accounts of the division between politics and economics in this period have little to say about the perceived role of 'public opinion' in the functioning of the economy.[13] This discourse rested on a presumption that a unified public existed which could regulate economic affairs without legal interference. This approach was not, however, incompatible with government involvement, though this was often understood in terms of the provision of information.[14] The idea of a unitary public relied upon a conception of the public cast in primarily consumerist terms. This was problematic for attempts to justify widespread industrial action of the sort apparent in 1911–14.

The notion of the consuming public was problematic for the Labour movement. Early Labour was not a purely productionist party, though it certainly wished to insist upon the meeting of basic human needs. The early twentieth-century labour movement contained a range of political perspectives, but it was importantly committed both to articulating the productionist demands of workers, and to arguing that capitalism was ill-placed in the long run to satisfy consumers. The relationship between ideas of the labour interest and the public was complex and contested, but its history demonstrates the movement's continuing efforts to develop a deliberative politics that embraced

---

[12] On populism, see Joyce, *Visions of the People* and *Democratic Subjects*; Vernon, *Politics and the People*; Biagini & Reid, *Currents of Radicalism*; J. Epstein, 'The populist turn', *Journal of British Studies*, 32, 2 (April 1993), 177–89; E. J. Yeo, 'Language and contestation: the case of "the People", 1832 to the present' in J. Belchem & N. Kirk, eds., *Languages of Labour* (Aldershot, 1997). Helpful reflections on this literature are to be found in Lawrence, *Speaking for the People*, pp. 54–8, 62–3, 65.

[13] See the influential essay by A. Reid, 'The division of labour and politics in Britain, 1880–1920' in W. Mommsen & H. Husung, eds., *The Development of Trade Unionism in Great Britain and Germany, 1880–1914* (London, 1985), pp. 150–66.

[14] Much valuable information on the working of the Labour department of the Board of Trade is contained in R. Davidson, *Whitehall and the Labour Problem in Late-Victorian and Edwardian Britain: A Study in Official Statistics and Social Control* (London, 1985).

public reason through which the difficulties of currently existing capitalism might be transcended.

The first chapter began with a reference to the important work of Ross McKibbin on interwar Conservatism.[15] It may be possible to find the roots of his dichotomy between the unions and the public in the idiom of the consuming public discussed in Chapter 1. However, important work on the interwar right has emphasised the inclusive, albeit hierarchical, nature of conservative visions of the public, while acknowledging that these were mobilised against assertive trade unionism.[16] Students of the interwar left have drawn attention to Labour's efforts to place its constituency at the heart of the political public, in a manner already evident in the defence of miners' patriotism offered by Vernon Hartshorn, who insisted, 'England is not represented by the pleasure-seekers of society, but by the artisan and the miner, the railwayman, the agricultural worker, the docker, the factory hand, the shop assistant, the doctor, the inventor, scientist, the men of the Army and Navy, and all who render service to the national well-being'.[17] Recent work on associational culture has sought to show that more active conceptions of 'public opinion' endured beyond 1918, reflecting a fundamentally different view of interwar Britain from that advanced by McKibbin in work old and new.[18]

This book focuses upon the period before 1914. It reveals a language of public opinion that was as much about producers and consumers as about class, and which appears, at least potentially, more inclusive than that sketched by McKibbin. While the interwar period witnessed the beginnings of opinion polling, which in time both reflected and encouraged a distinctly less activist conception of 'public opinion', the more

[15] R. McKibbin, 'Class and conventional wisdom: the Conservative Party and the "public" in inter-war Britain' in his *Ideologies of Class*, pp. 259–94.

[16] P. Williamson, *Stanley Baldwin: Conservative Leadership and National Values* (Cambridge, 1999), esp. pp. 200, 353. For a view closer to McKibbin's see B. Schwarz, 'The language of constitutionalism: Baldwinite Conservatism' in Formations Editorial Collective, *Formations of Nation and People*, Formations 7 (London, 1984), pp. 1–18.

[17] Lawrence, 'Labour and the politics of class'; L. Beers, 'Counter-Toryism: Labour's response to anti-socialist propaganda, 1918–39' in M. Worley, ed., *The Foundations of the British Labour Party: Identities, Cultures and Perspectives, 1900–39* (Farnham, 2009), pp. 231–54.

[18] McCarthy, 'Parties, voluntary associations and democratic politics'; H. McCarthy, 'Service clubs, citizenship and equality'; McKibbin, *Parties and People*.

participatory and inclusive picture of the imagined public identified in recent work on interwar Britain might suggest important connections with the debates addressed here. The pre-war language of 'public opinion' depicted in this book was part of the self-understanding of a complex political culture that remained strongly attached to the virtues of public spirit and civic activism. The history of a popular concept is well placed to demonstrate the prevalence of such values. The career of 'public opinion' in this period indicates the capacity for both inclusion and exclusion of a vanished political culture. While it was, in many respects, an exclusive political culture, it was also one committed to an ideal of public activism, which contrasts sharply with modern opinion polling. It may be possible to detect in the rise of the focus group an attempt to capture the dynamics of public debate, but the more strenuous commitment to deliberative engagement characteristic of the political culture of the late nineteenth and early twentieth centuries compels recognition and reflection.

Bibliography

Primary sources

Private papers

Bryce papers, Bodleian Library, Oxford
  Campbell-Bannerman papers, British Library, London
  Eliot papers, Harvard University Archive, Cambridge, Mass.
  Ensor papers, Bodleian Library, Oxford
  Godkin papers, Houghton Library, Harvard University, Cambridge, Mass.
  John Johnson Collection, Bodleian Library, Oxford
  Herbert Gladstone papers, British Library, London
  Norton papers, Houghton Library, Harvard University, Cambridge, Mass.
  Ponsonby papers, Bodleian Library, Oxford
  Poster collection, University Library, Cambridge

Official papers

Hansard, 3rd, 4th and 5th series
Report on strikes and lockouts, PP (1888–1914)
Reports of the Select Committee on Public Petitions
Royal Commission on Labour, PP 1894, XXXV
Royal Commission on Trade Disputes and Trade Combinations, PP 1906
Royal Commission Reports on the Trades Unions, PP 1867, XXXII; 1876–8, XXXIX; 1868–9, XXXI
Royal Commission Reports on the Working of the Master and Servant Act, 1867, and the Criminal Law Amendment Act, 1871, PP 1874, XXIV; 1875, XXX

Journals and reports

Blackwood's Magazine
Contemporary Review

Economic Journal
Economic Review
Edinburgh Review
Fortnightly Review
Journal of the Royal Statistical Society
Labour Representation Committee, *Annual Reports*
Macmillan's Magazine
Monthly Review
National Review
New Review
Nineteenth Century
Quarterly Review
Review of Reviews
Review of Review's Index of Periodicals
Sell's World's Press
Sessional Proceedings of the National Association for the Promotion of Social Science
Trades Union Congress, *Annual Reports*
Transactions of the National Association for the Promotion of Social Science
Westminster Review

Newspapers (daily and weekly)

The Bee-Hive
Capital and Labour
Clarion
Cotton Factory Times
Common Cause
Daily Chronicle
Daily News
Daily Telegraph
The Echo
The Economist
Industrial Review
Industrial Syndicalist
Justice
Labour Leader
Lloyd's Weekly
Manchester Guardian
The Nation
The Observer

Pall Mall Gazette
Railway Review
Reynolds's Newspaper
The Speaker
The Spectator
The Times
Truth
The Vote
Votes for Women
Westminster Gazette

Contemporary works

Acton, J. E. E. D., *The History of Freedom; and Other Essays* (London, 1907)

Adams, W. E., *Memoirs of a Social Atom* (2 vols., London, 1903)

Amos, S., *Fifty Years of the Constitution* (London, 1880)

Anon., 'The book of the month', *Review of Reviews*, 12 (April 1896), 366–73

Anon., 'The British press: its growth, liberty and power', *North British Review*, 30 (May 1859), 367–492

Anon., 'Democracy and liberty', *London Quarterly Review*, 27 new ser. (Oct. 1896), 137–59

Anon., 'The Labour party and the books that helped to make it', *Review of Reviews*, 32 (June 1906), 568–82

Anon., 'Lecky's Democracy and liberty', *Church Quarterly Review* 42 (Oct. 1896), 132–55

Anon., 'The paralysis of parliament', *Quarterly Review*, 194 (Oct. 1901), 601–36

Anon., 'The residuum', *Contemporary Review*, 30 (Nov. 1877), 1088–93

Arnold, M., 'Bishop Butler and the *Zeit-Geist*', in *Last Essays on Church and Religion* (London, 1903), pp. 45–107

Culture and Anarchy (London, 1869)

The Popular Education of France – with Notices of That of Holland and Switzerland (London, 1861)

'Up to Easter', *Nineteenth Century*, 21 (May 1887), 629–43

Arnold, T., 'Mill, *On Liberty*', *The Rambler*, 2 (Nov. 1859), 62–75, and (Mar. 1860), 376–85

Ashley, W. J., *The Adjustment of Wages: A Study in the Coal and Iron Industries of Great Britain and America* (London, 1903)

The Early History of the English Woollen Industry (Oxford, 1887)

The Economic Organisation of England: An Outline History (London, 1914)

An Introduction to English Economic History and Theory (Oxford, 1888)

Bain, A., *Mental and Moral Science: A Compendium of Psychology and Ethics* (London, 1868)

Bagehot, W., *Economic Studies*, ed. R. H. Hutton (2nd edn, London, 1895)

The English Constitution (2nd edn, London, 1872)

'Letters on the French *coup d'état* of 1851', in *The Collected Works of Walter Bagehot*, IV, ed. N. St. John-Stevas (London, 1968), pp. 29–84

Physics and Politics (London, 1872)

'The position of the metropolitan press', in *The Collected Works of Walter Bagehot*, VII, ed. N. St. John-Stevas (London, 1974), pp. 296–9

Balfour, A. J., *Foundations of Belief* (London, 1895)

Barnes, R. W., *Public Opinion Considered in Letters* (London and Truro, 1855)

Barnett, S., 'A scheme for the unemployed', *Nineteenth Century*, 24 (Nov. 1888), 753–63

Belloc, H. and Chesterton, C., *The Free Press* (London, 1918)

The Party System (London, 1911)

Beveridge, W., 'The reform of trade union law', *Economic Review*, 15 (Mar. 1905), 129–49

Billington-Greig, T., *The Militant Suffrage Movement* (London, 1911)

Blauvelt, M. T., *The Development of Cabinet Government in England* (London, 1912)

Blumenfeld, R. D., *The Press in My Time* (London, 1933)

Bohm-Bawerk, E., *Positive Theory of Capital* (London, 1889)

Booth, C., *Industrial Unrest and Labour Policy* (London, 1913)

Bosanquet, B., *The Philosophical Theory of the State* (London, 1899)

'The reality of the general will' in D. Boucher, ed., *The British Idealists* (Cambridge, 1997), pp. 130–42

Bosanquet, H., *The Strength of the People: A Study in Social Economics* (London, 1902)

Bourne, H. R. F., *English Newspapers: Chapters in the History of Journalism* (London, 1887)

Boutmy, E., *Studies in Constitutional Law*, trans. E. M. Dicey, intro A. V. Dicey (London, 1891)

Bowles, T. G., 'Newspapers', *Fortnightly Review*, 36 new ser. (July 1884), 17–29

Brassey, T., *Lectures on the Labour Question* (London, 1878)

On Work and Wages (London, 1872)

Brentano, L., *Hours and Wages in Relation to Production* (London, 1894)

On the History and Development of Gilds, and the Origin of Trade Unionism (1870)

The Translation of Labor to the Law of To-day, trans. P. Sherman (New York, 1891)

Brodrick, G. C., *Political Studies* (London, 1879)

Brooks, S., 'On national character', *Monthly Review*, 1 (Nov. 1900), 11–20

Browne, B. C., *Selected Papers on Social and Economic Questions by Benjamin Chapman Browne, Knight*, ed. E. M. B. and H. M. B. Browne (Cambridge, 1918)

Bryce, J., *The American Commonwealth* (3 vols., London, 1888)

Modern Democracies (2 vols., London, 1921)

'The study of popular governments', *Quarterly Review*, 203 (July 1905), 170–92 and (Oct. 1905), 387–411

Bull, J., Jr., 'Parliament and the party system', *Macmillan's Magazine*, 84 (Oct. 1901), 471–80

Burke, E., *Reflections on the Revolution in France* (London, 1790)

'Speech at Bristol', September 6 1780 in *The Writings and Speeches of Edmund Burke, vol. III: Party, Parliament, and the American War 1774–1780*, ed. W. M. Elofson and J. A. Woods, (Oxford, 1996), pp. 623–63

Thoughts on the Present Discontents (1770) in *Pre-Revolutionary Writings* (Cambridge, 1993)

Butler, G. C., *The Tory Tradition: Bolingbroke – Burke – Disraeli – Salisbury* (London, 1914)

Chamberlain, J., 'Labourers' and artisans' dwellings', *Fortnightly Review*, 34 new ser. (Dec. 1883), 761–76

Mr Chamberlain's Speeches, ed. C. W. Boyd (2 vols., London, 1914)

The Radical Programme (1885), ed. D. A. Hamer (Brighton, 1971)

Speeches of the Right Hon. Joseph Chamberlain, ed. H. W. Lucy (London, 1885)

Christensen, A., *Politics and Crowd Morality: A Study in the Philosophy of Politics*, trans. A. C. Curtis (London, 1915)

Clark, J. B., *The Distribution of Wealth* (New York, 1899)

Church, R. W., 'Mill's 'On Liberty'', *Bentley's Quarterly*, 2 (Jan. 1860), 173–95

Collins, G., *Trades' Unions: An Essay on the Struggle Between Capital and Labour, and the Agitation Amongst Agricultural Labourers* (London, 1872)

Colomb, Admiral P. H., 'The patriotic editor in war', *National Review*, 29 (April 1897), 253–63

Conservative journalist, A., 'Why is the provincial press radical?', *National Review*, 7 (July 1886), 678–82

Conway, M., *The Crowd in Peace and War* (London, 1915)

Courthope, W. J., 'The Conservative defeat', *Quarterly Review*, 149 (April 1880), 549–79

Courtney, L., 'The decline of parliament', *Monthly Review*, 17 (Dec. 1904), 13–21

'The making and reading of newspapers', *Contemporary Review*, 79 (Mar. 1901), 365–77

Cowell, H., 'Lecky's "Democracy and Liberty', *Blackwood's Magazine* CLIX (May 1896), 749–66

'Liberty, equality, fraternity: Mr John Stuart Mill', *Blackwood's Magazine*, 114 (Sep. 1873), 347–62

Cox, H., *The British Commonwealth: Or a Commentary on the Institutions and Principles of British Government* (London, 1854)

Croker, J. W., *The Croker Papers: The Correspondence and Diaries of the Late Right Honourable John Wilson Croker* (3 vols., London, 1884)

Crump, A., *A Short Enquiry into the Formation of Political Opinion from the Reign of the Great Families to the Advent of Democracy* (London, 1885)

Cunningham, W., *Politics and Economics: An Essay on the Nature of the Principles of Political Economy together with a Survey of Recent Legislation* (London, 1885)

Cygnus, 'The story of the Penrhyn quarries, 1865–1902', *Fortnightly Review*, 72 new ser. (June 1903), 1017–29

Dale, D., *Thirty Years' Experience of Industrial Conciliation and Arbitration* (London, 1899)

de Rousiers, P., *The Labour Question in Britain*, trans. F. L. D. Herbertson (London, 1896)

Devonshire, S. P. C., *An Address Delivered Before the University of Edinburgh, on His Inauguration as Lord Rector, January 31, 1879* (London, 1879)

Dicey, A. V., Bryce's American Commonwealth', *Edinburgh Review*, 169 (April 1889), 481–518

Lectures on the Relation Between Law and Public Opinion in England During the Nineteenth Century (London, 1905)

Memorials of Albert Venn Dicey, ed. R. S. Rait (London, 1925)

Dickinson, G. L., *The Development of Parliament During the Nineteenth Century* (London, 1895)

Disraeli, B., *Selected Speeches of the Late Right Honourable the Earl of Beaconsfield*, ed. T. E. Kebbel (London, 1882)

Whigs and Whiggism: Political Writings by Benjamin Disraeli, ed. W. Hutcheon (London, 1913)

Dobbs, M., 'A sceptical view of the theory of wages', *Economic Journal*, 39 (1929), 506–19

Dorman, M. R. P., *Ignorance: A Study of the Causes and Effects of Popular Thought* (London, 1898)

   The Mind of the Nation: A Study of Political Thought in the Nineteenth Century (London, 1900)

Drage, G., *The Labour Problem* (London, 1896)

Dückershoff, E., *How the English Workman Lives*, trans. C. H. d'E. Leppington (London, 1899)

Edgeworth, F. Y., *Mathematical Psychics: An Essay on the Application of Mathematics to the Moral Sciences* (London, 1881)

Edwards, C., 'Do trade unions limit output?', *Contemporary Review*, 81 (Jan. 1902), 113–28

Eggleston, E., 'A full-length portrait of the United States: James Bryce's "The American commonwealth"', *Century Magazine*, 15 (Mar. 1889), 789–98

Ensor, R. C. K., ed., *Modern Socialism* (London, 1904)

Escott, T. H. S., *England: Its People, Polity and Pursuits* (London, 1885)

   Essays on Reform (London, 1867)

   'Old and new in the daily press', *Quarterly Review*, 227 (April 1917), 353–69

   Social Transformation of the Victorian Age: A Survey of Court and Country (London, 1897)

Fawcett, H., *Manual of Political Economy* (London, 1884)

Fisher, W. J., 'The Liberal press and the Liberal party', *Nineteenth Century*, 56 (Aug. 1904), 190–206

Flint, R., 'Associationism and the origin of moral ideas', *Mind*, 1 (1876), 321–34

Foxwell, H. S., 'The growth of monopoly, and its bearings on the fluctuations of the state', *Papers on Current Finance* (London, 1919)

   Irregularity of Employment and Fluctuation of Prices (Edinburgh, 1886)

Freeman, E. A., *The Growth of the English Constitution from the Earliest Times* (London, 1872)

   Historical Essays (4th ser., London, 1892)

   'Progress in the nineteenth century', *The Chautauquan*, 14 (Jan. 1892), 434

Frere, H. C. P. B., *The Means of Ascertaining Public Opinion in India* (London, 1871)

Gardiner, A. G., *Prophets, Priests, and Kings* (London, 1908)

   'The Times', *Atlantic Monthly*, 119 (Jan. 1917), 111–22

Giffen, R., *The Progress of the Working Classes in the Last Half Century* (London, 1884)

Gladstone, W. E., 'The county franchise and Mr Lowe thereon', *Nineteenth Century*, 2 (Nov. 1877), 537–60

'The declining efficiency of parliament', *Quarterly Review*, 99 (Sep. 1856), 520–71

Gleanings of Past Years (London, 1879)

'The platform, its rise and progress', *Nineteenth Century*, 31 (April 1892), 686–9

Gleig, G. R. 'The government and the press, *Blackwood's Magazine*, 102 (Dec. 1867), 763–83

Gneist, R., *The History of the English Constitution* (2nd edn, London, 1889)

Gostick, J., 'Trade-unions, and the relations of capital and labour', *Cobden Club Essays*, 2nd ser., 1871–2 (1872), 357–99

Grant, J., *The Newspaper Press: Its Origin, Progress and Present Position* (London, 1871)

Great Central Gas Consumers Company, *A Letter to the Gas Consumers of the City of London, with an appendix, illustrating the force of public opinion and the advantages of free trade by the rise, progress, proceedings, position and prospects of the Great Central Gas Consumers' Company* (London, 1851)

Green, J. R., *A Short History of the English People* (London, 1874)

Green, O. M., 'The people and modern journalism', *Monthly Review*, 10 (Feb. 1903), 81–94

Greenwood, F., '*England at war*', *Nineteenth Century*, 43 (Feb. 1898), 171–81

'The newspaper press', *Blackwood's Magazine*, 161 (May 1897), 704–21

'Public opinion in public affairs', *Macmillan's Magazine*, 79 (Jan. 1899), 161–70

'Sentiment in politics', *Cosmopolis*, 4 (Nov. 1896), 340–54

Greville, C., *The Greville Memoirs: A Journal of the Reigns of King George IV and King William IV*, ed. H. Reeve (3 vols., London, 1874)

Grey, H. G., 'In peril from parliament', *Nineteenth Century*, 28 (Nov. and Dec. 1890), 694–8 and 1012–30

Parliamentary Government Considered with Reference to a Reform of Parliament (London, 1858)

Gross, C., *The Gild Merchant: A Contribution to British Municipal History* (2 vols., Oxford, 1890)

Hand, Rev. J. E., *Good Citizenship* (London, 1899)

Hardie, J. Keir *From Serfdom to Socialism* (London, 1907)

Keir Hardie's Speeches and Writings (from 1888 to 1915), ed. E. Hughes (3rd edn, London, 1928)

Harmsworth, A. C., 'The making of a newspaper' in A. Lawrence, *Journalism as a Profession* (London, 1903), pp. 167–89

Harrison, F., 'The good and evil of trade unionism', *Fortnightly Review*, 3 (Nov. 1865), 33–54

'The limits of political economy', *Fortnightly Review*, 1 (Aug. 1865), 356–76

'Mr Brassey on work and wages', *Fortnightly Review*, 12 (Sep. 1872), 268–86

Order and Progress (London, 1875)

Haslam, J., *The Press and the People: An Estimate of Reading in Working-Class Districts* (Manchester, 1906)

Hatton, J., *Journalistic London: Being a Series of Sketches of the Famous Pens and Papers of the Day* (London, 1882)

Hill, F., 'Are strikes necessary for the protection of workmen, or lock-outs for that of employers?', *Transactions of the National Association for the Promotion of Social Science* (1871), 566–71

Hitschman, F., 'The newspaper press', *Quarterly Review*, 40 (Oct. 1880), 498–532

Hobhouse, L. T., *Democracy and Reaction* (London, 1904)

The Labour Movement, ed. P. P. Poirier (3rd edn, 1912, Brighton, 1974)

Hobson, J. A., *The Economics of Distribution* (New York, 1900)

Imperialism: A Study (London, 1902)

The Psychology of Jingoism (London, 1901)

Holland, B., *Imperium et Libertas: A Study in History and Politics* (London, 1901)

Holyoake, G. J., *Sixty Years of an Agitator's Life* (2 vols., London, 1893)

Honeyman, J., *Trades Unionism the Blight on British Industries and Commerce* (London, 1877)

Hopkins, E., 'Social wreckage', *Contemporary Review*, 44 (July 1883), 94–104

Howell, G. J., 'The caucus system and the Liberal party', *New Quarterly Magazine*, 10 (Oct. 1878), 579–90

Conflicts of Capital and Labour (2nd edn, London, 1890)

Howell, G. J., ed., *Trade Unionism Old and New* (Brighton, 1973; reprint of 4th edn, 1907)

Hueffer, F. M., *The Spirit of the People: An Analysis of the English Mind* (London, 1907)

Industrial Remuneration Conference: The Report of the Proceedings and Papers (London, 1885)

Innes, A. T., 'Trade unionism; its limits and its future', *Transactions of the National Association for the Promotion of Social Science* (1874), 915–22

Jackson, M., *The Pictorial Press: Its Origin and Progress* (London, 1885)

Jephson, H., *The Platform: Its Rise and Progress* (2 vols., London, 1892)

Jennings, L. J., 'Parliamentary and election prospects', *Quarterly Review*, 174 (Jan. 1892), 254–85

Jevons, W., 'The future of political economy', *Fortnightly Review*, 20 new ser. (Nov. 1876), 617–31
  The State in Relation to Labour (London, 1882)
  The Theory of Political Economy (London, 1871)

J. G. L., 'The newspaper', *Macmillan's Magazine*, 87 (April 1903), 429–35

Johns, B. G., 'The literature of the streets', *Edinburgh Review*, 165 (Jan. 87), 40–65

Jones, E. R., *The Life and Speeches of Joseph Cowen, MP* (London, 1885)

Jones, K., *Fleet Street and Downing Street* (London, 1919)

Kebbel, T. E., 'Conservative instincts in the English people – the middle classes', *National Review*, 5 (July 1883), 687–701
  'England at war', *Nineteenth Century*, 253 (Mar. 1898), 337–44
  A History of Toryism (London, 1886), ed. E. J. Feuchtwanger (reprinted London, 1972)
  'Is the party system breaking up?', *Nineteenth Century*, 45 (Mar. 1899), 502–11
  Lord Beaconsfield and Other Tory Memories (London, 1907)

Kinnear, A., 'Parliamentary reporting', *Contemporary Review*, 87 (Mar. 1905), 369–76
  'The trade in great man's speeches', *Contemporary Review*, 75 (Mar. 1899), 433–44

Knight, C., *Charles Knight's School History of England; From the Earliest Period to our Own Times* (London, 1865)

Knoop, D., *Industrial Conciliation and Arbitration* (London, 1905)

Kydd, S., *A Sketch of the Growth of Public Opinion; Its Influence on the Constitution and the Government* (London, 1888)

Lambert, B., 'The outcast poor – I. Esau's cry', *Contemporary Review*, 44 (July 1883), 916–23

Lane, R. [Norman Angell], *Patriotism under Three Flags: A Plea for Rationalism in Politics* (London, 1903)

Lawrence, A., *Journalism as a Profession* (London, 1903)

Le Bon, G., *The Crowd: A Study of the Popular Mind* (London, 1896)

Leigh, J. G., 'What do the masses read?', *Economic Review*, 14 (April 1904), 166–77

Levi, L., *Work and Pay; Or, Principles of Industrial Economy* (London, 1877)

Lightbody, W., 'The awakening of democracy', *Westminster Review*, 165 (April 1906), 370–9

Llewellyn-Smith, H. and Nash, V., *The Story of the Dockers' Strike, Told by Two East Londoners* (London, 1890)

Lowe, R., 'A new reform bill', *Fortnightly Review*, 22 new ser. (Oct. 1877), 437–52

'Recent attacks on political economy', *Nineteenth Century*, 4 (Nov. 1878), 858–68

Lowell, A. L., *The Government of England* (2 vols., London, 1908)

Public Opinion and Popular Government (London, 1913)

MacDonald, J. R., *Labour and Empire* (London, 1907)

'Outlook', *Socialist Review*, 15 (Dec. 1919), 305–29

Parliament and Democracy (London, 1920)

'The people in power' in S. Coit, ed., *Ethical Democracy: Essays in Social Dynamics* (London, 1900), pp. 60–80

Ramsay MacDonald's Political Writings, ed. B. Barker (London, 1972)

Syndicalism (London, 1912)

Socialism and Government (2 vols., London, 1909)

Socialism and Society (London, 1905)

What I Saw in South Africa, September and October 1902 (London, 1903)

Macfie, M., 'Is parliamentary government compatible with democracy?', *Westminster Review*, 142 (Sep. 1894), 323–37.

Mackenzie, J. T., 'Professor Max Muller and Mr Mill on liberty', *Contemporary Review*, 37 (April 1880), 548–64

Mackinnon, W. A., *On the Rise, Progress and Present State of Public Opinion* (London, 1828)

Mackintosh, J., 'Parliamentary reform', *Edinburgh Review*, 34 (Nov. 1820), 461–501

Maine, H., *Ancient Law: Its Connection to the Early History of Society, and Its Relation to Modern Ideas* (London, 1861)

Malcolm, W. R., 'Socialism and the man in the street', *Monthly Review*, 22 (February 1906), 62–78

Mallock, W. H., *Aristocracy and Evolution* (London, 1898)

Classes and Masses: Wealth, Wages and Welfare in the United Kingdom (London, 1896)

Labour and the Popular Welfare (London, 1893)

Social Equality; A Short Study in a Missing Science (London, 1882)

Marshall, A., *Alfred Marshall's Lectures to Women*, ed. T. Raffaelli, E. F. Biagini and R. M. Tulberg (Aldershot, 1995)

Elements of the Economics of Industry: Being the First Volume of the Elements of Industry (London, 1892)

'A fair rate of wages' in *Memorials of Alfred Marshall*, ed. A. C. Pigou, pp. 212–26

Official Papers, ed. J. M. Keynes (London, 1926)

Principles of Political Economy (London, 1891)

'Some aspects of competition' in *Memorials of Alfred Marshall*, ed. A. C. Pigou (London, 1925), pp. 256–91

and M. P. Marshall, *Economics of Industry* (London, 1879)

Martin, K., *The British Public and the General Strike* (London, 1926)

Massingham, H. W., *The London Daily Press* (London, 1892)

'The need for a radical party', *Contemporary Review*, 85 (Jan. 1904), 12–24

Massingham, H. W., ed., *Labour and Protection* (London, 1903)

Masterman, C. F. G., *The Condition of England*, ed. and intro. J. T. Boulton (London, 1960)

Masterman, C. F. G., ed., *The Heart of Empire* (London, 1901)

May, T. E., *The Constitutional History of England Since the Accession of George III* (3rd edn, 3 vols., London, 1871)

Mayhew, H., *London Labour and the London Poor* (London, 1862)

Metcalfe, A. E., *Women's Effort* (Oxford, 1917)

Mill, J. S., 'Appendix' to *Dissertations and Discussions* in *Collected Works*, XIX, ed. J. M. Robson, intro. A. Brady (Toronto, 1977), 648–53

Autobiography (London, 1873)

'Civilisation' in *Collected Works*, XVIII, ed. J. M. Robson, intro. A. Brady, pp. 117–47

Considerations on Representative Government (London, 1861)

'De Tocqueville on democracy in America' in *The Collected Works of John Stuart Mill*, XVIII, ed. J. M. Robson, intro. A. Brady (Toronto, 1977), pp. 47–90 and 153–204

Letter to James Beal in *Collected Works*, XVI, ed. F. E. Mineka and D. N. Lindley (Toronto, 1972), pp. 1033–4

On Liberty and Other Writings, ed. S. Collini (Cambridge, 1989)

Principles of Political Economy, Collected Works, II and III, ed. J. M. Robson, intro. V. W. Bladen (Toronto, 1965)

'Thornton on labour and its claims', *Fortnightly Review*, 5 new ser. (May 1869), 505–18 and (June 1869), 680–700

Thoughts on Parliamentary Reform (London, 1859)

Utilitarianism (London, 1863)

Milman, A., 'Parliamentary procedure versus obstruction', *Quarterly Review*, 178 (April 1894), 486–503

'The peril of parliament', *Quarterly Review*, 178 (Jan. 1894), 263–88

Morley, J., 'The death of Mr Mill', *Fortnightly Review*, 13 new ser. (June 1873), 669–76

'Lancashire', *Fortnightly Review*, 24 new ser. (July 1878), 1–25

'Mr Lecky on democracy', *Nineteenth Century*, 39 (May 1896), 697–720

'Mr Mill's autobiography', *Fortnightly Review*, XV new ser. (Jan. 1874), 1–20

On Compromise (London, 1874)

Moseley, J., *Political Elements; or The Progress of Modern Legislation* (London, 1852)

Muller, F. M. 'On freedom', *Contemporary Review*, 36 (Nov. 1879), 369–97

Nicholson, A. P., 'Parliamentary reporting – a reply', *Contemporary Review*, 87 (April 1905), 577–82

Nicholson, J. S., *Strikes and Social Problems* (London, 1896)

O'Connor, T. P., 'The new journalism', *New Review*, 1 (Oct. 1889), 423–34

Oldershaw, L., ed., *England: A Nation, Being the Papers of the Patriots' Club* (London, 1904)

Oliphant, J. ed., *The Claims of Labour* (London, 1886)

Ostrogorski, M., *Democracy and the Organisation of Political Parties* (2 vols., London, 1899)

Otway, J. H., *Public Opinion: A Lecture* (Dublin, 1854)

Pankhurst, E., *My Own Story* (New York, 1914)

Paris, Comte de, *The Trade Unions of England* (London, 1867)

Paterson, A., 'Two centuries of daily journalism', *Sell's World's Press* (1902), 37–47

Pattison, M., 'Books and critics', *Fortnightly Review*, 22 new ser. (Nov. 1877), 659–79

Pebody, C., *English Journalism and the Men Who have Made It* (London, 1882)

Phelps, E. J., 'The American commonwealth and its lessons', *Quarterly Review*, 169 (July 1889), 253–86

Philips, E. M., 'The new journalism', *New Review*, 13 (Aug. 1895), 182–9

Pigou, A. C. *Principles and Methods of Industrial Peace* (London, 1905)

Ponsonby, A., *Falsehood in War-time* (London, 1928)

Porritt, E., 'The value of political editorials', *Sell's World's Press* (1910), 508–13

Portsmouth, 'Executive government and the unionists', *Quarterly Review*, 173 (Oct. 1891), 536–54

Potter, B., *The Co-operative Movement in Great Britain* (Aldershot, 1987, reprint; 1st edn 1893)

Pratt, E. A., *Trade Unionism and British Industry: A Reprint of 'The Times' Articles on 'The crisis in British industry'* (London, 1904)

Price, L. L. F., *Economic Science and Practice; or, Essays on Various Aspects of the Relations of Economic Science to Practical Affairs* (London, 1896)

   Industrial Peace (London, 1887)

   'The relations between industrial conciliation and social reform', *Journal of the Royal Statistical Society*, 53 (Jun. 1890), 290–302

Redlich, J., *The Procedure of the House of Commons: A Study of its History and Present form* (3 vols., London, 1908)

Reid, A., *The New Party* (London, 1894)

Reid, T. W., 'Public opinion and its leaders', *Fortnightly Review*, 28 new ser. (Aug. 1880), 230–44

Revised Report of the Proceedings at the Dinner of 31st May, 1876, in Celebration of the Hundredth Year of the Publication of the 'Wealth of Nations' (London, 1876)

Reynolds, S., Wooley, B. and Wooley, T., *Seems So! A Working-Class View of Politics* (London, 1911)

Ritchie, D. G., 'The rights of minorities' in D. Boucher, ed., *The British Idealists* (Cambridge, 1997), pp. 142–56

Robertson, J. M., *Patriotism and Empire* (London, 1899)

Rogers, J. E. T., *Six Centuries of Work and Wages* (London, 1884)

Rowland, D., *A Manual of the English Constitution; With a Review of its Rise, Growth, and Present State* (London, 1859)

Roylance-Kent, C. B., 'The future of party government', *Macmillan's Magazine*, 68 (June 1893), 102–8

Russell, B., *Anti-Suffragist Anxieties* in *The Collected Papers of Bertrand Russell, vol. 12: Contemplation and Action, 1902–1914* (London, 1985), 304–18

'Liberalism and women's suffrage', *Contemporary Review*, 94 (July 1908), 11–16

Salisbury, Lord, 'Extra-parliamentary utterances', *Saturday Review*, 5 Dec. 1863, 715–16

Lord Salisbury on Politics: A Selection of his Articles in the Quarterly Review, 1860–1883, ed. P. Smith (Cambridge, 1972)

Schooling, J. H., 'Strikes and lock-outs, 1892–1901', *Fortnightly Review*, 75 new ser. (May 1904), 849–63

Schulze-Gaevernitz, G. von, *The Cotton Trade in England and on the Continent*, trans. O. S. Hall (London, 1895)

Social Peace: A Study of the Trade Union Movement in England, trans. C. M. Wicksteed (London, 1893)

Scott-James, R. A., *The Influence of the Press* (London, 1913)

Seal, H., 'The electorate supreme', *Westminster Review*, 157 (Aug. 1904), 135–50

Seeley, J. R., 'The English revolution of the nineteenth century', *Macmillan's Magazine*, 22 (Aug. and Oct. 1870), 241–51, 347–58, 444–51

The Impartial Study of Politics, Being the Inaugural Address to the Cardiff Society for the Impartial Discussion of Political and Other Questions (London, 1886)

Shadwell, A., 'Mesmerism and hypnotism', *Quarterly Review*, 171 (July 1890), 234–59

'Proprietors and editors', *National Review*, 35 (June 1900), 592–601

Shore, A., 'The present aspect of women's suffrage considered' (1877) in J. Lewis, ed., *Before the Vote was Won: Arguments For and Against Women's Suffrage* (London, 1987), pp. 282–315

'What women have a right to' in J. Lewis, ed., *Before the Vote was Won: Arguments For and Against Women's Suffrage* (London, 1987), pp. 354–66

Sidgwick, H., 'The wages-fund theory', *Fortnightly Review*, 26 new ser. (Sep. 1879), 401–13

Simonis, H., *The Street of Ink: An Intimate History of Journalism* (London, 1917)

Smith, G., 'The American commonwealth', *Macmillan's Magazine*, 59 (Feb. 1889), 241–55

Spender, J. A., *Life, Journalism and Politics* (2 vols., London, 1927)

'The patriotic election – and after', *Contemporary Review*, 78 (Nov. 1900), 746–60

The Public Life (2 vols., London, 1925)

Spenser, H., *Principles of Sociology* (London, 1876)

Spiers, H. A., *The Art of Publicity – and its Application to Business* (London, 1910)

Stead, W. T., 'The future of journalism', *Contemporary Review*, 50 (Nov. 1886), 663–79

'Government by journalism', *Contemporary Review*, 49 (May 1886), 653–74

'Her Majesty's public councillors: to wit, the editors of the London daily papers', *Review of Reviews*, 30 (Dec. 1904), 593–606

A Journalist on Journalism (London, 1891)

'The London morning dailies that are and are to be', *Sell's World's Press* (1892), 107–16

Stephen, J. F., 'Journalism', *Cornhill Magazine*, 6 (July 1862), 52–63

Stephen, L., 'Anonymous journalism', *St Paul's Magazine*, 2 (May 1868), 217–30

'Mr Gladstone and Sir George Lewis on authority', *Nineteenth Century*, 1 (April 1877), 270–97

Swinny, S. H., 'Lecky's liberty and democracy', *The Positivist Review*, 4 (August 1896), 163–7

Symon, J, D., *The Press and its Story* (London, 1914)

Tarde, G., 'The public and the crowd' in T. N. Clark, ed., *Gabriel Tarde: On Communication and Social Influence* (London, 1969), pp. 277–96

Taylor, F., *The Newspaper Press as a Power Both in the Expression and Formation of Public Opinion* (London, 1898)

Taylor, H., *The Origin and Growth of the English Constitution* (London, 1898)

Thompson, G. C., *Public Opinion and Lord Beaconsfield* (2 vols., London, 1886)

Todd, A., *On Parliamentary Government* (2nd edn, London, 1887)

Toynbee, A., *Lectures on the Industrial Revolution in England* (London, 1884)

    Progress and Poverty: A Criticism of Mr Henry George (London, 1883)

Traill, H. D., 'What is public opinion?', *National Review*, 5 (July 1885), 652–64

Trant, W., *Trade Unions: Their Origins and Objects, Influence and Efficacy* (London, 1884)

Tregathen, H. P., 'Pauperism, distress and the coming winter', *National Review*, 10 (Nov. 1887), 382–94

Urquhart, D., *Public Opinion and its Organs* (London, 1855)

Various, 'A modern "symposium": is the popular judgment in politics more just than that of the higher orders?', *Nineteenth century*, 3 (May 1878), 797–832 and 4 (July 1878), 181–92

Various, 'Are papers too cheap?', *Sell's World's Press* (1914), 10–22

Villiers, B. [Shaw, F. J.], *Modern Democracy: A Study in Tendencies* (London, 1912)

Wallas, G., *The Great Society: A Psychological Analysis* (London, 1914)

    Human Nature in Politics (London, 1908)

Watney, C. and Little, J. A., *Industrial Warfare: The Aims and Claims of Capital and Labour* (London, 1912)

Watney, D., *An Appeal to the Men on Strike at Bolton, Containing Extracts from Letters in the Manchester Guardian as well as a Letter Suppressed by the Editor* (London, 1887)

Watson, W. L., 'The press and finance', *Blackwood's Magazine*, 164 (Nov. 1898), 639–50

Webb, S. and B., *History of Trade Unionism* (rev. edn, London, 1920)

    Industrial Democracy (2 vols., London, 1894 and 1897)

White, A., *Efficiency and Empire*, ed. G. R. Searle (Brighton, 1973; 1st edn 1901)

    The English Democracy: Its Promises and Perils (London, 1894)

Wilson, J., 'Liberty, equality, fraternity: John Stuart Mill', *Quarterly Review*, 135 (July 1873), 178–201

Wilson, W., 'Bryce's American Commonwealth', *Political Science Quarterly*, 4 (1889), 153–97

Wright, T., *The Great Unwashed* (London, 1868)

    'On a possible popular culture', *Contemporary Review* (July 1881), 25–44

    Our New Masters (London, 1873)

    Some Habits and Customs of the Working Classes (London, 1867)

Secondary Sources

Baker, K. M., *Inventing the French Revolution: Essays on Political Culture in the Eighteenth Century* (Cambridge, 1990)

Barrow, L. and Bullock, I., *Democratic Ideas and the British Labour Movement, 1880–1914* (Cambridge, 1990)

Barrows, S., *Distorting Mirrors: Visions of the Crowd in Late Nineteenth-Century France* (New Haven, 1981)

Belchem, J., *Popular Radicalism in Nineteenth-Century Britain* (London, 1996)

Belchem, J. and Epstein, J., 'The nineteenth-century gentleman leader revisited', *Social History*, 22, 2 (1997), 174–93

Beers, L., 'Counter-Toryism: Labour's response to anti-socialist propaganda, 1918–39' in M. Worley, ed., *The Foundations of the British Labour Party: Identities, Cultures and Perspectives, 1900–39* (Farnham, 2009), pp. 231–54.

Your Britain: Media and the Making of the Labour Party (Cambridge, Mass., 2010)

Bevir, M., *The Logic of the History of Ideas* (Cambridge, 1999)

Biagini, E. F., *British Democracy and Irish Nationalism, 1876–1906* (Cambridge, 2007)

'British trade unions and popular political economy, 1860–1880', *Historical Journal*, 30, 4 (1987), 811–40

'Liberalism and direct democracy: John Stuart Mill and the model of ancient Athens' in Biagini, ed., *Citizenship and Community: Liberals, Radicals and Collective Identities in the British Isles, 1865–1931* (Cambridge, 1996), pp. 21–45

Liberty, Retrenchment and Reform: Popular Liberalism in the Age of Gladstone, 1860–1880 (Cambridge, 1992)

Biagini, E. F. and Reid, A. J., eds., *Currents of Radicalism: Popular Radicalism, Organised Labour and Party Politics in Britain, 1850–1914* (Cambridge, 1991)

Black, A. and Brooke, S., 'The Labour party, women, and the problem of gender, 1951–1966', *Journal of British Studies* (1997), 419–52

Black, L., '"What kind of people are you?" Labour, the people and the "new political History"' in J. T. Callaghan, S. Fielding and S. Ludlam, eds., *Interpreting the Labour Party: Approaches to Labour Politics and History* (Manchester, 2003), pp. 23–38

Blackbourn, D. and Eley, G., *The Peculiarities of German History: Bourgeois Society and Politics in Nineteenth-Century Germany* (Oxford, 1984)

Blake, R. and Cecil, H., *Salisbury: The Man and his Policies* (Basingstoke, 1987)

Blaug, M., *Economic Theory in Retrospect* (3rd edn, Cambridge, 1978)

Blewett, N., *The Peers, the Parties and the People: The General Elections of 1910* (London, 1972)

Blumer, H., 'Public opinion and public opinion polling', *American Sociological Review*, 13, 5 (1948), 542–9

Brooks, P., *The Melodramatic Imagination: Balzac, Henry James, Melodrama, and the Mode of Excess* (New Haven, 1976)

Brown, L., *Victorian News and Newspapers* (Oxford, 1985)

Bryce, G., Curran, J. and Wright, P. eds., *Newspaper History from the Seventeenth Century to the Present Day* (London, 1978)

Burrow, J. W., *The Crisis of Reason: European Thought, 1849–1914* (New Haven, 2000)

    Evolution and Society: A Study in Victorian Social Theory (Cambridge, 1966)

    A Liberal Descent: Victorian Historians and the English Past (Oxford, 1981)

    'Some British views of the United States Constitution', in R. C. Simmons, ed., *The United States Constitution: The First 200 Years* (Manchester, 1989), pp. 116–37

    '"The village community" and the uses of history in late nineteenth-century England' in N. McKendrick, ed., *Historical Perspectives: Studies in English Thought and Society in Honour of J. H. Plumb* (London, 1974), pp. 255–84

    Whigs and Liberals: Continuity and Change in English Political Thought (Oxford, 1988)

Cain, P., *Hobson and Imperialism: Radicalism, New Liberalism and Finance, 1887–1938* (Oxford, 2002)

Chartier, R., *The Cultural Origins of the French Revolution* (Durham, 1991)

Clark, A., 'Gender, class and the constitution: franchise reform in England, 1832–1928' in J. Vernon, ed., *Re-reading the Constitution: New Narratives in the Political History of England's Long Nineteenth Century* (Cambridge, 1996), pp. 239–54

Clegg, H. A., Fox, A. and Thompson, A. F., *A History of Trade Unionism since 1889, vol. 2: 1911–1933* (Oxford, 1985)

Cohen, D. *Household Gods: The British and their Possessions* (New Haven, 2006)

Collini, S., *Absent Minds: Intellectuals in Britain* (Oxford, 2006)

    Liberalism and Sociology: L. T. Hobhouse and Political Argument in England, 1880–1914 (Cambridge, 1979)

    Public Moralists: Political Thought and Intellectual Life in Britain 1850–1930 (Cambridge, 1991)

Collini, S., Winch, D. and Burrow, J. W., *That Noble Science of Politics: A Study in Nineteenth-Century Intellectual History* (Cambridge, 1983)

Cosgrove, R. A., *The Rule of Law: Albert Venn Dicey, Victorian Jurist* (London, 1980)

Curthoys, M., *Government, Labour, and the Law in Mid-Victorian Britain: The Trade Union Legislation of the 1870s* (Oxford, 2004)

Daunton, M., *Trusting Leviathan: The Politics of Taxation in Britain, 1799–1914* (Cambridge, 2001)

Daunton, M. and Hilton, M., *The Politics of Consumption: Material Culture and Citizenship in Europe and America* (Oxford, 2001)

Davidson, D., 'On the very idea of a conceptual scheme' in D. Davidson, *Inquiries into Truth and Interpretation* (Oxford, 1984), pp. 183–99

Davidson, R., *Whitehall and the Labour Problem in Late-Victorian and Edwardian Britain: A Study in Official Statistics and Social Control* (London, 1985)

Davis, Jennifer, 'From "rookeries" to "communities": race, poverty and policing in London, 1850–1985', *History Workshop Journal*, 27 (Spring 1989), 66–85

'Jennings' buildings and the royal borough: the construction of the underclass in mid-Victorian England' in D. Feldman and G. Stedman Jones, eds., *Metropolis – London: Histories and Representations since 1800* (London, 1989), pp. 11–39

Davis, John, 'Radical clubs and London politics, 1870–1900' in D. Feldman and G. Stedman Jones, eds., *Metropolis – London: Histories and Representations since 1800* (London, 1989), pp. 103–28.

Dennis, B. and Skelton, D., *Reform and Intellectual Debate in Victorian England* (London, 1987)

Desrosières, A., 'The part in relation to the whole: how to generalise? The prehistory of representative sampling' in M. Bulmer, K. Bales and K. K. Sklar eds., *The Social Survey in Historical Perspective, 1880–1940* (Cambridge, 1991), pp. 217–45

Dewey, J., *The Public and its Problems* (London, 1928)

Dunn, J., 'Revolution' in T. Ball, J. Farr and R. L. Hanson, eds., *Political Innovation and Conceptual Change* (Cambridge, 1989), pp. 333–57

Dworkin, R. *Taking Rights Seriously* (London, 1977)

Eagleton, T., *The Function of Criticism: From the 'Spectator' to Poststructuralism* (London, 1984)

Ellenberger, H., *The Discovery of the Unconscious: The History and Evolution of Dynamic Psychiatry* (London, 1970)

Emy, H. V., *Liberals, Radicals and Social Politics, 1892–1914* (Cambridge, 1973)

Epstein, J. A., 'The populist turn', *Journal of British Studies*, 32, 2 (April 1993), 177–89

Radical Expression: Political Language, Ritual, and Symbol in England, 1790–1850 (Oxford, 1994)

Farr, J. 'Understanding conceptual change politically' in T. Ball, J. Farr and R. L. Hanson, eds., *Political Innovation and Conceptual Change* (Cambridge, 1989), pp. 24–50

Ford, T. H., *Albert Venn Dicey: The Man and his Times* (Chichester, 1985)

Francis, M. and Morrow, J., *A History of English Political Thought in the Nineteenth Century* (London, 1994)

Fraser, P., 'The growth of ministerial control in the nineteenth-century House of Commons', *English Historical Review*, 75 (July 1960), 444–63

'Public petitioning and parliament before 1832', *History*, 46 (1961), 195–211

Fraser, W. H., *Trade Unions and Society: The Struggle for Acceptance 1850–1880* (London, 1974)

Freeden, M., *Ideologies and Political Theory: A Conceptual Approach* (Oxford, 1996)

Liberal Languages: Ideological Imaginations and Twentieth-Century Progressive Thought (Princeton, 2005)

The New Liberalism: An Ideology of Social Reform (Oxford, 1978)

Freeden, M., ed., *Minutes of the Rainbow Circle, 1894–1924* (London, 1989)

Freeden, M., ed., *Reappraising J. A. Hobson: Humanism and Welfare* (London, 1990)

Gallie, W. B., 'Essentially contested concepts', *Proceedings of the Aristotelian Society*, 56 (1956), 167–98

Gatrell, V. A. G. and Hadden, T. B., 'Criminal statistics and their interpretation' in E. A. Wrigley, ed., *Nineteenth-Century Society: Essays in the Use of Quantitative Methods for the Study of Social Data* (Cambridge, 1972), pp. 336–96

'The decline of theft and violence in Victorian and Edwardian England' in V. A. G. Gatrell, B. Lenman and G. Parker, eds., *Crime and the Law: The Social History of Crime in Western Europe since 1500* (London, 1980), pp. 238–337

Ghosh, P., 'Gladstone and Peel' in P. Ghosh and L. Goldman, eds., *Politics and Culture in Victorian Britain* (Oxford, 2006), pp. 45–73

Goldman, L., *Science, Reform and Politics in Victorian Britain: The Social Science Association, 1857–1886* (Cambridge, 2002)

'The Social Science Association: a context for mid-Victorian Liberalism', *English Historical Review*, 101 (Jan. 1986), 95–134

Gollin, A. M., *'The Observer' and J. L. Garvin, 1908–1914: A Study in a Great Editorship* (London, 1960)

Gordon, S., 'The wages fund controversy: the second round', *History of Political Economy*, 5, 1 (1973), 14–35

Gray, R., 'The languages of factory reform in Britain, c. 1830–1860' in P. Joyce, ed., *The Historical Meanings of Work* (Cambridge, 1987), pp. 143–79

Green, E. H. H., *The Crisis of Conservatism: The Politics, Economics and Ideology of the British Conservative Policy, 1880–1914* (London, 1995)

Ideologies of Conservatism: Conservative Political Ideas in the Twentieth Century (Oxford, 2002)

'The strange death of Tory England', *Twentieth Century British History*, 2, 1 (1991), 67–88

'Radical conservatism: the electoral genesis of tariff reform', *Historical Journal*, 28, 3 (1985), 667–92

Green, E. H. H. and Tanner, D., eds., *The Strange Survival of Liberal England: Political Leaders, Moral Values and the Reception of Economic Debate* (Cambridge, 2007)

Griffin, B., *The politics of Gender in Victorian Britain: Masculinity, Political Culture and the Struggle for Women's Rights* (Cambridge, 2012).

Groenwegen, P., *Alfred Marshall: Critical Responses* (London, 1998)

Gunn, J. A. W., *Beyond Liberty and Property: The Process of Self-Recognition in Eighteenth-Century Political Thought* (Kingston, Ont., 1983)

'Public opinion' in T. Ball, J. Farr and R. L. Hanson, eds., *Political Innovation and Conceptual Change* (Cambridge, 1989), pp. 247–65

'"Public opinion" in modern political science' in J. Farr, J. S. Dryzek and S. T. Leonard, eds., *Political Science in History: Research Programs and Political Traditions* (Cambridge, 1995), pp. 99–123

Gurney, P., *Co-operative Culture and the Politics of Consumption in England, 1870–1930* (Manchester, 1996)

Habermas, J., *The Structural Transformation of the Public Sphere: An Inquiry into a Category of Bourgeois Society*, trans. T. Burger (Cambridge, Mass., 1989)

Hacking, I., *The Taming of Chance* (Cambridge, 1990)

Hall, C., 'Private persons versus public someones: class, gender and politics in England, 1780–1850' in C. Steedman, C. Urwin and V. Walkerdine, eds., *Language, Gender and Childhood* (London, 1985), pp. 10–33

'Rethinking imperial histories: the reform act of 1867', *New Left Review*, 208 (December 1994), 3–29

Hall, C., McClelland, K. and Rendall, J., *Defining the Victorian Nation: Class, Race, Gender and the British Reform Act of 1867* (Cambridge, 2000)

Hamer, D. A., *Liberal Politics in the Age of Gladstone and Rosebery* (Oxford, 1972)

Hampton, M. 'The press, patriotism, and public discussion: C. P. Scott, the *Manchester Guardian* and the Boer War, 1899–1902', *Historical Journal*, 44 (2001), 177–97

Visions of the Press in Britain, 1850–1950 (Urbana, 2005)

Hanham, H. J., *Elections and Party Management: Politics in the Time of Disraeli and Gladstone* (London, 1959)

The Nineteenth-Century Constitution 1815–1914: Documents and Commentary (Cambridge, 1969)

Harris, J., 'Labour's political and social thought', in D. Tanner, P. Thane and N. Tiratsoo, eds., *Labour's First Century* (2000), pp. 8–45.

'Platonism, positivism and progressivism: aspects of British sociological thought in the early twentieth century' in E. F. Biagini, ed., *Citizenship and Community: Liberals, Radicals and Collective Identities in the British Isles, 1865–1931* (Cambridge, 1996), pp. 343–60

'Political thought and the welfare state 1870–1940: an intellectual framework for British social policy', *Past and Present*, 135 (May 1992), 116–41

Private Lives, Public Spirit: Britain 1870–1914 (Oxford, 1993)

'The transition to high politics in English social policy, 1880–1914' in M. Bentley and J. Stevenson, eds., *High and Low Politics in Modern Britain: Ten Studies* (Oxford, 1983), pp. 58–79

Unemployment and Politics: A Study in English Social Policy, 1886–1914 (Oxford, 1972)

Harris, J., ed., *Civil Society in British History: Ideas, Identities, Institutions* (Oxford, 2003)

Harrison, B., *Drink and the Victorians: The Temperance Question in England, 1815–72* (London, 1971)

Peaceable Kingdom: Stability and Change in Modern Britain (Oxford, 1982)

Separate Spheres: The Opposition to Women's Suffrage in Britain (London, 1978)

Hawkins, A. H., '"Parliamentary government" and Victorian political parties, c. 1830–1880', *English Historical Review*, 104 (July 1989), 638–69

Hennock, E. P., 'Poverty and social theory in England: the experience of the eighteen-eighties', *Social History*, 1 (1976), 67–91

Hilton, B., *The Age of Atonement: The Influence of Evangelicalism on Social and Economic Thought, 1795–1865* (Oxford, 1988)

'Gladstone's theological politics' in M. Bentley and J. Stevenson, eds., *High and Low Politics in Modern Britain* (Oxford, 1983), pp. 28–57

Hilton, M., *Consumerism in Twentieth-Century Britain: The Search for a Historical Movement* (Cambridge, 2003)

Smoking in British Popular Culture, 1800–2000: Perfect Pleasures (Manchester, 2000)

Himmelfarb, G., *Poverty and Compassion: The Moral Imagination of the Late Victorians* (New York, 1991)

Holton, S. S., *Feminism and Democracy: Women's Suffrage and Reform Politics in Britain, 1900–1918* (Cambridge, 1986)

Hoppen, K. T., 'Grammars of electoral violence in nineteenth-century England and Ireland', *English Historical Review*, 109 (June 1994), 597–620

Howe, A., *Free Trade and Liberal England, 1846–1946* (Oxford, 1997)

'Towards the "hungry forties": free trade in Britain, 1880–1906' in E. F. Biagini, ed., *Citizenship and Community: Liberals, Radicals and Collective Identities in the British Isles, 1865–1931* (Cambridge, 1996), pp. 193–218

Hutchison, T. W., *A Review of Economic Doctrines, 1870–1929* (Oxford, 1975)

Ironside, P., *The Social and Political Thought of Bertrand Russell: The Development of an Aristocratic Liberalism* (Cambridge, 1996)

Jarvis, D., 'British conservatism and class politics in the 1920s', *English Historical Review*, 111 (Feb. 1996), 59–84

'"Mrs Maggs and Betty": the Conservative appeal to women voters in the 1920s', *Twentieth Century British History*, 5, 2 (1994), 129–52

'The shaping of conservative hegemony, 1918–1939' in J. Lawrence and M. Taylor, eds., *Party, State and Society: Electoral Behaviour in Britain since 1820* (Aldershot, 1997), pp. 131–52

Jenkins, T. A., *Gladstone, Whiggery and the Liberal Party, 1874–1886* (Oxford, 1988)

Jones, A., 'Local journalism in Victorian political culture' in L. Brake, A. Jones and L. Madden, eds., *Investigating Victorian Journalism* (London, 1990), pp. 63–71

Powers of the Press: Newspapers, Power and the Public in Nineteenth-Century England (Cambridge, 1996)

Jones, G., *Social Darwinism and English Thought* (Brighton, 1980)

Jones, H. S., 'The idea of the "national" in Victorian political thought', *European Journal of Political Theory*, 5 (2006), 12–21

Victorian Political Thought (Basingstoke, 2000)

Jordan, H. D., 'The reports of parliamentary debates, 1803–1908', *Economica*, 34 (1931), 431–49

Joyce, P., *Democratic Subjects: The Self and the Social in Nineteenth-Century England* (Cambridge, 1994)

Visions of the People: Industrial England and the Question of Class, 1848–1914 (Cambridge, 1991)

Kadish, A., *Historians, Economists and Economic History* (London, 1989)

Kadish, A. and Tribe, K., eds., *The Market for Political Economy: The Advent of Economics in British University Culture, 1850–1905* (London, 1993)

Keynes, J. M., *Essays in Biography* (London, 1951)

King, J. E., '"We could eat the police": popular violence in the north Lancashire cotton strike of 1878', *Victorian Studies*, 28, 3 (1985), 439–71

Kinzer, B. L., *The Ballot Question in Nineteenth-Century English Politics* (London, 1982)

'J. S. Mill and the secret ballot', *Historical Reflections/Réflexions historiques* 5, 1 (1978), 19–39

J. S. Mill Revisited: Biographical and Political Explorations (Basingstoke, 2007)

Kinzer, B. L., Robson, A. P. and Robson, J. M., *A Moralist In and Out of Parliament: John Stuart Mill at Westminster, 1865–1868* (Toronto, 1992)

Kirk, N., *The Growth of Working Class Reformism in Mid-Victorian London* (London, 1985)

Knight, M., 'Petitioning and the political theorists: John Locke, Algernon Sidney and London's "Monster" petition of 1680', *Past and Present*, 138 (1993), 94–111

Koot, G. M., *English Historical Economics, 1870–1926: The Rise of Economic History and Neomercantilism* (Cambridge, 1987)

Koss, S., *The Rise and Fall of the Political Press in Britain* (2 vols., London, 1976 and 1984)

Koven, S. *Slumming: Sexual and Social Politics in Victorian London* (Princeton, 2004)

Kripke, S., *Naming and Necessity* (Oxford, 1980)

Kuhn, T. S., *The Structure of Scientific Revolutions* (Chicago, 1963 and 1970)

Lawrence, J., 'Contesting the male polity: the suffragettes and the politics of disruption in Edwardian Britain' in A. Vickery, ed., *Women, Privilege, and Power: British Politics, 1750 to the Present* (Stanford, 2001), pp. 201–26

Electing our Masters: The Hustings in British Politics from Hogarth to Blair (Oxford, 2009)

'Labour and the politics of class, 1900–1940' in D. Feldman and J. Lawrence, eds., *Structures and Transformations in Modern British History* (Cambridge, 2011), pp. 237–60

'Popular radicalism and the socialist revival in Britain', *Journal of British Studies*, 31 (1992), 183–6

Speaking for the People: Party, Language and Popular Politics in England, 1867–1914 (Cambridge, 1998)

'The transformation of British public politics after the First World War', *Past and Present* (2006), 185–216

Lazarsfeld, P., 'Public opinion and the classical tradition', *Public Opinion Quarterly*, 21, 1 (1957), 39–53

Lee, A. J., *The Origins of the Popular Press in England 1855–1914* (London, 1976)

Lewis, J., ed., *Before the Vote was Won: Arguments For and Against Women's Suffrage* (London, 1987)

Leys, C., 'Petitioning in the nineteenth and twentieth centuries', *Political Studies*, 3 (1955), 45–64

Lippincott, B., *Victorian Critics of Democracy* (London, 1938)

Lippman, W., *The Phantom Public* (New York, 1925)

Macintyre, A., 'The essential contestability of some social concepts', *Ethics*, 84, 1 (1973), 1–9

Maloney, J., *Marshall, Orthodoxy and the Professionalisation of Economics* (Cambridge, 1985).

Mandler, P., *The English National Character: The History of an Idea from Edmund Burke to Tony Blair* (New Haven, 2006)

Marsh, P., *The Discipline of Popular Government: Lord Salisbury's Domestic Statecraft, 1881–1902* (Hassocks, 1978)

Mason, A., *Explaining Political Disagreement* (Cambridge, 1993)

Matthew, H. C. G., 'Disraeli, Gladstone, and the policy of mid-Victorian budgets', *Historical Journal*, 22, 3 (1979), 615–43

The Liberal Imperialists: The Ideas and Politics of a Post-Gladstonian Elite (London, 1973)

'Rhetoric and politics in Britain, 1860–1950' in P. J. Waller, ed., *Politics and Social Change in Modern Britain: Essays Presented to A. F. Thompson* (Brighton, 1987), pp. 34–58

Matthew, R. C., 'Marshall and the labour market' in J. Whittaker, ed., *Centenary Essays on Alfred Marshall* (Cambridge, 1990), pp. 14–43

McCarthy, H., Democratizing British foreign policy: rethinking the peace ballot, 1934–35', *Journal of British Studies*, 49 (2010), 358–87

'The League of Nations, public ritual and national identity in Britain, c. 1919–56', *History Workshop Journal*, 70 (2010), 108–32

'Parties, voluntary associations and democratic politics in interwar Britain', *Historical Journal*, 50 (2007), 891–912

'Service clubs, citizenship and equality: gender relations and middle-class associations in Britain between the wars', *Historical Research*, 81 (2008), 531–52

McClelland, J. S., *The Crowd and the Mob: From Plato to Canetti* (London, 1989)

McClelland, K., 'Rational and respectable men: gender, the working class and citizenship in Britain, 1850–1867' in L. Frader and S. Rose, eds., *Gender and Class in Modern Europe* (Ithaca, 1995), pp. 280–93

'Time to work, time to live: some aspects of work and the re-formation of class in Britain, 1850–1880' in P. Joyce, ed., *The Historical Meanings of Work* (Cambridge, 1987), pp. 182–210

McKibbin, R., *Classes and Cultures: England, 1918–45* (Oxford, 1998)

The Evolution of the Labour Party, 1910–24 (Oxford, 1974)

The Ideologies of Class: Social Relations in Britain, 1880–1950 (Oxford, 1990)

Parties and People: England 1914–1951 (Oxford, 2010)

'Why was there no Marxism in Britain?', *English Historical Review*, 99 (April 1984), 297–331

McNiece, G., 'Shelley, John Stuart Mill, and the secret ballot', *Mill Newsletter*, 8, 2 (1973), 2–7

McNulty, P. J., *The Origins and Development of Labour Economics: A Chapter in the History of Social Thought* (London, 1980)

McCormack, N., ed., *Public Men: Masculinity and Politics in Modern Britain* (Basingstoke, 2007)

Meadowcroft, J., *Conceptualizing the State: Innovation and Dispute in British Political Thought 1880–1914* (Cambridge, 1995)

Meisel, J. *Public Speech and the Culture of Public Life in the Age of Gladstone* (New York, 2001)

Minar, D., 'Public opinion in the perspective of political theory', *Western Political Quarterly*, 13, 1 (1960), 31–44

Morgan, J., *Conflict and Order: The Police and Labour Disputes in England and Wales, 1900–1939* (Oxford, 1987)

Nicholson, P. J., *The Political Philosophy of the British Idealists* (Cambridge, 1990)

Nye, R. A., *The Origins of Crowd Psychology: Gustave Le Bon and the Crisis of Mass Democracy in the Third Republic* (London, 1975)

O'Leary, C., *The Elimination of Corrupt Practices in British Elections* (Oxford, 1962)

Owen, J., 'Triangular contests and caucus rhetoric at the 1885 general election', *Parliamentary History* 27, 2 (2008), 215–35

Ozouf, M., '"Public opinion" at the end of the old regime', *Journal of Modern History*, 60 (Sep. 1988), S1–21

Palmer, P. A., 'The concept of public opinion in political theory' in *Essays in History and Political Theory in Honor of Charles Howard McIlwain* (Cambridge, Mass., 1936), pp. 230–57

Parry, J., *The Politics of Patriotism: English Liberalism, National Identity and Europe, 1830–1886* (Cambridge, 2006)

   The Rise and Fall of Liberal Government in Victorian England (New Haven, 1993)

Parsons, T., 'Economics and sociology: Marshall in relation to the thought of his time', *Quarterly Journal of Economics*, 46 (1931–2), 316–47

Pedersen, S. and P. Mandler, P., eds., *After the Victorians: Private Conscience and Public Duty in Modern Britain: Essays in Memory of John Clive* (London, 1994)

Pelling, H., *America and the British Left: From Bright to Bevan* (London, 1956)

Perkin, H., 'The origins of the popular press' in *The Structured Crowd: Essays in English Social History* (London, 1981), pp. 47–57

Petridis, A., 'The trade unions in the Principles: the ethical versus the practical in Marshall's economics,' *Economie Appliquée*, 42, 1 (1990), 161–86

Petridis, R., 'Brassey's law and the economy of high wages in nineteenth-century economics', *History of Political Economy*, 24, 4 (1996), 583–606

Pickering, P., '"And your petitioners &c": Chartist petitioning in popular politics 1838–48', *English Historical Review*, 116 (2001), 368–88.

Pombeni, P., 'Starting in reason, ending in passion: Bryce, Lowell, Ostrogorski and the problem of democracy', *Historical Journal*, 37, 2 (1994), 319–41

Porter, B., *Critics of Empire: British Radical Attitudes to Colonialism in Africa, 1895–1914* (London, 1968)

Porter, T., *The Rise of Statistical Thinking, 1820–1900* (Princeton, 1986)

Price, R., *An Imperial War and the British Working Class: Working-Class Attitudes and the Reactions to the Boer War, 1899–1902* (London, 1972)

Pyle, A., ed., *Liberty: Contemporary Responses to John Stuart Mill* (Bristol, 1994)

Quagliariello, G., *Politics without Parties: Moisei Ostrogorski and the Debate on Political Parties on the Eve of the Twentieth Century* (Aldershot, 1996)

Rapp, D., 'The early discovery of Freud by the British general educated public, 1912–1919', *Social History of Medicine*, 3 (1990), 217–43

Rees, N., *Dictionary of Popular Phrases* (London, 1990)

Reid, A., 'The division of labour and politics in Britain, 1880–1920' in W. Mommsen and H. Husung, eds., *The Development of Trade Unionism in Britain and Germany* (London, 1985), pp. 150–66

Rendall, J., 'Citizenship, culture and civilisation: the languages of British suffragists, 1866–74' in C. Daly and M. Nolan ed., *Suffrage and Beyond: International Feminist Perspectives* (Auckland, 1994), pp. 127–50

Richter, D. C., *Riotous Victorians* (London, 1981)

Robbin, L., *The Evolution of Modern Economic Theory and Other Papers on the History of Economic Thought* (London, 1970)

Roberts, B. C., *The Trades Union Congress, 1868–1921* (London, 1958)

Roberts, M. 'Constructing a Tory world-view: popular politics and the Conservative press in late-Victorian Leeds', *Historical Research*, 20 (2006), 115–43.

  Political Movements in Urban England, 1832–1914 (Basingstoke, 2009)

  '"Villa toryism" and popular Conservatism in Leeds, 1885–1902', *Historical Journal*, 49 (2006), 217–46

Rogers, L., *The Pollsters: Public Opinion, Politics and Democratic Leadership* (New York, 1949)

Rorty, R., *Contingency, Irony and Solidarity* (Cambridge, 1989)

Rose, J., *The Intellectual Life of the British Working Classes* (New Haven, 2001)

Saab, A. P., *Reluctant Icon: Gladstone, Bulgaria, and the Working Classes, 1856–1873* (Cambridge, Mass., 1991)

Saville, J., 'Trade unions and free labour: the background to the Taff Vale decision' in A. Briggs and J. Saville, eds., *Essays in Labour History* (London, 1960), pp. 317–51

Schapin, S., *A Social History of Truth: Civility and Science in Seventeenth-Century England* (Chicago, 1994)

Searle, G. R., *Eugenics and Politics* (Leyden, 1976)

  The Quest for National Efficiency: A Study in British Politics and Political Thought, 1899–1914 (Oxford, 1971)

Shannon, R. T., *Gladstone and the Bulgarian Agitation, 1872* (London, 1963)

Shattock, J. and Wolff, M., *The Victorian Periodical Press: Samplings and Soundings* (Leicester, 1982)

Sheehan, J. J., *The Career of Lujo Brentano: A Study of Liberalism and Social Reform in Imperial Germany* (London, 1966)

Siedentop, L., *Tocqueville* (Oxford, 1994)

Skinner, Q., 'Language and political change' in Ball, Farr and Hanson, eds., *Political Innovation and Conceptual Change* (Cambridge, 1989), pp. 6–24

'Language and social change' in J. Tully, ed., *Meaning and Context: Quentin Skinner and his Critics* (Cambridge, 1988), pp. 119–32

'Meaning and understanding in the history of ideas', *History and Theory*, 8 (1969), 3–53

'Some problems in the analysis of political thought and action', *Political Theory*, 2 (1974), 277–303

'The state' in T. Ball, J. Farr and R. L. Hanson, eds., *Political Innovation and Conceptual Change* (Cambridge, 1989), pp. 90–132

Visions of Politics, vol. 1: Regarding Method (Cambridge, 2002)

Soffer, R. N., *Ethics and Society in England: The Revolution in the Social Sciences, 1870–1914* (Berkeley, 1978)

Spring, D., 'Walter Bagehot and deference', *American Historical Review*, 81, 3 (1976), 524–31

Stedman Jones, G., *Languages of Class: Studies in English Working Class History, 1832–1982* (Cambridge, 1983)

Outcast London: A Study in the Relationship between Classes in Victorian Society (Oxford, 1971)

'The redemptive power of violence? Carlyle, Marx and Dickens', *History Workshop Journal*, 65, 1 (2008), 1–22.

Stocking, G. W., *Victorian Anthropology* (New York, 1987)

Sutherland, G., 'Education' in F. M. L. Thompson, ed., *The Cambridge Social History of Britain 1750–1950, vol. 3: Social Agencies and Institutions* (Cambridge, 1990), pp. 119–71

Swanton, C., 'On the "essential contestedness" of political concepts', *Ethics*, 95 (1985), 811–27

Tanner, D., 'Ideological debate in Edwardian labour politics: radicalism, revisionism and socialism' in E. F. Biagini and A. J. Reid, eds., *Currents of Radicalism: Popular Radicalism, Organised Labour and Party Politics in Britain, 1850–1914* (Cambridge, 1991), pp. 271–94

Taylor, H. A., *Robert Donald: Being the Authorized Biography of Sir Robert Donald* (London, 1934)

Taylor, M., *The Decline of British Radicalism, 1847–1860* (Oxford, 1995)

'John Bull and the iconography of public opinion in England c. 1712–1929', *Past and Present*, 134 (Feb. 1992), 93–128

Thompson, J., 'After the fall: class and political language in Britain, 1780–1900', *Historical Journal*, 49, 3 (1996), 785–806

'Democracy, monism and the common good: rethinking William Clarke's political religion', *History of European Ideas*, 38 (2012), 233–47

'The genesis of the 1906 Trades Disputes Act: liberalism, trade unions and the law', *Twentieth Century British History*, 9, 2 (1998), 175–200

'The great labour unrest and political thought in Britain, 1911–1914', *Labour History Review* (forthcoming 2014)

'Modern liberty redefined' in G. Stedman Jones and G. Claeys, eds., *The Cambridge History of Nineteenth-Century Political Thought* (Cambridge, 2011), pp. 720–47.

'"A nearly related people": German views of the British labour market, 1870–1900' in D. Winch and P. K. O'Brien, eds., *The Political Economy of British Historical Experience, 1688–1914* (Oxford, 2002), 93–119

'A people's voice?', *History Workshop Journal*, 47 (1999), 283–4

'Political economy, the labour movement and the minimum wage, 1880–1914' in E. H. H. Green and D. Tanner, eds., *The Strange Survival of Liberal England: Political Leaders, Moral Values and the Reception of Economic Debate* (Cambridge, 2007), pp. 62–88.

'"Pictorial lies"? Posters and politics in Britain, 1880–1914', *Past and Present*, 197 (2007), 177–210

'Printed statistics and the public sphere: numeracy, electoral politics and the visual culture of numbers, 1880–1914' in T. Crook and G. O'Hara, eds., *Statistics and the Public Sphere: Numbers and the People in Modern Britain, c. 1800–2000* (Abingdon, 2011), pp. 121–43

Tickner, L., *The Spectacle of Women: Imagery of the Suffragist Campaign 1907–14* (London, 1987)

Todd, N., *The Militant Democracy: Joseph Cowen and Victorian Radicalism* (Whitley Bay, 1991)

Tomes, J., *Balfour and Foreign Policy: The International Thought of a Conservative Statesman* (Cambridge, 1997)

Trentmann, F., 'Civil society, commerce and the "citizen-consumer": popular meanings of free trade in modern Britain' in F. Trentmann, ed., *Paradoxes of Civil Society: New Perspectives on Modern German and British History* (Oxford, 2000), pp. 306–31

Free Trade Nation: Commerce, Consumption and Civil Society in Modern Britain (Oxford, 2008)

'National identity and consumer politics: free trade and tariff reform' in D. Winch and P. O'Brien, eds., *The Political Economy of British Historical Experience, 1688–1914* (Oxford, 2002), pp. 215–44

'Wealth versus welfare: the British left between Free Trade and national political economy before the First World War', *Historical Research*, 70 (1997), 70–98

Trentmann, F. and V. Taylor, 'From users to consumers: water politics in nineteenth-century London' in F. Trentmann, ed., *The Making of the Consumer: Knowledge, Power and Identity in the Modern World* (Oxford, 2006), pp. 53–79.

Tuck, R., *Free Riding* (Cambridge, Mass., 2008)

Tulloch, H., *James Bryce's American Commonwealth: The Anglo-American Background* (Woodbridge, 1988)

Vernon, J., *Politics and the People: A Study in English Political Culture, c. 1815–67* (Cambridge, 1993)

Vile, M. J. C., *Constitutionalism and the Separation of Powers* (Oxford, 1967)

Vint, J., *Capital and Wages: A Lakatosian History of the Wages Fund Doctrine* (Aldershot, 1994)

Wahrman, D., *Imagining the Middle Class: The Political Representation of Class in Britain, c. 1780–1840* (Cambridge, 1995)

  '"Middle-class" domesticity goes public: gender, class, and politics from Queen Caroline to Queen Victoria', *Journal of British Studies*, 32, 4 (1993), 396–432

  'The new political history', *Social History*, 21 (1996), 343–54

  'Public opinion, violence and the limits of constitutional politics' in J. Vernon, ed., *Re-reading the Constitution: New Narratives in the History of Britain's Long Nineteenth Century* (Cambridge, 1996), pp. 83–122

Waites, B., 'The government of the home front and the "moral economy" of the working class', in P. H. Liddle, ed., *Home Fires and Foreign Fields* (1985), pp. 175–94

Walkowitz, J. R., *City of Dreadful Delights: Narratives of Sexual Danger in Victorian London* (London, 1992)

Weston, C. C., *The House of Lords and Ideological Politics: Lord Salisbury's Referendal Theory and the Conservative Party, 1846–1922* (Philadelphia, 1995)

Whitaker, J. K., 'Some neglected aspects of Alfred Marshall's economic and social thought', *History of Political Economy*, 9, 2 (1977), 161–97

Williams, K., *From Pauperism to Poverty* (London, 1981)

Williams, R., *Keywords: A Vocabulary of Culture and Society* (2nd edn, Oxford, 1981)

Wilson, K., *The Sense of the People: Politics, Culture and Imperialism in England, 1715–1785* (Cambridge, 1995)

Winch, D., *Wealth and Life: Essays on the Intellectual History of Political Economy in Britain, 1848–1914* (Cambridge, 2009)

Windscheffel, A., *Popular Conservatism in Imperial London, 1868–1906* (Woodbridge, 2007)

Wittgenstein, L., *Philosophical Investigations*, trans. G. E. Anscombe (Oxford, 1958)

Yeo, E. J., 'Language and contestation: the case of "the People", 1832 to the present' in J. Belchem and N. Kirk, eds., *Languages of Labour* (Aldershot, 1997), pp. 41–65

Zaret, D., *Origins of Democratic Culture: Printing, Petitions, and the Public Sphere in Early-Modern England* (Princeton, 2000)

Unpublished theses and papers

Buchanan, R. A., 'Trade unions and public opinion, 1850–1875', Ph.D. thesis, University of Cambridge (1957)

Gurowich, P. M., 'Party and independence in the early and mid-Victorian House of Commons: aspects of political theory and practice, 1832–1868, considered with special reference to the period 1852–1868', Ph.D. thesis, University of Cambridge (1986)

Kelvin, P., 'The development and use of the concept of the electoral mandate in British politics, 1867 to 1911', Ph.D. thesis, University of London (1977)

Jones, D. M., 'The liberal press and the rise of labour: a study with particular reference to Leeds and Bradford: 1850–1895', Ph.D. thesis, University of Leeds (1973)

Lee, M. J., 'John Stuart Mill, George Jacob Holyoake and the "social question": themes of continuity in mid-nineteenth century radicalism and socialism', Ph.D. thesis, University of Cambridge (1995)

McWilliam, R., 'The Tichborne claimant and the people: investigations into popular culture 1867–86', Ph.D. thesis, University of Sussex (1989)

Palmer, P., 'The concept of public opinion in political theory', Ph.D. thesis, Harvard University (1936)

Petridis, A., 'The economic analysis of trade unions by British economists, 1870–1930', Ph.D. thesis, Duke University (1974)

Rush, G. W. 'The activism of ideas: J. A. Hobson's opposition to aggressive imperialism, 1896–1902', Ph.D. thesis, University of Cambridge (1998)

Taylor, M., 'Public petitioning in the nineteenth century: a reinterpretation' (1995)

Index